D0221499

Organizing Knowledge in Libraries

An Introduction to Information Retrieval

WITHDRAWN

Organizing Knowledge in Libraries

An Introduction to Information Retrieval

C. D. Needham

Fellow of the Library Association

Principal Lecturer, School of Librarianship,
Polytechnic of North London

Second Revised Edition

Grafton Library Science Series

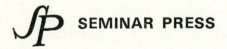 **SEMINAR PRESS**

Published in the Americas
by the Seminar Press, Inc.

Library of Congress Catalog Number: 72 176298
Copyright © 1964, 1971 by C. D. Needham

{WITHDRAWN}

Contents

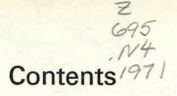

YOUNGSTOWN STATE UNIVERSITY
LIBRARY

292682

Z
695
.N4
1971

List of Figures

YOUNGSTOWN STATE UNIVERSITY
LIBRARY

292682

Preface to the Second Edition

Despite a remarkable increase in the number of books on index-ing published over the last few years, there seemed to be some justification in contemplating a second edition of this book. For one thing there was evidence of a measure of student demand. It is one of a still small number of books concerned with the basic range of approaches – author, title, and subject – to the retrieval of documents. Additionally it includes chapters on certain broader matters of organization and policy. It aims to provide an introductory survey, assuming neither prior knowledge nor a satisfactory supporting full-time course of study.

Those familiar with the first edition will note a number of changes. Most obvious are the new chapters on index languages and post-coordinate systems. The appearance of the Anglo-American Cataloguing Rules in 1967 and the ALA Filing Rules in 1968, the new editions (completed or in progress) of several schemes of classification, and the emergence of Shared Cata-loguing, PRECIS and MARC, have necessitated substantial revision of the greater part of the book. In the circumstances a second edition could lapse into a Five Years' Work, and one of the greatest problems has been to try to maintain a realistic view of students' requirements.

I am glad to acknowledge my obvious debt to the writers cited in the text. I am also indebted to those who have com-mented on the book over the past seven years. Above all, I should like to record my appreciation of the wide variety of instruction, encouragement and support given, always with good grace, by colleagues and members of my family.

The following abbreviations have been used:

AA	*Anglo-American cataloguing code*
AACR	*Anglo-American cataloguing rules*

ALA	American Library Association and the Association's *Cataloging rules for author and title entries*
BC	*Bibliographic classification* (Bliss)
BM	British Museum and the Museum's *Rules for compiling the catalogues*
BNB	*British national bibliography*
BTI	British Technology Index
BUCOP	*British union catalogue of periodicals*
CBI	*Cumulative book index*
CC	*Colon classification* (Ranganathan)
CIS	See page 112 (footnote)
DC	*Decimal classification* (Dewey)
FID	Fédération Internationale de Documentation
Hertis	Hertfordshire Technical Information Service
IFLA	International Federation of Library Associations
IIB	Institut International de Bibliographie
KWIC	Keyword-in-context
KWOC	Keyword-out-of-context
LA	Library Association
LADSIRLAC	Liverpool and District Scientific, Industrial and Research Library Advisory Council
LC	Library of Congress and the Library of Congress *Classification*
LULOP	*London union list of periodicals*
MARC	Machine-Readable Cataloguing
PRECIS	Preserved Context Subject Index
SC	*Subject classification*
Sinto	Sheffield Interchange Organization
SLIC	Selective Listing in Combination
TLS	*Times Literary Supplement*
UDC	*Universal decimal classification*

Chapter 1
Introduction

All societies depend for their very existence on the communication of knowledge. The more complex the society and the more complex its knowledge, the more complex does this matter of communication become; an ever-increasing amount of information must flow smoothly and accurately, not only between the members of the society but between one society and another and from generations past. Accordingly, the means of communication also become more complex: primitive sounds and signs give way to highly developed spoken and written languages; invention and technical skill produce varied media – printed books, telecommunications, films, sound recordings, and so on; education becomes a matter of increasing importance; conferences proliferate. By these and other means is knowledge communicated, and the proper organization of these means is one of the most pressing problems of today.

Bibliographic Organization

Bibliographic organization is that part of the organization of the means of communication which is concerned with the organization and control of publication and publications.

The *function* of bibliographic organization is to ensure that documents are adequately published, housed and recorded; its *purpose* is the efficient identification, selection, and location of these documents as required.

Reasons why adequate bibliographic organization and control is becoming increasingly difficult:

(i) *The number of documents.* Thirty thousand books are published annually by the British book trade alone; it is estimated that there are over 100,000 periodicals in science and technology; over 90,000 articles on chemistry are now abstracted each year by *Chemical abstracts*.

(ii) *The language of documents.* Important documents are published in an increasing number of languages as developing countries produce more literature. Bibliographical insularity in such conditions cannot be tolerated – and the language barrier is only one of several to be overcome before documents flow freely between the countries of the world.

(iii) *The complexity of documents.* With the increase in specialization and the discovery of new relationships between many areas of knowledge hitherto considered separate, the subject matter of documents is becoming more and more complex, giving rise to problems in classification and cataloguing, arrangement of bibliographies and so on. Complexity also arises through the growth of composite and multi-topical documents, of which periodicals are the most important single example. More and more are periodical articles and similar small units of publication sources of important information, and this means that such units must be separately recorded, though this is an immense task.

(iv) *The numerous forms of documents.* Documents produced on what might be called a form basis, e.g. standards, theses, patents, are not easily organized and tend to be neglected. For example, although patents are listed regularly by the Patent Office, they are often ignored by indexes and abstracts, even though they usually contain important contributions to the subjects concerned.

(v) *Complexity of publication.* The development of non-conventional methods of printing has facilitated publication by all kinds of organizations outside the book trade. Such publications are often missed by national bibliographies and reviewing sources and consequently are less easily controlled.

(vi) *The complexity of approaches to documents.* Almost any document, even the simplest, may be required for a variety of reasons; for example, its author may be of interest to one, its subject to another. Many documents are not simple in this respect: they have several authors, several subjects. Again, the same subject may be required for a number of reasons, e.g. an article on population trends in a certain area may be of interest to the statistician, the actuary, the market research worker, the economist, the sociologist, and so on. Clearly, the same document may need to be recorded in many different bibliographies designed for different needs.

Bibliographic devices are devices used to facilitate bibliographic control and so, broadly, they include all forms of librarianship and bibliography. Thus control of publication as envisaged by Bernal,[1] among others, is a bibliographic device, as are the cooperative purchase and storage of documents, interlending schemes, the arrangement of documents in libraries, the recording of documents in various forms of bibliographies, and so on.

If fully integrated, the sum total of these devices will be a *system of bibliographic organization.* In most subjects, the system is only partial; for example, in medicine the recording of documents in bibliographies of many kinds is better than in most other fields, but the organization of the purchase and storage of such documents in this country leaves much to be desired.

To deal with the whole system is well beyond the scope of this book, but the student should remember when considering any single device that it is related to other devices. Thus the effectiveness of union lists as location devices may be weakened by faults in the housing of the documents they record. The final assessment of particular examples of any device cannot be made except by reference to the state of the other devices in the system.

Retrieval Devices

The two bibliographic devices selected for examination in this book are known as *retrieval devices.* They are prepared specifically to facilitate the retrieval of documents from a particular store, the store, for our purposes, being a library. They are:

(i) the arrangement of documents on the shelves, and

(ii) the catalogues (including booklists, etc.), recording the documents.

PURPOSE AND FUNCTION

We have already said that the function of bibliographic organization is the adequate housing and recording of documents. In terms of a particular library, this means that the documents should be adequately arranged and catalogued. But what we mean by 'adequately' will vary according to the purpose of the devices.

Purpose will be dictated mainly by the needs of the users. The librarian must study the requirements (both actual and potential) of his clientele before he can assess the purpose of the devices he is creating. And only when purpose is understood can the functions of the devices, i.e. the means by which the purpose is to be achieved, be satisfactorily determined. For example, the librarian of a technical college should have a clear idea of the subjects taught in the college, the level of the courses, the teaching methods used, and so on, if he is to be able to define the purpose of the library in general and the catalogue in particular, in relation to real needs. He will then be able to particularize about the functions of the catalogue and shelf arrangement – whether, say, periodical articles should be indexed, whether abstracts would be useful and what points should be emphasized in such abstracts, whether select lists should be produced on certain subjects and the style to be adopted in such lists. At the same time, such alternative devices as bibliographies must be remembered, for, as we have seen, no device exists in isolation and the functions of a particular device should be integrated into the overall pattern of bibliographic organization.

Although the precise purposes of retrieval devices will vary, they can be broadly summarized in the terms used by Cutter[2] as long ago as 1876 when he defined the purpose of the catalogue:

(i) To enable a person to find a document of which
    (a) the author, or
    (b) the title, or ⎬ is known.
    (c) the subject

(ii) To show what the library has
    (d) by a given author
    (e) on a given subject (and related subjects)
    (f) in a given kind (or form) of literature.

(iii) To assist in the choice of a document
    (g) as to its edition (bibliographically)
    (h) as to its character (literary or topical).

Point (iii) as we shall see is largely a matter of document description in the catalogue: the description should be such that it enables the user to distinguish between one edition of a work and another; it may also assist in the choice of a document by giving information about its content and character.

It is the function of retrieval so to arrange documents and to provide catalogues that these purposes – or those of them which the librarian considers relevant – can be achieved.

DOCUMENT ARRANGEMENT

Documents are usually arranged by their authors, titles, subjects, or forms because, as we have seen, readers usually ask for them by these characteristics. Thus, for fiction, author arrangement is common; for periodicals, title arrangement; for most non-fiction, subject arrangement.

The great advantage of document arrangement as a retrieval device is *immediacy*: the reader, having found the relevant section of the library, can then browse through the documents immediately. Everyone prefers this to browsing through second-hand devices like catalogues and bibliographies.

It has, however, the following limitations:

(a) *Documents can be arranged in one order only.* Any document may be required by author, title, subject, or form, but it can be arranged by only one of these. Moreover, within any of these characteristics, it may be complex – it may, for instance, have several authors or several subjects. Again, it may be approached from several different points of view – as in the case of the article on population mentioned above. The arrangement will allow the document to be retrieved according to only one of its characteristics. In some cases guiding and displays can help, but these are relatively crude methods.

(b) *The arrangement is often broken.* Documents in a library are rarely shelved in a single sequence. Reference books, pamphlets, periodicals, outsize material, and other special categories may be shelved separately – and documents may be out on loan. Each break, even when related material is shelved in a near-by parallel sequence, as in the case of outsize books, reduces the efficiency of document arrangement as a retrieval device.

CATALOGUES

Catalogues are simply one of the many forms of bibliographies, differing from the other forms in that they record only the documents in one collection. They are prepared mainly to overcome the limitations of document arrangement.

Basically, like other bibliographies, a catalogue is an arrangement of *entries* representing documents. Each entry is in two parts, a *heading* and a *description*, as the following example illustrates:

HEADING	Damsell, Dennis Henry.
	⎧ Modern everyday science. London:
DESCRIPTION	⎨ Dent, 1961.
	⎩ 92 p.; illus. 26 cm.
	For children.
	9357 500

Description

The description should contain the author's name if it is to be self-contained, but as the name is in the heading, it is often, in practice, omitted. If there are other authors unmentioned in the heading, they may be included in the description. Note that the description includes the class number of the document by which it is arranged on the shelves. In this case the class number 500 represents the subject Science in the Dewey *Decimal classification scheme*. The number on the left is the accession number, individualizing the particular copy.

Headings and Varieties of Catalogues

The *heading* is the element by which the entry is filed in the catalogue. In the above example the heading is the author and if the entry is filed by this heading, it is called the *author entry*. A catalogue which is composed of author entries only (including added entries for editors, translators, etc.) is called an AUTHOR CATALOGUE. An example of an author catalogue is the British Museum's *General catalogue of printed books* (though books *about* authors, etc., are also included).

Now consider the following entry:

SCIENCE
   Damsell, Dennis Henry.
     Modern everyday science. London:
   Dent, 1961.
     92 p.; illus. 26 cm.
     For children.
   9357   500

Here the heading by which the entry is filed is the *subject heading* SCIENCE, the author heading being secondary and used only for the sub-arrangement of all entries having the same subject heading. (It is important to note – we shall return to this later – that whatever the filing heading, the author heading is always retained as in this example.) Such an entry is called a *subject entry*, and a record which contains only subject entries is called a SUBJECT CATALOGUE.

In the above example the subject heading is a term in *natural language* and, as the entries will be arranged alphabetically by such terms, such a catalogue is more specifically defined as an ALPHABETICAL SUBJECT CATALOGUE. An example of this type is the Library of Congress *Catalog: Books: Subjects*.

The subject heading could have been a *class number* representing the subject and chosen from a classification scheme such as DC; such a catalogue, of which the main arrangement, as with documents on the shelves, is by class numbers, is called a classified subject catalogue – or CLASSIFIED CATALOGUE for short:

   500
     Damsell, Dennis Henry.
       Modern everyday science. London:
     Dent, 1961.
       92 p.; illus. 26 cm.
       For children.
     9357   500

Here again, entries having the same class number would be sub-arranged by the author heading. Students should refer to the *British national bibliography* (BNB) for a good example of classified arrangement.

Similarly entries can also be made under *title headings* and *form headings*:

Modern everyday science
Damsell, Dennis Henry.
    Modern everyday science. London:
Dent, 1961.
    92 p.; illus. 26 cm.
    For children.
9357   5̲0̲0̲

ENCYCLOPAEDIAS
Larousse, P. A.
    Grand dictionnaire universel du
XIXᵉ siècle. Paris: Larousse & Bover,
1865–76.
    15 v. 35 cm.
6840–54   0̲3̲4̲

Catalogues which contain only title or form entries are called
TITLE or FORM CATALOGUES, but they are rarely found in
libraries in their pure forms, being usually filed with author
and subject catalogues respectively.

Often catalogues contain *more than one type of entry.* Subject
catalogues usually contain some form entries; title entries are
often interfiled with author entries to form AUTHOR/TITLE
CATALOGUES. Catalogues which combine author, title, subject
and form entries in one alphabetical sequence are called
DICTIONARY CATALOGUES. Such interfiling of entries is
impossible in the case of the classified catalogue: here entries
for subjects and forms are found under the appropriate class
number in the classified file itself, which is supported by
separate alphabetical *author/title* and *subject indexes.*

The main types of catalogue will be considered later in more
detail.

*The great advantage that catalogues have over document arrangement
as a retrieval device should now be clear: within economic limits any
number of entries can be made for a single document.* Whereas the
librarian has to decide whether to arrange a particular document on the shelves according to its author or title or subject
or form, knowing that it may be asked for by any of these, he
can make entries for it under each, thus catering for any
approach. And for complex documents theoretically any
number of author entries or subject entries, etc., can be made

as required. We shall have to qualify this later, but this main point the student should grasp at the outset.

To illustrate some of the points already made, below are the entries for a single document as recorded in the *Cumulative book index* (CBI), a bibliography using the principles of the dictionary catalogue. (The alphabetical order is retained here.)

Dictionary of obsolete English. Trench, R. C.—*Title added entry*
    35s. Owen, P.   *(catering also for form approach for this document).*

English language – Dictionaries   —*Subject added entry*
    Trench, R. C. Dictionary of obsolete   *(with form sub-*
    English. [New ed.] 35s. '59. Owen, P.   *division).*

Trench, Richard Chenevix, bp. 1807–1886   —*Author entry.*
    Dictionary of obsolete English [New ed.]
    35s. '59. Owen, P.

And here are the entries for the same book in the *British national bibliography*, a classified bibliography:

420.0—1350—1800 DICTIONARIES
    TRENCH, Richard Chenevix, *Anglican*   —*Entry in Classified*
    Archbishop of Dublin   *section (where 420*
    Dictionary of obsolete English [New ed.]   *stands for English*
    London, Owen, 35s. Apr. [1959]. xii,   *language).*
    275 p. 19 cm. (B59—5711)
    Originally published as *A select glossary*
    of English words used formerly in senses
    different from the present. 1859.

Dictionary of obsolete English, *see* Trench, Richard—*Title* ⎤
    Chenevix, *Anglican Archbp. of Dublin*   ⎥
Trench, Richard Chenevix, *Anglican Archbp.*   —*Author* ⎥
    of Dublin   ⎥ *index*
    Dictionary of obsolete English. New ed. *Owen*,   ⎥ *entries*
    35s. 420.9 (B59—5711)   ⎥

English language 420   —*Subject* ⎥
Languages 400   —*Subject* ⎦

Main Entries, Added Entries, References

It will be noticed that in both the CBI and BNB not all entries carry the same amount of description. In the case of the CBI the fullest entry is the *author entry*; in the case of BNB it is the entry in the *classified file*. In other words, in each case one entry is chosen as the *main entry*, to which the reader must refer if he wants all the details. One reason for this is clear: the expense of making full entries under every heading in a printed catalogue could not be contemplated. Similarly, in library catalogues one entry is selected as the main entry; in the *dictionary catalogue* it is traditionally the *author entry*; in the *classified catalogue*, the entry in the *classified file*. All other entries are called *added entries*. The degree of description called for in main and added entries will be discussed in Chapter 14.

Sometimes even an added entry is considered an extravagance. Then a *reference*, i.e. a direction from one heading to another, may be used instead. This can be seen in the BNB example above where a reference is made from the title to the author entry for details. In many cases, whether to use an added entry or reference will be a matter of policy, but there are some occasions when references are to be preferred, the economy being so great. These occasions arise *whenever the use of a reference will result in the curtailment of further added entries under a particular heading at a later date*. For example, we could make entries for a novel by Sheila Kaye-Smith under both Kaye-Smith, Sheila, and Smith, Sheila Kaye-. If we do, we shall be bound to do the same for every other book by this writer. It will therefore pay to select one heading – say Kaye-Smith, Sheila – and then refer from the other:

> Smith, Sheila Kaye-
> *see* Kaye-Smith, Sheila

The same principle applies to synonyms in subject headings. A book on radio could be entered under the heading RADIO and a further entry made under WIRELESS, but to select one and to refer from the other will result in a great saving whenever further documents on that subject are being catalogued.

References are divided into two kinds: those which refer from a heading which is never used to a heading which is (*see references*), and those which refer from a heading that is used to a related heading (*see also references*):

> WIRELESS   TELECOMMUNICATIONS
> *see* RADIO   *see also* RADIO

It may be remarked that the use of *unit entry* invalidates much of what has here been said on added entries and references. A unit entry consists of a filing heading (a subject heading, for example) placed above a unit consisting of author heading and description, the unit being mechanically reproduced from a master using a machine such as manufactured by Banda, Gestetner, Addressograph, etc. The method can be used with any flexible form of catalogue, such as card or sheaf. BNB cards are unit cards and can be converted into any type of entry simply by adding a new heading above the unit. The example on page 16 can be interpreted as a unit and the example on page 17 as a subject entry produced from it, simply by the addition of the subject heading SCIENCE. Clearly an unlimited number of entries can be mechanically produced once the master has been made; each entry will contain exactly the same amount of description, and because the only additional labour involved in making an entry is the typing of the filing headings, the method is less expensive than the making of even abbreviated added entries.

This being the case, *why bother to distinguish between main and added entries and references?*

(i) *Firstly, not all libraries use unit entries, and the student must therefore be able to think in these terms.* For example, in a library where the number of entries required per document is limited, mechanical reproduction methods may not be economical and in such circumstances added entries having less information than the main entry will be used. Such a library may find it practicable to buy BNB cards but this may not be so in the case of a special library where many non-British books and other materials excluded from BNB are acquired.

(ii) Differentiation between main and added entries may be necessary on economic grounds if the catalogue or part of the catalogue is at some stage to be *printed*, whether by conventional or computer processes.

(iii) Even where unit entries are used it will still be helpful to designate one as main entry, this entry then carrying the *tracings* on the reverse side, i.e. an indication of the other entries and references made for that particular document to facilitate the removal of all relevant entries when the document is withdrawn.

(iv) *An abundance of entries is a mixed blessing* because the ease with which a catalogue is used is in inverse relation to its growth and therefore what has been said about *references* still holds true – they should always be used whenever their use will obviate the need for further added entries under a particular heading – and the use of such *see references* presupposes the selection of a main entry.

(v) The idea of a main subject, a main author, and a main title, where the document has several of each, follows naturally from the need to select these for *the arrangement of the document on the shelves.*

The student may now question the inclusion of the author heading in the basic unit. *Why not restrict the unit to the description?*

(i) Many cataloguers today do not include the name of the author in the description and *without the heading the authorship would remain unknown* in entries other than the author entry itself.

(ii) Without this author heading, *entries under a particular subject or form heading would file in title order*, i.e. by the next element after the heading; clearly the organization of the catalogue is better if all the documents that one author has written on a subject or in a certain form file together within that heading. For this reason alone the choice of main author heading is very important.

To sum up: document arrangement and catalogues are known as retrieval devices; they are part of a system of bibliographic organization, the latter being in turn part of the organization of communication. The limitations of document arrangement are overcome by the various types of entries and references in the catalogue.

CONSISTENCY AND COMMON SENSE

In the chapters that follow many rules for the cataloguing and classification of documents will be noted. One of the aims of these rules is consistency, and the student may ask whether the desire for consistency may not in some cases result in practices which seem contrary to common sense. Cutter has said: 'The convenience of the public is always to be set before the ease of the cataloger. In most cases they coincide. A plain rule without exceptions is not only easy for us to carry out, but easy for the public to understand and work by. But strict consistency in a rule and uniformity in its application sometimes lead to practices which clash with the public's habitual way of looking at things. When these habits are general and deeply rooted, it is unwise for the cataloger to ignore them, even if they demand a sacrifice of system and simplicity.'[3]

Minto commented: 'Mr Cutter's dictum has sound common sense at the bottom of it but there is a good deal to be said for the point of view of consistency particularly as the public's habitual way of looking at things is by no means a constant way and liable to change.'[4]

A report on the Institute on Catalog Code Revision held at Stanford University in 1958[5] puts it this way: 'Now the "convenience of the public" is like Virtue. Everybody is for it. Probably every cataloger who lived would claim that he had only "the convenience of the public" in mind. But how define "convenience"? As with Virtue it is not easy. For Cutter, "convenience of the public" was a maze of bypaths down which he led catalogers to psychoanalyze the absent reader. Codes became an infinite variety of intricate exceptions to rules and exceptions to exceptions each to provide some special case of suspected "convenience".'

This is the view generally held today. Rigid adherence to merely *ad hoc* rules is not desirable, but rules and procedures based on the careful assessment of the principles underlying the problems involved should not be overruled to cater for particular cases simply because of the 'public's habitual way of looking at things' – or 'common sense':

(i) Common sense is not so common; what is 'common sense' to one is frequently anything but to another.

(ii) It is doubtful whether the public has 'an habitual way' of looking at most retrieval problems (as Cutter himself pointed out) and even if it has, librarians rarely agree as to what it is. The attempt to discover it may lead to ineffective 'psychoanalysis of the absent reader'.

(iii) The public's habitual way is temporary as Minto pointed out – and as Cutter showed in his discussion of the treatment of pseudonyms.[6]

(iv) Serious users including members of staff may be expected to learn a few basic rules if the results are worth the effort; on the other hand, they will soon become dissatisfied with devices that have no consistency.

READINGS

1. Royal Society Information Conference. London, 1948. *Report and papers submitted.* p. 253.
2. CUTTER, C. A. *Rules for a dictionary catalog.* 4th ed. Washington, GPO, 1904. p. 12.
3. CUTTER, C. A. op. cit. p. 6.
4. MINTO, J. 'The Anglo-American cataloguing rules.' *Library Association Record,* 11 (7), July 1909, 296.
5. 'Institute on Catalog Code Revision'. *Library Resources and Technical Services,* 3 (2), Spring 1959, 124.
6. CUTTER, C. A. op. cit. p. 28.

An interesting set of readings on communication, bibliographic organization, and the growth of the world's literature can be found in:

KOCHEN, M. ed. *The growth of knowledge.* New York, Wiley, 1967.

Part One
The Author/Title Approach

Chapter 2
The Author Approach – Introduction

Purpose

The author of a document is the person or organization responsible for its writing as distinct from its publication. In the 1967 *Anglo-American cataloguing rules* (AACR) the following definition of authorship is provided: 'The person or corporate body chiefly responsible for the creation of the intellectual or artistic content of the work.'[1] *Author* is a comprehensive term. On occasion the author may be an editor, compiler, illustrator, etc. The author is, of course, one of the main identifying features of a document, and for this reason author entries are, for most documents and in most libraries, of fundamental importance.

Two basic reasons why readers make the author approach:
(a) to discover a *particular document* whose author is known, or
(b) to discover what documents by a *particular author* are in the library.

In the first case the emphasis is on a particular document; in the second on the author's total production. (These two objectives of the author catalogue are frequently referred to in succeeding chapters and the student should memorize them.)

Entry under the author's name as found on the title page will normally ensure that both objectives are catered for. Problems arise, however, when an author uses *variant names in different documents*, e.g. when he has changed his name or when he uses pseudonyms. In such cases, entry under the author's name as found on the title page will clearly not collocate all the writings of a particular author, i.e. it will not satisfy objective (b). However, it will usually (though not always) be the best heading for that particular document, i.e. it will satisfy objective (a); this is because readers learn of particular documents through reviews, hearsay, citations in other documents, and so on – sources which usually quote the author's name as found in the document. Thus, entry of *End of a chapter,* by Nicholas Blake (a pseudonym of C. Day Lewis), under Blake, and *The poet's way of knowledge,* by C. Day Lewis, under Lewis, will satisfy readers with objective (a), but not those with objective (b), who will want all the books by C. Day Lewis together, whatever the name used on the title page. To satisfy these latter, a *uniform heading* (Lewis, say) will have to be chosen and adhered to, whatever the name used in the document. Whichever method is chosen, references will be made to cater for the objective that has been ignored: thus, if Lewis is chosen as a uniform heading, a *see reference* will be made from Blake to Lewis; whereas if Blake *and* Lewis are used, a linking *see also* reference will have to be made between each.

The first thing that a cataloguer has to decide is whether his catalogue is to cater primarily for objective (a) *or objective* (b) *whenever a choice is necessitated.*

Objective (a) results in what may be called a *direct catalogue,* because it will give direct access to a particular document, having in most cases headings chosen directly from the title page of the document. Because its prime purpose is the finding of particular documents, such a catalogue has also been called a *finding list catalogue.* It has also been called an *inventory catalogue.*

Objective (b) results in what might be called a *collocative catalogue,* because it will collocate the writings of each author, whatever names he uses. It has also been called a *bibliographical catalogue* to distinguish it from the inventory catalogue.

In practice most cataloguers would seem to favour the *direct catalogue* because it results in the most frequently sought headings being used. It is also much simpler for the cataloguer because it means that in most cases he accepts the name found on the title page and so there is relatively little biographical and bibliographical checking involved; and when new information about an author's identity comes to light, all that is needed is a reference in the catalogue – as against the revision of headings and entries associated with the collocative catalogue with its uniform headings. A more wary attitude can be found in the codes of rules. The new *Anglo-American cataloguing rules* (1967), for example, though favouring simplification and advocating the use of information as found in the document being catalogued, nevertheless abides by the principle of collocating an author's work – at least so far as personal authors are concerned.

Once one objective has been chosen, the cataloguer should abide by it in all its applications. Consistency saves members of staff and readers who use the catalogue regularly from having to follow up unnecessary references, an irritating and time-consuming business as can be seen from a study of some of the headings in Cassell's *Encyclopaedia of literature* (1953). In this encyclopaedia George Eliot is recorded under Eliot, suggesting that pseudonyms are accepted as headings; for Lewis Carroll, however, the reader is referred to the real name, Dodgson; and to add spice to the chase, Mark Twain is found under neither Twain nor Clemens but under Mark. In such conditions it is a matter of pure luck if the reader hits the bull's eye at the first shot.

We have seen that a *uniform heading* will often have to be selected if the catalogue is to be collocative, and there are occasions when one will have to be chosen even if the catalogue is direct – as when differences between variant names on title pages are slight and will be ignored by readers (e.g. George Bernard Shaw and Bernard Shaw). One general principle should be borne in mind when choosing a uniform heading: *the name should be one used by the author somewhere in his writings.* Simply to say real name is not good enough, because if the real name has never been used, it will never be sought by readers, and in using it the cataloguer is making readers use references unnecessarily. This is the great fault of the rule for pseudonymous writers, rule (38), in the Anglo-American code (1908).

Variant name should not be confused with the possibility of *citing one name in a number of ways.* For example, the fact that the name De la Roche can be entered under De, La, or Roche, does not alter the fact that it is still the same name, not a variant. In these cases a uniform heading must always be adopted, and *see references* made from alternative citation orders.

Code of Rules

Without a code the cataloguer would be reduced to making individual decisions for every document catalogued and inconsistencies would be inevitable. There would be inconsistencies for the same type of author, e.g. the Ministry of Agriculture might be entered under Agriculture, Ministry of, the Ministry of Defence under Ministry of Defence, and the Ministry of Transport under Great Britain, Ministry of Transport. There might be inconsistencies in the same author – the Institution of Electrical Engineers, for example, being entered under Institution of Electrical Engineers on one occasion, and under the inverted form on another.

The cataloguer can either choose an existing code of rules or create his own. (The latter possibility is hardly practicable in a large system with an existing catalogue, though modifications of practice must be made from time to time.) The advantages and disadvantages of the former course are the advantages and disadvantages of standardization: the rules, usually the work of a group of librarians and therefore impersonal, will be the basis of many other catalogues and bibliographies and the resulting familiarity will assist both the cataloguer and the reader. On the other hand they may not in every instance suit the requirements of the particular catalogue; change may be discouraged and fossilization set in through inadequate revision.

The AACR published in 1967 shows a marked improvement over previous codes. The real problems that arise in author cataloguing have been more carefully analysed and the rules display, to a far greater degree than before, a logical order and consistency. It is likely that as a result there will be a greater measure of standardization in catalogues and bibliographies in future.

The remainder of this chapter will be devoted to a brief examination of the principles and procedures involved in making a code: for although students are unlikely to find themselves in the position of having to create a code, such an analysis provides a valuable tool by which existing codes can be assessed. (The method can also be applied to making codes for title entry – see Chapter 5.)

MAKING A CODE

Choose author headings for the following documents:

(a) *The record guide*, by Edward Sackville-West and Desmond Shaw-Taylor, with Andrew Porter and William Mann.

(b) *Schubert: thematic catalogue of all his works in chronological order*, by Otto Erich Deutsch in collaboration with Donald R. Wakeling.

(c) *The poetical works of Wordsworth*, edited by E. de Selincourt.

(d) *Studies in the social psychology of adolescence*, by J. E. Richardson, J. F. Forrester, J. K. Shukla, and P. J. Higginbotham; edited with a foreword by C. M. Fleming.

(e) *Oxford book of English verse, 1250–1918*, chosen and edited by Sir Arthur Quiller-Couch.

(f) *Ambit* (a periodical), edited by M. C. O. Bax and Edwin Brock.

(g) *The Library Association Record*, edited by Edward Dudley.

(h) *Essays and studies, 1962: being volume fifteen of the new series of Essays and studies*; collected for The English Association by Beatrice White.

(j) *The tropics*, by Edgar Aubert de la Rue, François Bourliére, Jean-Paul Harroy.

(k) *Making magical apparatus*, by Jane Reid (i.e. Mrs David Johnstone).

(l) *Lord Jim*, by Joseph Conrad (i.e. Josef Teodor Konrad Korzeniowski).

(m) *The far country*, by Neville Shute (i.e. Neville Shute Norway).

(n) *The trimmed lamp, and other stories*, by O. Henry (i.e. William Sydney Porter).

(p) *The scene of the crime*, by John Creasey.

(q) *The man I killed*, by Michael Halliday (i.e. John Creasey).

(r) *A branch for the baron*, by Anthony Morton (i.e. John Creasey).

(s) *The Aeneid of Virgil*, retold by N. B. Taylor.

(t) *Chisholm's handbook of commercial geography*; entirely re-written by L. Dudley Stamp and S. Carter Gilmour.

(u) *Shakespeare's 'Much ado about nothing'*, by N. T. Carrington (Notes on chosen English texts). Text and commentary.

(w) *Billy Budd* (libretto) adapted from the story by Herman Melville by E. M. Forster and Eric Crozier.

(y) *A concordance to the poems of William Wordsworth*, by Lane Cooper.

(z) *Iban agriculture: a report on the shifting cultivation of hill rice* ... prepared for the Colonial Office by John Derek Freeman.

(za) Ministry of Education. *15–18*. (The Crowther report.)

(zb) *Yearbook* of the Institution of Agricultural Engineers (originally the Institution of British Agricultural Engineers).

(zc) National Physical Laboratory. *Mathematical tables*. (The National Physical Laboratory is a branch of the Department of Trade and Industry.)

(zd) *Farm business statistics for south-east England*. Wye College (London University).

(ze) *Annual report* of the Association of Assistant Librarians (a division of the Library Association).

In each of these examples authorship complications arise and the cataloguer must choose between two or more possible headings. (Some of these complications will be discussed in Chapter 4.) The first task in codification is the study of a wide range of documents as well as existing codes, *listing instances of complications in authorship*. The list will be an extended version of the one given here. In this way, the codifier will have a clear view of the problems that actually arise in the literature. *Next, the problems must be defined and then classified*. This involves:

(1) asking why the problems arose in the first place, and

(2) grouping related problems.

If, for example, we examine document (s) above, we see that it presents a problem because it can be entered under Virgil or Taylor; (t) can be entered under Chisholm or Stamp; (u) can be entered under Shakespeare or Carrington. If we now ask why the problems arise, the answer is clear: not because they are epitomes, revisions or commentaries, but because in each case the document depends for its existence on another document, and therefore it may be considered as legitimate to enter each under the original author as to enter under the author of the new document. *Thus a number of particular classes of document (in this example, epitomes, or revisions or commentaries) can be said to present the same kind of cataloguing problem and they should therefore be grouped together as* DEPENDENT DOCUMENTS. Again, if we examine document (zd) above, we see that a problem arises because it can be entered under Wye College or London University; document (zc) can be entered under National Physical Laboratory or the Department of Trade and Industry; (ze) under Association of Assistant Librarians or

Library Association. Why do the problems arise? Not because one is a college, one a government department, one an affiliated society, but because in each case the organization producing the document is associated with another organization in some way. *Thus a number of different types of organization (colleges of a university, government departments and affiliated societies) are seen to present the same kind of cataloguing problem and they should be grouped together as* ASSOCIATED ORGANIZATIONS.

This initial analysis is very important, and (1) *above must precede* (2) *if the final groups are to reflect the real cataloguing problems involved.*

The number of real problems arising in the selection of headings for author catalogues is limited, as has been shown by Lubetzky,[2] to whom we are indebted for his important work on this subject. He lists the following *problems arising in cases of personal authorship*:

(i) The document* is one prepared by an author with the aid of collaborators or contributors.

(ii) The document is one composed by an editor or compiler from the writings of other people.

(iii) The document is one by several authors with no one author more responsible for it than any of the others.

(iv) The document is one in which the writer reports the communications of another person.

(v) The document is the report of a person made in the name of a certain body or organization, not a personal statement.

(vi) The author has changed his or her name.

(vii) The author writes under an assumed name different from his real name, or under his title of nobility, or under part of his name.

(viii) The author writes under his real name but also uses a pseudonym in a special literary genre.

(ix) The author's name appears in translation in varying forms.

(x) The document is dependent, i.e. not written for its own sake but to accompany another document upon which it depends for its interest.

They can be grouped again as follows:

(a) Documents having more than one author: groups (i)–(v) above.

* *Document* has been substituted in these conditions for *work*.

2

(b) Authors having more than one name: groups (vi)–(ix) above.

(c) Dependent documents.

Corporate authors give rise to a further group of problems which, because of their exclusiveness demand separate treatment – though, as far as possible, where the problem is related to a similar problem in personal authorship, the solution should be consistent.

(i) The document is a report or a statement prepared by one of the officers of the organization or by some other person engaged to make the statement for it, or by one of its subdivisions assigned to prepare the statement.

(ii) The name of the organization as it appears in the document may differ from its official name.

(iii) The organization has no proper identifying name of its own but only a generic name describing its type and common to most bodies of its type, e.g. public library, technical college, women's institute, and so on.

(iv) The name of the organization may change. Though this is related to change of name in personal authors, there are special considerations here.

(v) The organization may be associated with another organization, e.g. it may be affiliated, or it may be a division, section, committee of the parent organization.

(vi) The document may be produced by a collective body which has no formal characteristics, e.g. a body of citizens acting collectively for a particular purpose.

These problems will be examined in Chapter 4.

Having defined the various groups in this way, the codifier will now proceed to list under each heading the various types of document or organization relevant to each group. For example, under the heading *Dependent documents* will be listed concordances, indexes, glossaries, supplements, appendices, digests, commentaries, and so on; within the group *Change of name* will be listed those occasions which give rise to a change of name – such as marriage, joining a religious order, change of citizenship, and so on. In other words, all those *cases* will be listed in which the general *condition* denoted by the heading is operative.

The term *condition* has been used by Lubetzky to denote a relevant code problem; a *case* is simply a class of documents, organizations, etc. in which that problem is found.

It may be possible to supplement or amend these groups – in fact the committees working on AACR, though using Lubetzky's original analysis, considered it necessary to make a number of modifications. What is significant here is not the precise detail but the method. Lubetzky's method – his analysis of relevant authorship problems, of conditions and cases – is more rigorous than anything so far achieved. All major codes have faults arising from inadequate prior analysis of the problems involved. And as we noted in Chapter 1, consistency in the application of code rules can be fairly maintained only if the rules are based on clear definition of underlying principles.

The next job will be the making of the rules. Rules will, of course, be needed only for the conditions (though this is not to deny that some cases – periodicals, government publications, music, for example – will need additional detail for their unique problems). As each condition represents the problem common to all cases listed under it, the solution will apply to all cases; to repeat the rule for every case obviously would be uneconomic. A guiding principle in the making of the rules will be the *purpose* of the code, and in particular whether its object is a collocative or direct catalogue, for many of the controversies in cataloguing can be settled once this point has been decided.

The Advantages of the Analytical Method Just Outlined

The only other 'method' is to try to *enumerate* all cases, i.e. all classes of documents, organizations, etc., which give rise to problems and then to make a rule for each. The older codes are all basically enumerative – for example, many of the rules 1–22 in the 1908 Anglo-American code (AA) are rules for cases of dependent works. The advantages of this analytical method over such enumeration are as follows:

(i) *Once the real problems are analysed, the solutions are likely to be more satisfactory.* Knowing the problem is half the battle. In the past, the lack of such prior analysis and the consequent misunderstandings of the problems have led to much confusion in the rules, as for example in the rules for societies and institutions in AA. Again, this can be seen in the treatment of noblemen in the codes, where the only problem seems to be whether they should be entered under family name or title of nobility. In fact, as we shall see, several problems are involved (e.g. change of name, constant use of one name – family *or* title; use of both names in different documents – or same document). Many of these problems are common to other classes of writer also.

(ii) *Consistency*. Where rules are made for cases rather than conditions there are likely to be inconsistencies because of the lack of clearly established principles. For example, if rules are made independently for glossaries, revisions, indexes, and so on, on an *ad hoc* basis, it is not likely that the same consistency will be achieved as if they were all covered by a general rule for dependent works.

(iii) *Reduction in the number of the rules*. As Lubetzky has clearly demonstrated and as can be understood from the above, the creation of rules to deal with cases rather than the conditions operating in them is one of the main reasons for prolificity in codes of rules. Such prolificity makes the work of the cataloguer unnecessarily difficult and, when added to the inevitable inconsistencies, greatly reduces the efficiency of rules.

(iv) *Greater coverage*. Despite the reduction in the number of rules, a code based on the sound analysis of conditions is likely to cater for a greater variety of documents than an enumerative code. This is because new cases frequently arise whereas the cataloguer will meet few new conditions. For example, a code produced in 1908 could not be expected to cater specifically for radio adaptations, but if it had a rule for the general condition *Dependent works*, there would be little difficulty in accommodating the new type. Enumerative codes soon date and need frequent revision. Until a new edition appears, new cases will be accommodated by *ad hoc* rules because of the lack of general principles, and these may well differ from the rules introduced later into the revision.

READINGS

1. *Anglo-American cataloguing rules* (British text). London, Library Association, 1967 (footnote 2).
2. LUBETZKY, S. *Cataloging rules and principles*. Washington, GPO, 1953.

Chapter 3
Major English-Language Codes

In this chapter I have attempted to outline the essential features of the major English-language codes, beginning with the British Museum code, first published in 1841, and ending with the Anglo-American rules of 1967. Although I have had to refer to particular rules,* I wish to emphasize that such references are merely illustrative: I certainly do not intend to encourage students to undertake the tedious and unprofitable business of memorizing rules parrot-fashion. In studying author cataloguing the important thing is to grasp the fundamental problems – the 'conditions' that arise from particular 'cases' – and the possible solutions to those problems. It is as background to such study, which we shall turn to in the next chapter, that a knowledge of the essential features of existing codes will prove valuable. (Each of the codes also caters for title entry, but the title entry rules will be examined in Chapter 5.)

The British Museum Rules
(1841. Latest Revision 1936)

The oldest code of importance in English. Panizzi was largely responsible. When published, it aroused great controversy – the ninety-one rules covering author and title headings and description were said to be too complex.

BM has had a great *influence* directly or indirectly on all subsequent codes. Its direct influence can be seen in the codes of some other national and academic libraries, e.g. the Bodleian. Its indirect influence has been through the British Museum

* Throughout Chapters 3–5 numbers given in brackets refer to rules in the code being discussed at that point.

representatives on various code committees and through the printed catalogues of the British Museum.

Designed for a single large library. In such libraries change in the catalogue is expensive and choice of heading is affected by this practical consideration. Example: (11) change of name, specifies entry under earliest name used as author thus obviating change in entries. *Collocation* – in this case, under earliest name – is thus forced by practical considerations.

However BM often favours *direct* entry; it is a practical location tool in many respects. Example: the basic rule that headings should be chosen from information found in the book (4). Other examples: pseudonyms and initials are allowed as main entry headings (20) and (12).

References frequently give some information (35). Although the indiscriminate use of added entries is avoided, so is the use of simple references from one part of the catalogue to another. To that extent the resultant catalogue is collocative *and* direct.

The concept of *corporate authorship* was first formulated in BM and has been adopted by all subsequent English codes – though continental countries have been slower to accept the idea, preferring to treat works by corporate authors as anonymous. Primary rules here: (5, 16, 17b, 22). In general, preference is for entry under place, e.g. Paris. Bibliothèque Nationale; only international societies, commercial firms and some religious bodies being entered directly under name.

Form headings are a feature. There are sequences in the catalogue under such headings as: Congresses, Ephemerides, Dictionaries, Encyclopaedias, Directories, Liturgies, and so on. Some of these – in particular, Academies – have now been abandoned and the material dispersed under other headings.

BM has faults associated with inadequate analysis and enumeration. It is badly in need of revision and now would seem to be the time for this, following completion of the *General catalogue of printed books*, and in view of the proposals for automation at the British Museum. In particular, the rules for corporate authors and such quaint survivals as Anonymous books (18), need overhauling. The code needs to be rearranged according to some more easily recognizable pattern.

Cutter. Rules for a Dictionary Catalog
(1876. 4th ed., 1904)

A comprehensive code, having sections on author, title, subject, and form entry, description, and the filing of entries.

Cutter has had an immense *influence*, especially on dictionary cataloguing in the US, and many of its rulings on subject headings still remain almost unquestioned. Its influence on AA is evident in the American alternative rules particularly, and in the treatment of corporate authors. Its frequent discussion of rules has made it a useful handbook for students and practising cataloguers.

Pragmatic approach: alternative rules are frequently suggested – according to the nature and size of the library and the physical form of catalogue. Cutter's attitude is expressed in the famous *Prefaces* and *General remarks* which all students should read: 'No code of cataloging could be adopted in all points by every one . . .' *Three styles* of cataloguing are formulated: Short, Medium, and Full. Where he considers no absolute ruling can be laid down, the 'convenience of the public is to be the final guide' and the cataloguer is to choose the *best known name*. Examples: (24c) Married women ('let him follow rather than lead the public'); (40) Change of name; (7) Pseudonyms; (25) Noblemen; (28) Compound names. Frequently *double entry* is suggested where no alternative is perfectly satisfactory, e.g. (8) Illustrations; (11) Music; (20) Concordances. In aiming at sought heading – for example in allowing initials and pseudonyms, Cutter in general favours a *direct* catalogue.

Rules for *corporate authorship* are more detailed than those in BM, and they grow in number through the four editions. They are prefaced by an interesting and still useful introduction and there are many notes on the rules themselves. In general preference is for entry under *name* of organization (contrast BM) but there are many exceptions – in particular, official organizations go under place. The basic rule is (61). These rules are by no means satisfactory but are of great historical importance.

General *arrangement* is sound: Part A – Entry (where to enter), Part B – Style (how to enter). Within A are further divisions for types of entry, author entry being divided into Personal and

Corporate Authors. However the detailed grouping is less satisfactory, some problems being scattered through several sections, e.g. Pseudonyms (7) and (97).

Cutter recognized the distinction between conditions and cases. In the preface to the 4th edition he states: 'The number of . . . rules is not owing to any complexity of system, but to the number of widely varying cases to which a few simple principles have to be applied.' However, these principles are not clearly isolated and the code enumerates many types of documents and organizations.

The Anglo-American or Joint Code (1908)

This code is a result of the combined effort of Committees of the Library Associations of Great Britain and America, 'with a view to establishing unity of practice throughout the English-speaking race' (*Preface*). The committees represented various types and sizes of libraries. The historical background can be read in the two *Prefaces*.

AA has had a greater *influence* than any other code in English. Although the Americans brought out a revision in 1949, it persisted as a *joint code*, unrevised, for fifty years – and even today, despite the gradual acceptance of the new *Anglo-American cataloguing rules* (1967), the Joint Code is still the basis of cataloguing in countless libraries and bibliographies.

Aim: 'larger libraries of a scholarly character' – *Preface.* The detail in the rules for descriptive cataloguing, as compared with BM, suggests that the compilers had in mind libraries somewhat larger than the British Museum.

One hundred and seventy-four rules, covering author and title headings and description. *The two committees differed over only eight rules:* (16) Concordances; (32) Princes of the blood; (33) Noblemen; (40) Change of name; (41) Married women; (116) Anonymous – different spelling; (118) Anonymous – translations; (121) Periodicals – change of title. Many of the differences concern the problem of *authors having more than one name,* and in general the Americans prefer collocation of an author's works under latest name or tend to advocate 'best known' name, following Cutter; the British prefer collocation under earliest name.

Arrangement is better than in previous codes. Two broad sections: Entry and heading (1–135) and Description (136–174). Rules for author heading are in two sub-sections: Personal authors and Corporate authors. The Personal authors section is further subdivided into (a) Under whom as author? and (b) Under what part or form of name?

A A *has the following limitations:*

(i) Despite the arrangement, *analysis into conditions and cases is by no means complete*; there is frequent enumeration of types of document (libretti, concordances, etc.) and types of organization (alumni associations, churches, agricultural experimental stations, etc.). Therefore there are:

(a) *Inconsistencies* – e.g. Thematic catalogues (10) under composer but Concordances (16 – American) under compiler. And see (113) and (116).

(b) *Too many rules* – thus many of the first twenty-two rules are simply examples of dependent works.

(c) *Many ommissions* – enumeration if attempted must be as complete as possible, yet there are no rules in the section on government publications for reports by committees, royal commissions, etc., or for government institutions such as the Science Museum. Again, there is no rule for change of name in corporate authors.

(ii) *Inadequate definitions.* Examples: overlappings and confusion in (101) and (105 – 1 and 2), where the examples add to the difficulties. The phrase 'minor divisions' in (59) Subordinate departments, is vague. 'Societies' and 'institutions', though major divisions in the code, are defined only by means of specifications. The word 'usually' in the definition of 'joint author' allows some documents by several authors to be catalogued according to (2) or (126).

(iii) The *examples* are one of weakest elements of the code (recognized in the *Preface*, but neglected since). Many are in German or Latin. In the section on corporate authors parts of headings are italicized without apparent reason; many of the rules for government publications have only American examples. In (32) the language of the designations in some of the examples does not conform to the ruling in (35).

(iv) *Tendency to ignore author's identity as found in document.* Thus

Initials (115) are never to be used as headings and Pseudonyms (38) must not be used if the real name can be found, even though author may never have written under his real name.

(v) *Whether the catalogue is to be basically direct or collocative is not finally settled.* There is no introductory statement of principles. Many rules, e.g. (38, 40, 121, 123), favour collocation, but there are inconsistencies – especially in the American rules, e.g. by (116) they prefer to follow the spelling of title page where spelling differs in various editions of an anonymous book – and see (118 – American).

(vi) *Non-author headings are sometimes suggested.* Thus (62) and (71) advocate form headings for laws and treaties – though not sought headings – and the resulting collocation will rarely be required.

(vii) *Corporate authors.*

(a) *Primary division into governments, societies, and institutions, results in the neglect of problems common to each,* e.g. change of name, subordinate divisions.

(b) *Division into societies and institutions is not relevant to the cataloguing problem underlying this division.* (An account of the historical reasons for the division can be found in the Lubetzky Report.) The basic problem is whether to enter corporate authors under *name* or *place.* Organizations having distinctive names will be sought under name (e.g. Library Association) and should be so entered; those without such names (e.g. public library) will be sought under place and should be so entered. A rule to this effect would appear to suffice.* Instead, the main rules (72) and (82) call for entry of societies under name, and institutions under place – even though societies with common names (e.g. Dramatic Society, Antiquarian Society) will be sought under place, while institutions with distinctive names (e.g. Science Museum) will be sought under name. The inadequacy of these two rules is

* The question arises: what is a name? If the place name is considered to be part of the name of the organization, e.g. Barnet Film Society, then a simple rule calling for entry under name may well be sufficient (cf. Post Office Telephone directories). But this would appear to give rise to a further set of problems, e.g. whether in any individual instance (say, Lambeth Public Libraries) the place name is a part of the official name. As we shall see, the British and American editions of the new *Anglo-American cataloguing rules* differ in their treatment of this problem.

the cause of most of the other rules for societies and institutions, which make exceptions or modifications for certain cases. Thus, (83) allows entry of institutions having *proper names* under name (e.g. Victoria and Albert Museum). This makes matters worse: some distinctive names are not proper (e.g. Science Museum) and some proper names are not distinctive (e.g. names of churches). A special rule (96) accommodates the latter (this becoming an exception to an exception), but the former is ignored.

(c) *Government bodies (central and local)*. Why enter one's own central government publications under country, e.g. Great Britain, Ministry of Agriculture? Theoretically, of course, the State is responsible, but this does not result in the sought heading – and is collocation by country desirable? Entry under organization directly (with country following, if foreign) has been advocated by many writers.[1] There are examples of non-author headings (see (vi) above). Several classes of government publication are not catered for by these rules (see (ic) above). On the other hand, some of the rules, e.g. (59) and (60) are concerned with problems common to all forms of corporate authorship.

By the 1920's AA was under criticism and the need for revision was repeatedly expressed. Some called for simplification, saying the rules were too fussy, others wanted more detail. Both were right: enumerative codes always appear too fussy, yet are not capable of meeting all cases, as we have seen. Revision of principles was really needed – but this had to wait till Lubetzky in 1953. Those who called for greater detail won. In the 1930's Committees of the American Library Association (ALA) and the Library Association (LA) began revision. The LA dropped out at outbreak of war. The ALA continued alone, producing a draft code in 1941. The final version appeared in 1949, covering author and title headings. The rules for description were published separately by the Library of Congress as *Rules for descriptive cataloging*.

The ALA Code (1949)

Though containing rules for headings only, ALA has 250 pages as compared with the 60 of AA. It was immediately criticized for over-elaboration. It can more truthfully be criticized for doing the wrong thing: supplementing and amending the 1908 Code rather than defining principles. (This is, of course, more easily seen in retrospect.) In her *Introduction* the editor says: 'Dissatisfaction with the 1908 Code rested not with its inclusions but rather with its omissions.' Reliance on principles alone is specifically rejected and in its place an attempt is made to codify 'experience'. 'The exceptions to the general principles and general rules result from practical experience' (*Introduction*).

Despite statements to the contrary, this gives a certain arbitrary quality to the rules, and faults of enumeration already mentioned under the 1908 Code apply equally here – as do most of the specific faults listed above. Lubetzky's report is basic reading on this.

In certain details it improves on AA:

(a) *Some rules are rearranged to make the sequence more logical,* e.g. joint author and collections rules are associated, as are rules for all kinds of religious bodies (though this latter group is not based on a real cataloguing problem).

(b) There are better *examples* and more of them.

(c) As an enumerative code, it is better in *listing more types of literature,* e.g. scenarios, radio scripts, adaptations; and the rules for *government publications* are extended.

There are a few alterations to specific rulings: joint authorship (3), librettos (12A2), thematic catalogues (12F), encyclopaedias and dictionaries (5B), pseudonyms and anonymous classics (33A). And all American alternatives in AA are incorporated.

Lubetzky and Catalogue Code Revision since 1953

ALA was the result of an impetus originating in the 1930's. By 1949 the real requirements of a new code were widely recognized and from the first ALA was unsatisfactory. In 1951 the ALA invited Lubetzky, consultant on bibliography and cataloguing policy to the Library of Congress, to 'prepare a general analysis of the 1949 Code . . . with special consideration of the rules for corporate authors and a discussion of the objectives and principles which should underlie a revision of the rules'.

The Report[2] was published in 1953. Many of its observations can be applied to codes other than ALA. Only the briefest outline is given here. It is in three parts:

Part One. Is this rule necessary? Many rules are not properly related to each other and are inconsistent. Due to: poor wording, irrelevant definitions and distinctions, and cases being made the subject of rules rather than conditions.

Part Two. The corporate complex. Traces the historical development of the corporate authorship rules. Main point – the idea of distinctive name, already introduced in the above notes on AA.

Part Three. Design for a code. A direct catalogue is to be preferred, collocation being left to references. Lubetzky's conditions, put forward as a basis for a code, are listed in Chapter 2 and discussed in Chapter 4 (see also Chapter 5 for Lubetzky's code outline for title cataloguing).

The ALA accepted the Report and began work on a new code based on it. (No longer merely a revision of the existing code.) Meanwhile, in 1951, the LA reconstituted its Catalogue Code Revision Committee. The Committee spent several years discussing the obsolescent 1949 Code. In 1956 the American Committee published a 'Statement of objectives and principles for catalog code revision'.[3] By 1960 a draft code had been produced[4] and from this time on the British and American committees worked closely together. In 1961 an International Conference on Cataloguing Principles[5] was held in Paris and the statement of principles which emerged (known as the Paris Principles) was largely endorsed by the Revision Committees. Lubetzky, who had edited the work in progress since 1956, resigned in 1962 and was replaced by C. Sumner Spalding. After much discussion and the appearance of numerous interim reports and comments in the professional press,[6] the new code was finally published in 1967, the British text by the Library Association, the North American text by the American Library Association.[7]

Anglo-American Cataloguing Rules (1967)*

Although the Code is designed primarily to meet the needs of

---

* Unless otherwise stated subsequent reference is to the British text of this code.

research libraries, other kinds of libraries have not been forgotten and in some cases alternative rules are provided.

Apart from rules for choice and style of author and title *headings*, the Code includes sections on *descriptive cataloguing*. And in addition to monographs, certain categories of *special materials* (maps, films, music, etc.) are given separate treatment, the rules for several of these types of materials, and for descriptive cataloguing, being based on Library of Congress practice.

Multiple entry through the use of unit cataloguing is accepted, but the need to distinguish between main and added entries and references is recognized throughout.

The most significant feature is the attention paid to matters of *principle*. The influence of Lubetzky and the Paris Principles has been profound. It can be seen in the general structure of the Code and in the systematic arrangement of the rules; in the provision of a basic statement of intent – which is to produce a more direct form of entry based on information found in the document and, in particular, on the title page; and in the consistent attempt to distinguish between conditions and cases.

It is in this latter feature that the Code represents such a marked advance over earlier formulations The number of its rules is due less to old-style enumeration than to the comprehensive nature of the Code. In each section the underlying condition is defined and a fundamental rule formulated; subsequent rules usually do no more than develop that rule, without conflict, to meet specific cases. To a considerable degree, therefore, the advantages of an analytical approach (outlined on pages 30–36) are realized.

Although it has been rightly stated that the rules will, in general, result in a more direct form of entry than was often the case with earlier codes, it must be emphasized that collocation is also an important – and frequently paramount – objective. Indeed, it is a basic principle of the Code that the writings of one person should, so far as possible, be collocated. For example, though the rule for pseudonymous works (42) allows the use of pseudonym as a heading – thus accepting the 'direct' principle of adopting for headings information found in books – the same rule states that whenever an author uses more than one name in his books only one must be used, thereby collocating an author's works. Books by Lewis Carroll, for example, must be entered under Charles Lutwidge Dodgson, and those by Ashe, Halliday, Morton, etc., under Creasey. As we shall see, the principle of collocation also underlies the rules for uniform titles.

The main rules for ENTRY AND HEADING are to be found in *Part I* (rules 1–6). The first rule states: 'Enter a work, a collection of works, or selections from works by one author under the person or corporate body that is the author, whether named in the work or not.' *Anonymous works*, works of 'unknown or uncertain authorship' are entered, by rule (2), under title. Rule (3) concerns the problem of *shared authorship*: where the principal author is indicated, his name is used as the main heading; where there is no such indication, the first-named is selected for the heading unless there are more than three authors, in which case entry is under title. Rule (3), however, covers only certain prescribed categories of shared authorship, and in (4–6) further rules are laid down for *works produced under editorial direction, collections,* and *serials*. Rules (1–6) contain numerous sub-sections in which the application of rules to special cases is demonstrated – joint pseudonyms and authors represented on their title pages by initials, for example.

Insofar as rules (7–19), dealing with *mixed authorship* and *related works*, are concerned with problems that arise when responsibility for the existence of a document is shared, forcing a choice between alternatives – between, for example, adapter and original author, artist and author of text, corporate author and personal author – it can be said that these rules are further extensions of the basic rules for shared authorship. And throughout this section the guiding principle is that of the 'principal responsibility' enumerated in (3) and defined by reference to the 'relative importance of the different activities', the 'relative proportions of the work that have resulted from the activities', and the 'emphasis given to each on the title page'. Whether all these cases need have been elaborated – and the editors admit that no listing can be comprehensive – is questionable. But at any rate they are seen in the context of a general principle and not as independent cases requiring *ad hoc* rules.

The rest of Chapter 1 is devoted to special problems arising from *legal* and *religious publications*. It concludes with a summary (33) of circumstances in which *added entries* should be made.

Having determined authorship the next step in cataloguing is to decide upon the form of heading, and Chapter 2 of the code, (40–58), is concerned with the problems of *names of persons*. The basic rule (40) prescribes entry under the 'name by which he is commonly identified, whether it is his real name, or an assumed name, nickname, title of nobility, or other appellation'. (41) gives a general rule for choosing among *different names*, and this is followed by amplified rules for specific cases (pseudonyms, shortened forms of name, variations arising through language – forms and spelling). (46–53) cover *style of heading* (compound surnames, names with prefixes, titles of nobility, etc.), and there are additional rules (54–58) to assist in coping with foreign names.

Rules covering *headings for corporate bodies* are given in Chapter 3, and the basic rule (60) states: 'Enter a corporate body directly under its name except when the rules that follow provide for entering it under a higher body of which it is a part, or under the name of the government of which it is an agency.' These two exceptions give rise to a number of special rules for *subordinate and related bodies* (69–71) and *governments* (75–86).

(69) advocates entry of a subordinate body as a subheading under a higher body only in certain specified circumstances – e.g. when the name 'includes the entire name of the higher body' or 'contains a term that by definition implies that the body is a component of something else'.

(75) provides that the 'conventional name of a country, province, state, county, municipality, or other political jurisdiction' is to be used as the heading for its government. (78), following the general principle that 'agencies through which the basic legislative, judicial, and executive functions of government are exercised should be entered as subheadings under the heading for the government', specifies such headings as: Great Britain. *Department of Education and Science*, and Kent. *County Council*. However, the basic principle also allows that 'other bodies created and controlled by the government should be entered under their own name', and (78) gives examples of the types of organizations that should be thus

directly entered, e.g. institutions (Kent County Library), authorities and trusts for the operation of utilities and industries (National Coal Board), etc.

Other rules for corporate bodies cover *choice and form of name* (61–68), and certain special categories – *conferences*, etc. (87–91), *religious bodies* (92–97), and *radio and television stations* (98).

Chapter 4 is devoted to *uniform titles*, an issue which the 1908 Code dealt with only incidentally and with some inconsistency. The chapter begins: 'The following rules for uniform titles provide the means for bringing together catalogue entries for all editions of a given work when its editions, translations, etc., have appeared under various titles, and for properly identifying a given work when its title is obscured by the wording on the title-page.' The rules refer both to title as heading and title as part of the description, and their purpose is to facilitate collocation and also, frequently, identification. Further examination of these rules is reserved for Chapters 5 and 14 below.

The rules in Chapter 5 (120–126) 'summarize the requirements for *references*'. Although many of the rules in the Code indicate when references should be made, the various provisions are outlined systematically in this chapter.

Part II, headed DESCRIPTION, comprises rules (130–191) for the descriptive cataloguing of monographs and a variety of special materials. Rules on recording the parts of the description follow a general statement of the objectives of descriptive cataloguing and the general principle that 'information presented by the author, publisher or other issuing authority in or on their items generally forms the basis of catalogue description'.

Part III, rules (200–272), concerns NON-BOOK MATERIALS and opens with the following statement: 'The rules for entry, heading and description for books and book-like materials (Parts I and II) are applied also in the cataloguing of non-book materials (Part III) ... to the extent that they are pertinent and unless they are specifically contravened or modified by the rules in the following chapters.' Parts II and III, will be discussed further in Chapter 14 below.

The Code ends with a number of appendices – on glossaries, capitalization, abbreviations, numerals, punctuation and diacritics – and a statement of those rules in the Code whose American text differs from the British.

A valuable analysis of the new Code has been made by Michael Gorman.[8] He points out two general weaknesses:

(i) A lack of adequate definition of the nature of authorship and responsibility, both personal and corporate.

(ii) An occasional failure of nerve: an unwillingness to accept the consequences of its decisions on principles. This can be seen particularly in the American rules allowing for entry of certain classes of organizations under place rather than name; and in rule (43) where the cataloguer is advised always to give full forenames even though this will not result in the sought heading for those writers who habitually use, and are known by, their initials – D. H. Lawrence, for example.

The overall tenor of Gorman's study is favourable, however, and the new Rules have, justifiably, met with general approval.[9]

A revision programme for AACR has been instituted,[10] and the question of more widespread international cooperation on the basis of AACR is being studied.[11]

READINGS

1. PIGGOTT, M. 'The cataloguing of government publications'. *Library Association Record*, 58(4), April 1956, 129–35. A useful account of practices in various libraries. See also: HORROCKS, S. *The State as publisher*. London, Library Association, 1952.

2. LUBETZKY, S. *Cataloging rules and principles*. Washington, GPO, 1953.

3. 'Statement of objectives and principles for catalog code revision'. *Journal of Cataloging and Classification*, 12(2), April 1956, 103–7.

4. LUBETZKY, S. *Code of cataloging rules: author and title entry – an unfinished draft*. Chicago, American Library Association, March 1960.

5. International Conference on Cataloguing Principles, Paris, 1961. *Report*, edited by A. H. Chaplin and Dorothy Anderson, London, IFLA, 1963. See also the subsequent *Statement of principles: annotated edition,* edited by Chaplin and Anderson (IFLA, 1967). Summaries and comments were, of course, published in periodicals – e.g. PIGGOTT, M. 'International agreement on cataloguing principles'. *Assistant Librarian*, 55(11), November 1962, 212–15.

6. For example: 'Cataloguing rules: progress in code revision'. *Library Association Record*, 62(8), August 1960, 248–53.
7. *Anglo-American cataloguing rules: British text*. London, Library Association, 1967.
8. GORMAN, M. *A study of the rules for entry and heading in the Anglo-American cataloguing rules, 1967 (British text)*. London, Library Association, 1968. See also Gorman's review article: 'A-A 1967: the new cataloguing rules'. *Library Association Record*, 70(2), February 1968, 27–32.
9. Apart from various review articles, the following offer valuable interpretations and commentaries:
   Seminar on the Anglo-American cataloguing rules (1967) . . . London, Library Association, 1969.
   ALLEN, THELMA E. *and* DICKMAN, DARYL ANN. *ed.* *New rules for an old game: Proceedings of a workshop on the 1967 Anglo-American cataloguing code*. London, Bingley, 1968.
   DOWNING, J. C. 'The Anglo-American cataloguing rules, 1967'. *Library World*, 70 (824), February 1969, 199–204.
10. See *Catalogue and Index*, 17, January 1970, 1.
11. GORMAN, M. 'International meeting of cataloguing experts: a report from Copenhagen'. *Catalogue and Index*, 16, October 1969, 12.

Some of the earlier commentaries and articles resulting from the renewed interest in codes are still valuable also, e.g.:

STOUT, R. F. *ed.* *Towards a better cataloging code*. University of Chicago, Graduate Library School, 1956. (These articles are also in *Library Quarterly*, 26 (4), October 1956.)

INTERNATIONAL FEDERATION OF LIBRARY ASSOCIATIONS. Working Group on the Co-ordination of Cataloguing Principles. 'Report on anonyma and corporate authorship'. *Libri*, 6 (3), 1956, 271–97. (This is one of several examples of IFLA's work, published in *Libri*.)

VERONA, E. 'Literary unit versus bibliographical unit'. *Libri*, 9 (2), 79–104.

Chapter 4
The Author Approach:
Conditions and Cases

Chapter 3 indicated in broad terms the kind of knowledge that a student should aim to acquire in his study of cataloguing codes. Here a method is outlined: the main problems of author cataloguing as isolated by Lubetzky are stated, and for each problem (i) the possible solutions are set out, (ii) Lubetzky's solution as found in his *Report*[1] is given, and (iii) the various code rules are referred to. Reference is also made on several occasions to pages 30–32 where examples of documents illustrating the problems will be found. Of course the major codes, being enumerative, do not have the same classification of problems and so it is not easy on every occasion to demonstrate how they would solve them. However I have pointed out what seem to me to be the more important of the relevant rules and I have tried to summarize their main pronouncements without misrepresentation, despite the unavoidable simplification. Although many rules are referred to, it is not suggested that students attempt to memorize them; rules are given to illustrate solutions to problems and rule numbers are given so that the student who wishes to verify a particular point can do so. Clearly the student who has the codes at hand when reading this section will derive the greatest benefit.

In this and the succeeding chapter on title entries, under each condition I have given the AACR rulings first when discussing the codes so that the student may, if he wishes, refer only to these, thus gaining a general impression of one code before entering upon a comparative study.

Condition One: Documents having more than one Author

Lubetzky has distinguished the following sub-conditions:

1. THE DOCUMENT IS PREPARED BY AN AUTHOR WITH THE AID OF COLLABORATORS OR CONTRIBUTORS (e.g. a, b*).

Possible Solutions:

Entry under (i) author first-named on the title page, or (ii) title, or (iii) author chiefly responsible.

Lubetzky's Solution:

The document will be cited by the author chiefly responsible; therefore enter under his name, with possible added entries for collaborators or contributors.

Codes Solutions:

AACR agrees with Lubetzky. The general rule (3A) for this kind of shared authorship states: 'Enter a work of shared authorship under the person or corporate body, if any, to whom principal responsibility is attributed, e.g. by wording or typography.'

The treatment of this condition is unsatisfactory in all other codes except ALA, which by (4) broadly agrees with Lubetzky, though the definition of 'composite work' here limits the scope of this rule. None of the other codes isolates the problem and therefore such documents have to be treated either by the rules for joint authorship and composite works, or by the rules for collections, always assuming that the definitions allow this. If documents are treated by the joint author/composite-works rules, then all codes would enter them under first-named author on the title page, which will not be the chief author in documents where his name appears last and is distinguished typographically. If treated by the collections rules, a better result will be achieved so long as the chief author is regarded as editor, because by all codes collections are entered under editor.

2. THE DOCUMENT IS ONE COMPOSED BY AN EDITOR OR COMPILER FROM THE WRITINGS OF OTHER PEOPLE

i.e. in the plural – this does not refer to collected editions or selections of a single author, as in (c) – such works would obviously be entered under the original author, (e.g. e/h).

* The examples denoted by lower case letters here and elsewhere in this chapter refer to pages 30–32.

Possible Solutions:

These will differ according to whether the document is a monograph or a periodical (i.e. any work appearing regularly: periodicals as commonly understood, directories, annuals, year-books, etc.).

Monographs: (i) editor, or (ii) title.

Periodicals: (i) editor, or (ii) title, or possibly (iii) the organization, society, etc. responsible.

Lubetzky's Solution:

Monographs: entry under editor or compiler will result in the sought heading; if no editor is named enter under title.

Periodicals: there are bound to be successive editors; therefore entry under title will result in sought heading and will collocate the work (except, perhaps, where several titles are possible – see Chapter 5).

Codes Solutions:

In general each agrees with Lubetzky on *monographs.* AACR by (4A) – works produced under editorial direction, and (5A) – collections, prescribes entry under the editor's name except in certain circumstances (e.g. if the editor is not named on the title page or, in the case of works produced under editorial direction, if the publisher is named in the title). The exceptions, attempting to provide for those cases where the sought heading is unlikely to be the editor, are relatively clear-cut, and examples are given to clarify the points.

AA (126) and ALA (5A1a) prefer title entry if the editor's work is slight and his name does not appear on the title page, and Cutter (104) also advocates the use of title for those collections 'chiefly known by their titles'. Both qualifications are vague, though intended to produce the sought heading, and inconsistency is likely to follow. (Note example (e). By all codes, except possibly Cutter, this would be entered under editor: clearly an added entry should be made for title.)

Periodicals: AACR (6) rules that entry should be under title, with added entry for the corporate body responsible (other than one acting solely as commercial publisher). However, certain exceptions are indicated: in particular, by (6B) the name of the corporate body is to be used as the heading if the title of the serial includes its name or consists solely of a 'generic term or phrase which does not adequately identify the serial except when taken in conjunction with the name of the body'.

Other codes do not isolate this problem satisfactorily, preferring to list some of the classes of documents exhibiting this condition and making rules for each. Thus AA (121–127) has rules for periodicals, encyclopaedias and dictionaries, directories; ALA (3–5) has a similar, though extended, enumeration; Cutter (98–104) is more analytical and lists the various classes of documents as examples, while BM uses form headings for many of these categories. So far as periodicals in the narrow sense are concerned, BM (17) excepted, all agree on title entry; however, AA (121) and ALA allow entry under organization in certain circumstances, e.g. if the periodical is infrequent in its appearance or composed only of the routine transactions, etc. of the organization. (BUCOP enters under title except (a) where the name of the organization forms 'a direct or indirect part of the main title' or (b) where 'the title is not specific in itself' – e.g. *Arbitrator, The.* Organ of the Workingmen's Peace Association; but, Association of American Geographers. *Annals.*) BUCOP's ruling, and that of AACR, is more satisfactory than AA's because it concentrates on the wording of the title, etc., and it is this that determines the reader's approach. The enumerative method causes difficulties when the cataloguer is dealing with types of periodical publications that are not specifically listed, e.g. *Year's work in . . .*

3. **THE DOCUMENT IS ONE BY SEVERAL AUTHORS WITH NO ONE AUTHOR MORE RESPONSIBLE FOR IT THAN ANY OF THE OTHERS** (e.g. j).

Possible Solutions:
(i) First-mentioned author (or where two only, first and second in one heading), or (ii) title.

Lubetzky's Solution:
Lubetzky advocates title entry. Though he argues the case for title entry at some length, few cataloguers have been convinced of the efficacy of this solution. Traditionally such documents have been entered under the first-mentioned author and there

is little doubt that in many cases this is the sought heading. A factor which seems to influence this is the number of authors – the more authors the greater the prominence of the title. The problem is to discover how many authors have to be named before title takes precedence over author.

Codes Solutions:

AACR by (3B) specifies entry under first-named author unless there are more than three authors. In the latter case entry is under title unless the work is produced under the direction of an editor named on the title page (in which case rule (4) applies – see above).

In general, other codes enter such works under the first-named author (or first and second in one heading), but all are bedevilled by the distinctions they make between a work of 'joint authorship' and a 'composite work', the distinction being that in the first case the parts written by each author are not specified, while in the second, they are. (Cutter makes the distinctions but reverses the definitions.)

Two points to note here: (a) the distinctions are not relevant to cataloguing because both types of document are sought by readers in the same way and therefore repetition of the rules is inevitable (as to some extent in ALA (3) and (4)); (b) having made the distinction, both AA and Cutter fail to provide all the rules, AA (2) neglecting composite works, Cutter neglecting joint authorship – (3) caters for composite works by his definition.

4. THE DOCUMENT IS ONE IN WHICH THE WRITER REPORTS THE COMMUNICATION OF ANOTHER PERSON.

Possible Solutions:

Entry under (i) the original person, or (ii) the writer.

Lubetzky's Solution:

If the person is real, enter under his name, with added entry under writer.

Codes Solutions:

This problem is neglected by most of the codes. AACR (16)

states: 'Enter a work written by one person for another person, [and] in whose name it is presented, under the latter person . . .' (16B) makes an exception to this general rule: 'If a work written by one person for another person to present as his own is never so presented (e.g. a ghost-written speech that was never delivered by the other person or published under his name), enter it under the person who wrote it.'

Condition Two: Authors having more than one Name

Choice of name is often a further complication once the authorship has been established. In Chapter 2 – headings for persons – AACR gives a general rule (40): 'Enter a person under the name by which he is commonly identified, whether it is his real name, or an assumed name, nickname, title of nobility, or other appellation.' An exception is made in the case of an author using initials only (e.g. H. D.), when entry should be under full name if known (Doolittle, Hilda). (Compare (43) which specifies full forenames even when authors habitually use initials.) Rule (41) extends this basic rule: 'Enter an author who is not commonly identified in his writings by one particular name according to the following order of preference: (1) under the name by which he is generally identified in reference sources; (2) under the name by which he is most frequently identified in his works; (3) under the latest name he has used. If, however, a person changes his name, if he acquires or becomes identified by a title of nobility, or if the title by which he is identified is changed, enter him under the latest name or form of name or title unless there is reason to believe that an earlier one will persist as the one by which he will be better known.'

It should be noted that the Code, rather than accepting the name found in the document and thus running the risk of scattering an author's works (or even editions of his works) thus seeks to establish *one* form of heading. The remaining rules elaborate on these general directions.

Lubetzky distinguishes between authors who have several names and elect to use one consistently, and those who use different names in successive documents (Condition 4). His sub-conditions are as follows:

I. THE AUTHOR HAS CHANGED HIS OR HER NAME IN
CONSEQUENCE OF MARRIAGE, ADOPTION OF NEW CITIZEN-
SHIP, JOINING A RELIGIOUS ORDER, OR FOR ANY OTHER
REASON (e.g. k/l).

Note that here, in contrast to the conditions listed below, the
change of name is not primarily a matter of authorship: the
new name has a validity beyond the author's writings.

Possible Solutions:
Entry under (i) earliest name, or (ii) latest, or (iii) best known.

Lubetzky's Solution:
Enter under latest name if used in the author's books, on the
grounds that this will be the sought heading (even if he has used
the earlier one at some stage in his career), because he will be
known by this later name and all re-issues of his works will bear
the later name.* Such a solution satisfies the reader wanting a
particular document and also leads to collocation of an author's
works.

Codes Solutions:
AACR (41) agrees with Lubetzky, advocating entry under the
latest name, with the qualification 'unless there is reason to
believe that an earlier one will persist. . . .'
    In the older codes the Americans agree with Lubetzky – AA
(40) and ALA (45). The British – AA (40) and BM (11) – would
agree only if the earlier name has never been used in the author's
writings, for if it has, the earliest name is preferred.
    Entry under earliest name when two or more names have
been used is administratively convenient: it requires fewer
alterations in the catalogue than the Lubetzky solution, by which
entries have to be brought up to date when a person changes
his or her name. On the other hand, earliest name is rarely, if
ever, the sought name. Thus the convenience of the reader is
sacrificed to administrative convenience.
    Cutter (40) offers the third solution: best known name. But

---

* This would apply equally well to a nobleman who, on receiving a title –
or discarding one – uses his new name in his publications and becomes
known by it (Hailsham, for example).

'best known' is a temporary criterion and in practice merely delays alteration to the latest name; this may be no bad thing but the danger lies in the fact that entries will probably not be altered before many readers have been inconvenienced.

All older codes, BM excepted, provide examples of enumeration here. Thus, AA (41) repeats the rule for the specific case of married women; ALA (46) and Cutter (24C) do likewise; and ALA has further enumeration for Jews who have settled in Palestine (65B2), and for change of name in religious orders (53).

2. THE AUTHOR ALWAYS WRITES UNDER AN ASSUMED NAME DIFFERENT FROM HIS REAL NAME, OR UNDER HIS TITLE OF NOBILITY, OR UNDER PART OF HIS NAME (e.g. m/n).

Possible Solutions:

Entry under (i) real name or (ii) assumed name, etc.

Lubetzky's Solution:

Use the assumed name, etc. because readers will identify an author by the name he uses in his writings. Here again direct entry results in both a sought heading and collocation of an author's works, thus satisfying both objectives of an author catalogue.

Codes Solutions:

AACR agrees with Lubetzky – rules (40) and (42A) would apply. The older codes give different degrees of recognition to pseudonyms, i.e. assumed names (for a further discussion of this problem, see Chapter 5). AA (38) never allows it as a heading if the real name can be found, though the real name may never have been used in the author's works. This solution is clearly unhelpful. ALA (30) allows the use of pseudonym on specific occasions, e.g. if it has become 'fixed in literary history'. Cutter (7 and 97) allows pseudonym when a writer habitually uses it or is generally known by it (his discussion of the problem should be read). BM (20) allows pseudonym in accordance with (4) – with some slight exceptions. There is little to be said for this grudging acceptance or utter rejection of pseudonyms. If a writer constantly uses one, then only by entering the author under that name will both objectives of the catalogue be satisfied. Our concern is bibliography not biography. This also applies to titles of nobility. Where family name is never used the title should be adopted as heading with a reference from family name, e.g. *The case of Timothy Evans*, by Lord Altrincham and Ian Gilmour, should be entered under Altrincham and Gilmour rather than Grigg and Gilmour. The style of the heading can be devised so that it differentiates between different Lord Altrinchams:

> Altrincham, Edward William Macleay Grigg, *1st Baron*
> Altrincham, John Edward Poynder Grigg, *2nd Baron.*

In the case of noblemen BM (14) and AA (33 – British) call for entry under family name always. AA (33 – American), ALA, and Cutter (25) suggest latest title unless the writer is decidedly better known by family name or earlier title.

3. and 4. HERE LUBETZKY CONSIDERS THE PROBLEM OF AN AUTHOR WHO USES MORE THAN ONE NAME IN SUCCESSIVE DOCUMENTS

– and who thus forces the cataloguer to choose between the two objectives of the author catalogue (e.g. p/r). See also earlier notes in Chapter 2.

Possible Solutions: entry under (i) real name, or (ii) earliest name used, real or assumed, or (iii) latest name used, or (iv) whatever name is used on the title page of the particular document being catalogued.

Lubetzky's Solution: enter under the names as found on the title pages unless an author uses pseudonyms 'indiscriminately', in which case real name should always be used – so long as the author has used it in some of his writings.

Writers often use different names when they write in a number of different genres or styles (e.g. C. Day Lewis – Nicholas Blake). In such cases particularly readers enquire after their works by the names used on the title pages – few even know of the relationships between pseudonyms. Thus direct entry according to the title page is certainly the most generally useful mode of entry and the qualification Lubetzky makes about 'indiscriminate' use of pseudonyms should be warily applied. One can see its point however when there is little significance in the different names used, e.g. entry under the name found on the title page would be of little value in the case of a nobleman who sometimes used family name, sometimes title of nobility, more or less by accident, or a married woman variously identified. In such cases a uniform heading is essential for both objectives of the author catalogue.

Thus generally speaking Lubetzky – here as elsewhere – prefers the direct catalogue. References would be used to reveal related names.

Codes Solutions:

AACR departs here from Lubetzky. (41), as we have seen, gives an order of preference for determining the heading when an author 'is not commonly identified in his works by one particular name'. (42B), part of the rule for pseudonyms, amplifies this: 'If the works of an author appear under several pseudonyms or under his real name and one or more pseudonyms, enter him under the name by which he is primarily identified in modern editions of his works and in reference sources. In case of doubt, prefer the real name.'

The older codes are much more cautious than Lubetzky. AA never allows an author's works to be entered in more than one place; a uniform heading is always called for, cf. (33), (38), (40/41). BM (4) is nearer to Lubetzky. Cutter (7) allows such scattering: 'If any author uses two different pseudonyms enter under each the works written under it'; and ALA (30A) allows it on certain specified occasions.

5. AUTHORS WHOSE NAMES APPEAR IN TRANSLATION IN VARYING FORMS.

Possible Solutions:
Entry under (i) English form, or (ii) vernacular form.

Lubetzky's Solution:
Vernacular form – thus collocating original works and translations. However, well-known foreign authors whose names

are generally read in translation should be entered under the name which appears in the translations, e.g. Rabindranath Tagore.

Codes Solutions:

AACR (44A) specifies the name 'most firmly established in reference sources' for names in the Roman alphabet. This general rule is amplified in several sub-sections covering particular cases.

In general AA (23) agrees with Lubetzky, but there are some exceptions, e.g. saints better known by the English form of name; and Greek and classical writers, where the Latin form is specified (resulting in headings like Homerus). ALA (36) and Cutter (32–34) differ little from AA. In BM there is no general rule, but the preference in (4) and (6–9) is for the English form of name (a further example of BM preference for sought heading at the expense of collocation).

Condition Three: Dependent Documents (e.g. t/y)

I have extended Lubetzky's conception of dependent documents to cover the following categories:

(i) Modified documents: e.g. revisions, epitomes, selections.

(ii) Dependent documents proper: works which are separate but which depend for their interest and existence on other documents. Two groups: (a) those which depend on a single document, e.g. librettos, continuations, scenarios, indexes of single documents, and (b) those which depend on the total output of an author, e.g. thematic catalogues, concordances.

Lubetzky's Solution:

(i) and (iia) give rise to the same real problem: is the new document to be placed under the author of the original, or entered as a separate document in its own right (with the necessary references in either case)? Lubetzky considers (iia) only and states that they should be entered under the author and title of the document to which they belong, unless they have an interest and value of their own, in which case they should be entered as independent documents. This could be extended to include category (i): where the revision, etc., is virtually a new work, entry should be made under reviser. This would meet the requirements of a direct catalogue, and, in the case of entry under the original, will also result in collocation of dependent documents with the originals. However, it should be noted that it is by no means always easy to decide whether a document has an interest and value of its own. Its treatment in reviews and the layout of the title page might help in practice. For (iib) entry should be under the author of the new document; entry under the author whose output is treated constitutes subject (form) entry, e.g. SHAKESPEARE, WILLIAM – CONCOR-DANCES.

Codes Solutions:

AACR has two sections which include rules relevant to this issue: Works with authorship of mixed character (7–18), and Related works (19). In the introduction to the first section the following statement is made: 'The determination of main entry, or the person or body to be considered primarily responsible, depends variously on such considerations as the relative impor-tance of the different activities as such, the relative proportions of the work that have resulted from these activities, and the emphasis given to each on the title page. . . . Since no rules can anticipate all of the possible combinations of mixed authorship responsibility that may arise, the general principle of assigning main entry to the person or body judged to be principally responsible for the intellectual or artistic content of the work as a whole should be followed whenever sufficient specific guidance is not provided in the rules.'

This is in line with Lubetzky's recommendation, as are the general provisions of rule (19) where related works are classified into those with dependent titles and those without, the former being entered under the author of the original work. Although the rules in these sections are enumerative of particular cases, the enumeration might be justified on the grounds that without amplification determination of responsibility is a vague directive.

None of the older codes has general rules for dependent documents; instead there are separate rules for types (revisions, commentaries, etc.) – enumeration resulting in omissions and inconsistencies.* In very general terms all codes follow the rulings given above for groups (i) and (iia), e.g. AA (19), BM (24), Cutter (18). In the case of group (iib) the British rules in AA prescribe entry under original author (subject entry); Cutter (20) however recognizes the difference between author entry and subject entry and prescribes the former.

Condition Four: Corporate Authors[2]

Lubetzky distinguishes the following sub-conditions:

I. THE REPORTS AND STATEMENTS OF A CORPORATE BODY ARE USUALLY PREPARED BY ONE OF ITS OFFICERS OR BY ANOTHER PERSON ENGAGED TO PREPARE THE STATEMENT FOR IT (e.g. z/za).

Possible Solutions:
Entry under (i) person, or (ii) corporate body.

Lubetzky's Solution:
Enter under the name of the corporate body publications issued in its name, that is, communications purporting to be those of the corporate body and bearing the authority of that body. Other publications should be entered under the person who prepares the work (as in example (z)). Added entry should usually be made for the personal author where the main entry is under organization, and in the case of committee reports (e.g. (za)) added entry under chairman is essential. Individual cases may still be difficult to decide, but no better solution has been discovered. For the basic question here is: in what circumstances can a corporate body be considered as author? As Michael Gorman has pointed out in his discussion of AACR,[3] it is a question that will remain unanswered until further investigations have been made into the nature of the relationships that exist between organizations and the documents bearing their names.

Codes Solutions:
AACR (17) deals with 'works issued by or bearing the authority

* Related rules: AA (9, 10, 13–19); ALA (20–29, 12A2, 12F); BM (24); Cutter (14–20).

of a corporate body, but with authorship or editorship specifically and prominently attributed to one or more persons, either by name or by official title'. Following Lubetzky, it calls for main entry under corporate body when the work 'is by its nature necessarily the expression of the corporate thought or activity of such a body'. This general rule is amplified by specification of types of document and by examples. In case of doubt (17B) prescribes entry 'under the heading under which it would be entered if no corporate body were involved'. The net result of this is likely to be emphasis on personal author. As Gorman states: 'These definitions and rules work very well as an aid to practical cataloguing in a situation where personal authorship is preferred for catalogue headings, and a corporate heading is only used for want of anything better.'[4] Gorman sums up this section in the following words: 'One has some generalized statements, some guide lines, and some indications. All these manifestations of the unstated basic theory will probably serve as more than adequate practice, certainly as good as, probably better than, the same rules in previous codes. What they will not do is clear up the foggy area in most cataloguers' minds, the area that leads to an inconsistent application of half-understood principles'.[5]

By AA (60) – a rule which is, strictly speaking, confined to *government* publications – the criterion is whether or not the person is an official. This has little to do with the way the report is asked for and may be especially difficult to determine in the case of non-governmental organizations (to which this rule also applies, though listed under government bodies). ALA (75 C–E) corresponds to AA, with the addition that 'non-administrative or routine' reports should go under personal author. (More elaborate but less comprehensive as the rules apply to government reports only.) BM has no general rule but (16) shows distinct preference for entry under the society and in part will be determined by the stress given on the title page. Cutter (55) – as AA, and refers to government reports only.

Partial coverage, such as is found in ALA and Cutter for example, is almost inevitable when there are no general rules for all classes of corporate authorship. It shows the weakness of primary division of codes by classes of organization rather than by the authorship problems common to each.

3

2. MANY CORPORATE BODIES HAVE NO PROPER IDENTIFY-
ING NAMES OF THEIR OWN BUT ONLY GENERIC NAMES
DESCRIBING THEIR TYPE AND COMMON TO MOST BODIES
OF THAT TYPE e.g. public library, historical society, dramatic
club, etc.

Possible Solutions:

Entry under (i) name followed by place to distinguish between
them, or (ii) place followed by the name of the body.

Lubetzky's Solution:

Those which need the name of the place (e.g. country, city,
county, etc.) for their identification should be entered under
such place names, e.g. Taunton. Public Library. All other
organizations should be entered under name.

This rule refers especially to non-governmental authors; the
problem of entry under country of central government authors
was mentioned briefly on page 43.

It could be argued that this condition arises from a misunderstanding – and that, in fact, place is an essential part of
the *name*: thus the corporate body in the above example is
Taunton Public Library (see the British rule in AACR).

Codes Solutions:

AACR (60), accepting that all organizations have names,
words its basic rule thus: 'Enter a corporate body directly
under its name except when the rules that follow provide for
entering it under a higher body of which it is a part, or under
the name of the government of which it is an agency.' (In
general this rule is also applied to organizations set up for a
specific purpose – e.g. *ad hoc* conferences; these too are entered,
by rule (87), under name.) This represents a major departure
from conventional practice and the Americans have found it
necessary to make some exceptions in rules (98) and (99),
which advocate entry under place for certain categories of
churches and other types of corporate bodies closely associated
with place – educational institutions, libraries, galleries, museums, etc. The British procedure has the virtues of simplicity
and consistency. Where there is likely to be confusion between
names, place can be added after the heading, e.g. St Clement's

Church, *Leigh-on-Sea*. (It seems possible that the Americans will revise these rules to bring them in line with the British solution.)

Other rules in Chapter 3 of AACR (Headings for corporate bodies) deal with such matters as variant forms of name, conventional name, language, etc. There are special rules for certain classes of publications, notably government documents, where a distinction is made (78) between those to be entered directly under their names (e.g. Medical Research Council) and those to be entered under the country or other area of jurisdiction (e.g. Great Britain. *Foreign Office*, and Kent. *County Council*). This distinction is based on the general principle that 'agencies through which the basic legislative, judicial, and executive functions of government are exercised should be entered as subheadings under the heading for the government; other bodies created and controlled by the government should be entered, if possible, under their own names.'

The problems which arise from the fact that 'many corporate bodies have no proper identifying name' has given rise to many of the rules for organizations in the older codes. Each of them enumerates types of organizations and makes rules for each. They have been discussed briefly in Chapter 3; note especially the section on the AA code. We saw that BM preferred place; Cutter, name; AA and ALA, place and name (institutions and societies). All have exceptions.

3. CHANGE OF NAME IN CORPORATE BODIES (e.g. zb).

Possible Solutions:

Entry under (i) earliest name, or (ii) latest, or (iii) successive names as they arise.

Lubetzky's Solution:

Lubetzky points out that the problem is different in kind from the problem of change of name in personal authors (see above, p. 58). Here change of name often reflects a change in structure or constitution. Having regard to this and to the fact that works are often sought under the names in which they were issued, Lubetzky prefers to consider change of name as the end of one organization and the beginning of another, and therefore suggests entry under each successive name, except where the change is slight or of such short duration as to be of little significance to the enquirer. A direct form of entry leaving collocation to cross references.

A further advantage of this solution is that it presents the cataloguer with little extra work.

A disadvantage is that particular editions of a work may be scattered according to whether they were issued under one name or another. Again cross references would relate them.

Codes Solutions:

AACR (68) agrees with Lubetzky, specifying the style of cross references to be made between the various names of an organization. A footnote allows collocation under the latest form of name 'if the change is so slight that the distinction between names might be easily confused in citations or escape notice by users of the catalogue'.

Apart from two comparatively minor rules in ALA (91A and 144D) none of the codes has any rules on this and therefore the rules for change of name in personal authors must be used. AA (40 – British) and BM (11) stipulate earliest form of name – collocation and little work, but less satisfactory from the enquirer's point of view; AA (40 – American) and ALA (45) choose latest form – more satisfactory than earliest name for the enquirer in so far as most requests are likely to be for recent publications, but hard work for the cataloguer. Cutter (40) prefers 'best known' name.

4. AN ORGANIZATION MAY ACT OR SPEAK AS A WHOLE OR THROUGH ONE OF ITS BRANCHES, DIVISIONS, OFFICES, ETC. (e.g. zc/ze).

Possible Solutions:

Entry under (i) main body alone, or (ii) main body with subheading for subordinate body, or (iii) subordinate body. For example, the Association of Assistant Librarians may be entered as:

Library Association.
Library Association. Association of Assistant Librarians.
Association of Assistant Librarians.

Each has its advantages and disadvantages, discussed by Lubetzky in his *Report*.

Lubetzky's Solution:

If the subdivision has a proper and self-sufficient name of its own (as the AAL has), it should be entered under its own name directly. Cross references should be made to show relationships.

This solution aims at the sought heading rather than collocation of all branches of an organization, for the latter will occur only when the branches have no proper and self-sufficient names (e.g. Statistics Division). It should be remembered when considering this problem that affiliations change and too much subordination in the catalogue must lead to frequent change of entries, or of cross references if entered successively by the different names – not to mention the problems facing the reader when searching for information.

Codes Solutions:

AACR (69–71) provides for various kinds of relationships among corporate bodies. The principle behind these rules is that the name of a subordinate body should stand as a heading so long as it makes sense without the name of the parent body – that is, in Lubetzky's words, 'if it has a proper and self-sufficient name.' Furthermore, even when the unit has no such name it should be entered 'subordinately as a subheading of the lowest element in the hierarchy above it that may be independently entered. Omit intervening elements in the hierarchy that are not essential to clarify the function of the smaller body as an element of the larger one. In case of doubt, interpose the lowest element of the hierarchy above it that serves the purpose' (69A). Examples given include:

> Central Electricity Generating Board. *Education and Training Branch* (*Hierarchy:* Central Electricity Generating Board. Personnel Department. Education and Training Branch).
>
> and: Public Library Association. *Military Library Standards Committee* (*Hierarchy:* American Library Association. Public Library Association. Armed Forces Librarians Section. Military Library Standards Committee).

Again, the older codes lack general rules here. AA (79) gives a ruling similar to Lubetzky's for affiliated societies, and

AA (59) similarly prescribes direct entry (under country) for subordinate departments of government bodies except for 'minor divisions'; but there is no rule for subordination in institutions, though examples of it, e.g. colleges of a university, are catered for. ALA (99 and 100) are like AA but more confusing, and ALA (75) is as AA (59) but improves on the 'minor divisions' phrase by replacing it with the concept of distinctive name, which is the real problem. Although Cutter (90) specifies subdivided headings, the examples in (324) show that he is thinking only of those sections, etc., without distinctive names; his comments (pp. 117–18) are worth reading.

Style of Heading

These are some of the main problems arising in the choice of author headings. However, it should be recognized that once the heading has been selected, there may still be the question of style of heading. For example, having decided to enter a book under, say, Walter de la Mare, should the heading be under Mare, La Mare, or De la Mare? Should compound names be entered under the first or last part of the compound? Should names of organizations ever be inverted, e.g. Electrical Engineers, Institution of? When should forename entry be used and what style should be adopted? All codes have rules for these problems – or for some of them, e.g. AACR (46–51), AA (25, 26). While the student should note these, he would do well to concentrate particularly on the major problems of choice of heading as outlined above.

Added Entries and References

We have been concerned throughout mainly with main entry. Added entries and references will be made in the author catalogue for subordinate authors (joint authors, editors, translators, illustrators, etc.). In deciding whether to make such added entries and references the cataloguer will consider (a) whether the reader is likely to search for a particular document by these subordinate authors, and (b) whether the subordinate author is sufficiently well-known to warrant an entry under his name so that entries for all his writings may be seen in one place.

AACR summarizes its provisions for added entries and references in rules (33) and (120–6).

READINGS

1. LUBETZKY, S. *Cataloging rules and principles*. Washington, GPO, 1953.
2. TAUBE, M. 'The cataloging of publications of corporate authors'. *Library Quarterly*, 20(1), January 1950, 1–20. *See also:* LUBETZKY, S. 'The cataloging of publications of corporate authors: a rejoinder'. *Library Quarterly*, 21(1), January 1951, 1–12; *and* TROTIER, A. H. 'The draft code and problems of corporate authorship'. *Library Resources and Technical Services*, 6(3), Summer 1962, 223–7.
3. GORMAN, MICHAEL. *A study of the rules for entry and heading in the Anglo-American cataloguing rules, 1967 (British text)*. London, Library Association, 1968.
4. GORMAN, op. cit., p. 13.
5. GORMAN, op. cit., p. 14.

JOLLEY'S *Principles of cataloguing* is particularly relevant here—as are many of the readings noted in Chapter 3. Still well worth reading is: OSBORN, A. D. 'Cataloging costs and a changing conception of cataloging'. *Catalogers and classifiers yearbook*, 1936, 45–54.

Chapter 5
The Title Approach

A reader is as likely to remember a document by its title as by its author, but cataloguers usually consider title to be secondary when choosing the main heading There are three main reasons for this:

(a) entry under title has little collocative value because titles are unique, whereas entry under author not only gives direct access to a particular document but also results in collocation of documents related by authorship;

(b) though titles may be remembered, readers often misquote them, and certainly they are more difficult to memorize accurately than authors – though there are some striking titles which are exceptions to this;

(c) titles present filing problems because many begin with common elements such as *Introduction to . . . History of . . .*, and so on. The cataloguer must then either create long sequences under such headings, or invert the title bringing the key word to the fore. The latter method is called catchword entry and is not recommended because the choice of significant word is highly subjective (but see p. 87).

Title entry is therefore usually an *added entry*, often filed with author entries to make an author/title catalogue, or filed in a separate sequence but still secondary. The making of such added entries is left to the cataloguer's discretion; striking titles often receive an entry, but many cataloguers omit them altogether, relying on bibliographies to ascertain author when a reader makes a title request, or, where the title indicates the subject (e.g. *Introduction to transients*), using the subject catalogue.[1] This contrasts with the method employed in certain bibliographies, e.g. *Cumulative book list*, and HMSO lists, where catchword title entry is a very rudimentary substitute for the subject entry. One type of title added entry often made is the *Series entry*, e.g.:

Man and society series
Williams, Raymond
Reading and criticism. 1950.

Such entries are not normally made for amorphous series such as *World's classics, Everyman,* and so on. However, they are useful when the series has a particular subject value or level or purpose (*Methuen's monographs on applied physics; Nurses' aids series*).

There are occasions however when a reader will make a title request because the author's name is not found in the document (anonymous), or because, for a variety of reasons, the author is subsidiary. In such cases, the title entry may be the *main entry*, and problems connected with such anonymous and quasi-anonymous documents are considered below.

The *layout* of title *added* entry can be seen on page 285. Title *main* entries are usually displayed as in the following example:

Isle of Ely: the official guide. Croydon,
Home Publishing Company, 1959.
86 p.; illus., plate (map). 21 cm.

This form – the 'hanging indentation' – saves repeating the title under a separate title heading.

Anonymous Documents

I. DEFINITIONS AND PROBLEMS

When the author's name is not found in the document it is said to be anonymous, and in general such documents are entered under title. But there are degrees of anonymity. Consider the following list of 'authors': Lewis Carroll, Aunt Jane, Harassed Housewife, A gentleman of low descent, Boz, and By the author of *The storm in a teacup, Mountains and molehills,* etc.

Documents by authors like these are anonymous in the sense that the real identity of the author is not revealed, though sufficient information is given for at least some of the works of one author to be recognized (which is not the case in works which are purely anonymous).

It is not easy to say exactly what constitutes *anonymity* and *pseudonymity*. The latter can be regarded as a species of the former. AACR defines a pseudonym as 'an assumed name used by an author in his works'; and an anonymous document as one 'of unknown authorship'. An examination of the rules – particularly (1), (2), (40) and (42) – will reveal that 'assumed name' is strictly limited to works having a *name* on the title-page, and rule (42) for pseudonyms does not cover documents whose authorship is masked by initials, phrases, etc. The latter are regarded as anonymous and treated accordingly. The distinction and consequent rules and procedures are clear, except in one detail: by (1B) 'erroneous' and 'fictitious' authorship is treated as a category distinct from pseudonymity – a differentiation which is clear in the examples but may well prove confusing in practice.

AA defines a pseudonym as 'an assumed name under which a person writes', while 'a book is considered anonymous if the author's name does not appear in the book itself'. These definitions give rise to the question: what is a name? AA does not answer this but its examples indicate that name is meant to cover only proper names, and thus a book by someone calling himself 'The Gardener' or 'G.A.' is anonymous and by (112) and (115) is entered under the title if the real name cannot be found, 'never under the appellation or the initials'. On the other hand, a book by Mary Adams (an assumed name) is pseudonymous and is entered under the pseudonym if the real name cannot be found. AA's definition and practice has the virtue of simplicity lacking in all the other older English codes. Though the definitions themselves leave something to be desired, in practice the distinction between an anonymous document and a pseudonymous one is evident and it is quite clear how they are to be treated. Whether the treatment is sound is another matter and one to which we shall return.

BM gives different treatment to the different degrees of anonymity. It distinguishes between pure anonymity (18) and (19), official designations or descriptions 'which render [the author's] identity unmistakable', assumed names (in the AA sense), single words (e.g. A Gardener) or combinations of single words that can be written as one word (e.g. Bull's Eye, which may be written Bullseye), Christian names that are accompanied by an epithet (e.g. Uncle John), circumlocutions (e.g. A Merchant of London), and initials. These degrees of anonymity are grouped together under the rule for 'pseudo-nyms and descriptive names' (20) – with the exception of initials (12).

Distinctions of this kind are also made by Cutter. His definitions are simple: anonymous means 'published without the author's name'; a pseudonym is 'a fictitious name assumed by the author to conceal his identity'. And the basic rules (97) and (120) are straightforward. But there are many qualifications, e.g. see (96) and the footnote to rule (97) in which Cutter distinguishes between names, initials, phrases, and forenames with epithets. He even distinguishes between phrases like 'A Lawyer' and those beginning with definite articles like 'The Prig', and prescribes different treatment for each.

ALA is much closer to Cutter than to AA. It counts as pseudo-nyms specific words or phrases with or without the definite article (e.g. by Ex-intelligence officer, and by The Prig (30)) but not phrases beginning with an indefinite article (e.g. By a physician). Whether such precision will result in a catalogue more satisfactory to readers than that produced by the reasonable application of the vaguer AA rules is a moot point.

The practice of distinguishing between degrees of anonymity and making rules accordingly is not helpful to readers, who will usually identify a document by the name or other identifying mark appearing in the document. An examination of the rules made by the various older codes on the basis of these distinctions will reveal their arbitrary quality.

2. SOLUTIONS

Anonymous documents can be entered:

(i) under the real name of the author, if it can be found, or

(ii) under the title, or

(iii) under the pseudonym or other identifying element wherever there is one, otherwise under title.

The first solution will result in the collocation of an author's works, but the heading will not always be the one sought by the reader and its discovery may involve the cataloguer in much bibliographical and biographical checking. It will also involve alterations in the catalogue as unsuspected pseudonyms are identified.

The second solution will result in a satisfactory finding list for purely anonymous documents, but it will not collocate books by one author, and in those cases where a pseudonym is used or some degree of authorship established, it will not lead to the sought heading.

The third solution will result in a satisfactory direct catalogue in so far as readers ask for documents by pseudonym or other identifying element. It will also give some degree of collocation (for example, all documents in which the author uses the same pseudonym will be collocated). It is the easiest method for the cataloguer. On balance, therefore, it is the most generally helpful solution, though modifications may have to be made in particular circumstances.

As can be imagined from our examination of the distinctions made between the various degrees of anonymity, *the four codes offer different solutions* to the problems that arise in dealing with such documents.*

AACR (1) states: 'Enter a work, a collection of works, or selections from works by one author under the person or corporate body that is the author, *whether named in the work or not.*' Thus, anonymous works are to be entered under author if the authorship can be discovered. (Otherwise, by (2), entry must be under title.) The name to be chosen must, by (40), be 'the name by which he is commonly identified, whether it is his real name, or an assumed name, nickname, title of nobility, or other appellation'. Thus the general tendency of AACR is towards the first of the solutions noted above, except that where an author is commonly identified by a name other than his own, this is to be used. Other rules are consistent with this basic provision. Thus, writers using more than one name (several pseudonyms, or real name and pseudonym), are to be entered under one heading only (42). Initials, even when used consistently, are never to be employed as headings; when they are used consistently, the name for which the initials stand must be chosen (if it can be discovered), otherwise entry must be made under title (2c) and (40). Similarly, documents which conceal an author's identity behind phrases, etc., are to be

---

* The general remarks to students of the Part I examination – see the opening of Chapters 3 and 4 – apply in this chapter. The student should not lose sight of principles in the detail of specific rules.

entered, if the authorship cannot be determined, under title (2C). In all cases appropriate references are to be made.

In very general terms it can be said that AA prefers the first of the alternatives listed above. All pseudonymous and anonymous works are to be entered under the real name of the author if this can be discovered; otherwise they are to be entered under the title (with no inversion) unless the pseudonym is a proper name. (It is not quite clear what is to be done with Aunt Jane.) Initials, typographical devices, phrases, etc. are to be ignored, except for the purpose of added entries or references. The most significant difference here between AA and AACR is in the former's emphasis on *real* name.

The other codes are more complex but in general tend towards the third solution. At the other extreme from AA is BM, which avoids prescribing entry under the real name for pseudonymous or anonymous documents unless the designation is an official one such as 'The Chancellor of the Exchequer' (20). 'In the absence of declared authorship' the cataloguer is not to spend time trying to track down the author but instead is to enter the document according to some element found in the document itself. Thus by (20) pseudonyms (in the sense of proper names) are legitimate headings, and so are single words or groups of words that can be written as single words (Merchant, Bullseye, and so on), initials, and Christian names accompanied by an epithet (Aunt Jane, for example). In the absence of any of these features, the document is to be treated as anonymous according to rules (18) and (19). These latter rules differ from the other codes in preferring as heading elements in the document other than title – 'biographee', for example, and even where title is prescribed, inversion to allow catchword entry is suggested. It is interesting to note (18) states that even when the real author can be ascertained his name is to be used only in the description. BM is thus in some respects, nearer to solution (iii) above, but is marred by (a) the elaborate distinctions drawn between types of pseudonymity and anonymity, and (b) the rejection of title entry for anonymous documents.

Cutter stands midway on this subject between the AA and the BM. Purely anonymous works are to be entered under the name of the author if it can be ascertained, otherwise under the title (without inversion). In this respect Cutter is identical with AA. Again, like the AA, he prefers entry of pseudonymous books under the real name if known (97) but is willing to make an exception to this, e.g. if the pseudonym is 'generally used by the writer or is much better known by the public'; thus George Eliot's books would be entered under this name and not, as by AA, under Marian Evans. He also, unlike AA, allows initials, typographical devices, appellatives beginning with a definite article (The Prig, and so on), and Christian names accompanied by an epithet (Aunt Jane, for example) to be used as headings for the main entry.

ALA has to some extent returned to Cutter. Although both (30) and (31) still emphasize entry under real name for pseudonymous and anonymous works, there are exceptions: thus, the pseudonym can be used if the real author wishes his name withheld, if it represents two or more real persons, or if it is fixed in literary history.

QUASI-ANONYMOUS DOCUMENTS

Authorship of such documents, e.g. collections, encylopaedias, periodicals, directories, and so on, though often known, is less important for bibliographic purposes than the title. Such documents are often not, strictly speaking, anonymous but, because they are written by several authors or appear at intervals over an indefinite period of time – as in the case of periodicals and directories – they tend to be known by their titles, as already discussed in Chapter 4.

Conditions and Cases in Title (Main) Entry

If a document is entered under its title, several problems arise for which rules are necessary. Lubetzky has distinguished them as follows:

(i) The title differs in the several volumes of a document.

(ii) The title of the document differs in the various editions.

(iii) The document is known in several countries under different titles.

(iv) The document has no title of its own – as in the case of some manuscripts.

The following brief notes give Lubetzky's solutions to these problems and comment on some of the relevant code rules.

Purpose.

In the selection of author headings we have seen that two basic questions have to be answered:

(a) What is the sought heading for this particular document?

(b) What is the heading that will collocate all documents by this particular author?

Where the answers to these questions conflict in any single case preference is, in practice, usually given to (a), thus producing a direct catalogue.

Similarly in choosing title headings two basic questions must be asked:

(a) What is the sought title for this particular document?

(b) What is the heading that will collocate the various editions, translations, and other manifestations of this document?

Again, where the answers to these questions conflict in any single case (and examples of such conflict will be found below) preference is normally given to (a), references or added entries being made to show relationships between documents. In this way title headings will be consistent in principle with the author headings.

Although in this chapter we are concerned with problems arising from the use of title as *main* entry, the basic question underlying many of these problems – namely, whether to use the title found on the title page or to select another in order to collocate the various editions and forms of a work under a *uniform title* – reappears as a subsidiary problem within entries using a main author heading. For example, if *Fiesta* is entered under its author, Ernest Hemingway, there remains the problem of whether to adopt that title or its American counterpart (*The sun also rises*), or indeed whether to follow the title pages in each case, thus scattering editions of a work within an author heading. Though subsidiary, this issue is by no means insignificant, especially in large catalogues covering extensive collections of works by major writers. It is easy to comprehend the scale of the problem if one examines the entries for *Hamlet* in the *British Museum catalogue*, where variant spellings and elaborations of the title, not to mention translations, would, if the title pages were slavishly followed, result in such scattering as would serve the functions neither of a finding list nor of a bibliographical tool. Students should recognize that the conditions outlined below are also relevant to this subsidiary issue. However, we shall return to this matter in Chapter 14.

It is one of the striking features of AACR that the rules for choice of title, whether regarded as a main entry or as part of the description, have been brought together in a separate chapter entitled *Uniform entry*. It thus gives systematic consideration to a set of problems which were covered relatively cursorily in previous codes.

The basic rule (100A) states: 'When the editions (other than revised editions as specified in E below), translations, etc., of a work appear under various titles, select one title as the uniform title under which all will be catalogued.' The only exception is in the case of 'an edition purporting to be a revision or updating of the original work': in this case a uniform title is not to be used, but editions are to be related 'by noting the earlier or later title on each entry'. In all cases adequate references are called for. This collocation of the various forms of a work is consistent with the Code's basic policy, noted earlier, of collocating all documents by a single author.

Where main entry is under title the uniform title will be the heading, the particular title used in any edition etc., being the first element in the description; where the main entry is under author it is recommended that the uniform title be placed in brackets between the heading and the actual title. For example:

Shakespeare, William.
   [Hamlet]
  The tragicall historie of Hamlet, Prince of Denmarke ... 1603.
Trial of treasure.
  A new and mery enterlude, called The Triall of treasure ... 1567.

Condition One: The Title Differs in the Several Volumes of a Document

(a) MONOGRAPHS

Monographs in several volumes are normally catalogued under one title and usually there is an overall title, e.g.

The new Cambridge modern history. Cambridge, University
Press, 1957–
    v. 27 cm.
    v. 1 The Renaissance, 1493–1520; ed. by G. R. Potter
    v. 2 The Reformation, 1520–1559; ed. by G. R. Elton
    etc.

When there are different titles in the various volumes and no
comprehensive title, which title should be chosen?

Possible Solutions:

Entry under (i) first volume title, or (ii) most frequently used
title if there is one.

Lubetzky's Solution:

Enter under the title of the first volume – the monograph will
be known by this. Added entries under other titles.

Codes Solutions:

AACR treats this problem as a part of the rules for descriptive
cataloguing. (132C) states: 'A monographic publication in
several volumes is, as a rule, catalogued from the title page of
the first volume.' Other codes agree – AA (113); ALA (32A –
with qualification); Cutter (143) though (147) makes an
exception for those anonymous works generally known by later
title; BM has no specific rule, though (27) calls for 'fullest title'.

(b) PERIODICALS

(Includes serial publications generally.) The problem of change
of name in successive issues frequently arises.

Possible Solutions:

Entry under (i) earliest title, or (ii) latest title, or (iii) successive
titles as they occur.

Lubetzky's Solution:

Enter under successive titles. 'It is not to be expected', he writes,
'that a writer citing a given volume will enquire what the
original title was, or what the relation of the given title is to
any other title, and the purpose of the catalogue will be better

served if each title is entered separately and provided with notes indicating its relationship to other titles'.

This solution is consistent with Lubetzky's preference for a direct catalogue, and, as the number of occasions on which a reader will want all issues of a periodical collocated are rare, this would seem the most convenient solution. It is usual to find union lists of periodicals using this method, though BUCOP prefers the first of the alternatives, which makes it an admirable guide to the history of any periodical but less satisfactory as a speedy location list.

Codes Solutions:

AACR agrees with Lubetzky. The main rule for serials (6) – amplified in the special rules in Chapter 7 – states: 'If the title of a serial changes, if the corporate body under which it is entered changes or undergoes a change of name, or if the person under whom it is entered ceases to be its author, make a separate entry for the issues appearing after the change.' An exception is made for changes 'of very short duration or of a very minor character'.

AA (121 – British) specifies entry under earliest name as in BUCOP, and collocation is thus preferred at all costs. By this rule the whole history of a periodical can be seen in one place, but the results are a little grotesque at times, e.g. *The Times* would be entered under *Daily universal register*, and *Flight* under *Automotor and horseless vehicle journal*. The rule has the advantage that no catalogue changes are required when a periodical changes its name – all that is needed is a reference from the new title to the old. This is a consideration, especially in printed lists where alterations of this kind may prove expensive. However, the third solution is almost as economical.

AA (121 – American) and ALA (5ci) suggest latest title. Like the British rule this collocates all issues of a periodical, and under a title more likely to be sought because the majority of requests for most periodicals are for recent issues. However, like the first solution it is less satisfactory than the third solution in those cases where a periodical is sought for an article noted in an abstract journal or cited in another document, because these will quote the title current at the time of the article. Again, this solution achieves collocation only at a price to the cataloguer, who will have to revise entries for a periodical every time it changes its title. In a printed list this is a formidable task, and even in a card catalogue where the method suggested by the Library of Congress note under AA (121) is in use, the work involved is great.

Cutter (133 and 145) allows alternative practices – earliest name or successive entry, preferring the latter, and thus anticipating Lubetzky.

BM has no specific rule for this: periodicals are in any case separately entered under the form heading *Periodical publications* subdivided by place of publication; except for periodicals which are the 'organ of a society or institution', which are entered under the appropriate body.

Condition Two: The Title of the Document Differs in the Various Editions

Possible Solutions:

Here again there are three possible ways of entry as in section (b), page 81. And again direct entry under successive titles will usually result in the most frequently sought headings, especially as a change in title usually indicates substantial revision so as to make the work virtually a new one. Collocation has to be left to references.

However, there is one important qualification to be made: where works are sufficently established to have a commonly known title – for example, classics and religious texts – both identification and collocation will best be met if the commonly known title is adopted as a uniform heading, whatever happens to be on the title page. For in such cases many editions appear (complete, select, epitomes, etc.) under a variety of titles. A uniform title, e.g. Beowulf, Bible, Everyman, no matter what the title of the particular document at hand, will not only collocate the work but, if well chosen, will also result in the most frequently sought heading for the particular document. (Added entries or references will be made under other titles, editors, etc.) Example:

> Everyman.
> The summoning of Everyman . . .

Lubetzky's Solution:

Lubetzky concentrates on works having a 'generally-known title' and prescribes such titles as uniform headings.

Codes Solutions:

As already noted AACR (100 E) calls for entry of successive editions incorporating revised matter under their particular titles. Cutter (144) agrees with direct entry here, though if a choice between earliest and latest has to be made he prefers the earliest title. The other codes have no specific rules, though BM (27) calling for fullest title could be used again; AA (143) calls for entry of works under successive titles within an author but this is not consistent with the general tenor of at least the British rules for anonymous works, e.g. (118) calls for entry of anonymous translations under original title, and (116) suggests earliest form of spelling when it differs in different editions. We could adapt the author rule (19) for revisions which specifies entry under earliest name unless the revision is 'substantially a new work'.

A different treatment is usually prescribed for works having a generally known title. As indicated above AACR (100) generally requires a uniform title. (101) and (102) elaborate on the choice and form of such a title. In general, for works written after 1501, whether anonymous or not, earliest title is preferred, but if a later title is better known 'through use in editions of the work or in reference sources' – as is often so with the classics – this better known title is to be adopted. (Works written before 1501 usually involve language problems and will be treated as primarily illustrative of the next condition.) Rules (108) – (119) present special rules for creating uniform headings for sacred scriptures and liturgical texts. All codes have rules for such works – e.g. AA (119–120). Notice too that within the uniform heading subdivisions are usually made, e.g. Bible – Selections, Bible – Old Testament, etc. The problems of order of subdivisions are akin to the problems of classification, and there are several schemes, e.g. those in the various codes and ALA *Filing rules*.

Condition Three: The Document Is Known in Various Countries under Different Titles

Possible Solutions:

The direct entry principle will call for entry under successive titles and this will result in the sought headings because a translation into one's native tongue is usually asked for in that language, whilst a foreign version is asked for by the foreign title, except perhaps in non-Western languages. The alternatives are, (a) entry under original title, or (b) entry under English title as uniform heading whatever the title on the title page.

Lubetzky's Solution:

Always enter under English title. Collocation is thus gained, but the heading may not be that sought by a reader wanting the original.

Codes Solutions:

The basic preference of AACR, for works published both before and after 1501, is for original title, (101) and (102). An example of this can be found in (105) – translations – though in this case the work is not anonymous:

> Maurois, André.
>   [Magiciens et logiciens. English.]
>   Prophets and poets . . .

Note here that the language of the translation is added after the original title. However, as noted below, there are certain exceptions.

AA (118 – American) and ALA (32G) agree with Lubetzky, but AA (118 – British) and Cutter (132) and BM (23) prefer to collocate the various translations with the original title – less frequently the sought heading in popular libraries.

As in Condition Two, special consideration must be given to translations of works with well-known titles, such as anonymous classics and religious texts. Having agreed to select a *uniform title* (according to the rules given in Condition Two) – should this title be in English or the language of the original? Again Lubetzky chooses the 'English title best known to the English-speaking reader' as being the form most usually sought, e.g. Arabian nights *not* Alif Laila. AACR's general preference for original title would apply here also, but there are exceptions. For example, (102B) allows the use of 'a well-established English title, when there is one, for a work in classical Greek'; and (102C) states: 'If the original language of an early anonymous work is not written in the Roman alphabet, prefer a title in English, when there is one.' Examples of the latter are: Arabian nights and Book of the dead.

AA (120), though emphasizing English form, makes exception for those works well known in England by their original titles, e.g. Nibelungenlied. The phrasing of ALA (32) emphasizes the original or traditional language, with the qualification that if the document is well known in many languages, the English title will be selected. Cutter (132) stipulates the original always, and by (23) so does BM.

Condition Four: The Document Has No Title of Its Own

This condition rarely arises except in the case of manuscripts and incunabula.

Style

One important question of style remains. Having selected the title, shall it be used as it stands or inverted: Journal of scientific instruments or Scientific instruments, Journal of? With periodicals[2] the uninverted form is usual today; where a form of visible index (see Chapter 17) is in use, the build-up of entries under common words such as *Journal of* . . . is of little consequence, and is likely to cause less trouble than inversion, which tends to be subjective. However, some librarians make exception for a few selected common phrases, e.g. *Journal of* . . ., always inverting when these are used, and making a note to that effect for the convenience of the user. With monographs inversion is of even more dubious value.

Titles and Subjects

Earlier in this chapter we referred to the practice, fairly common in trade bibliographies, of using title entry as a rudimentary form of subject approach. Traditionally such bibliographies have tended to enter each title under its keywords, a practice long referred to as *catchword entry*. Thus the title *How to find out in philosophy and psychology* would be entered not only under *How* but also under *Philosophy* and *Psychology*.

The use of computers greatly facilitates the compilation of published indexes in which each title is arranged according to its keywords. In some examples the titles are rotated around the various words in turn (as in the example reproduced in Figure 1), in others they file under an alphabetically arranged list of the keywords extracted from the titles. The first method is referred to as KWIC (Keyword-in-context), the second as KWOC (Keyword-out-of-context).

IPPURAN RENOGRAM IN	RENAL HOMOTRANSPLANTATION* SEQUENTIAL R	07 0556
ENTIAL DIAGNOSIS OF	RENAL INSUFFICIENCY FOLLOWING VASCULAR S	04 0106
REMENT OF EFFECTIVE	RENAL PLASMA FLOW BY EXTERNAL COUNTING M	08 0077
	RENAL RETENTION OF HG–203 NEOHYDRIN*	07 0308
L VASCULAR DISEASE*	RENAL SCINTISCANS IN THE DIAGNOSIS OF RE	02 0272
HIPPURAN RENOGRAM*	RENAL TRANSIT TIME. ITS MEASUREMENT BY T	06 0269
RENAL CLEARANCE AND	RENAL TUBULAR MASS* 1–131 DIODRAST FOR	01 0041
IN THE DIAGNOSIS OF	RENAL VASCULAR DISEASE* RENAL SCINTISCA	02 0272
THE RADIOISOTOPE	RENOCYSTOGRAM*	02 0008
QUANTITATION OF THE	RENOGRAF IN 1–131 RENOGRAM FOR RENAL CLEA	07 0442
LUMINE DIATRIZOATE	(RENOGRAF IN) IN MAN* THE RENAL CLEARANCE	06 0183
HE RENOGRAFIN 1–131	RENOGRAM FOR RENAL CLEARANCE DETERMINATI	07 0442
RADIOISOTOPE	RENOGRAM IN KIDNEY TRANSPLANTS*	05 0807
THE 1–131 HIPPURAN	RENOGRAM IN RENAL HOMOTRANSPLANTATION*	07 0556
OF THE RADIOISOTOPE	RENOGRAM IN THE DIFFERENTIAL DIAGNOSIS O	04 0106
FOR EVALUATING THE	RENOGRAM OF HYPERTENSIVE PATIENTS* A DI	05 0180
OF THE RADIOISOTOPE	RENOGRAM TEST* IN-VITRO ANALYSIS	04 0045
E* THE RADIOISOTOPE	RENOGRAM. ADVANCES IN TEST SUBSTANCE AND	03 0067
OR THE RADIOISOTOPE	RENOGRAM. DISA–1–131, EDTA–CR–51, AND HI	03 0273
THE 1–131 HIPPURAN	RENOGRAM* A THEORETICAL APPROACH TO	05 0555
OF THE RADIOISOTOPE	RENOGRAM* EVALUATION OF QUANTITATIVE AS	04 0117
THE 1–131 HIPPURAN	RENOGRAM* RENAL TRANSIT TIME. ITS MEASU	06 0269
ANDARDIZED HIPPURAN	RENOGRAM* RESULTS OF A ST	04 0446
A CHAIR FOR	RENOGRAMS*	06 0075
MEDICINE*	REPORT OF SURVEY ON TEACHING OF NUCLEAR	05 0400
TASES A PRELIMINARY	REPORT* THE USE OF SR–85 IN THE EVALUAT	04 0009
T* A	RESCANNER WITH PHOTOGRAPHIC COLOR READOU	07 0501
H A COLOR-RECORDING	RESCANNER* CLINICAL RESULTS WIT	08 0437
SING COLLIMATOR FOR	RESEARCH IN SCANNING* A FOCU	03 0010
ON UCLIDES* NEED FOR	RESEARCH PROGRAMS TO PROVIDE DATA APPLIC	06 0079
PORT OF THE MEDICAL	RESEARCH REACTOR* CONTROL OF RADIATION	03 0360
3 TEST*	RESIN SPONGE MODIFICATION OF THE 1–131 T	05 0112
ECHNIQUE* 1–131 T–3	RESIN SPONGE UPTAKE USING ICE WATER BATH	07 0072

1. An extract from *Kwic Index to the Journal of Nuclear Medicine 1960–1967* (U.S. Department of Health, Education and Welfare, Public Health Service Publication No. 1831).

As they can be produced very speedily, no intellectual effort being involved, such indexes provide a useful, if rudimentary current awareness service. Their limitations when judged as *subject* retrieval devices are obvious. In particular, they fail unless the titles are explicit – i.e. adequate summarizations of subject content – a fact which reduces their value in some fields more than in others and partly accounts for their being found almost exclusively in science and technology. Even when explicit, however, the lack of subject analysis embodied in a structure of references to and from related terms, synonyms, etc., means that they can hardly be relied upon to bring to the user's attention all (or even the most important) items relevant to the subject of his search.

READINGS

1. LUBETZKY, S. 'Titles: fifth column of the catalog'. *Library Quarterly*, 11 (4), October 1941, 412–30.
2. LANCASTER-JONES, E. 'Listing titles of periodical publications'. *Proceedings of the British Society for International Bibliography*, v. 111, part 3, pp. 56–7. See also the readings on periodicals listed in Chapter 14.

_____

It need hardly be said that the Lubetzky report and several of the works cited in Chapters 3 and 4 are essential reading for this chapter. A reading which supplements the Lubetzky article quoted above is: DEWEY, H. *Specialized cataloguing and classification*. 3rd ed. Wisconsin College Typing Co., 1956. v. 2, Chapter 40.

Part Two
The Subject Approach

Chapter 6
The Subject Approach –
Introduction

The importance of the subject approach has been particularly accentuated by the growth of science and technology where authorship is of slight importance as compared with subject content. Again, most documents are arranged by subject in all kinds of libraries and although in many catalogues and bibliographies author/title entries have been traditionally regarded as the main entries, librarians with special collections pay relatively scant attention to authorship and if they had to choose between author and subject entries, would certainly choose the latter. In the classified catalogue, found in a majority of libraries in this country – and in nearly all special collections – the main entry is the subject entry in the classified file, the author entry being an index entry in added entry style.

Enquirers approach subjects in terms of *natural language*; they ask for documents and information on Physics, Coal-mining, Shakespeare, and so on. Documents on these subjects and entries in catalogues referring to the documents can therefore be arranged alphabetically by means of headings using such natural language terms, with strict adherence to the natural form of phrase used, e.g. ORGANIC CHEMISTRY not CHEMISTRY, ORGANIC; FURTHER EDUCATION not EDUCATION, FURTHER. *Such headings – those using natural language and the natural form of phrase – can be called direct headings*, being taken directly from ordinary usage. (An example of a catalogue entry using such a heading can be seen on page 17.) They are found traditionally in the DICTIONARY CATALOGUE where they are interfiled alphabetically with author/title entries and where they are secondary or added entries, the main entry for any document being the author entry. For an example of entries in such a catalogue see page 19 and CBI. Here we shall speak of catalogues using this style of heading as ALPHABETICO – DIRECT CATALOGUES and the term can be regarded as referring to separate subject catalogues or the sum total of subject entries in dictionary catalogues. (Note that Coates uses the term *alphabetico-specific* with the same meaning in his book, *Subject catalogues*.)

The great advantage of direct headings lies in their immediacy; once the request has been stated, the relevant documents or catalogue entries can be found – ideally at any rate (we shall have to make qualifications later).

There are two important objections however:

(i) *Length of heading needed.* Words are cumbersome. In practice, it is quite impossible to use them for shelf arrangement and even in vertical files they become unwieldy as the files grow. In catalogues recording complex subjects, words are similarly awkward.

(ii) *Unhelpful order.* Although it is not true to say that the alphabetico-direct catalogue does not collocate related subjects, it certainly does not collocate the subjects that are usually studied together. Thus the chemist will not find all documents on Chemistry collocated because some will be scattered alphabetically under such headings as ANALYTICAL CHEMISTRY, ORGANIC CHEMISTRY; the psychologist will have to search through such headings as CHILD PSYCHOLOGY, EDUCATIONAL PSYCHOLOGY, SOCIAL PSYCHOLOGY; and the metallurgist will have to refer to COPPER METALLURGY, STEEL METALLURGY, and so on. However the use of direct headings as we shall see more clearly later does result in a degree of collocation of what have been called concretes,* i.e. tangibles such as steel, children, prefabricated buildings, etc. rather than traditional disciplines or operations – as can be seen from the following groups of headings:

STEEL, STEEL ENGRAVING, STEEL METALLURGY, STEEL PRICES, STEEL PRODUCTION.

RAILWAY LAW, RAILWAY MANAGEMENT, RAILWAY MODELS, RAILWAY STATIONS, RAILWAYS, RAILWAYS AND STATE.

RADIO, RADIO ANNOUNCING, RADIO APPARATUS, RADIO ASTRONOMY, RADIO BROADCASTING, RADIO ENGINEERING, RADIO INDUSTRY AND TRADE, RADIO NEWS, RADIO PLAYS, RADIO RECEIVERS.

* Compare SC.

Many catalogues use this style of heading and it is claimed that the consequent immediacy of access more than offsets the deficiencies of collocation. Other relationships are in fact revealed by a secondary network of *references*, e.g.:

METALLURGY *see also* STEEL METALLURGY
ENGRAVING *see also* STEEL ENGRAVING
ENGINEERING *see also* RADIO ENGINEERING

A greater degree of collocation could be achieved if terms were manipulated, e.g.:

ENGINEERING
ENGINEERING: ELECTRICAL
ENGINEERING: ELECTRICAL: INSULATION
ENGINEERING: ELECTRICAL: SWITCHGEAR
ENGINEERING: ELECTRICAL: WIRING
ENGINEERING: MECHANICAL
ENGINEERING: NUCLEAR
ENGINEERING: TRANSPORT
ENGINEERING: TRANSPORT: MOTOR
ENGINEERING: TRANSPORT: RAILWAY

This method, using such *indirect headings* in contrast to the direct headings already illustrated, results in what has been called the ALPHABETICO-CLASSED CATALOGUE. It has a number of limitations (see page 221) the most obvious being that the terms no longer reflect natural language style and thus immediacy, the main advantage of using words as headings, is lost. Moreover, collocation is still limited: thus in the above example it would be impossible to place INSULATION next to WIRING or MECHANICAL before ELECTRICAL; the alphabet will not allow it.

Satisfactory systematic collocation in practice requires the use of notation. Thus if we wish to arrange Electrical engineering after Mechanical engineering, the first can be given the symbol B, the second the symbol A; if Insulation were B2 and Wiring B1, the sequence would now be:

A   Mechanical engineering
B   Electrical engineering
B1   Wiring
B2   Insulation

Notation thus mechanizes a preferred order (and we use it daily, e.g.

whenever we write a list of jobs to be done and number it in order of priority). It cannot, of course, create an order – that has to be settled first and written down in the form of a *classification scheme* or *schedule*.

Another advantage of notation as compared with natural language headings is *brevity*. In DC the three digits 621 are the equivalent of: TECHNOLOGY : ENGINEERING : MECHANICAL.

Thus by notation we overcome the two objections to natural language formulated above. And notation is clearly necessary for the *shelf arrangement* of documents. Catalogues which use notational symbols as headings to maintain systematic order of entries are called CLASSIFIED CATALOGUES. An example of an entry in such a catalogue can be seen on page 17. For a printed example see BNB.

Such catalogues have been objected to on the grounds that unlike the alphabetico-direct catalogue their use demands the prior use of an *index of terms in alphabetical order:* the symbol representing the subject sought has to be discovered first before the classified file can be used. (see page 19 for an example of the index entries in BNB). The force of this objection is much reduced when we realize how often references have to be followed up in alphabetical subject catalogues.

The alphabetico-direct, the classified, and to a lesser extent the alphabetico-classed catalogues, are the main traditional types of catalogue used in libraries. Some other forms will be mentioned briefly in Chapter 11.

Purpose

The basic purposes of any subject device (shelf arrangement or catalogue) are:

(i) To show what the library has on a *particular subject* (or to reveal further details of a particular document whose subject is known).

(ii) To show what documents exist on subjects *related* to the subject of the enquiry.

The importance of the first is self-evident; the second is equally important. Documents on related subjects *are* documents on the subject sought – to a greater or lesser degree. A book on Physics is a book on Science and vice versa; a book on

Social psychology is also a book on Psychology and Sociology. Moreover, readers wanting material on Physics may consult the catalogue under SCIENCE (i.e. the wrong concept); those wanting material on Social psychology may consult the catalogue under PSYCHOLOGY, SOCIAL instead of the heading that is used: SOCIAL PSYCHOLOGY (i.e. the wrong combination order of concepts). As Vickery[1] has clearly shown, only a display of relationships can correct these faults.

The differences between the various types of catalogue outlined in the introduction to this chapter are differences of priorities and method rather than purpose. All attempt to fulfil the purposes listed here. The classified and alphabetico-classed catalogues with their systematic collocation of related subjects, allowing access to particular subjects only indirectly through indexes and references, give the second purpose priority. The alphabetico-direct catalogue which uses sought terms in natural language and allows direct access to particular subjects gives the first purpose priority; for whilst incidental collocation (mainly of 'concretes') is achieved, systematic collocation is left to secondary references.

All who are engaged in *subject retrieval* – those who classify and catalogue documents, who make the schemes of classification or the lists of subject headings and who carry out reference work – must be able to define subjects and comprehend relationships between them. The basis of all this is *classification*. A cataloguer who makes an entry under the heading PHYSICS in an alphabetico-direct catalogue and who then makes a reference SCIENCE *see also* PHYSICS is engaged in classification just as surely as the cataloguer who makes an entry under the respective class number for physics in a classified catalogue and an alphabetical subject index entry for it. Both are defining subjects in relationships. The principles of classification must therefore be studied carefully before considering the various types of catalogue. But first we must examine a number of basic concepts underlying subject retrieval systems.

Indexing

The term index has been traditionally used in cataloguing to refer to the creation of an index to a classified file. More recently, however, its use has widened and today it can be regarded as covering all the processes involved in the *input* to the system – the analysis of the subject content of documents, classifying, and the creation of catalogue entries.

Terms, Concepts, and Index Languages

Documents are composed of words and readers enquiring after information on subjects use words, but those who organize retrieval systems cannot simply accept the words they use. Our concern is with the *concepts* that underlie the words. Documents containing information on a subject will not be retrieved in response to an enquiry on that subject unless the terms used to describe the document in the system match those of the enquirer – and very often they will not match unless we have carefully analysed both conceptually. To take a simple example: there are books with more or less identical content-matter calling themselves variously *Anthropology, Sociology, The study of man*, and *The study of society*. All should be retrieved in response to an enquiry using any of these terms. But this will happen only if we analyse the actual concepts dealt with in documents and enquiries and create an intermediate language into which both can be translated and matching effected. This intermediate language we refer to as an *index language*. Classification schemes are an example of index languages, as are lists of subject headings for use in alphabetical subject catalogues. In the creation and use of index languages all depends on the adequacy of our conceptual grasp of subject knowledge, of the meanings of terms and the relations between them. *Subject analysis* is a fundamental process in indexing and enquiry work, and no retrieval system can make good deficiencies in subject analysis. (Of course, there are systems that rely solely on the words as used in individual documents, and in particular on the words used in their titles – e.g. KWIC and similar computer produced indexes. Whatever their merits they are no substitute for subject indexing – and indeed are best considered as title indexes.)*

---

* *Automatic indexing* – the use of machines to read and index documents may one day be a practical reality, but at present systems using such techniques can be regarded as largely experimental.

Pre-coordination

Many subjects can be expressed in a single term – Libraries, Cataloguing, Administration, Universities, etc. Others are made up of *compounds* of these, e.g. Cataloguing in libraries, Administration of universities. The cataloguer may attempt to create headings representing such compounds – e.g. LIBRARIES-CATALOGUING, UNIVERSITIES-ADMINISTRATION; or, in terms of the classified catalogue, their equivalents in notational terms, e.g. by UDC: 025·3 (where 02 stands for libraries, 025 for library methods, and 025·3 for cataloguing); 378·4:378·11 (where 378·4 represents universities, and 378·11 stands for administration). When the cataloguer devises compounds in this way so as to arrange entries in a series of classes, simple and compound, according to the subject content of the documents, the resulting system is referred to as a *pre-coordinate system:* whatever coordination of simple subjects there has been has taken place at the *input* stage. The traditional forms of catalogue mentioned earlier in this chapter are all pre-coordinate catalogues. Similarly, all classification schemes allow a measure of coordination, either by including compound subjects or by providing facilities for creating them out of simple elements. The same goes for lists of headings for use in alphabetical subject catalogues. Such schemes and lists of headings can therefore be regarded as *pre-coordinate languages*. In the four chapters which follow this we are assuming a pre-coordinate system.

Post-coordination

If, however, the cataloguer deals only in simple concepts, providing a device or devices through which the *user* can combine them to create the compound subjects in which he is interested and so retrieve the relevant documents, then the resulting system is referred to as *post-coordinate:* the coordination takes place at the *output* stage. Further discussion of such devices will be left to Chapter 11.

Specificity*

A specific heading (and here we are assuming a pre-coordinate system)

* A somewhat narrower definition of this term is found on page 119. *Specific* is a term used in textbooks with a variety of meanings.

4

whether a term in natural language or a notational symbol, is one which is co-extensive with the subject of the document. For example, a document on the subject of Electricity may be given one of the following headings: (a) SCIENCE, or (b) PHYSICS, or (c) ELECTRICITY, or (d) 5, or (e) 53, or (f) 537 (where 5, 53 and 537 stand for Science, Physics, and Electricity, respectively in a scheme of classification); (g) SCIENCE: PHYSICS, or (h) SCIENCE: PHYSICS: ELECTRICITY, or (i) SCIENCE: ELECTRICITY, or (j) PHYSICS: ELECTRICITY. Only those which include the concept Electricity are co-extensive with the subject of the document and therefore specific (i.e. c, f, h, i, and j). The rest are representative of broader concepts – Science and Physics. Similarly, headings like MAGNETISM and CURRENT, or the class numbers representing these headings, are narrower than the total content of the document. *Headings which represent subjects broader or narrower than the subject of the book are not specific headings.* (Note that style of heading – direct or indirect – has nothing to do with the concept of specific heading; thus ELECTRICITY and PHYSICS: ELECTRICITY are equally specific for a document on Electricity; the difference is that one is more indirect than the other – they represent different degrees of collocation.)

A fundamental theoretical rule of subject cataloguing is that each heading, whether a notational symbol or a term in natural language, should be co-extensive with the subject of the document. If we imagine headings to be a succession of labelled pigeon holes each carrying documents – or records of documents – then the contents and labels should match. If the label is for Chemistry then the pigeon hole should contain material on neither Science in general nor Inorganic chemistry. For it can be appreciated that the enquirer will not want to weed out material on General science and specific aspects of Chemistry if he is simply seeking material on Chemistry. These other subjects should themselves have distinct pigeon holes. Of course it can be said that these other materials may be of interest to the enquirer – but this is simply an argument for bringing their existence to his notice (by collocation or cross references or indexes) not for filling the Chemistry pigeon hole with anything but Chemistry.

In practice, this principle is often modified: at a certain degree of specialization, an alphabetical heading or a class number broader than the subject of the document is selected. For example, in D C (16th ed.) we find:

> 659.134 Outdoor and transportation advertising.
> (Including billboards, signs, car cards, moving signs.)

Thus a document on Billboards must be classified at the more general number 659.134. Again:

> 809.91 Literary movements and schools.
> (Including realism, idealism, naturalism, romanticism, symbolism, in literature.)

Documents on any one of these special subjects will be scattered at 809.91 according to author. To find what documents the library has on Romanticism in literature the enquirer will have to search through all entries at 809.91.

Thus several subjects carry the same class number. Some libraries carry this a stage further and restrict class numbers in subjects on which they have only few documents to a certain number of digits; for example, all documents on Petroleum manufacture whether or not they deal with more specific subjects would carry the D C class number 665.5 because the use of numbers with over four digits had been prohibited.

These practices are called *broad classification* – as distinct from *close or specific classification.* They are found also in catalogues using natural language terms, e.g. in Sears' *List of subject headings* (9th ed.) the general heading ENDOWMENTS will be used for all forms of Endowments (hospital, school, etc.); entries for documents on Slum clearance are to be filed under HOUSING; those on Public libraries under LIBRARIES; those on Inspection of schools under SCHOOL ADMINISTRATION AND ORGANIZATION, and so on.

This question of specificity will be raised on several occasions in the chapters that follow. Suffice to say here that all broad subject work should be practised very carefully – for one thing, as libraries grow it becomes increasingly difficult to sort through documents and entries which have been placed at broad class numbers and headings – and the final result is re-classification and cataloguing. On the other hand it must be recognized that in the alphabetico-direct catalogue, the greater the degree of specificity the greater the degree of scattering of subjects often required at one time.

Summarization

A specific heading in a catalogue is a *summarization* of a document's subject. It may be difficult to achieve. If the document is on two or more distinct subjects, for which no comprehensive heading exists two or more entries may have to be made for the document. Thus a document on Anatomy and Physiology will have entries under both ANATOMY and PHYSIOLOGY – or 611 and 612 if the catalogue is classified, one of these being chosen as the shelf number.* (Such multi-topical documents should not be confused with those with titles like Mathematics for engineers or Business English which are really about only one subject – Mathematics or English. Though treated from a particular viewpoint, they should be entered under the heading for the main subject though an extension may be added to indicate the bias and achieve specificity, e.g. ENGLISH LANGUAGE – *for business*, or 51:62 – where 51 signifies Mathematics and 62 Engineering. Similarly a document called 'The use of visual aids in secondary schools' is on one subject only: Visual aids and Secondary schools are in a relationship to each other; they are not distinct as in the case of the document on Anatomy and Physiology.)

Exhaustive Indexing

It should be noted that there is an alternative approach to summarization variously referred to as *exhaustive indexing, depth indexing,* or *extraction.* In brief, the attempt to create a specific catalogue heading summarizing the essential nature of the document is abandoned and, instead, entries are made for each of the topics treated in the document – or, more precisely, for such of them as are regarded as being significant or relevant to the users of the collection. Taken to its extreme this

---

* *Shelf number:* the symbol by which the document is shelved. Apart from the classification number it may include a number representing author, date, etc.

practice would result in a catalogue comprising the indexes to all the books in the library. As a method it is employed chiefly in specialized libraries for collections of periodical articles, reports, etc.; moreover, it is not a common practice in systems using the traditional (i.e. pre-coordinate) forms of catalogues outlined above.

The Process of Indexing

Two basic processes can be identified: analysis of the subject content of the document, and translation of the analysis into the terms of the index language.

ANALYSIS

If the aim of a retrieval system is the recall of documents relevant to demands, then the analysis of subject content is basic. On it depends the quality of the subsequent retrieval process.

Yet even the simplest document may – and often does – contain information on several topics, and it may be relevant to a person interested in any one of these topics. The article abstracted on p. 282, for example, may be of interest to someone wanting information on Southampton, public libraries, library surveys, readership and the effect of social and environmental factors, the siting of libraries in urban systems, etc. An average-length book may have hundreds of topics listed in its index, and it may be that a reader will need it for its contribution on just one of these. At the same time, most documents can be regarded as being on a unified subject – there will be a basic theme which can normally be identified and stated. The article already referred to is essentially about the factors affecting the use of public libraries in Southampton.

How, then, are we to answer the first question in indexing: what is the subject of this document? Imagine two people being questioned on the subject content of a book they have just read. One may well plunge into an enthusiastic account: 'Oh, it's got a marvellous account of A, and there's a remarkable section on B, and the author argues that . . .' etc. We can say that such a response is atomistic, designed to convey the whole by the naming of parts. The other will pause for a moment and say: 'Well, it's about the influence of A on B during the nineteenth century in X.' Here the person is trying to capture the essence of the document through a process of succinct summarization – the whole is named rather than the parts, though the parts may be inferred or implied by the delineation of the whole. Broadly speaking, the first is the method of the book's index, the second that of its title.

We can add that in each case the speaker may bear in mind the interests of the questioner and modify his answer accordingly, emphasizing those aspects of the book that are most likely to appeal to the listener and ignoring or playing down others. However, the scope for such interpretation is reduced when a summarization is attempted: here the focus is mainly on the document and the aim is to capture its essence in a compact statement.

Traditionally, indexing in libraries has been based on *summarization*. The aim has been to express verbally or in the form of a notational symbol the essential nature of a document, i.e. to find a heading co-extensive with what is regarded as *the* subject. (The limitations of index languages may have modified this ideal in practice, as we shall see, but the general intention has remained constant.) Beyond this the structure of the language – the cross references, systematic arrangement, etc. – has achieved a degree of movement from part to whole, and vice versa. In this way the implications of the basic summary have been made more or less explicit: a reader wanting information on readership will be led to documents on library surveys and thence to library surveys in Southampton. For the rest other tools have to be used – bibliographies, for example, and of course the indexes to the documents themselves (which points to the importance of such indexes – an importance they are all too frequently unfitted for[2]).

More recently, however, the alternative approach has been tried – and the term *exhaustive* indexing coined to differentiate it from summarization. Particularly in special libraries where the interests of the clientele can, to some extent, be predicted, the indexing of a document under all of the topics of which it is composed (or such of them as are deemed to be relevant or significant) is not unusual.

Exhaustive indexing is usually associated with post-coordinate systems, summarization with pre-coordinate. There is no inherent reason for this association: it would be theoretically possible to index exhaustively in a pre-coordinate system by making entries for a document under all the subjects contained within it – just as, conversely, entries in a post-coordinate system may be confined to terms from a summarization. Indeed, the use of certain kinds of added and analytical entries in a pre-coordinate system may be regarded as a form of exhaustive indexing. However, the economics of indexing and sheer convenience suggest that pre-coordinate systems are best used for summarization and post-coordinate for exhaustive indexing. (Bastard forms which mix the two indiscriminately – as in the stringing together in a single heading, in a UDC file, the class numbers representing bits of a document – are the result of confused thinking and in the end serve no one.)

Thus how we answer our initial question – what is the subject of this document? – depends to some degree on the system in use. If we are aiming at exhaustive indexing we shall go through the document picking out what we consider to be significant concepts and making an initial enumeration. Where summarization is the aim we shall scan the document more broadly and our first enumeration of contents will tend to be limited to those necessary for defining its essence.

TRANSLATION

The second stage is one of translating the basic analysis into the index language used in the system. In a pre-coordinate system, which is our main concern here, the first step will be to place the terms of our analysis into an order of priority. (As we shall see, there are various generalized statements of 'citation orders' that will help us in this procedure.) Suppose, for example, that we are dealing with a document which we have summarized as being about Working conditions of civil servants at the Home Office. The basic terms are: Working conditions, Civil servants, Home Office. We might consider that the key term, the one on which the others depend and which will juxtapose the document most usefully with others of a like kind, is Home Office. The document is about civil servants in the Home Office, and the working conditions of civil servants. The best order might therefore be:

Home Office: Civil servants: Working conditions.

Home Office implies Great Britain, but we may wish to specify this in order to distinguish it from other documents on equivalent organizations in other countries. We may therefore add this to our analysis:

Home Office: Civil Servants: Working conditions: Great Britain.

The next step is to decide on the general class into which such a subject would fall – in this case, Public administration, and in particular Central government administration. Our final string of terms might therefore be:

Public administration: Central government: Civil servants: Working conditions: Great Britain.

Turning now to the index language, and assuming that for purposes of illustration this is UDC, we can do one of two things. Either we can turn to the broad class – Public administration – and search the schedules for subdivisions related to the document; or we can turn to the index of the scheme and search it for key words, e.g. Home Office or Civil servants. If we are unfamiliar with the scheme we shall certainly have to do both.

Public administration in UDC is given the notation 35 and a major subdivision is 354: Central government. Home Office is specified at 354.31. The scheme has thus so far followed the terms of our analysis. To any of the divisions of 354 we can add concepts from a series of divisions placed at the head of 35, among which is .08 Civil servants and .088.2 Working conditions. So far all conforms with our analysis:

35	Public administration
354	Central government
354.31	Home Office
354.31.08	Civil servants
354.31.088.2	Working conditions

To this we could add (41) for Great Britain to complete the chain, but a note at 354 suggests the placing of the concept

Great Britain after either Home Office or Central government. And, of course, if we pause to think for a moment it is unlikely that we should want a mixture of documents on the working conditions of civil servants in various countries filed by country, thus separating the one on the working conditions at the Home Office from other documents on the Home Office. The concept Great Britain should therefore be moved up the chain at least as far as Home Office. The order would then be:

354.31(41)088.2

Even this, however, might still be regarded as unsatisfactory. For it will result in documents on the Home Office (Great Britain) being separated from other documents on departments of British government. If we wish to collocate documents on all departments of British government we must move the (41) a notch further:

354(41)

Now we have ensured the collocation of all aspects of British central government and can go ahead with further subdivisions:

354(41)31.088.2

This example illustrates the modification of an initial analysis by the index language, for although UDC lays down no citation order it does offer the suggested order accepted here. In this case it is for the better, but it may well happen that the language will force upon us an order that is not ideal.

Let us now imagine ourselves using an alphabetical index language (Sears' *List of subject headings*, 9th ed.) and trying to find a heading for the same document. A note under CIVIL SERVICE directs us to use this heading only for works 'on the history and development of public service. Works on public personnel administration, including the duties of civil service employees, their salaries, pensions, etc., are entered under the name of the country . . . with the subdivision *Officials and employees*'. The subject heading might therefore be:

GREAT BRITAIN – OFFICIALS AND EMPLOYEES

There would appear to be no provision for specific departments

(Home Office), nor for the concept of Working conditions. However, we might make a reference:

GREAT BRITAIN. *HOME OFFICE*–OFFICIALS AND EMPLOYEES
see
GREAT BRITAIN – OFFICIALS AND EMPLOYEES

It is clear that the subheading OFFICIALS AND EMPLOYEES is intended to cover all aspects of working conditions, and that no further specificity is advocated.

The heading is an example of relatively broad subject work frequently practised in alphabetical subject headings. It will be noted too that the language has modified the order of terms as set out in our initial analysis. The new order reflects a traditional view that in certain circumstances country should take precedence over subject – and in fact it is in line with the reasoning behind the transposition of country suggested in the UDC schedules.

Having determined the heading – whether a class number or natural language terms – there remains the further stage of providing alternative approaches to the document, i.e. relating it to broader and collateral concepts, ensuring that users who approach the subject from synonymous terms are catered for, etc. In the case of the classified catalogue the class number will itself result in the collocation of related subjects. An index is necessary, however, to lead the reader from possible keywords into the classified sequence – e.g.:

Home Office (Great Britain) *see* Great Britain. *Home Office*
Great Britain. *Home Office*: Public administration 354(41)31
Great Britain: Central government 354(41)
Government, Central: Public administration 354
Public administration 35
etc.

In the alphabetical subject catalogue references will have to be made from alternative approaches – e.g.:

GOVERNMENT EMPLOYEES *see* GREAT BRITAIN – OFFICIALS AND EMPLOYEES
CIVIL SERVICE *see also* GREAT BRITAIN – OFFICIALS AND EMPLOYEES
PUBLIC ADMINISTRATION *see also* CIVIL SERVICE
etc.

(These are only a few of the index entries and references that should be made in this case. The aim here is simply to illustrate the processes involved in indexing. We shall look more closely at these matters in subsequent chapters.)

We can now summarize the steps taken:

(i) Scan the document, noting key topics.

(ii) Convert into a succinct summary.

(iii) Place the terms of this summary into an order of priority.

(iv) Add the broad general class into which the summary falls.

(v) Add other concepts (e.g. Great Britain in our example, or Central government) as steps of division.

(vi) *Classified catalogue:* Search the schedules under the broad class, and the index for key concepts. Build up the class number – if possible avoiding the modification of term order, unless improvements are obvious.

Alphabetical catalogue: Search under basic concepts, noting related terms, until the appropriate heading is found. The heading should be as specific as the language permits.

(vii) Provide for alternative approaches. In the *classified catalogue* this will be through the index which will lead the reader to the relevant class numbers whatever the terms sought. In the *alphabetical subject catalogue* the same function will be served by a series of references which will be indicated in the index language.

(viii) Check that all major keywords have been indexed.

READINGS:

1. VICKERY, B. C. *Classification and indexing in science.* 2nd ed. London, Butterworth, 1959. p. 4.
2. Interesting comments on book indexing can be found in the following symposium:
   KNIGHT, G. N. ed. *Training in indexing: a course of the Society of Indexers.* Cambridge, Mass. and London, MIT Press, 1969.

Basic readings on subject work include:

COATES, E. J. *Subject catalogues: headings and structure.* London, Library Association, 1960.

FOSKETT, A. C. *The subject approach to information.* London, Bingley, 1969. A valuable new textbook with an integrated, systematic approach.

MILLS, J. A *modern outline of library classification.* London, Chapman and Hall, 1960.

There are also valuable chapters in:

ASHWORTH, W. *ed. Handbook of special librarianship and information work.* London, Aslib, 1967.

Other readings will be indicated in the chapters that follow.

Chapter 7
Classification

The *Shorter Oxford English Dictionary* defines a class as 'a number of individuals (persons or things) possessing common attributes, and grouped together under a general or "class" name; a kind, sort, division'. Classification, 'the action of classifying', is a basic process in indexing – whether the final product of the process be a systematic sequence of classes known as a classification scheme, a sequence of documents systematically ordered into subject classes on the shelves (or a similar sequence of entries in a catalogue), or an alphabetical sequence of classes (as in an alphabetical subject catalogue or a list of subject headings). In creating any of these tools we are naming classes of things – documents and the subjects contained within them – according to the presence or absence of attributes. Further, by the arrangement of classes and through systematic references etc., we are demonstrating the relationships that exist between them. Classification is also a fundamental operation in reference work, and Coates has written an interesting chapter on this use of classification in his book *Subject catalogues*.

Although in this and the next chapter we shall be dealing with *schemes* of classification, the basic theoretical points concerning the analysis and categorization of subjects underlie all forms of subject indexing.

The Making of a Classification Scheme for a Particular Subject

A classification scheme is simply defined as 'an orderly arrangement of terms or classes'. Given a notation, a classification scheme can be used to arrange documents or entries in the catalogue and is, as we have seen, the only way of achieving a preferred order of subjects.

Examine the following titles: (i) *The literature of the Eighteenth* *century,* (ii) *A history of English literature,* (iii) *French drama,* (iv) *Russian influence in the English short story.* A good scheme for Literature should be able to accommodate each of the subjects denoted by these titles with a distinct place set aside for that subject only – otherwise specific entry will not be possible* – and setting each in proximity to related subjects.

Of the making of such subjects there is no end. Hundreds pour off the presses each week. How then can a scheme be made to accommodate them whenever they occur? Clearly *enumeration* of all subjects is impossible.

STAGE ONE: ANALYSIS

As all substances are either simple chemical elements or compounds† of such elements, so subjects in documents are either simple concepts or compounds of such concepts. The subjects expressed in the titles listed above are compounds of: (i) Literature, Eighteenth-century, (ii) History, English, Literature, (iii) French, Drama, (iv) Russian, English, Short story. Although the number of such simple concepts increases with the increase in knowledge, the rate of increase is slight compared with the rate at which new compounds are created. It follows that if a classification scheme is composed of simple concepts only, and if some means of combining them in a preferred order is devised, then the scheme will be capable of accommodating the vast majority of new subjects as they arise. For example, if the notational symbol L represents Literature, b Novel and e English, then the combination 'Leb' will stand for the subject 'The English novel'. *Synthesis* is a term used to refer to the creation of compound subjects by the combining of simple elements.

---

   * A classification scheme should allow specific entry even if the classifier using the scheme prefers broad classification.

   † In this chapter and elsewhere in the book I have not differentiated between 'compound' and 'complex': both terms are used to connote subjects comprising more than one simple element. However, other writings on classification make the following distinction.

Compound: a subject comprising a relationship between two or more foci within a class, e.g. the use of visual aids in teaching mathematics.

Complex: a subject comprising a relationship between two or more foci from different classes, e.g. mathematics for engineers, psychology of politics. Complex relationships are sometimes referred to as *phase relations.*

Number-building refers specifically to the notational aspects of this process.

The first job of a maker of a subject classification scheme will be to examine a representative sample of documents in that subject, covering all topics within the subject and all levels – such as could be found in a bibliography of the subject – listing concepts as they arise. In this way all simple concepts will be discovered and they will be concepts actually arising in documents – they will have *literary warrant*. Concepts in this unorganized state are often called *isolates*.

Vickery has advocated the use of organized textbooks in the subject to discern the general structure of the subject. He also shows how glossaries of the subject can be of assistance, particularly in connection with Stage Two – the creation of facets.[1]

STAGE TWO: CREATION OF FACETS

The isolates now need grouping so that those which are related are proximate. Examine the following isolates in Education: (i) Primary, (ii) Secondary, (iii) Further, (iv) Visual aids, (v) Tutorials, (vi) Geography, (vii) Mathematics. (i)–(iii) are obviously related, so are (iv)–(v), and (vi)–(vii). There are three basic groups here: (a) Education according to age, (i)–(iii); (b) Teaching methods, (iv)–(v); (c) Subjects taught, (vi)–(vii). The relationships arise because in each group the concepts have one characteristic in common (Age or Method or Subject).

A *characteristic* is an attribute by which concepts are grouped or subjects divided. Traditionally we talk of *characteristics of division*, because, following logical analogy, the process of division predominated. The isolates listed above could have been arrived at had we divided the class Education by the characteristics Age, Method, and Subject. The grouping process has this advantage: the isolates have literary warrant. However, division might help to yield isolates which by chance have remained undiscovered in the survey of the literature.

Other examples:

Subject	*Characteristic*	*Examples of isolates*
Literature	Period	Eighteenth century, Nineteenth century

Subject	Characteristic	Examples of isolates
	Form	Ode, Ballad, Drama, Novel
	Author	Shelley, Blake, Hugo
	Language	English, German
Occupational safety and health (cis)*	Industries	Agriculture, Food, Textiles
	Source of hazard	Fires, Tools, Electricity
	Industrial disease	Asthma, Eczema

The sum total of isolates formed by the division of a subject by one characteristic of division is called a *facet*. In the above examples we may refer to the Form facet, the Period facet, the Source of hazard facet, and so on. The isolates within a facet are called *foci* to distinguish them from the unorganized concepts called isolates. This process of analysis is called *facet analysis* and a scheme produced after such analysis a *faceted classification*.†

Characteristics of division should be *mutually exclusive*. Thus the Period facet in Literature should not include foci belonging to the Form facet, nor the Hazard facet in Occupational safety and health include foci belonging to the Industry facet. This is very important. Where such impurities occur there is liable to be *cross classification*: the situation where documents on the same subject are to be found classified at different places in the scheme.

The enumeration of foci should be *exhaustive* according to the literary warrant. That is, all foci should be listed and there should be room for expansion as new foci arise, e.g. Esperanto in the Language facet for Literature. The latter is a notational problem that will be discussed below.

It has been discovered that there are recurrent *categories of facets* in many subjects. For example, a Materials facet appears in Engineering, Building, Architecture, Painting, and so on;

* A scheme for this subject devised by D. J. Foskett and others, was published by International Occupational Safety and Health Information Centre, Geneva, 1960, and is referred to in this book as cis.

† Many of the terms and concepts in this chapter – and indeed throughout this book – are based on the fundamental research of S. R. Ranganathan.

an Operations facet appears in these subjects also; an Age facet appears in many subjects in the Social sciences, e.g. Education, Social Services, Labour, Economics. The foci within these categories may vary according to subject, of course, as the following table illustrates:

Category of facet	Subject	Examples of foci
Operations	Librarianship	Cataloguing, Reference work
	Building	Site preparation, Bricklaying
	Medicine	Surgery, Nursing
Materials	Engineering	Steel, Plastics, Copper
	Textiles	Wool, Cotton, Nylon
	Painting	Water paints, Oils, Crayon

This fact – that categories of facet recur – is of great assistance to the maker of a scheme as an aid to the initial definition of relevant characteristics and, consequently, facets. By asking what is the Materials facet, the Operations facet, and so on, the grouping of isolates is facilitated. Ranganathan has suggested that there are, basically, five categories which he calls Personality, Matter, Energy, Space, and Time (PMEST). Other fundamental characteristics have been suggested. Vickery,[2] with particular reference to scientific literature, has postulated the following: Thing (product) – Part – Constituent – Property – Measure – Patient – Process/Action/Operation – Agent (Space – Time). Differences between sets of fundamental categories arise from differences in level of generality and differences in the purposes for which they have been created. The important thing to grasp here is the principle of facet analysis and the recurrence of categories of facet.

Once the facets are established, the foci within them may need further grouping into subordinate facets or *sub-facets* according to subordinate characteristics applicable only to the facet under consideration. Thus in the CIS scheme, the foci in the Pathology facet (M – N) are grouped according to the location of the disease (diseases of the eye, respiratory system, nervous system, and so on); in the Safety and health engineering facet (S) there are sub-facets for fire protection, explosive prevention, radiation and electrical protection, and so on, and within each of these a cluster of related foci. Again, in the class Literature, foci in the Form facet may be grouped as follows:

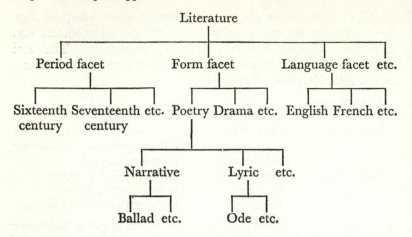

Care must be taken to see that elements from other facets are not introduced, for, as we have seen, characteristics of division should be mutually exclusive. For example, it would be wrong to sub-divide the Language facet of Literature by divisions from the Period facet, e.g.:

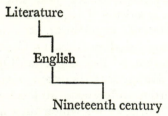

because this results in a compound: Nineteenth-century English literature. It is better to form such compounds by synthesis rather than by enumeration.

The groups of foci could be listed in a classification schedule as follows:

> Literature
> *Period facet, e.g.*
> Sixteenth century
> Seventeenth century
> *Form facet, e.g.*
> Poetry
> Narrative
> Ballad

Lyric
Ode
Drama
Language facet, e.g.
English
French

Such a series of ranked classes and subclasses reflecting various steps of division through the application of a variety of characteristics, as shown here, is referred to as a *hierarchy*. Within the hierarchy foci of equal status, i.e. those formed by dividing a class by *one* characteristic, are called *coordinate foci* or *coordinate classes* or *arrays*. Thus (a) Poetry and Drama are coordinate, as are (b) Narrative and Lyric. This distinguishes their relationship from the *subordinate* relationship existing between, respectively, Poetry, Narrative, and Ballad, and Poetry, Lyric, and Ode, for here, in each case, the second and third foci are produced after further steps of division. Hierarchy can only be properly demonstrated by a two-dimensional 'family tree' layout; classification schedules with a *linear* or one-dimensional sequence demonstrate it with only partial success by indentation and typography, and on the shelves and in catalogues the order is even less apparent.

Each stage in the creation of sub-facets is called a *step of division*.* It is important that relevant steps of division (i.e. those for which there is a literary warrant, such as Narrative and Lyric in the above example) are not missed. As Mills has pointed out in his *Modern outline of library classification, the* omission of a division for Prose in DC Class 800 has led to the lack of accommodation for documents on Prose.

STAGE THREE: ARRANGEMENT OF FOCI

So far we have a series of facets and sub-facets with coordinate foci enumerated in each. The next task is to arrange the foci in some order. Ranganathan[3] has listed the following principles for the arrangement of foci: evolutionary, chronological, geographical, increasing complexity, alphabetical, canonical

---

* This term is also used, as we shall see, to refer to steps in the formation by synthesis of a compound subject, e.g. Literature – English – Nineteenth century, see p. 183.

and consistent. What order is chosen for a particular group of foci will depend on the subject: thus, arrangement of Place names according to geographical proximity is superior to the arbitrary alphabetical arrangement; some foci – Biological species, for example – are best arranged according to the evolutionary principle; chronological arrangement is clearly called for whenever the development or sequence of a subject is to be stressed – in Printing processes or Agricultural operations for example. Arrangement of coordinate foci has been called *order in array*.

STAGE FOUR: DECIDING ON THE COMBINATION ORDER OF FACETS

Remember that the scheme will consist of simple concepts which will have to be combined or synthesized to accommodate the complex subjects found in documents. A combination order (or citation order as it is sometimes called) must therefore be laid down, i.e. *a combination order of facets*. Without this documents on the same subject may be classified at different places. For example a person classifying a document called *Sixteenth-century English literature* may, unless he is given an indication of combination order, place it in the Period facet or the Language facet. Again, a person classifying a document called *English language teaching in secondary schools* must know whether to place the document in the Subject facet or the Grade facet; if the notational symbol for English language is Eb and the symbol for Secondary schools is Gd, shall the final symbol be EbGd or GdEb? In the first place the combination order is Subject – Grade, in the second Grade – Subject. *This is a very important point, for it determines the extent of collocation.* If the order is Subject – Grade, then the teaching of a particular subject will be collocated whatever the type of school involved, but a person wanting all material on, say, Secondary schools will have to search not only under the symbol for Secondary schools, where he will find documents on Secondary schools in general only, but also under the various *subjects* taught in Secondary schools.

Classification inevitably separates as it collocates because a document can go in only one place on the shelves, no matter how complex its subject; and though in theory any number of entries can be made in the catalogue, there are economic limits, and few cataloguers would make entries for books on the teaching of subjects in certain types of schools under both subject *and* school. And the more complex the subject the greater the separation; if the combination order for Literature is Language – Form – Period, as in DC, then all the Literature in a particular Language is collocated, but Forms of literature (Drama, Poetry, etc.) are scattered through those Languages, and Periods of literature are further scattered through the Forms – and thus a person who wants all documents on the Literature of a certain period, regardless of Language or Form, will have a long search. Related subjects scattered by the classification in this way are called *distributed relatives,* a term which we shall use frequently when discussing the subject index to the classified catalogue (Chapter 9). The index to the scheme itself – particularly if enumerative – should gather together any distributed relatives.

The best combination order for a subject will depend to some extent on *the needs of users,* and their approaches to the subject should be carefully analysed. This is impossible if the library caters for a wide variety of readers, but even here there is, to use Bliss's phrase, an *educational and scientific consensus of opinion.* Thus in the field of Literature, students normally confine their studies to the Literature of a particular Language, rather than Period or Form, hence Language should take precedence in the combination order for compounds; within a particular Language they normally study Period rather than Form (see the style of GCE examinations) and therefore the combination order should be Language – Period – Form.

There have been several attempts to express a standard citation order in terms of fundamental categories. The catagories of Ranganathan and Vickery have already been noted (p. 113), and the order in which they are given (PMEST, Thing – Part, etc.) is, in each case, the one regarded by its author as being most appropriate for general application. However, Vickery makes the point that 'such a set can only serve as a guide, a reminder of a pattern that has been helpful in other situations'.

STAGE FIVE: ARRANGEMENT OF FACETS IN THE SCHEME:
SCHEDULE ORDER

The final decision before the notation is added is the relative
order of the facets *in the scheme itself* (i.e. the facets as wholes –
not the foci within them as already discussed above). For
example, shall the layout be:

(a) Education	OR	(b) Education
Grade facet		*Subject taught facet*
Primary		Science
Secondary		Literature
Higher		History
etc.		etc.
Subject taught facet		*Grade facet*
Science		Primary
Literature		Secondary
History		Higher
etc.		etc.

This is relatively unimportant compared with the question of
combination order. However it is traditional for 'general' to
precede 'special', e.g. Wheat and Harvesting in general would
precede the compound Harvesting of wheat; Secondary schools
and The teaching of mathematics would file before The teaching of mathematics in secondary schools. If we wish to achieve
this order of *increasing speciality* (and some recent schemes have
abandoned it), then *the order of facets in the scheme must be the
reverse of the combination order*. For example, if the combination
order in Education is Grade – Subject, then the schedule order
must be Subject – Grade; in this way the most significant facet
(the one which collects most compounds – and is therefore more
specialized) will file after the less significant (the one where
there are fewer compounds and which is therefore more
general). If however an order of increasing speciality is not
considered important the order of facets in the schedule should
be simply that of the combination order (as in CIS).[4]

STAGE SIX: NOTATION

The last stage apart from the index, is to add a notation to
mechanize the arrangement. This subject will be treated below.

STAGE SEVEN: MAKING THE INDEX

An index is necessary: (a) to indicate the location in the schedules of a sought term, and (b) to collocate distributed relatives (see page 117). Indexes which meet the second objective have been called *relative indexes*. We shall investigate the purpose and construction of a relative index in Chapter 9. Suffice to say here that *the index should not repeat the order of the schedules* as this adds greatly to the length of the index, is uneconomic, and is likely to be unsystematic. For example, the index to the partial schedule given above (list (a)) should read:

		Class number
	Education	. . .
	Higher education	. . .
	History: Teaching: Education	. . .
	Literature: Teaching: Education	. . .
	Primary education	. . .
	Science: Teaching: Education	. . .
	Secondary education	. . .
NOT	Education	. . .
	Education: Higher	. . .
	Education: Primary	. . .
	Education: Secondary	. . .
	Education: Teaching: History	. . .
	etc.	

Traditional Classification Theory

The method outlined here is today recognized as being superior to the traditional methods of library classification. It has been used in several special classification schemes, e.g. CIS and the BNB *Music classification* used in the *British catalogue of music*. The traditional methods were based on a close analogy with logical classifications where the classification structure is a hierarchy formed by the *successive* application of characteristics of division thus enumerating compounds. This can be diagrammatically expressed on the next page.

Its main purpose is the *definition* of terms and categories, and it is concerned with relations between *Genus* (e.g. Corporeal substance) and *Species* (e.g. Organic substance) – the *thing* and its *kinds*. Strictly *specificity* should be used only to refer to this

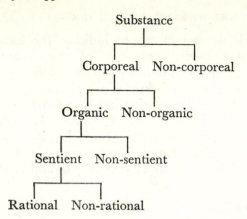

relationship between a thing and its kinds (but see page 97).
In library classification we are not concerned solely with the
Genus-species relationship (Harvesting is not a *kind* of Agriculture, Electricity is not a *kind* of Physics), nor is our aim
definition. The limitations of the traditional hierarchical
structure for our purposes are easily demonstrated by the following diagram where the subject Literature is divided successively by various characteristics by analogy with the above
pattern.

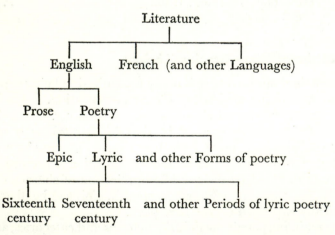

Similar divisions would be found under each of the Languages.
Because all Forms can only be expressed as sub-divisions of
Languages, documents *simply* on Poetry, Prose, Epic, etc.,

cannot be accommodated; documents on Periods of literature cannot be accommodated either – except where the document also concerns a particular Form and Language,'e.g. Seventeenth-century English lyrics. Moreover, *just as simple subjects cannot be accommodated, neither can compounds other than those enumerated in the hierarchy* – thus the scheme above could not accommodate Seventeenth-century English literature. This is what invariably happens in enumerative classification schemes.[5]

Clearly the method outlined earlier in this chapter (contrast the hierarchy on page 114), where, instead of creating hierarchies based on the successive application of characteristics, simple subjects only are listed with the means of combining them whenever necessary, is much more satisfactory. Ranganathan has likened the latter method to a Meccano set – the pieces and fixings are provided, and innumerable compounds can be created.

General Classification Schemes: Special Problems and Traditional Features

The general principles and methods outlined above, though relating specifically to the creation of classification schemes for particular subjects, could no doubt be used in the creation of a general scheme of classification. A major problem here is that of 'main classes'.

(a) 'MAIN CLASSES'

With the exception of sc all existing schemes choose the major disciplines as their 'main classes': Economics, Medicine, Law, Engineering, and so on. Apart from the fact that the barriers between these main disciplines are increasingly difficult to distinguish, there is a further disadvantage in having such disciplines as the primary divisions of a scheme: documents which concern subjects (often 'concretes') treated from several aspects cannot be classified satisfactorily. For example, a book on Railways dealing with the Economic, Administrative and Engineering aspects, has to be classified according to *one* of these aspects – under Economics for example – with the result that it is lost to the students of Transport organization and

Engineering. Nor is it an easy matter to rectify this in the catalogue, as we shall see. The problem arises frequently, e.g. documents on *substances* (Oil, Coal, etc.), on *processes* (Measuring, Testing, etc.), *places* (GB, USA), *periods* (Eighteenth century), and so on. Investigation of this problem is in progress at the present time;[6] though there are difficulties, there seems to be no fundamental objection to the faceted method outlined in this chapter being applied to knowledge generally in order to produce a general scheme of classification. The basis of such a scheme will not be the traditional 'main classes' but a series of facets capable of being compounded according to a preferred order with the possibility of alternative orders to suit particular needs.

The Classification Research Group has been largely responsible for exploratory work on a new general scheme, their investigations having been assisted for a time with a research grant from Nato. The Group has, through its members, close connections with BNB, and Derek Austin of the BNB has written several papers on the progress of the research.[7]

It would be optimistic to suggest that a new general classification is imminent, but certain fundamental features appear to have been established. The 'vocabulary' of the scheme is to consist of two schedules of terms designated *Entities* and *Attributes*. Examples of the former include terms arising from energy (force, gravity, heat), matter (molecular states, elements, compounds), earth, plants, animals, man. Attributes include such 'positional terms' as time and space; properties such as shapes, sounds, states, structures; and activities, e.g. equilibrium, kinetic conditions, motions and transfers. The order of these vocabularies is based on the philosophy of 'integrative levels', whereby terms are categorized according to level of complexity and arranged in an ascending order – as can be glimpsed from the outline of Entities given above. Each concept is represented once only in the vocabularies and it is hoped that basic generic relationships will be accounted for by the hierarchies of terms. Compounds will be built up according to an established citation order and the relationships between elements in the compounds will be made explicit by the use of a series of *Relational Operators* (e.g. property of a system, subsystem, interaction within the system, effect produced on the system, attribute defining a type or class). The notational symbols for these operators will link the symbols representing Entities or Attributes to demonstrate the precise relationships between them.

Austin has stated that such a highly specific, synthetic scheme will inevitably produce lengthy class numbers: '. . . any idea of a short notation will now have to be abandoned. This is where enumerative schemes must score every time, but it should be remembered that an enumerated scheme fed into a computer will not allow retrieval of any particular element, whereas this proposed system of organized concepts will, and the computer, thank goodness, has no aesthetic scruples about long numbers.'[8]

To illustrate the sort of class number that could arise Austin gives the following: c35(2)q24(29)x75(299)v6(22)B(223)t44 – a hypothetical number standing for the document 'Energy balance in the turbulent mixing layer of a gas'. The basic citation order is Gases/Turbulent mixing layers/Energy balance. The numbers introduced by capital letters (c35 and B) are taken from the Entities schedule and stand for gases and energy respectively. Those introduced by lower case letters (q24, x75, v6 and t44) are taken from the Attributes schedule and stand in turn for layers, to mix, turbulence, and to balance. The numbers in brackets are Relational Operators all stemming from the basic operator (2), standing for a subsystem: thus layers is seen as a part of gases and so we get the sequence c35(2)q24.

Whether or not a new general scheme emerges in the next few years the work of analysing concepts and relationships is fundamental. Its influence can be seen already in the development of PRECIS indexing at BNB (see Chapter 9). There is no doubt that a new general scheme is badly needed to provide an alternative to the essentially nineteenth-century conceptions in general use today. A scheme such as this with its systematic analysis of concepts and relationships would also provide an extremely valuable basis for the creation of special schemes, effecting a much-needed measure of standardization.

Where *traditional* 'main classes' are used, some criterion for determining schedule order must be devised. (In a faceted scheme this would be determined largely by the combination order of facets.) Bliss, who has systematically investigated this problem[9] has said that 'main classes' should be carefully collocated so that related subjects are proximate. For example, Literature and Language should be proximate, as should Commerce and Economics and Business, Psychology and Medicine, and so on. Of course, there are limits to such collocation in schemes which are essentially one-dimensional linear sequences. In some cases *alternative locations* should be allowed to cater for special needs (some examples of these will be found in the section on BC below). The prefaces to BC are extremely valuable commentaries on the content of 'main classes' and the relationships between subjects.

(b) FACET ANALYSIS IN TRADITIONAL SCHEMES

Although enumeration of compounds is the traditional basis using the hierarchical model shown on page 120, all schemes have some degree of facet analysis – and in some it is considerable. The outstanding examples found in all schemes (save LC) are the *common subdivisions*, the main ones being for Place, Period, and Form of presentation.* These divisions can be applied at most points in the schedules – thus, in UDC (41) stands for Great Britain and 62 (41) would therefore represent the compound Engineering in Britain (where 62 means Engineering); similarly 338 (41) would stand for Economic situation in Great Britain. Again '19' stands for Twentieth century and thus 8 '19' would stand for Literature in the twentieth century. (03) represents the form Encyclopaedias and therefore 62 (03) would represent Encyclopaedias of Engineering. Further examples can be found in the notes on the schemes (Chapter 8).

By definition these are common *subdivisions* and cannot be used except in conjunction with a subject in the main schedules. The *Generalia class* results from this limitation; basically it houses *general forms* (general encyclopaedias, general collected essays, general periodicals, etc.). Such a class would be unnecessary if a *common facet* were created which could accommo-

* See Chapter 13.

date such documents and also be applied to any subject in the schedules in the manner of common subdivisions. Note: in practice the generalia class, as we shall see, is also used as a rag-bag for miscellaneous items that will not fit anywhere else.

Other examples of facet analysis in general schemes will be noted in Chapter 8. In general it is sporadic – for example, in DC there is the occasional instruction to *'divide like . . .'* as in the Literature class where all Languages can be further subdivided by the divisions enumerated under English; thus 820 is English literature, 821 English poetry, and the 1 can be added to any other literature to stand for poetry, e.g. 831 German poetry, 841 French poetry, etc. However, in recent years there has been a notable trend in DC towards a more systematic analysis of categories and the use of synthetic devices. The most extensive use of analysis and synthesis in general schemes is to be found in UDC and, of course, in Ranganathan's *Colon classification*.

Notation

Ranganathan has defined notation as 'the system of ordinal numbers used to represent the classes in a scheme of classification'. To be efficient each class number should be unique, standing for only one distinct subject and used constantly for that subject.

PURPOSE

As already noted (page 93), the main purpose of notation is the mechanization of a preferred order; the order must be decided first. *Yet without notation the classification scheme cannot be put into operation at all*, for the only order without a notation is the alphabetical order of terms. A notational symbol is a shorthand sign and as such necessary for the arrangement of documents on the shelves; it also provides briefer and more satisfactory headings than words for the filing of entries for complex documents in the catalogue. The notational symbol is an easily memorized link between catalogue and shelves.

KINDS OF NOTATION

Notation can be *pure* or *mixed*: a pure notation uses only one kind of symbol (e.g. arabic numbers *or* roman letters), a mixed notation uses more than one kind of symbol (e.g. arabic numbers *and* roman letters). Numbers can be used as decimal *fractions* (e.g. 0 . . . 1 . . . 12 . . . 13 . . . 131 . . . 2 . . . 21 . . . etc.) or as *integers* (e.g. 1 . . . 2 . . . 12 . . . 13 . . . 21 . . . 131 . . . etc.).

Notation can be *expressive* or *non-expressive*. Expressive notation not only mechanizes the order but reveals the structure of the classification scheme. For example, in the Literature class in DC the hierarchy is reflected in the notation, a further digit being added at each stage of division:

8	Literature
82	English literature
821	English poetry
821.3	Sixteenth-century English poetry

Again, subjects of equal status in the hierarchy (coordinate subjects) have class numbers that *look* equal (82 English literature, 83 German literature, 84 French literature, etc.).

Expressiveness is not always found and is generally considered less important than it once used to be. In UDC, though this scheme is largely expressive, we find:

531	Mechanics
532	Fluid mechanics
533	Gas mechanics

and

450	Italian language
459.0	Roumanian language
459.0	Ladin-Romansch. Rhaeto-Romanic
460	Spanish language
469.0	Portuguese language
469.9	Galician language

A distinction should be made between the expression of generic relations (i.e. those existing between simple foci within a facet) and compound relations (i.e. those between two or more foci from different facets). As we shall see there is no inherent difficulty in expressing compound relations through the use of facet indicators, retroactive notation, etc. Generic relations are another matter: there are obvious limits to the number of co-ordinate divisions that can be placed within any facet or sub-facet so long as we are aiming at expressiveness – the number being determined by the notation employed. Thus a numerical base will allow only ten such divisions, whilst an alphabetical base will allow twenty-four. Ranganathan has suggested the use of the various *sectorizing devices* for extending the capacity of a numerical base. One of these, the *octave device,* reserves the final digit 9 for a further set of coordinate divisions. With such a device 9 is never used alone but always introduces a further series of coordinate divisions: 91, 92 . . . 991, 992 . . ., etc. Though this certainly provides places for any number of co-ordinate divisions the resulting numbers do not *look* coordinate and are evidently so only to the initiated. Moreover this device alone is still incapable of allowing insertion of a new focus at a predetermined point in the schedule: for example, it will not allow the placing of a division between 2 and 3 which is still expressive.

REQUIREMENTS OF NOTATION

(i) *Hospitality*

The basic purpose of notation is to mechanize a preferred order, and if knowledge were static it would be easy to add a notation to the final scheme and there the matter would end. But new subjects are constantly being created and therefore notation must be able to accommodate these subjects as they arise – and in their proper place in the scheme: in a word, it must be hospitable. If the notation is inhospitable, it will *determine* order not merely mechanize it; the cart will be before the horse. For example, in an arithmetic notation (i.e. one using integers) if 62 represents the Novel and 63 Drama, there is no means of placing the Historical novel in its correct place – which is clearly *between* 62 and 63. Instead the nearest vacant number will be used (numbers are always left free for this purpose in an arithmetic notation). An arithmetic notation can never be fully hospitable because no amount of foresight can ensure that gaps will always be left as required. A decimal notation, on the other hand, is infinitely hospitable; had the numbers in the above example been decimal fractions, the Historical novel could have been accommodated at, say, 625 (or 62.5); again, if 010 represents Bibliography and 020 Librarianship, and Documentation (considered as a subject including both Bibliography and Librarianship) had to be placed ahead of 010, then 009 might be used – or, if that were already in use, 0099, and so on. This is equally true of an alphabetical notation. For example, if Gb represents Bibliography and Gc Librarianship, them Gab could be used for Documentation and if Gab were already in use Gaab could be used, and so on.

No notation can ever be fully hospitable and maintain its expressiveness; in the examples above, the symbols for Librarianship and Bibliography do not *look* subordinate to the symbol chosen for Documentation. Nor is there any symbol that would look superordinate to these. Expressiveness is useful in that it expresses the structure of the scheme to some extent, but it must be sacrificed in the interests of hospitality – and many modern schemes have abandoned the concept, at least, so far as generic relations are concerned.

So far we have considered hospitality to *new foci* and simple *steps of division*; equally important is hospitality to *new compounds*. Such compounds are, as we have seen, the result of synthesis – the combining of foci from different facets in a scheme.*

One of the problems in notation is to create a device to indicate that the resulting symbol *is* a compound so that it cannot be confused with a straight division within the facet; for example, in UDC 531 stands for Mechanics and 62 for Engineering, but the compound Mechanics for engineers cannot be expressed as 531.62 because this is a division of 531, standing for Law of conservation of energy – in other words, the point cannot be used as a facet indicator in a scheme using a decimal notation and a point separator. *Combination cannot be indicated by an indicator that is already used for class divisions.*

Bearing this general consideration in mind, *combination can be indicated by the following methods*:

(a) *By such devices as colons, brackets, inverted commas, and so on –* as in UDC, e.g. 531:62 Mechanics for Engineers; 373.5:371.27

---

* The process of combining notational symbols to cater for compounds has been called *number building*.

Examinations in Secondary schools (where 373.5 stands for Secondary schools and 371.27 for Examinations); 5(09) History of science (where (09) stands for History).

(b) *By capital letters being used to indicate the different facets* – as in CIS where Gtz means Dust (in the Substance facet G) and Qfz means Sampling (in the Method of investigation facet Q) and so GtzQfz means Dust sampling.

(c) *By the reservation of certain sections of the base for certain facets* – thus, for example, in UDC class 656 (Transport organization) the series .01/.09 is reserved for the Operations facet and .1/.9 is reserved for the Type of transport facet. 656.032 stands for Passenger rates and 656.132 for Buses and motor coaches. As .032 is used here in the Operations facet only, the compound, Bus fares, can be expressed as 656.132.032.

A scheme which sets out its facets in inverted citation order, reserving sections of the base for each facet as illustrated here, is said to employ a *retroactive notation*.

When symbols with no ordinal value – such as brackets, colons, etc. – are used, they have to be given one and this makes filing and searching more difficult (thus in UDC, colons file before inverted commas, which in turn file before brackets, and so on). On the other hand it gives a certain measure of flexibility to the classifier who, by the simple expedient of altering the filing value of the connecting symbols, can achieve a filing order to suit his requirements.

(ii) *Notation should be easily comprehensible and have ordinal value*

This means that only roman letters and/or arabic numbers should be used; other symbols (triangles, for example) being unusual and having no ordinal value. It also means that as far as possible, facet indicators should also be symbols having ordinal value as seen already.

(iii) *Notation should be easily memorized, written and spoken*

This is partly dependent on its *comprehensibility*. It is also and primarily dependent on the *simplicity* of symbol. In general, numbers are more easily remembered than letters, but they have some disadvantages (see *Length of symbol*, below). It has been shown (Coates)[10] that too much mixing of letters and figures is detrimental to memory and that much depends on the

5

placing and style of *separators* to break a long sequence (e.g. the point in DC and UDC). The best separators are those which have that function in everyday usage (points, brackets, and so on). 33847 (62148) and 33847K62148 are better than 3384762148 (no separators) or 3384U2K21P8 (three separators), and so on. If the function of separator is combined with that of facet indicator (as in CIS), and letters or figures are used to indicate order, this may lead to compounds with rather too many separators for easy memorizing. The use of such mixtures as BB211 is to be avoided. *Pronounceable* or *syllabic notation*, pioneered by Cordonnier and others, may well be increasingly used in new schemes – see, for example, D. J. Foskett's *London education classification*.

Another factor here is *length of symbol*. Inevitably class numbers will become longer as more complex subjects are specified. *Maximum brevity can be achieved by:*

(a) *A long notational base:* in a decimal system a numerical base (0/9) will result in longer class numbers than an alphabetical base (A/Z) – because whilst the former can accommodate only ten classes using one digit and a hundred using two digits (00/99), etc., the latter can accommodate twenty-six classes using only one letter, and 676 classes using two letters (AA/ZZ), etc. Bliss uses a base of thirty-six digits – 0/9 followed by A/Z.

(b) *The proper allocation of the notation:* subjects on which there is much literature and which are rapidly expanding (as Science and Technology) should be given more space than the relatively static subjects. DC gives Philosophy and Religion (100 and 200) the same space as the whole of Science and Technology (500 and 600) and therefore, as may be expected, class numbers in the former classes are much shorter than those in the latter where important classes start from a four-figure symbol or more (e.g. Electrical engineering 621.3, Aeronautical engineering 629.13).

(c) *Rejection of expressiveness.* Expressiveness will also lengthen class numbers – as every new subdivision will require a further digit in the notation.

(d) *Synthesis also tends to lengthen numbers.* The compound subjects on page 129 could be more shortly expressed if, instead of forming them by synthesis, they had been enumerated, e.g. Examinations in secondary schools could have been 373.51 (or

373.6). But enumeration is, as we have seen, to be avoided. Good allocation of notation and carefully designed synthesis can do much to reduce length.

Memory may also be assisted by *mnemonics*, i.e. the constant expression of certain concepts by particular symbols so that they become familiar in time to staff and even perhaps to users – e.g. periodicals (05), Great Britain (41). In this way enquiries can be rapidly translated into class numbers and class numbers on documents and in catalogues translated back into natural language. This is clearly an aid in reference work – not to mention its value in the process of classification and cataloguing. Sometimes 'literal' mnemonics are used (e.g. in LC the letter T is used for the class Technology, in BC Chemistry is C, and U stands for Useful arts). Literal mnemonics should be incidental – there is danger that in striving for them order and economy may be affected.

Throughout these brief notes on notation a manual system has been assumed. Where machine systems are in operation the characteristics and the priorities given to them will change. For example, length of notation is no longer a great handicap as the computer can search long numbers easily. The same goes for complexity of notation. Expressiveness for generic relations becomes more desirable if hierarchical searching is envisaged. Relationships may need to be made explicit through notational symbols – as in the example cited by Austin earlier in this chapter.

READINGS

1. VICKERY, B.C. *Faceted classification*. London, Aslib, 1960.
2. VICKERY, B.C. *Classification and indexing in science*. London, Butterworths, 1959. p. 35.
3. RANGANATHAN, S. R. *Elements of library classification*. 3rd ed. London, Asia Publishing House, 1962.
4. MILLS, J. *A modern outline of library classification*. London, Chapman & Hall, 1960. The principle of inversion is discussed on pp. 18–19. See also p. 44 – retroactive notation Also Mills' paper at the Dorking Conference (item no. 6 below).
5. For a further account see MILLS, J. op. cit. pp. 25–30.
6. FOSKETT, D. J. 'Classification and integrative levels' (*In*

Classification Research Group. *Sayers memorial volume.* London, Library Association, 1961. pp. 136–50.) See also: VICKERY, B. C. 'Relations between subject fields: problems of constructing a general classification' (*In* International Study Conference for Information Retrieval, Dorking, 1957. *Proceedings.* London, Aslib, 1957. pp. 43–9).

7. (i) AUSTIN, D. 'Development of a new general classification: a progress report'. *Information Scientist,* 3 (3), November 1969, 93–115.

(ii) Also the same author's 'Prospects for a new general classification'. *Journal of Librarianship,* 1 (3), July 1969, 149–69. And:

(iii) LIBRARY ASSOCIATION. *Some problems of a general classification scheme.* London, Library Association, 1964.

8. AUSTIN, D. op. cit. – 7 (i). p. 99.

9. BLISS, H. E. *The organization of knowledge and the system of the sciences.* New York, Holt, 1929. *The organization of knowledge in libraries.* New York, H. W. Wilson, 1939.

10. COATES, E. J. 'Notation in classification' (*In* International Study Conference for Information Retrieval, Dorking, 1957. *Proceedings.* London, Aslib, 1957. pp. 53–4.)

In addition to the titles mentioned above and those found at the end of Chapter 6, the student will find the following useful:

Classification research: proceedings of Second International Study Conference, held at Elsinore, Denmark, 1964. Edited by Pauline Atherton. Copenhagen, Munksgaard, 1965. An advanced work.

FOSKETT, D. J. *Classification and indexing in the social sciences.* London, Butterworths, 1963.

PALMER, B. I. *Itself an education:six lectures on classification.* London, Library Association, 1962.

PALMER, B. I. *and* WELLS, A. J. *Fundamentals of library classification.* London, Allen and Unwin, 1957.

RANGANATHAN, S. R. *Prolegomena to library classification.* 3rd ed. London, Asia Publishing House, 1967.

SAYERS, W. C. B. *Manual of classification for librarians.* 4th ed. by A. Maltby. London, Deutsch, 1967.

Chapter 8
Schemes of Classification

This chapter examines briefly the more important of the general schemes of classification. All were first produced before the theories of facet analysis had been fully established. All – except Colon, in which Ranganathan has experimented with the ideas of facet analysis and which is placed first for this reason – are, to a greater or lesser extent enumerative, and inevitably the schemes suffer from the limitations associated with enumeration; in particular:

(i) the enumeration is incomplete; many compound – and at times even simple subjects (concretes, for example) – are not catered for;

(ii) number-building facilities are limited and therefore many compound subjects cannot be accommodated;

(iii) a preferred combination order is too seldom observed and therefore cross classification is likely;

(iv) schedule order is confused because facets are not clearly distinguished and compounds made up of the same categories (e.g. Operations and Materials), and even simple foci belonging to the same facet, may be found in more than one place.

Clearly it is no reflection on the original producers of these schemes that they were unaware of methods created after their work was finished, but we can legitimately criticize any scheme for not meeting the basic requirements of a classification scheme mentioned at the beginning of Chapter 7. And we can legitimately use the principles outlined in Chapter 7 to indicate more clearly why the faults arise. This is, in fact, the method used in this chapter. Each scheme is examined broadly under such headings as: schedule order, combination order, hospitality of notation, and so on, to try to indicate why the limitations of the schemes arise.

Note: this chapter does not attempt to give a detailed description of the schemes but rather to use the schemes as examples of theoretical points already made.

S. R. Ranganathan. Colon Classification

This scheme is of particular interest because Ranganathan has used it to test his theories of facet analysis, theories which have revolutionized classification theory and practice since the last war. Each edition since the first in 1933 has included significant modifications, and in 1957, with the fifth edition, it was decided to publish the scheme in two parts: Part 1 the 'basic classification', having sufficient detail for the general run of books; Part 2 for 'microthought' as found in periodical articles, patents, etc. The 5th and 6th (1961) editions of the scheme consist of only the basic classification; so far Part 2 has not yet appeared; it will be published in separate fascicules.* Some of these depth schedules have appeared as journal articles – notably in *Library science with a slant to documentation*.

MAIN CLASSES

The scheme uses the traditional main classes, the basic outline being as follows:

a/z Generalia
1/9 Preliminaries, e.g. 2 Library Science, 4 Journalism
A/M divisions for Science, Technology, Useful arts
ΔSpiritual experience and mysticism
N Fine Arts   o Literature   p Language
Q Religion   R Philosophy s Psychology
T Education u Geography v History   w Politics   x Economics
Y Sociology   z Law

As can be seen, the overall pattern is: Science and Technology – Humanities – Social sciences.

FACET ANALYSIS

It is here that the scheme differs markedly from other general schemes. All classes are comprised of simple isolates grouped as foci within facets and sub-facets, e.g.:

* The 6th ed. (1963 reprint with amendments) has been used for examples in this chapter.

s Psychology
>   Entity facet (Child, Adolescent, etc.)
>   Problem facet (Nervous reaction, Cognition, Feeling, etc.)

t Education
>   Grade/Person educated facet (Pre-secondary, Secondary, Adult, University, etc.)
>   Operations or Problem facet (Curriculum, Educational measurement, Management, etc.)

l Medicine
>   Organ facet (Stomach, Heart, etc.)
>   Problem facet (Disease, Surgery, etc.)

Students should not be misled by the brevity of the scheme into thinking that few specialized subjects can be catered for; in fact, some highly specialized compounds can be accommodated by synthesis, as we shall see.

In each class the most significant facet is placed first, the next most significant second, and so on. The final order on the shelves is the reverse of this so that an order of *increasing speciality* is achieved; this is accomplished through the facet indicators (see below).

At the head of each class the *combination order* is given, and in preliminary notes to the scheme, these orders are discussed. The statement of combination order is always in terms of the *fundamental categories* (see page 113) – p Personality, m Matter, e Energy, s Space, and t Time in that order. For example, at the head of Class s Psychology, we find:

s [p]: [e] [2p]

This means that foci from the Personality facet (in this case the psychological Entity – Child, Adolescent, etc.) must be placed first, foci from the Energy facet (in this case the Psychological Problem – e.g. Cognition, Reasoning, etc.) second, and further manifestations of the p facet, third. For example:

>   Adolescence has the class number 2 in the Personality facet
>   Reasoning has the class number 44 in the Energy facet

and therefore s 2:44 will be the class number for Reasoning in adolescence.

Again, in Class m 7 Textiles we find a combination order:

[p] : [e] [2p]

Here the Personality facet p is considered to be the Fibre

(Cotton, Flax, Hemp, etc.) and in the Energy facet are found the operations (Spinning, Weaving, Carding, etc.). In the Energy facet 13 stands for Carding and 2 for Spinning; in the Personality facet 1 stands for Cotton. Thus:

M71 is the class number for Cotton textiles
M71:13 is the number for Carding cotton
M71:2 is the number for Spinning cotton

and M 7:13 would stand for Carding generally, and M 7:2 for Spinning generally.

Again, in Class L Medicine, the Organ facet is considered to be the Personality facet, and the Operations constitute the Energy facet. In the P facet 24 is the symbol for Stomach, and 7 is the symbol for Nervous system; in the Energy facet 4 is the symbol for Disease and as a second 'round' of the Energy applicable to 4 Disease we find 7 Surgery. Thus:

L:4	Disease
L:4:7	Surgery
L24	Stomach
L24:4	Diseases of the Stomach
L24:4:7	Surgery of the Stomach
L7	Nervous system
L7:4	Diseases of the nervous system

NOTATION

By now the student will have gathered that *capital letters* are used for the main classes. Within the classes, *roman numerals* are used for sub-facets and foci (4 Disease, 7 Nervous system, etc.). The numbers are used decimally, though without any decimal point separator. Clearly something must be done to avoid confusion when, as here, the same numbers are used to signify foci from different facets, e.g. in Class L, 7 can mean Surgery (in the E facet) or Nervous system (in the P facet). Without some facet indicator L 7 could mean Surgery or Nervous system. Ranganathan avoids such confusion by using a *colon* to indicate that the focus is from the E facet (as in the examples above). A *comma* is used to indicate a P focus in some cases (in the examples given it is not necessary because it can be assumed that a number following immediately after the main class symbol is a P focus if there is no indicator). A focus from the Materials facet (a rare occurrence in the scheme) is indicated by a *semi-colon*.

Space and Time are common facets, applicable throughout the scheme. Each used to be introduced by a point and no confusion was possible because different symbols are used: numbers for Space and capital letters for Time. However, the 1963 reprint of the scheme suggests that an inverted comma be used to introduce the Time facet:

L'N	Twentieth-century medicine
L.2	Medicine in Great Britain
	(where N stands for Twentieth century and 2 for Great Britain).
	The *combination order* is always Space – Time, e.g.
L.2'N	Medicine in Great Britain in the Twentieth century.

In the Space and Time facets, detailed specification is possible – particular years can be specified and also kinds of geographical region.

There are also common facets for Forms, where lower-case letters are used, e.g. a Bibliography, c Concordance, v History.

So far, then, we have a specified combination order and specified facet indicators within the compound class numbers. Finally, a *filing order* must be established. Without this, L 7 might file before or after L:7, L'N before or after L.2, and so on. The chosen order results in the more significant facets following the less significant, i.e. an order of increasing speciality. Lower-case letters file first,* inverted comma divisions next, point divisions next, then semi-colon, followed by colon, and lastly commas or direct foci (i.e. the P facet):

La	Bibliographies of medicine
L'M	Nineteenth-century medicine
L'N	Twentieth-century medicine
L.2	Medicine in Great Britain
L.2'Ma	Bibliography of nineteenth-century British medicine
L.2'M	Medicine in nineteenth-century Britain
L:4:7	Surgery
L:4:7'Ma	A bibliography of nineteenth-century surgery

* Some of these, called *anteriorizing common isolates* even file before the class number without a division, e.g. La would file before L, and L:4:7'Ma before L:4:7'M.

L:4:7'M   Nineteenth-century surgery
L24a   The stomach: a bibliography
L24   The stomach
L24:4:7   Surgery of the stomach
L24:4:7'M   Surgery of the stomach in the nineteenth century
L24:4:7.2'M Surgery of the stomach in nineteenth-century Britain

The notation is basically simple – letters and numbers – but the use of facet indicators with no ordinal value and Greek letters for certain main classes complicates matters, and the attempt at expressiveness lengthens class numbers. However, as can be seen from the examples quoted, the notation is completely hospitable to new foci and steps of division (by the decimal principle) and to compounds (by synthesis of simple elements). There is no allowance for alternative orders, however, and in some cases librarians may wish to alter the facet order in certain classes, e.g. in Literature, where form may be thought to have too great a priority.

INDEX

The index is very economic; it does not repeat the schedules but simply collocates the distributed relatives:

Heart G[P], K[P2], L[P], 32.

This means that the concept Heart will be found as Focus number 32 in the P facet of Class G, in the P2 facet of Class K, and the P facet of Class L.

This account of the CC has been highly simplified. In essence the method is indeed simple, but there are complications which to some extent arise from the use of the five fundamental categories and their extensions through *rounds* and *levels* (i.e. further manifestations of the categories, alluded to earlier) – and, for English readers, in the style used by Ranganathan to elucidate the scheme and his use of abbreviations. But the detail should not obscure the fundamental advances in classification theory and practice underlying the scheme.

THE SEVENTH EDITION

The 7th edition of CC is due to appear in 1971, and Ranganathan has given an extensive preview in an article in *Library science with a slant to documentation*, cited at the end of this chapter.

As usual the changes reflect further developments in Ranganathan's theoretical work on classification, and although he is at pains to stress that librarians using the scheme (and it is widely used in India) will not be faced with insurmountable problems of re-classification, it is clear that considerable alterations are envisaged. It would be out of place to elaborate on the changes in detail here, but certain basic features may be noted.

(i) The number of main classes (called *Main Subjects*) is increased from 46 to 105. This is largely a reflection of the rapidity with which new disciplines develop in the modern world, and such growth is an inevitable consequence of a discipline-oriented scheme (though in no other general scheme is this consequence accepted). Ranganathan illustrates how these Main Subjects have developed – by loose assemblage, dissection, denudation, distillation, etc. The list of subjects includes a type referred to as Partial Comprehensives, e.g. Natural Sciences, Humanities, Social Sciences – several of which had already emerged or were emerging in the 6th edition. It is difficult, however, at this stage to understand how certain subjects, e.g. Typewriting, Shorthand, can be considered Main Subjects in the same sense as Communication, Cybernetics, Astrophysics, and the traditional disciplines.

(ii) Main Subjects are a species of what are termed *Basic Subjects* – subjects that are more than mere Isolates (i.e. concepts that can only be regarded as components of a subject). Altogether there are about 900 Basic Subjects, arranged in order of the Main Subjects, e.g.:

N   Fine Arts
NA Architecture
NB Town Planning
NC Plastic art
ND Sculpture
    etc.

(iii) In a distinct category, over and above these Basic Subjects are the *Isolates* already referred to. For example, the following are cited as being 'organ isolates': 163 Arm, 36 Artery. They can be compounded and added to Basic Subjects to form Compound Subjects.

(iv) The intention behind these changes is to create a more

flexible, 'freely faceted' scheme. A distinction is made between earlier editions in which 'the facets that go with each Basic Subject and their sequence are predetermined, without reference to various possible Compound Subjects capable of going with that Basic Subject', and the 7th edition in which 'predetermination of the facets for all Compound Subjects likely to go with any Basic Subject is ruled out'. The term 'facet' is re-defined as 'a generic term used to denote any component – be it a Basic Subject or an Isolate – of a Compound Subject'; and it is stated that 'above all this Version recognizes that facets belong to Compound Subjects and not to Basic Subjects'.

(v) Notational provision for the increase in the arrays of classes within the Main Subjects is made by using the lower-case alphabet as well as numerals. This will necessitate the use of double inverted commas before anteriorizing common isolates – e.g. B"a for a bibliography of mathematics, not Ba. Similarly, the zero, hitherto reserved to indicate phase relations, is also to be used for the formation of arrays, whilst the ampersand is to be used for phase relations – e.g. s&bT for a book on Psychology for teachers, not so$b$T.

(vi) Fundamental work on the nature of many foci in the Energy facets – e.g. Anatomy, Physiology, Disease, and Development, in the Biology and Medicine classes – has resulted in their being reconstituted as Matter-Property Isolates. These will be introduced by the semi-colon as the facet indicator. Thus the compound, Morphology of the cow, will have the class number KX,311;2 not KX311:2 as in the 6th edition. (The Personality facet is always to be introduced by a comma, where this was – as already shown – frequently omitted for the first round, first level, of Personality in the 6th edition. The reason given for this change is that the longer notation resulting from depth classification is easier on the eye when broken by a facet indicator.)

Melvil Dewey. Decimal Classification and Relative Index

First published in 1876. The 14th edition (1942) was the

'fullest'; the 15th edition (1952) was virtually an abridged edition. The 16th edition, though still shorter than the 14th, was once again expanded. In 1965 the 17th edition appeared, incorporating a number of new features (see below). There is an abridged edition for use in schools – now in its 9th edition. The scheme has been translated into many languages.

The most extensive revision was in the 15th edition where more than a thousand topics were re-located in the scheme. This represented a change from the traditional revision policy which, whilst admitting the need to accommodate new subjects, had laid stress on the policy, initiated by Dewey, of 'integrity of numbers', i.e. the maintenance of existing class numbers; thus new editions had been concerned mainly with expanding existing numbers rather than structural reorganization, and revision had been uneven, extensions being made to suit pressing demand and interest. Many libraries complained of the re-locations and in the 16th edition about forty-five per cent of them were once again altered – back to their original and often less satisfactory places in the 14th edition. This shows the pressure that can be brought to bear on the editors of an established scheme by librarians who do not wish to go to the trouble of re-classifying sections of their libraries to keep pace with the growth of knowledge.

17TH EDITION

However, a bolder stand has been taken in the 17th edition. Although the total number of re-locations is modest, the changes are often fundamental. In his Introduction the editor states that 'even though the total number of re-locations in this edition is less than half the number in Edition 16, the average effect of each is probably greater . . .' The new features can be briefly summarized as follows:

(i) *Integrity of subjects*. 'Classification by attraction', i.e. the placing of a subject at the most concrete element represented in it, without regard to the basic discipline concerned, is renounced. Thus, it is affirmed that, for example, a book on the sociology of the Jews should go in class 301 with sociology and not at 296, the number for Judaism. 'Classification by attraction' has always been a tendency, especially among American librarians, and the practice had been given some support in the 16th edition.

(ii) *Facet analysis and synthesis.* Though still an essentially enumerative scheme, there is in this edition a distinct trend towards basic analysis into simple subjects with provision for combining them in a preferred order. For example, in class 630 Agriculture, it is now made clear that the citation order is to be Crop-Process, and notational devices allow such number-building as 633.155 Harvesting corn (where 633.1 is corn and the 55 has been detached from 631.55, the number for harvesting). Even when provision for compounding has not been made, there has been an attempt to suggest priority orders among facets to achieve consistency and to avoid cross classification. In his Introduction the editor gives certain general rules for combination order. Beyond the broad Subject-Place-Form, he suggests that 'the following precedence formula is a generally reasonable and helpful one to follow, although it may require modification in certain places: class the subject by (1) kinds, (2) parts, (3) materials, (4) properties, (5) processes within it, (6) operations upon it, (7) agents'. The increasing emphasis placed on synthesis can be seen both in the editorial remarks and the table, *Synthesis of Notation*, in Volume Two.

(iii) Allied to this concern with analysis and synthesis is the attention given to the general structure. Scope notes are improved and the use of black arrows to identify 'centered headings' is of great assistance in classifying and indexing. Again, the editor emphasizes the hierarchical structure and the schedules aim to demonstrate clearly the successive degrees of subordination. Where a subject is divided by more than one characteristic of division an effort has been made to spell this out, as for example in 373.2 where Secondary schools are categorized as follows: types as to control, types as to organization, and types as to curriculum.

(iv) Classes that have undergone major re-casting include Psychology, now provided with a new schedule at 150, leaving 130 for 'pseudopsychology, parapsychology, occultism'. The common form divisions have been re-labelled Standard Sub-divisions in recognition of the fact that they cover more than forms of material, and several of them have been revised, notably the divisions for historical periods at 090 which are a marked improvement on the skeletal divisions available in earlier editions. Particularly important is the removal of the place facet from the 900's and its presentation as an Area Table in Volume Two, emphasizing its general applicability throughout the scheme. It will be noted that the divisions in the Area Table have been revised and, in particular, provision is now made for concepts other than political boundaries – e.g. physiographic regions and socio-economic regions and groups.

The 18th edition, due in 1971, will no doubt develop these trends and we are promised some major revision in certain areas, notably in 340 Law and 510 Mathematics.

DC is still the most widely used of the general schemes of classification, though in recent years there has been a distinct movement towards the LC classification, and in the US in particular many librarians are busy re-classifying their stocks. The reasons for this change would seem to lie less in the superiority of LC than in the numerous advantages to be gained through the centralized services offered by the Library of Congress. Indeed, it might be argued that in terms of the basic criteria of classification LC can hardly stand comparison with DC (see Appendix), and that this process of re-classification is a reflection of the low esteem in which classification is generally held in the US where the dictionary catalogue is the main avenue for the subject approach, classification being regarded as little more than a shelving device.

The initial success of DC was immediate and has continued, despite its relatively slight decline, through the hundred years of its existence. The enthusiasm of its first reception was probably due to its uniqueness and to the following features in particular:

(i) relative location: then a new idea to overcome the disadvantages of 'fixed location', i.e. the reservation of certain shelves for set subjects;

(ii) the simplicity and hospitality of the decimal notation;

(iii) the relative index – always a good one and emphasized by Dewey as one of its most important features;

Its continuing use is largely due to:

(i) its being firmly established in so many libraries;

(ii) its permanent revision organization established in the Library of Congress;

(iii) its use in schemes of centralized cataloguing such as BNB and Wilson;

(iv) the continuing lack of a general scheme sufficiently excellent to convince librarians of the need for re-classifying their stocks.

Clearly there are advantages in adopting a scheme in general use – not only because of the consequent benefits of centralized cataloguing (see Chapter 20) but also for stock revision purposes, cooperative book acquisition, and so on.

Inevitably a scheme planned nearly a hundred years ago is bound to have its limitations. Over such a period of time even the basic structure of knowledge will undergo significant changes and it is hardly to be expected that even the most thorough revision will satisfactorily cope with the unprecedented growth of knowledge during this period and the increasing subject complexity of documents. Despite the improvements in the 17th edition, the scheme has been held back for years by the old policy of 'integrity of numbers' referred to above, the effects of which are not likely to be quickly mitigated. And it has to be recognized that the very popularity of the scheme will always act as a brake on the most radical editorial team.

In the following notes reference is made to both the 16th and 17th editions as both are widely used in libraries today.

MAIN CLASSES

As the notation used is one of decimal numerals, there are ten primary divisions, but in fact the first hundred divisions give a better impression of the major divisions of the scheme. The basic outline is as follows:

000 Generalities (including Bibliographies and Library science); 100 Philosophy (including Psychology); 200 Religion; 300 Social sciences (e.g. Political science, Economics, Law, Education, Commerce); 400 Language; 500 Pure sciences (e.g. Mathematics, Physics, Chemistry, Biology); 600 Technology (including Medical sciences,

Agriculture and agricultural industries, Domestic arts and sciences, Business); 700 Arts (including Photography, Recreation); 800 Literature; 900 Geography and history and related disciplines.

Collocation is limited in certain parts of the scheme, e.g.:

(i) Language 400 – Literature 800;

(ii) Technologies in 600 separated from their fundamental sciences in 500 (e.g. Electricity 537 – Electrical engineering 621.3; Chemistry 540 – Chemical technology 660);

(iii) Economics 330 – Commerce 380 – Business 650;

(iv) Buildings 690 – Architecture 720.

Within some of these main classes there are further anomalies, e.g. note the placing of Printing and Publishing in the following sequence:

650 Business, 651 Office services, 655 Printing (including publishing and related activities), 658 Management.

There are some examples of dated collocation, a particularly obvious one being the placing of Psychology in Class 100 (Philosophy).

There are a few examples of *alternatives*. Thus Bibliography at 010 allows for collocation of subject bibliographies, or they can be placed with subject; Biography 920 can be used to collect all biographies or they can be placed with relevant subjects associated with the person (the latter being preferred in the 17th edition).

INDEX

The index is detailed and relative, i.e. it concentrates on collocating distributed relatives. The following entry from the index to the 16th edition is typical:

Ships

Accident prevention	614.864
Canal transportation	386.22
Construction and engineering	623.8
Naval science	359.32
Ocean transportation	387.2

(Incidentally this is a good illustration of the difficulties of placing such concretes as Ships when treated from many viewpoints in one document.) In general the index does not wastefully repeat divisions found in the scheme itself, e.g. there are few numbers in the 800's to be found at the index entry Literature.

We have seen that two features of the 17th edition are the stress placed on the 'integrity of subjects' and the development of synthesis. Each of these underlines the need (always there, of course, though often ignored) to classify by the schedules rather than the index. In an attempt to force users to adhere to this basic rule the editors of the 17th edition pruned the index by omitting many 'minor' headings, referring the user to relevant broad terms and the schedules. Clearly, the more synthetic the scheme, the simpler the index (as illustrated by cc), but the mixed nature of DC creates difficulties in indexing and some of the simplifications did little more than involve the user in unnecessary searching. For example, the index entry Mysticism has the following subdivisions:

Religion
General works 291.14 (a misprint for 291.42?)
    see also Religious experience

Under Religious experience we find:

General works 291.42
    see also other spec. rel.

The schedules at 291.42, Religious experience, have the scope note: 'Mysticism, conversion, asceticism, self-discipline'. Specific religions can often be divided like 291, so 294.542 stands for Hindu religious experience (including mysticism).

So far so good – though why the user should make the journey from Mysticism to Religious experience in the index is not immediately clear as the latter makes no mention of Mysticism. However, the point here is that the reference *See also other spec. rel.* will work properly only if there is consistency in the schedules – i.e. if *each* religion is divided like 291.42. This could be assumed in a fully analytico-synthetic scheme, but the fact is that in DC there are exceptions – e.g. Mysticism in Judaism is at 298.71. To cover such exceptions additional index entries are required, e.g.:

Religious experience – Judaism 298.71

As a result of the complaints received on publication a new

index based on that of the 16th edition and appropriately modified, was distributed to users.

FACET ANALYSIS

Dewey was always aware of the necessity for number-building for compound specification and he was years ahead of his time in making some notational provision for this (see below). However the complementary measure of preliminary analysis of subjects into simple elements capable of being subsequently combined was generally unrecognized, and the scheme is still fundamentally enumerative of compounds.

As we have seen, the 17th edition moves in the direction of synthesis, and this is evident if we compare the following extracts. In the 16th edition we find levels of education isolated (e.g. 372 Elementary), but there is also the sequence:

371   Teaching, school organization, etc. (The Operations facet);
371.21   Admission;
371.211   Primary school admission standards (a compound due to the introduction of an element from the Level of education facet).

This has been revised in the 17th edition to give precedence to the level of education facet: Admission standards in elementary education is placed with Elementary education at 372.1216 (the final 216 being taken from 371.216 – Admission standards in general).
Again, in the 16th edition we find:

371.7   School health;
371.73   Physical education in schools (a compound due to the introduction of the Subject taught facet);
371.7322   Physical education in elementary schools (a triple compound due to the further introduction of the Level of education facet).

In the 17th edition physical education in elementary schools goes with Elementary schools at 372.86.

The successive application of characteristics of division and consequent enumeration of compounds is still characteristic of much of DC. One of the most exemplary of the exceptions to this is to be found in Class 400, Language, where essentially the Problem facet is outlined at 420 (covering such subjects as Etymology, Grammar, etc.) and each problem can be applied to most of the languages in the Language facet 430/499.

The inevitable results of this enumeration and limited analysis are, apart from the length of schedules:

(i) *Many simple subjects and compounds cannot be specified* (because not all of the latter can ever be listed). For example, in Class 800 (16th ed.), in some respects a good example of analysis, the Literary period facet has not been isolated, nor is there any General period facet of any consequence in DC, and therefore it is impossible to specify, for example, the simple subject Literature, 1837–1900, or the compound English literature, 1837–1900. But the compound English drama, 1837–1900 can be specified because it is enumerated (and in fact Period can be specified under any Form, but not elsewhere). There is some improvement in the 17th ed. where, at 809, divisions .01–.04 can be used for historical periods, though specification is limited to the periods listed in the *Table of Standard Subdivisions*. See page 150 for further examples.*

(ii) *Related material is scattered.* In the example quoted above (16th ed.) the teaching of a particular subject (Physical education) in elementary schools is separated from the teaching of other subjects in elementary schools at 372.3–372.8. In the 17th edition, despite the implicit rule that the Level of education facet takes precedence, we find at 376 (Education of women) a place for 'the education of women by level' – e.g. 376.63 Secondary. (However, this could be justified on the grounds that special categories of education take precedence over level.)

(iii) *Cross classification is likely.* For example, at 372.8 (under Elementary schools) in the 16th edition any subject taught in elementary schools can be classified – and therefore the subject Physical education could be placed here, with the risk of

---

* The premature listing of compounds is frequently found. Thus at 385/388 (16th ed.) there are divisions for Railway transport, Road transport, etc., but there is no place for Transport. At 757.4/.6 (17th ed.) there are divisions for Men's portraits, Women's portraits, etc., but there is no place for Portrait painting, the number 757 (Human figures and their parts) having to stand for this.

having material on the same subject in two places: here and at 371.7322. In the 17th edition there is a place for Public schools (i.e. State schools in the British sense) at 373.224, and a series of divisions at 373.3–.9 for Secondary education and schools by continent, country, and locality – but no clear indication of how to deal with a document on State schools in England. Again, Public libraries are given a place at 027.4 and Cataloguing can be found at 025.4 but what is the classifier to do with a document on Cataloguing in public libraries? Whenever a compound is not listed a document on that compound can be placed at any of the simple subjects that comprise it, and unless the cataloguer creates his rules for this, cross classification is inevitable. However, the scheme often contains instructions to assist here: for example, in Class 630 Agriculture (16th ed.), Harvesting is 631.55 and Wheat 633.11, and though the compound Harvesting of Wheat cannot be specified we are told to place such compounds with Crop rather than Operation. (As indicated above, the 17th edition has provided number-building facilities at this point.)

(iv) *The order of facets (schedule order) is frequently confusing.* For example, in Class 200 Religion (16th ed.), 260 is Christian Church (262 Church government and organization, 264 Ritual, 265 Sacraments, etc.) but Church and parish administration is at 254, Pastor (life, everyday duties of minister, priest, etc.) 253, Preaching 251. (There has been some attempt to clarify this area in the 17th edition, but little basic improvement is to be seen.) In Class 370, 371 accommodates various types of teaching Operation or Problem, 372/374 accommodate Grade of Education (Elementary, etc.), 375 returns to Problems (Curriculum), 376 Education of women (other special groups are at 371.9), 378 returns to Grade (Higher education) and 379 concerns an organization problem (Education and state). Again, confused order is found in Class 900: 900 General history, 910 Geography, 920 Biography, 930 Ancient history, 940/990 Modern history. However, there is a general tendency to place the Problem/Operation facet before the others (e.g. in Agriculture, operations such as Harvesting, Irrigation, etc. precede the Crop facet) and this is generally regarded as resulting in an order of increasing speciality.

Combination order

(a) *In enumerated compounds.* It is impossible to generalize about these as they do not follow a consistent pattern. (It should be remembered, however, that in the Introduction to the 17th edition the editor has suggested a basic citation order to be followed as a general guide.)

(b) *In synthesis.* The amount of number-building possible is much reduced in the 15th and 16th editions – and is in fact, confined to the common subdivisions (form, place, period) and to the instructions in the scheme 'divide like . . .' (for an example of the latter see page 151). The common subdivisions precede at 01/09 the special subdivisions of a subject in the approximate order: Form of presentation – Period – Place. For example (notation according to 16th ed.):

360.2	Handbook to social welfare
360.3	Encyclopaedia of social welfare
360.904	Social welfare twentieth century
360.942	Social welfare in Great Britain
360.942082	Social welfare in Great Britain in the twentieth century
361.5	Disaster relief
etc.	

NOTATION

Pure – numerals used decimally, with a point separator after the third place. Three figures at least are used: 100, 200, 250, etc., not 1, 2, etc.

Hospitality. The decimal notation allows virtually complete hospitality to new foci and steps of division, but the notation is less hospitable to compounds. As already pointed out the amount of synthesis possible is much reduced in the later editions. Up to the 14th edition it was always possible to join any two class numbers by the use of 0001, e.g. 532.000162 (Fluid mechanics for engineers) and although this was a cumbersome device it was better than nothing. Now, despite the improvements in the 17th edition, many compounds cannot be specified, e.g. Portrait painting in oils (Oil painting 751.45, Portraits 757).

Standard subdivisions (01/09) can be used at any point in the scheme (as shown in the above example). They cover common approaches to a subject (philosophy) and forms of presentation (encyclopaedias, periodicals) as well as periods of time. Although the common period divisions have been extended in the 17th edition they allow only limited specification – contrast the hospitality of UDC here. Place divisions have been removed to a separate Area table – see above.

'*Divide like . . .*' is a frequent instruction in the schedules, allowing compound subjects to be specified, e.g.

338   Production
338.47 Specific goods and services
     Divide like 001–999, e.g. Motor vehicle industry: 338.476292 (where 6292 is taken from the Engineering class to represent Motor vehicles).

Again:

823   English fiction
     Divide as instructed at 820–890. (Thus 823.91 stands for Twentieth-century fiction, the .91 representing Twentieth century being taken from the period divisions for English literature at 820.9001/.900914.)

The notation is frequently expressive:

600   Technology
620   Engineering
621   Applied physics (Mechanical engineering)
621.2   Power derived from liquids
621.21   Water wheels

Because of this expressiveness, the use of numbers only, the cumbersome synthesis ('divide like . . .'), and the fact that the notation is badly apportioned (e.g. 200 Religion and 400 Language have as much room as the whole of Science and Technology), the notation is lengthier than it need be, e.g. 610.73 Nursing, 150.195 Psychoanalysis, as against 221 Old Testament, 227 Epistles, 419 Non-verbal languages, etc. However its simplicity – through the use of numbers only and the lack of non-ordinal signs – helps to compensate for this defect to some extent.

Mnemonics. Clearly literal mnemonics are not possible but the use of certain numerals fairly regularly, though not always consistently, throughout the scheme (e.g. –42 for British Isles, –03 for Encyclopaedias, and in special sections, e.g. in Literature: 1 for Poetry, 2 for Drama, etc.) has an important mnemonic value.

Universal Decimal Classification

UDC was first introduced as a result of the Brussels Conference on Bibliography in 1895; the work was carried out by the old IIB and the first edition (in French) appeared in 1905. The aim was to create a scheme more suitable than any existing at the time for the classification of specialized pamphlets, articles, abstracts, and so on – and particularly for such materials in the fields of science and technology. DC was used as a basis for the new scheme.

Since 1905 several versions of the scheme have appeared, e.g. 2nd edition (again in French), 1927–33, 3rd edition (German), 1934–53. The 4th edition (English) was started in 1943 but is still not complete; however, an abridged English version was issued in 1948 (3rd edition of this 1961).* In addition to full and abridged editions (and, more recently, intermediate editions), individual classes have been separately issued – e.g. (in English) education, building, mineralogy. After the 1914–18 war FID became responsible for the central organization of UDC and various national bodies, in this country the British Standards Institution, have assumed responsibility for their own editions. Revision is constantly in progress, though the international nature of the scheme makes it a slow process at times. FID regularly publishes *Extensions and corrections to UDC* and what are known as 'P-notes' – working documents circulated among those actively engaged in the process of revision.

UDC is used by an increasing number of special libraries throughout the world and also in many published bibliographies, e.g. RIBA *Catalogue, Index bibliographicus, Aslib booklist, Electrical engineering abstracts*, etc. Its popularity can be attributed to its hospitality to specialized compound subjects and to the usual advantages arising from standardization. Moreover, the

* This version has been used for the examples in this chapter.

notation permits a variety of combination orders of facets (see below), frequently allowing any library to choose the order most suited to its particular purposes – clearly an advantage and one not found to the same extent in the other general schemes. No general scheme is more suited to the needs of special libraries, especially those in science and technology.

MAIN CLASSES

The basic outline is still that of DC – see the *Outline of main divisions* that prefaces the scheme. Two modifications are immediately apparent: the confinement of Psychology to 159.9 and History to 93/99. Thus to some extent the scheme still has the weaknesses of DC in its main class order (the separation of Economics, Commerce, and Business and of Language and Literature, for example) – though in fact the disadvantages have been minimized by more careful definition of the scope of overlapping classes, and in the case of Language and Literature suggestions are given for their amalgamation. Recently a decision has been taken to vacate Class 4.

INDEX

UDC like DC has a detailed relative index which concentrates on collocating distributed relatives rather than repeating unnecessarily the divisions of the classification (contrast BC index for example).

FACET ANALYSIS

It is in this respect that UDC differs so greatly from DC. The content of most classes has been radically revised. Enumeration has been pruned and many classes are now mainly composed of simple elements, rather than enumerated compounds. This accounts for the comparative brevity of the scheme: the abridged British version has some 119 pages for the scheme itself, yet despite this many more compound subjects can be specified than by the much larger DC. The Literature, Geography, Biography, and History classes are perhaps the best examples of this – three pages in all. Note also the −1/−09 divisions prefacing Class 62 and similar analysis of fundamental concepts at Class 3.

Facets are more clearly distinguished. For example, Class 37 (Education) has been reorganized so that the Problem facet is confined to 371 (e.g. .1 Management, .2 School organization, .3 Methods of instruction, etc.) whilst 372/378 cover Grade and type of institution, and 379 the State and education. In many subjects the Problem facet is isolated at the 'o' divisions – e.g. in 669 Metallurgy .046 stands for Heating processes, .05 for Fundamental processes, and each of these divisions can be applied to any of the metals listed in 669.1/.9 simply by adding the .o number.

Combination order. The notation allows many alternatives here, and the librarian must spend time carefully working out the facet order best suited to his needs – for example, in Class 8 (Literature) the Form, Period, and Language facets can be combined in any order.

NOTATION

Basically pure – decimal numbers as in DC. The three-figure base is dropped:

5 Science, 51 Mathematics, 52 Astronomy, etc.

The nought is sometimes added with special meaning (e.g. 3 Social sciences, 30 Sociology). The decimal point is used more freely as a separating device, e.g.:

69	Building industry
69.00	Building practice, procedure
69.001.3	Building specifications

Hospitality. As with DC the decimal system allows virtually infinite hospitality to new foci and steps of division.

The provision for number-building (synthesis) is greatly increased and this, along with the initial analysis of simple elements, allows extensive specification of compound subjects. It is in this respect that UDC differs so radically from and is such an advance on DC.

Number-building is possible through the use of the devices listed in *Table of Auxiliaries.* The more important of these are as follows:

(i) *Colon*. This is the most widely used device for it allows the linking of any two or more class numbers. For example 338 stands for Industrial economics and 62 for Engineering and therefore 338:62 for Economics of the engineering industry. Highly specialized compound subjects can be built up in this way, e.g. Science in the curriculum of secondary schools: 373.5:371.214:5 (where 373.5 means Secondary schools, 371.214 Curriculum, 5 Science). However it becomes cumbersome (see the UDC symbols on British Standards). Any combination order is possible and as we have already pointed out the librarian must decide on a preferred order so as to avoid cross classification. If necessary, added entries can be made under parts of the compound, e.g. for the above an added entry could be filed with Curriculum: 371.214:5:373.5* – though this (*rotation of entries*) can become very expensive and generally only one entry is made, the subject index isolating other elements in the usual way, e.g.

Science: Curriculum: Secondary schools	373.5:371.214:5
Curriculum: Secondary schools	373.5:371.214
Secondary schools: Education	373.5

(For an account of such indexing methods see Chapter 9). Each of the following can be added to any class number:
(ii) (o . . .) *Form of presentation*, e.g.

621.38(03)	Encyclopaedias of electronics
54(091)	History of chemistry

(iii) (1/9) *Place*, e.g.

369.4(430)	Youth movements in Germany

Note the special numbers here for physical features (mountains, seas, rivers, etc.) and zones, compass points, and so on.
(iv) '. . .' *Time*, e.g.

8—2'19'	Twentieth-century drama

Note the numbers for seasons (spring, summer, etc.), frequency (weekly, monthly, etc.) and so on. The time divisions are a great improvement on DC in that they allow specification freely

---

* The order could remain constant, underlining showing the filing position, e.g. 373·5:371·214:5.

and in detail. The system used allows even a particular day to be specified:

'1962.4.4'   4th April, 1962.

(v) oo. *Point of view*, e.g.

629.118.2.001.4   Motor cycle tests (where .001.4 stands for Testing)

There are also special auxiliaries for use with particular classes. These are listed with the relevant classes and are indicated by the use of a dash (–) or .o.

The notation is not brief – due to the poor allocation of the notational base (cf. DC) and the maintenance of expressiveness in many parts of the schedules. When already lengthy numbers are synthesized by the colon the resulting class number is often well over twelve digits. Some of the auxiliary devices are rather cumbersome, e.g. the Time divisions.

Though basically simple – numerals with a point separator – the use of colons, brackets, .oo, and other divisions each with their special indicators reduces comprehensibility. Moreover such devices have not always an ordinal value and so order is not immediately apparent. In practice an order has been created – colon files before (o . . .) which in turn files before '. . .', etc.

H. E. Bliss. A Bibliographic Classification

This is the result of a lifetime's effort. Theoretical principles on which the work is based are recorded in *The organisation of knowledge*, 1929, and *The organisation of knowledge in libraries*, 1933. A preliminary version of the scheme appeared in 1935 (2nd edition 1936): *A system of bibliographic classification*. Apart from the basic theories underlying classification, Bliss was particularly interested in defining and tracing the relationships between areas of knowledge, and there are many useful notes on the content of specific subjects in the works mentioned above as well as the introductions to the volumes of the final scheme. The superior order of main subjects in the BC is largely due to this effort.

MAIN CLASSES

The carefully planned sequence can be seen only in the two-dimensional Table II given in Volume One. All classes spring from four basic areas of knowledge: Philosophy, Science, History, Technologies and Arts. The final linear order, which uses the major disciplines as Main classes, benefits from this preliminary schematization, but the subtlety is lost.

A   Philosophy and general science (including fundamental sciences applied in many fields – Mathematics, Statistics).

B/D Physical sciences (Physics, Chemistry, Astronomy, Physical geography etc. – and the related technologies and industries).

E/G Life sciences (Biology, Botany, Zoology).

H/I Science of Man (Anthropology, Medicine, Psychology).

J/Z Social sciences (in the broadest sense, i.e. those based on Society, e.g. Education, History, Human geography, Religion, Law, Economics, Arts – Useful and Fine, Literature).

Collocation of related subjects can be seen in, for example, the grouping together of fundamental sciences and their applications, e.g. Electricity and Electrical engineering (BJ/BO), and throughout Chemistry (C); in the grouping together of Language and literature and Bibliography (W/Z); in classes M/O where various aspects of social life in a particular area are collocated; and in the way that classes modulate from one to the other: e.g. Botany>Zoology>Medicine>Psychology> Education.

Apart from the main classes outlined above, there are the *Anterior numeral classes* 1/9 which correspond in many ways to the Generalia classes in other schemes. Thus Class 1 (Reading-room collections) caters for general encyclopaedias and dictionaries, atlases, gazetteers, yearbooks, bibliographies, special collections – its aim being to provide a scheme for reference collections kept apart from the main library; Class 2 provides an alternative special scheme for bibliography and librarianship; Class 5 – Archives; Class 6 – Periodicals special collection. Note that the aim differs from that of the usual Generalia class in that a series of special collections is envisaged. There are alternative placings for many of these so that the contents can be accommodated in the main classification A/Z if required.

Alternatives. B C is unique in the number of alternative locations provided for. For example, many of the applied sciences and technologies can be classified with the respective sciences or together with the arts, e.g. Applied botany in Class F (Botany) or with WA (Agriculture); bibliographies may be distributed or kept together, as may the law of special subjects and also biography. And within many classes alternatives are frequently found, for example, in Class HM/HZ Medicine, surgery of particular organs can be classified with the Diseases of the organ or with Surgery (HS). This latter is an example of *alternative combination order* within a class (i.e. Organ – Problem or Problem – Organ) and there are many other examples, the chief being the alternative 'modes' allowed under Class W/Y Language and literature, where in Schedule 5b four modes are outlined; for example, by Mode 1 all works by and about a particular author may be grouped together regardless of form, the authors filing alphabetically, but by Mode 2 individual authors are scattered according to a classification by period and form. Obviously each library using B C must decide very carefully which alternatives it is going to use and then abide by its decision, or cross classification will result.

INDEX

The index is a relative index and occupies the whole of Volume Four. It is longer than it need be because Bliss tends to list the divisions of a subject already collocated in the classification, e.g.

Anatomy, Human	HD
Applied	HDB
External	HDC
Practical	HDB
Regional	HDN
Special	HDN

All entries except the first are unnecessary because they simply repeat the subdivisions at HD in the scheme. Other examples can be easily found by the student (e.g. see index entries under

Museums, Building, Forestry, etc.). This is not only wasteful; it also makes the index difficult to use. More will be said on this subject below (see sections on the Index to the classified catalogue in Chapter 9). Despite its length key words are sometimes not indexed; for example, there are no entries under the terms Backward, Deficient, Handicapped, Mental deficiency, Mentally deficient – despite the fact that Class JGJ is devoted to the teaching of Deficient, Handicapped, etc. . . . children – nor are any of these terms found as subdivisions relating to this class under the term Children or Childhood in the index.

FACET ANALYSIS

(i) *In many classes the facets are carefully distinguished and kept separate and within each the foci are listed without enumeration of compounds.* Examples:

J (Education)

    JA/JI Problem facet (e.g. JEI Learning and memory, JF Tests, measurements, standards, JI Teaching methods, JJ Curriculum)

    JK Subject taught facet (e.g. JKM – Teaching of mathematics)

    JL/JV Person and grade of education facet (e.g. JL – Elementary)

S (Law)

    SE/SO Type of law facet (e.g. SJ Civil, SM Property)

    SP/SQ Procedure and organization facets (e.g. SPH – Witnesses, SQC – Courts)

    ST/SY Country facet – law of nations other than English and American which take precedence at SE

UEK (Civil engineering)

    UEN/UET Structures facet (e.g. UEP – Wooden structures, UES – Stone structures)

    UEU/UEY Type of construction facet (e.g. UEV – Office buildings)

    UF/UFY Materials facet (e.g. UFQ – Lime)

(ii) *However, the analysis is not sustained throughout and compounds are enumerated.* For example, in the Problem facet in Education there is a class JG for Pupils and students – differences, diagnosis and guidance – which, apart from listing the problems, has such compounds as Conduct problems in unruly children;

in Class JL Elementary education, there is JLR – Methods (Basketry, Clay modelling, etc.).

(iii) *Sometimes simple elements are not isolated*. For example, in HM/HZ (Medicine) there is no Organ facet to accommodate documents treating of particular organs from a variety of standpoints; thus a book on the Kidney must be placed with Anatomy, or Diseases, or Surgery, etc. Where the basic analysis is thus insufficient, repetition in the schedules is found; thus, under the various divisions in Medicine (Anatomy, Diseases, etc.) organs have to be enumerated.

(iv) *Division is not always exhaustive*. For example, in the Types of building facets in Civil engineering (UEK/UFY) and Architecture (VA/VD) the listing of types seems almost arbitrary. On the other hand, in some parts of the schedules, e.g. in the Biological sciences, minute subdivision is found.

(v) *Facet order (schedule order) sometimes leaves much to be desired*. For example, in Education, the Person and grade facet is arranged thus:

JL/JM	Elementary
JN	Secondary
JO	Vocational
JP	Industrial
JQ	Education of women
JR/JS	Higher education
JT	Professional schools and colleges
JU	Adult education

(vi) *Combination order is frequently though not always, indicated*. For example, in Education, the order is Grade – Country – Problem, e.g. Guidance at evening high schools in New York state: JNwbc, MG (where JNW stands for Evening high schools, bc New York state, and MG Guidance). Again in class TS (Insurance) the order is: Type of insurance – Problem, e.g. TSS stands for Life insurance and ,v for Lapsed policies and therefore TSS,V means lapsed policies in life insurance. As we have already pointed out, alternative combination orders are often allowed.

NOTATION

(i) *Notation is mixed:* the base consists of the anterior numeral classes (1/9) and the main classes (A/Z). Lower-case letters are used for country divisions, and numerals are used for form divisions. Commas are frequently used as facet indicators (as in the examples above) and the dash (—) is used to synthesize elements from different main classes.

(ii) The long base and the generally careful apportionment of the notation results in *brevity* of notation, e.g. UOMT Wire ropes in mechanical engineering; UTHJ Water paints in interior house decoration. However, the use of numerals and upper and lower-case letters and commas and dashes sometimes results in not-easily comprehensible symbols, e.g.

JPOj7   Miscellanies on industrial education in Turkey today

JQHa,YZA3   History of the Association of University Women in America

Brevity is also assisted by the notation's being non-expressive, e.g.

HNP   Therapeutics
HNPA   Administration of medicines
HNPB   Internal
HNPC   Oral

(iii) Confusion may arise through the use of the numerals o and 1 and the letters o and 1.

(iv) *Order is not always apparent,* e.g. what is the relative filing order for letters, numerals, commas, dashes? Bliss fails to give definite guidance on this point.

(v) *Hospitality.* The use of alphabetical notation means virtually complete hospitality to new foci and steps of division. However, there is not complete hospitality to new compounds – as we have already seen some simple elements are not isolated and in some cases compounds are enumerated, with the inevitable omissions.

In fact specification of compounds is largely achieved through the use of the *Systematic Schedules,* which, though extensive, do not allow full freedom of synthesis. These schedules are an extension of the 'common subdivisions' found in other schemes but they do not follow the principle to its logical conclusion: a completely faceted classification composed of simple elements combinable according to preferred orders.

6

Some of the schedules are of general application; these correspond largely to the common subdivisions in other schemes:

Schedule 1 (1/9)   – basically form divisions (e.g. 2 Bibliography, 6 Periodicals)
Schedule 2 (a/z)   – geographical divisions (e.g. e England)
Schedule 3 (,A/,z) – Language, nationalities divisions (e.g. ,M English)
Schedule 4 (A/z)   – Period divisions (e.g. R Twentieth century)

Altogether there are over forty *Systematic Schedules* (including the special extensions of the twenty-two numbered schedules) and the rest are of special application only, i.e. they are to be used only in specified classes. In fact many of these correspond to particular facets in certain classes, e.g. Schedule 20a is essentially a Problem facet for use with Insurance (see example on page 160).

Although Bliss has this extensive system of number-building, he still lists many compounds. For example the dash (—) allows linking of subjects from different parts of the schedules but we find INC Psychology for lawyers. Similarly period divisions are enumerated under Art and Literature for example, in place of Systematic Schedule 4.

(vi) *Mnemonics*. Bliss uses a number of literal mnemonics, e.g. AL Logic, AM Mathematics, UA Agriculture, UE Engineering. The numeral (Form) subdivisions and the lower-case (Geographical) divisions also have mnemonic value, but the other symbols are used with various meanings. Mnemonics are not achieved at the cost of order.

BC is published by H. W. Wilson, New York. Unfortunately it has for years lacked adequate revision arrangements and is now seriously out of date. There is a British Committee for the Bliss Classification and a Journal, *Bliss Bulletin*, in which revisions of parts of the schedules have appeared, but little financial backing. However, with the help of a research grant, a new edition is at present being prepared at the Polytechnic of North London School of Librarianship.

Library of Congress Classification*

Although the Library of Congress was founded in 1800, the detailed classification scheme in present use was largely instigated by Herbert Putnam, Librarian of Congress, 1899–1939, and most of the scheme appeared between 1899 and 1920. Each main class is separately published. The schedule for Law first appeared in 1969, others have gone through several editions and in some cases supplementary revised schedules have been issued. Though designed for a large single library, it has been adopted by other libraries in different parts of the world and, as was pointed out in the section on D C above, its popularity is increasing.

Several features – the separate publication of classes and the lack of common subdivisions for instance – stem from the fact that the Library is organized on a subject department basis and to a large extent the main classes can be viewed as separate special schemes, though incorporating the same fundamental principles and practices.

It has been frequently said that, because the classification scheme was based on a large existing book stock, the scheme has a greater 'literary warrant' than schemes based on theoretical principles. It is difficult to understand what exactly is meant by this, though there are parts of the scheme which show a particular awareness of special categories of literature, e.g. in Class TH there is a section for books on Heating and ventilating, preceding the schedules for these subjects considered separately. Again, in many parts of the scheme compounds are enumerated which could have been conceived only after a careful study of the book stock, e.g. the schedules under authors in the Literature class. Nevertheless, a scheme using simple elements based on literary warrant will cater for compounds as required with even greater success.

MAIN CLASSES

The traditional disciplines are chosen as the main classes:

* The following editions of the various classes have been used in this chapter: Class H, 3rd ed. 1950; Class L, 3rd ed. 1951; Class P, 1928; Class R, 3rd ed. 1950; Class S, 3rd ed. 1948; Class T, 4th ed. 1948.

A General
B Philosophy and Religion
C/F History   G Geography, Anthropology
H Social sciences   J Politics   K Law   L Education
M Music   N Fine arts   P Language and Literature
Q Science   R Medicine   S Agriculture   T Technology
U/V Military and naval science
Z Bibliography

It should be remembered that in so far as the classes represent separate subject departments, to that extent collocation is irrelevant in the broad classes. Bliss has criticized it as showing no great degree of collocation, e.g. Logic and Mathematics are separate, as are Geology, Astronomy, and Geography; also many sciences are separated from their fundamental technologies, and though Language and Literature are found at class P, within this class the Language and Literature of major tongues are separate (e.g. English language at PE, English literature at PR).

INDEX

There is no general index to the whole scheme. Indexes to individual classes collocate distributed relatives:

Finance: Banking   HG 1501—3540
Crime   HV 6763—71
Crises   HB 3731.M7
Railroad   HE 2231—71

but they can also be wasteful, repeating sequences found in the classification:

Banking: Collections   HG 136—9
Dictionaries   HG 150
Directories   HG 65—96
Periodicals   HG 1—51

The lack of a complete index to the scheme is a serious weakness.

FACET ANALYSIS

LC is more enumerative than any other major general scheme. Even common form divisions are not found applicable to the whole scheme. There is some capacity for synthesis as we shall see, but it is limited. As examples of enumeration study the following:

HD   Economic history and conditions: here there is an enumerated list of industries (contrast DC – see example on page 151).
R   Medicine:
   RC Internal medicine – 254 Neoplasms
                   280 Neoplasms – by organ alphabetically, e.g. RC280.B7 Brain
   RD Surgery – 645 Neoplasms
            663 Neoplasms of the Brain
L   Education
   LB 1572 – Elementary– curriculum enumerated
   LB 1628 – Secondary – curriculum enumerated
P   Language and Literature
PA 4413 34—Sophocles – divisions enumerated include editions, translations, criticisms, biography, philosophy, treatment of topics (philosophy, religion, etc.). (Similar treatment is found under all authors of note.)

Frequently form, period, and country divisions are enumerated, e.g.:

R   Medicine
   Periodicals by country, e.g. 31 English periodicals
   History by country, e.g. 486—489 Great Britain
   Directories by country, e.g. 713.29 Great Britain
   Medical education by country, e.g. 772 Great Britain
   etc.
   (Many similar divisions are also found under Pathology, Surgery, etc.)

The reason for the length of the schedules will now be understood.

To some extent the schedules become guides to the subjects – as in the Literature class. However the inevitable results of the enumeration follow.

(i) *Simple subjects cannot always be specified.* For example, in Class L Education, the general problem of Curriculum, regardless of kind of school; the Teaching of, say, Mathematics, regardless of kind of school; the Education of Girls; the Education of Boys. It is important to recognize that a high proportion of the schedules does not consist of subject classification at all, but is merely the enumeration of forms, periods, places, and organizations. Thus, despite the detail, broad subject classification is the norm.

(ii) *Many compounds cannot be specified.* For example, although there are divisions for Church schools and Primary schools there is no place for Church primary schools; again, Liberal education can be specified and Technical colleges, but not Liberal education in Technical colleges; in class s Agriculture, we find:

SB 211.P8	Potatoes
SB 129	Storage
SB 741.M65	Mildew

– but not Storage of potatoes, or Mildew in potatoes, etc.

(iii) Following from (ii) it is not only impossible to specify these compounds in the notation, *it is also difficult to decide in which class to place the compound.* For example, shall the document on the Mildew of potatoes be placed with Potatoes or Mildew? In DC, though the compounds cannot always be specified, there are frequent directions: in LC such directions are all too few, and cross classification is likely.

(iv) *Facets are often clearly distinguished but not always.* An example of good differentiation is in Painting – divided by Form, Biography, History, Styles, Subjects and Materials. In Class TL Motor vehicle engineering, however, the main divisions are by type of vehicle (Gasoline, automobile, Motor buses, etc.); under Gasoline automobiles are divisions for construction details, which reappear as a separate facet: Design and construction. Cross classification is likely in such circumstances.

(v) *Order of facets in the schedules might be improved in places.* For example in Education, Grade (Elementary, etc.) is followed by the sequence: School architecture, Religious education, Education of special categories (negroes, women, etc.). However, an overall pattern is discernible: Form, Period, Country, preceding the specialized divisions of a class. Note that sometimes History is collocated, e.g. in the Education class L, the History of education, whether of Primary, Secondary, etc., is collocated at the general form division for history at the beginning of the class – in contrast to other schemes where History is usually secondary to specific subjects. Similarly Place may take precedence, e.g. Higher education LB 2300/2411 caters for only the general problems, Higher education in specific countries being at LD/LG where actual institutions (e.g. Lampeter College) are enumerated under country.

(vi) *Order of foci and sub-facets*. Alphabetical order is very often used. Chronological sequences frequently found in Operations facets, e.g. in Agriculture.

NOTATION

The notation is simple: letters are used for the main classes, integers for the divisions (up to four-figure maximum). Better apportionment would have reduced length (e.g. PE English language, UE Cavalry, QD Chemistry, NB Scripture). As with all integer notations, only broad expressiveness is achieved:

TH 6101—6729	Plumbing
7010—7975	Heating, ventilation, lighting, acoustics
8001—8901	Decoration
9031—9615	Protection of buildings

As a result of this and the fact that synthesis is rudimentary, there is little mnemonic value in the notation. There are some literal mnemonics, e.g. G Geography, T Technology. As the notation can hardly be said to display hierarchy and relationships, browsing in a large library classified by LC is an unsatisfactory business – a fact which, along with the relatively broad specification, results in great reliance being placed on the dictionary catalogues so often found where LC is used. Clearly, it is not the ideal scheme for use in a classified catalogue.

Hospitality. New foci and steps of division can be accommodated if a gap has been left in the sequence at the point required; to some extent, as we have seen, integers are almost certain to determine order because gaps cannot always be left as required. However, alphabetical extensions help here. Synthesis of compounds, so far as it exists (see above), is achieved by:

(i) *Common tables within particular classes*. For example, in most classes there are Place divisions that can be added to a subject number, e.g. in Class N Fine Arts there is a table of country divisions, numbers from which can be added to certain numbers in schedules, e.g.:

> NE 501–794 History of engraving in particular countries
> (US is 05 and thus NE 505 means History of engraving in US).

However, Place is often enumerated too, N 510–3990 Art Museum and galleries enumerated by county and town. There are also special subject divisions, e.g. in Education LF 1–1257 Universities and Colleges in Great Britain divided by a table (Charters, Policy, etc.) shown on page 176 of the scheme.

(ii) *The use of alphabetical extensions.* For example, RC 280 Neoplasms, RC 280.B7 Brain neoplasms – the organ being provided by the alphabetizing number, B7. Very many divisions in the scheme are arranged alphabetically in this way.

J. D. Brown. Subject Classification

First published 1906. The 3rd edition, edited by J. D. Stewart, appeared in 1939. It is the only English general scheme. At one time used by a number of libraries in this country, but the lack of revision (many of the classes in Science, Technology and the Social Sciences are particularly dated), the peculiar features of the scheme (see below) and the use of DC by BNB, have led to its decline in recent years. Today its interest is mainly due to the underlying theory.

In his *Introduction* Brown states: 'I incline to think that in book classification the constant or concrete subject should be preferred to the more general standpoint or occasional subject.' In complete contrast to all other schemes the SC *collocates concretes* instead of scattering them according to particular contexts; thus, whereas in DC, say, Restaurants will be found in a number of classes according to whether the Catering, Architecture, Management, or other aspects are being considered, in SC all aspects of Restaurants are gathered together:

I 984	Restaurants
I 984.183	Architecture
I 984.767	Management
I 984.769	Staff
etc.	

(a) *How is this achieved?* The scheme is divided into *Main Classes* which appear to be traditional:

A Generalia, B—D Physical Science, E—F Biological science, G—H Ethnology and Medicine, I Economic Biology, J—K Philosophy and Religion, L Social and Political science, M Language and Literature, N Literary forms, O—W History and Geography, X Biography.

All concretes are, however, found in *one class only* (hence the name a 'one-place scheme'); for example, Plants are in Class E Botany, Animals are in Class F Zoology, Railways are in Class B (where the Physical sciences and their applications are found). All aspects of these subjects are collocated at these places, e.g.:

Railway engineering	B500
Rolling Stock	B507
Signals	B512
Railway administration	B530
Freight rates	B535
Passenger fares	B538
Running powers	B541

This means that many classes contain simply the general Problem or Operation facets – the particular applications of the problems being elsewhere; thus at L 135 Administration and Business method there are divisions for Staff (Personnel), Bureaucracy, etc. but all the applications of Administration are classified with the applications (e.g. Railways and Restaurants, as above). Again, in Agriculture (I) there are divisions for general Operations (Irrigation, Draining, Plough-ing, Stock management, etc.), but all documents about individual animals and plants are classified with the animals in the Botany and Zoology classes whatever their context. In Architecture (B 300) there are only the generalities (Masonry, Brickwork, Pillars, Cornices, etc.) the type of building being elsewhere – Libraries with Librarianship, Banks with Banking, etc.

(b) *How did Brown decide on the location in the scheme of these concretes?* Why, for example, gather everything on Railways in Class B along with Physical sciences and Technologies rather than with Business organization in Class L? Brown writes: 'In general libraries the difficulty can be overcome in many cases by determining how far the subject has a constant or only occasional interest for the enquirer' and he quotes a book on Library law which he stated would be more regularly used by the Librarian and therefore ought to go with documents on Libraries rather than Law; again, in some cases the concrete would be placed with the more fundamental of the possible contexts, e.g. Plants with Botany and Animals with Zoology rather than with Agriculture – and presumably this would place Railways too because by the arrangement of Main Classes Brown gives Matter precedence over Life and the Social and Political sciences.

The disadvantage of this, despite Brown's carefully argued case, is that the majority of readers do in fact find related material scattered more frequently than in other schemes. There are no specialists in all aspects of Railways, for example; and the railway administrator would prefer to find material on Railway administration not with other aspects of Railways (Engineering, etc.) but with other documents on Administration because clearly many books on general administration will be of direct interest to him and documents on the administration of other services (Shipping, Air and Road Transport, for example) will frequently be consulted by him for a number of reasons (information on competitors, parallel problems, etc.). Similarly the Zoologist will not be particularly interested in having with Zoology documents on, say, Milk yields for Friesian herds in England and Wales, but the farmer will be downright annoyed at having to turn to the Zoology class every time he wants a document on a particular breed of cattle. At times, of course, and particularly where a subject is pervasive (e.g. Law and Architecture) the issue is not so clear-cut and a case can be made for scattering certain applications – but a general theory cannot be based on a few special cases.

MAIN CLASSES AND DIVISIONS

We have already noted that at first glance the outline of main classes appears traditional. The *Summary Table* reveals another feature – and Brown lays particular stress on it; namely, *the collocation of technologies and the fundamental sciences.* Thus Physics is followed by Mechanical engineering, Civil engineering, Architecture, Transport, Naval and Military science; Geology gives way to Mineralogy, Metallurgy, Mining, Metal trades; under the general heading Language and Literature are collocated Bibliography, Printing and Publishing, Librarianship; Drawing and Fine Arts follow Geometry; Music is collocated with Acoustics; all manufacturing industries are similarly treated, e.g. Food and Textile manufacturing are collocated with Economic biology – with their natural resources.

Brown comments: 'Classes like Literature, Useful arts, Fine arts, Extractive arts, Mechanic arts, etc. are examples of arbitrary or standpoint grouping that have been avoided.' However, in collocating Fine Arts and Mathematics, Music and Acoustics, Brown has carried his theory beyond practical utility.

Though s c has grave limitations, Brown's dissatisfaction with 'main classes' like Useful arts, Fine arts, and so on, and his attempt to cater for 'concretes', have a remarkably modern flavour (see page 121).

FACET ANALYSIS

(i) There is *relatively little enumeration* of compounds in the scheme – another characteristic in which Brown anticipates later developments. In Class G/H Medicine, for example, the Organ facet is clearly isolated and though diseases peculiar to certain organs are listed with the respective organs, other diseases are separately listed and grouped (Infectious diseases, Tropical diseases, etc.). Again in Class A, Education is analysed through two main facets – Grade and Problem and these are mainly kept separate. However, the analysis is not exhaustive in many places and in some cases a whole facet is ignored (e.g. in Education there is no mention of a Curriculum facet, though this could be catered for by synthesis).

(ii) *The order of facets (Schedule order) is not always satisfactory* – for example, in the Education Class, 'Systems of education' (Elementary, Secondary, etc.) are separated from Schools by the whole of the Problem facet.

(iii) *Combination order.* Brown, in his *Introduction* and in the schedules, occasionally indicates combination order, sometimes suggesting alternative orders – and there is the general rule that concretes take precedence (thus in Medicine, the Organ facet would take precedence, Surgery, Anatomy, etc., catering only for general studies). In fact the notation allows many alternative combination orders and the classifier will have to be careful to decide on a particular order or cross-classification is inevitable.

NOTATION

(i) Alphabetical (single letters only) followed by numbers used as integers up to 3 figures. Thus:

A 0—950	Generalia	
B 0—995	Physical sciences and applications	
C 0—965	Electricity, Heat, Acoustics, Astronomy, and applications etc.	

The use of 1 and o (letters) and 1 and 0 (numbers) may lead to confusion.

(ii) *Hospitality*. Integers always give rise to the problem of insertion of new foci and steps of division as we have seen. Brown suggests that this may be overcome by decimal extension, e.g.:

K 951	Catholic Apostolic Church
K 9511	Christadelphians
K 952	Christian Endeavour

but as a decimal point cannot be used (because of its use with the Categorical numbers – see below) this does not clearly indicate order as the number can be read as an integer (e.g. 9,511).

The scheme is particularly hospitable to new compounds, class numbers for which can be built in either of two ways – in the following order of priority:

(a) *By the use of the Categorical Table.* This table consists of 'forms, phases, standpoints, qualifications, etc. which apply more or less to every subject or subdivision of a subject'. Instead of 'loading the scheme' with the repetition of such categories, Brown placed them in this separate table, which is a much-extended version of the usual 'common subdivisions' and in fact forms a huge common facet – though some of the categories are relevant only to a limited number of subjects.

Again, the idea shows that Brown was ahead of his times. The notation for the table consists of integers following a point, e.g. .1 Bibliography, .2 Encyclopaedias, .121 Design, etc. Examples of compounds:

c 647.261   Scales for the piano
m 121.901   Slang in journalism

Note that the order of divisions in the Categorical Table is unsatisfactory.

(b) *By amalgamating class numbers* – made possible by the use of the initial capital letter which thus acts as an indicator (compare cis), e.g.:

h 050 g 572   Heart operations
e 154 i 222   Pruning of shrubs
i 420 u 505   Cotton spinning in Oldham

However, this method is not recommended whenever a categorical number is available – thus the first compound would be better expressed as:

h 050.544

The use of these two devices gives rise to a filing problem.

(iii) The notation is simple, using only letters and numbers and the point as a separator. Its apparent brevity in the schedules is misleading because the notation is not satisfactorily apportioned – far too much of the base is given to Geography and History (o–w) – and to cater for new subjects in Classes b, c, and d (Physical science, etc.) lengthy extensions would have to be devised. However, it is non-expressive and this helps to reduce length.

SPECIFIC INDEX

Because Brown considered his to be a 'one-place' scheme, he made a one-place index (sometimes called a 'specific index'). Thus he is content with such index entries as:

Agriculture   i 000
Management   l 135

It is satisfactory to make a single entry for a subject that is collocated, e.g.:

R oses e 600 (where all aspects of roses will be found)

but it is quite unsatisfactory elsewhere. The entries for Agriculture and Agriculture and Management are misleading because, as we have seen, documents on crops will be found in Botany, and the Management of Restaurants, Railways, etc., will be found under these subjects. Brown ought therefore to have made such entries as:

Agriculture	I 000
Crops (individual)	E 100
Management	L 135
Railways	B 530

All classification scatters as it collocates and the fact that Brown scatters aspects rather than concretes does not exempt either him or the classifier using the scheme from making entries that collocate distributed relatives.

READINGS

Students should read the chapters on the schemes in the various textbooks on classification. An up-to-date guide which expands on the account given here can be found in:

FOSKETT, A. C. *The subject approach to information*. London, Bingley, 1969.

It is also important to read the introductions to the schemes themselves.

Colon

BATTY, C. D. *Introduction to colon classification*. London, Bingley, 1966.

RANGANATHAN, S. R. *The colon classification*. Rutgers, the State University, Graduate School of Library Service, 1965.(Rutgers series on systems for the intellectual organization of information, v.4).

RANGANATHAN, S. R. 'Colon classification: edition 7 (1971): a preview'. *Library Science with a Slant to Documentation*, 6 (3), September 1969, 193–242.

Dewey

BATTY, C. D. *Introduction to the Dewey decimal classification*. London, Bingley, 1965.

BATTY, C. D. *Introduction to the seventeenth edition of the Dewey decimal classification*. London, Bingley, 1967.

COATES, E. J. 'The Dewey decimal classification, edition 16'. *Library Association Record*, 61 (8), August 1959, 187–90.

COATES, E. J. 'The decimal classification, edition 16: class 300'. *Library Association Record*, 62 (3), March 1960, 84–90.

UDC

BRITISH STANDARDS INSTITUTE. *Guide to the UDC* [by J. Mills]. London, B.S.I., 1963. (BS 1000 C: 1963).

KYLE, B. 'The Universal decimal classification . . . with particular reference to those schedules which deal with the humanities, arts and social sciences.' *Unesco Bulletin for Libraries*, 15 (2), March–April 1961, 53–69.

MILLS, J. *The universal decimal classification*. Rutgers, the State University, Graduate School of Library Service, 1964. (Rutgers series on systems for the intellectual organization of information, v.1.)

PERREAULT, J. *Introduction to the UDC*. London, Bingley, 1969.

VICKERY, B. C. 'The universal decimal classification and technical information indexing'. *Unesco Bulletin for Libraries*, 15 (3), May–June 1961, 126–138, 147.

WELLISCH, H. *UDC: a programmed instruction course*. College Park, Maryland, University of Maryland, School of Library and Information Services, 1970.

Bliss

The best introduction to BC is to be found in the various books written by Bliss and mentioned earlier. For example, many of the principles underlying the scheme can be found in *The organization of knowledge in libraries*, pp. 331–6; see also v.1–2 of the scheme, chapters 1–6 and pp. 20–5 in particular.

MILLS, J. 'Composite specification in the Bliss classification'. *Bliss Bulletin*, 2 (1), 1957, 6–15.

MILLS, J. 'A new edition of Bliss'. *Catalogue and Index*, 17, January 1970, 8–9.

Library of Congress

BLISS, H. E. *The organization of knowledge in libraries*. New York, H. W. Wilson, 1933. Chapter 12.

IMMROTH, J. P. *A guide to Library of Congress classification*. Rochester, N.Y., Libraries Unlimited Inc., 1968.

LAMONTAGNE, L. E. *American library classification, with special reference to the Library of Congress*. Hamden, Conn., Shoestring Press, 1961.

Special schemes demonstrating facet analysis include:
AITCHISON, J. ed. *Thesaurofacet: a thesaurus and faceted classification*

for electrical engineering and related subjects. Whetstone, Leics., English Electric Co. Ltd., 1969.

COATES, E. J. *The British catalogue of music classification*. London, BNB, 1961.

FOSKETT, D. J. *The London education classification*. London, University of London, Institute of Education, 1963.

INTERNATIONAL OCCUPATIONAL SAFETY AND HEALTH IN-FORMATION CENTRE (GENEVA). *Guide to the card service and CIS classification*. Rev. ed. Geneva, CIS, 1961.

VERNON, K. D. C. *and* LANG, V. *The London classification of business studies*. London, Graduate School of Business Studies, 1970.

Chapter 9
The Classified Catalogue

We have already seen (Chapter 6) that there are three traditional types of subject catalogues: the classified, the alphabetico-
direct, and the alphabetico-classified.

The classified catalogue using notation and with which we
are concerned in this chapter is usually in three parts:

(i) *The classified file* or section, which contains the main entries
arranged according to the classification scheme used in the
library. Note that it is not merely a duplication of the sequence
on the shelves; it contains not only the main entries which will
be filed by the same class number as the document, but also
added entries as necessary, e.g. a document on Radar *and*
Television must be shelved at the class number for Radar *or*
Television (assuming that there is no place for the composite
subject) but entries for this document can be made in the
classified file under both subjects. (For an example of an entry
see pages 17 and 19 and BNB.)

(ii) *The alphabetical subject index*
which does not include entries for
particular documents   } Sometimes combined.

(iii) *The alphabetical author index*
The main purpose of the classified catalogue is to collocate
documents on related subjects systematically and this is done
principally through the main and added entries in the classified
file; here all the entries for documents on Philosophy, Economics, Mathematics, Poetry, and so on, are brought into
proximity according to the classification scheme in use. However, no matter how perfect the scheme used, the only relationships that are immediately apparent are those between
a subject and the subjects immediately preceding and succeeding it in the file; this limitation is inevitable with linear order.
But there are usually many other relationships apart from those
revealed by juxtaposition; for example, the entry for a

document on Science teaching may be filed by UDC in Class 371, relating it to other documents on the teaching of various subjects, but an entry for Science teaching in technical colleges may be filed with other material on Technical colleges at 378.962. As we have already seen, the necessary imposition of a citation order in classifying compound subjects results in the successive scattering of concepts which are not primary. The alphabetical subject index helps to offset this limitation. A reader interested in science teaching will discover relevant documents filed at the number for technical colleges if we make an index entry:

Science teaching: Technical colleges 378.962: 371.214:5

As the entry will file alongside others on science teaching, e.g.

Science teaching 371.214:5
Science teaching: Secondary schools 373.5:371.214:5
Science teaching: Technical colleges 378.962:371.214:5

the index can be said to collocate distributed relatives (see page 117).

In this way the reader who wants to study documents on subjects scattered by the classification scheme can do so. However, it has to be admitted that such a system entails some inconvenience to the reader because the index only refers to the relevant classification symbols – he has then to consult the classified file in several places to discover the entries for the documents. This underlies the importance of choosing a citation order that reflects the needs of most users.

Of course it would be possible to enter a document on a compound subject under each of the major elements comprising the class number. For example, the document on Science teaching in technical colleges might be given a main entry at 378.962:371.214:5 and an added entry at 371.214:5:378.962. But the multiple entry of all compounds is expensive and in practice it is generally recommended that multiple entry be reserved for documents on two or more distinct subjects separately treated in a document (e.g. Radar and Television).

Nevertheless, there are circumstances in which the multiple entry of compound subjects may be advocated; these arise whenever enquiries for a subject scattered by the citation order are frequent. Then primary collocation in the classified file would be particularly desirable. In the above instance, if the approach by subject taught (Science) and that by type of institution (Technical colleges) were frequent among the users of the collection, then multiple entry in the classified file would be justified.

For the moment we shall assume that multiple entry is not the norm. Later in this chapter we shall return to this question.

The Author/Title Index

An index of authors must be provided in the classified catalogue and where unit entry is used there is no reason why it should not be as full in its details as the main entry in the classified file. Added entries and references will be made in the usual way for author records. In practice the index will also contain entries for titles, in accordance with the rules for title entry.

Where unit entry cannot be used it will not be possible to give full entries in the author/title index. Usually a brief added entry style is adopted, sufficient to identify the particular edition of the document. For further details, if needed, the reader can then refer to the main file, under the class number indicated. For obvious reasons, the style of index which simply gives an author's name and a string of page references or class numbers is to be avoided: Redmayne, P. B. 385, 620, 745, etc.

The Classified File

The classified file should be well signposted; far too many cataloguers leave the reader to struggle through a maze of unfamiliar notational symbols. It is this, far more than the classified sequence as such, that makes the catalogue difficult to use. How much guiding is done will depend to some extent on the size of the catalogue, but in general there should be:

(a) *Entries listing the main subdivisions in each major subject,* e.g. in a card catalogue:

> 500 Science
> 510 Mathematics
> 520 Astronomy
> 530 Physics
> etc.

At 510 another entry will indicate the main divisions of 510, and so on, according to the number of entries for any subject.

(b) *Verbal translations alongside headings* – see the careful use of these in BNB, e.g.

> 631.4   – SOIL
> 631.43 – Soil physics
> 631.432 – Humidity

This is sometimes referred to as featuring. To save having to give these verbal translations every time an entry is made under these headings, guides simply bearing the headings, 631.4 SOIL, 631.43 Soil physics, and so on, and filing before the appropriate entries, would be quite satisfactory.

(c) *Cross references*. These should be made with discretion, but when one considers the value to the classifier of cross references in the classification schedules that he uses daily, it is difficult to understand why more are not made in his catalogues. They are particularly useful in linking coordinate and collateral subjects, relationships not always brought out in the subject index; e.g. in UDC:

> (a) 327 International foreign affairs
>   *see also* 341 International law
> (b) 330 Economics
>   *see also* 380 Commerce
>   650 Business

All signposts should, in card and sheaf catalogues, be of a different colour from the entries themselves; too many white cards can be dazzling.

The Subject Index

Class numbers are meaningless to most users of the classified file and therefore an index of subjects is required by which terms in natural language can be converted into class numbers, e.g.

Science 500

Each index entry should normally show the *context* of the term indexed:

Railways: Engineering 625.1, NOT Railways 625.1

In any scheme of classification (even SC) many subjects appear at various points in the schedules. This fact must be remembered when making the index. It is wrong to make the entry, Railways 625.1, because it is misleading; not *all* documents on Railways are to be found at 625.1 – in fact, only those on the Engineering aspects of the subject will be found there; other material on Railways will be classified at (in DC) 338.476251 (Engineering economics), 385 (Transport economics), 656* (Transport operations), and so on. And so qualifying terms indicating context must be provided:

Railways: Engineering	625.1
Railways: Engineering: Economics	338.476251
Railways: Transport economics	385
Railways: Transport operations	656

The BNB index yields many examples:

Nervous system: Anatomy: Domestic animals	636.08918
Nervous system: Anatomy: Medicine	611.8
Nervous system: Anatomy: Vertebrates	596.[1]
Nervous system: Diseases	616.8
Nervous system: Diseases: Children	618.92m8
Nervous system: Physiology: Infants	612.65[1]
Nervous system: Physiology: Medicine	612.8
Nervous system: Physiology: Rabbits	599.322[1]
Nervous system: Physiology: Vertebrates	596.[1]
Nervous system: Physiology: Zoology	591.18
Nervous system: Psychology	131.2
Nervous system: Surgery	617.48

Such entries clearly indicate the aspects of the subject treated at each class number and thus save the searcher considerable time. In this way too, distributed relatives are collocated.

The *purpose* of the subject index is therefore twofold:

(i) To translate a natural language term into a class number;

(ii) to collocate distributed relatives.

Note that it does not include entries: it is simply a guide to the arrangement of entries in the classified file.

Such an index is called a *relative index,* and can be systematically made by a process called *chain indexing.* Chain indexing is an attempt to rationalize an operation that has

---

* This number has been discarded from the 16th ed.

existed at least since Dewey formulated the phrase 'relative index'. The theory of chain indexing was first propounded by Ranganathan. It was used for twenty years in BNB.

CHAIN INDEXING

In essence each index entry created by chain procedure is simply a statement *in reverse* of the elements that comprise the class number* for a particular document. For example, the class number 821 which represents the subject English poetry in DC is made up of the following elements: Literature (8), English (2), and Poetry (1); a reversal of this gives the index entry:

Poetry: English literature 821

By this method the qualifiers indicating the context (English literature) are *automatically* indicated and distributed relatives will, as the index grows, be collocated.

The reason for this is clear when we consider that this operation reverses the order of application of characteristics in the scheme, or the combination order for compounds: now it was precisely this order that scattered the elements in the first place – according to particular contexts. For example, in DC class 800 (Literature), the combination order is: Language – Form; this means that all the Literature in a particular Language is collocated, but equally certainly the Forms of literature (Poetry, Drama, etc.) are scattered according to Language context – thus English poetry is at 821 in the context of English literature (820), French poetry at 841 in the context of French literature (840), Spanish poetry at 861 in the context of Spanish literature (860) and so on. By the simple expedient of reversing this combination order in the index we gather together again all the elements that were scattered by it:

Poetry: English literature　821
Poetry: French literature　841
Poetry: Spanish literature　861

The method demands great care in its application especially when used with existing classification schemes where the steps of division are not always made clear; for example, in DC 200

* But note the qualification to this statement – page 183.

is the Religion class and 220 Scriptures. An indexer might be tempted to make an index entry:

Scriptures: Religion 220

but this would be a mistake because there is a hidden step of division – the divisions 220/280 relate only to the Christian religion and so the entry should be:

Scriptures: Christianity 220

This danger arises particularly in non-expressive notations where the steps of division are not represented in the class number (as above). *In fact the indexer must never work from the class number alone but from the actual steps of division*, i.e. *the chain* – and these should be written down before index entries are made using terms which consist, as far as possible, of nouns in plural form, e.g.

200	Religion	800	Literature
220/280	Christianity	820	English
220	Scriptures	821	Poetry

Note that each step in the chain should be composed only of *terms signifying that particular step* – thus for the step 821 the term is Poetry *not* English poetry (English having been listed already against 820). The reason for this will become clear.

Without the precaution of such a list the indexer is likely to create false entries.

We have noted that readers do not necessarily look up the exact terms used in the catalogue: they may consult a more general heading or a synonym for example. So the index entry produced simply by reversing the chain as described here is not in itself complete. Suppose for example that the reader consulted the index under the term Verse, not Poetry, in the example given above. To cater for such *synonyms* we can either make another entry, e.g.

Verse: English literature 821

or make a reference:

Verse *see* Poetry

In this case a reference will save many index entries, for if an index entry: Verse: English literature, is made, similar entries

will also be needed for other languages (Verse: French literature; Verse: Spanish literature, and so on) duplicating similar
entries already made under Poetry. Where large-scale saving
is achieved a reference is preferable, but it should be remembered that the reader has to consult the classified file after the
subject index and references are to be used only in extreme
cases so as to save the reader's time.

What of the reader who consults a *related heading* – for
example, he consults the index under English literature instead
of Poetry when what he wants is a book on English poetry? An
entry must be made for such a person:

English literature 820

Guiding in the classified file at 820 will now enable him to
discover the whereabouts of English poetry, the subject he was
really seeking. And for the person who consults the catalogue
under Literature a further entry should be made:

Literature 800

*To summarize: index entries must be made not only for the ultimate
term in the chain, but also for synonyms and for superordinate terms
whenever they are terms likely to be sought by readers.* In each case the
term indexed will be qualified by a superordinate term or
terms in the chain so as to place it in its context. To ensure that
this is properly done the actual steps of division should be listed
first. And though this might appear to be a lengthy business it
must be recognized that once a class number has been indexed
there will be no need for further index entries to that number
however many documents are placed there (except for occasional synonyms and keywords – see examples in Chapter 23 –
so far not indexed). Moreover, by making indexing systematic,
overall economy is achieved; without such a method cataloguers
tend to index all permutations of terms, e.g.

Literature, English 820
English Literature 820
English Poetry 821
Poetry, English 821
and so on.

Where such hit-and-miss methods are used no one can ever be
sure that all the information on a subject has been indexed.

There is another reason why it is legitimate to make several index entries in the way described: a document on a specific subject is to some extent a document on all (or many of) the subjects represented by the superordinate steps in the chain. Thus the document on English poetry is to some extent a document on English literature and also on Literature – and anyone interested in either of these two subjects may be interested in this document; without the index entries he will not find it – unless there are other documents already indexed at English literature and Literature.

Finally, the student may ask why an entry is not made: English poetry 821. The reason is that such an entry *repeats the combination order* and we have seen that the purpose of the index is to reverse this so as to bring to the fore elements scattered in the classification and thus to collocate these scattered elements. To make entries like the above is wasteful – they simply repeat the work done in the classified file. The person looking up English poetry will find English literature and having turned to the classified file at 820 will then be lead to 821. And remember that if this type of entry is made for English poetry it must be made for English drama, etc. – and similar entries must be made under all other languages (Spanish poetry, French drama, etc.). *So qualify only the superordinate terms in the chain.*

Another example (U D C):

Chain:

600	Technology	
620	Engineering	
621.3	Electrical	
621.39	Telecommunications	
621.396	Radio. Wireless (a synonym)	

Index entries:

Radio:Engineering	621.396
Wireless: Engineering	621.396
Telecommunications: Engineering	621.39
Electrical engineering	621.3
Engineering	620

Note that all superordinate terms do not need repeating as qualifiers in each entry – only sufficient to indicate unambiguously the context of the indexed term.

These notes on chain indexing do not attempt to give full practical instructions, but rather to show sufficient of the method at work to give a general introduction to the underlying principles. Students should try their hand at it: a simple method is to construct index entries for a document in the classified section of BNB (pre 1971) and then to check the index to compare entries. Further examples will be found in Chapter 23.

PRECIS INDEXING

The effectiveness of chain indexing is obviously related to the effectiveness of the classification scheme on which it is based. If, for example, the scheme is inhospitable to specific concepts, then unless further action is taken such specific concepts cannot be properly indexed. Thus, by DC (16th ed.) a document on Elites would have to be given the class number 301.44 which stands for the broader concept of Social classes. The steps of division are as follows:

> 301   Sociology
> 301.4   Social organization
> 301.44   Classes

The final step of division – Elites – is missing and therefore cannot be indexed except by reference to the broader concept of Class, where it will be hidden among a wide range of entries filing alphabetically by author.

BNB has for many years attempted to overcome this difficulty by using the symbol [1] to introduce steps of division not catered for in DC. The number assigned to this document would be 301.44 [1]. Following the [1] in the classified file would be the 'verbal extension' Elites. The filing heading would then be:

> 301.44 [1] Elites

In this way any class number may be followed by a series of alphabetically arranged subject divisions representing steps of division extending beyond those catered for by the scheme itself. The corresponding subject index entry would read:

> Elites: Sociology 301.44 [1]

The cooperative production and use of MARC tapes (see Chapter 20) by BNB has resulted in a reassessment of their classification and indexing procedures. One of the decisions recently taken is the adoption of standard DC for the arrangement of the classified section of the bibliography (as distinct from the modified BNB/DC used hitherto). Such practices as the use of [1] are no longer possible. As a result of this and other decisions a new system of machine indexing has been devised for use in the bibliography and is described in a BNB publication by Austin and Butcher, entitled *PRECIS: a rotated subject index system*.[1] PRECIS stands for PREserved Context Subject Index.

In brief, the new index will be compiled independently of the classified file. The first step (preceding both classification and indexing) will be to analyse the basic concepts representing the subject of the document. These elements will then be translated into terms acceptable for the index through the use of two vocabularies, one covering Entities (things – concrete objects and mental constructs), the other Attributes (properties of things, activities of things, and properties of activities). The terms in the vocabularies are hierarchically organized so as to indicate fundamental generic relationships and suggest references that should be made between one term and another.

Relevant terms selected from these vocabularies to express a compound subject will be cited in a predetermined order. One feature of this citation order is that Entity is to be given precedence. Beyond this, order will be determined by the kinds of relationships existing between the terms. For example, in the case of a possessive relationship the possessing system is cited first, e.g. Bicycles:Wheels:Spokes. Another type of relationship is one of interaction and in such instances a basic rule is that the passive system – i.e. the product, patient or system affected by or modified by the interaction – is to be cited first. Thus the string of terms: Rivers/Contamination/Power station feed water, would represent a document on the effect of power station feed water on rivers. On the other hand, Power stations/Feed water/Contamination/Rivers would refer to a document on the contamination of power station feed water by rivers.

As the index will be produced by computer the relationships between elements in the compound will be made explicit by the use of Relational Operators. These are symbols representing the particular relationships that have so far been defined. They will be placed between the terms comprising the compound and, when translated into machine terms, they will facilitate the automatic generation of index entries. For example:

(4) Bulgaria (3) Invasion (2) Greece

(where (4) represents the key system, (3) the effect, action, and (2) the active system);

(4) Food (3) Irradiation (1) Health aspect

(where (1) represents the viewpoint, perspective).

Once the accepted terms have been cited in their correct order and the Operators added, the whole will be coded for machine manipulation. The end-result in the printed BNB will be an index in which the terms representing compounds are rotated, each element being brought into the filing position with the remaining terms lying on each side of it indicating the context.

To give an example, a document entitled *The role of digital computers in planning the manpower requirements of British universities* would be analysed as follows:

(6) Great Britain (4) Universities (p) Manpower (3) Planning
(3) Role (2) Computers, digital.

The meaning of the Operators is as follows: (6) Environment, (4) Key system, (p) Subsystem, (3) Effect, action, (2) Active system.

Six index entries will result from this analysis:

(i) GREAT BRITAIN
Universities. Manpower planning. Role of digital computers
(ii) UNIVERSITIES. Great Britain
Manpower planning. Role of digital computers
(iii) PLANNING. Universities. Great Britain
Manpower planning. Role of digital computers
(iv) MANPOWER PLANNING. Universities. Great Britain
Role of digital computers
(v) COMPUTERS. Role in manpower planning. Universities.
Great Britain. Digital computers
(vi) DIGITAL COMPUTERS. Role in manpower planning.
Universities. Great Britain

Additionally, the generic relationships built into the vocabularies will give rise to the following references:

EDUCATION *see also* HIGHER EDUCATION
HIGHER EDUCATION *see also* UNIVERSITIES
COLLEGES *see also* UNIVERSITIES
EDUCATIONAL PLANNING *see also* MANPOWER PLANNING.
  Universities
LABOUR *see* PERSONNEL
STAFF *see* PERSONNEL
PERSONNEL *see also* MANPOWER
DATA PROCESSING *see also* DIGITAL COMPUTERS
ELECTRONIC COMPUTERS *see also* DIGITAL COMPUTERS

PRECIS has been referred to as a *rotated index*: the terms (with some modifications) rotate in order to bring each of them into the filing position in turn. Each concept moves into the lead position in the 'heading', the qualifiers giving the wider context of the term, while the 'display' in the line below indicates the more specific elements in the compound:

UNIVERSITIES. Great Britain.   – *Heading with qualifier*

Manpower planning. Role of digital computers.
          – *Display of more specific 'elements'*

Whatever term is sought the reader can, by reading the entry from right to left in the heading and then continuing from left to right in the display, build up the complete compound. The class number cited against any of the index entries for a compound will be the number at which the entry for the document is filed in the classified file.

This has been necessarily a brief resumé of the system, but certain points can be made:

(i) The initial analysis will be used as a basis not only for the index entries but for the classification also. As the MARC tapes will include, in addition to the standard DC number, those for BNB/DC and LC (and, later, UDC), as well as subject headings using the LC list, it is particularly important that fundamental analysis be undertaken without reference to any one scheme.

(ii) Index entries will no longer suffer from the limitations imposed by a standard classification scheme. Even though the Manpower planning document may have to be classified at a broad class number signifying Universities or Manpower planning, the index entries will systematically cover all key concepts. Within the classified file class numbers will be amplified by terms from the PRECIS analysis. Despite the use of [1] and other devices, the limitations of DC have never been fully overcome by chain indexing in BNB.

(iii) A major difference between PRECIS and chain indexing is the inclusion in the former of all elements in a compound in *each* index entry, i.e. the full compound is indexed at each step. To illustrate the difference, let us suppose that the chain for the document on Manpower planning had included the following steps of division:

> Universities
>   Manpower
>   Planning
>   Computers
>   Digital

Then by chain procedure the following index entries would have been created:

> Digital computers: Manpower planning: Universities
> Computers: Manpower planning: Universities
> Planning: Manpower: Universities
> Manpower: Universities
> Universities

Each entry would be given the class number *signifying that particular step of division.*

One consequence of this basic difference is that a PRECIS index gives more scope for sifting *in the index itself.* A reader will find under Manpower a full statement of all compounds which include that concept. The index thus gives more information than a chain index and serves as a basis for selection *before* the classified file is consulted. Only by searching the classified file will a reader using a chain index discover whether the index entry Manpower: Universities indicates that there is a document on that precise subject as distinct from one on a more specific division of it.

(iv) A further difference is the use of cross references in the PRECIS index. This follows from the dissociation of the index from the classification scheme: generic relationships have to be displayed in the index itself. As we have seen these relationships are built into the vocabularies on which the system is based. Two advantages are gained by this: in the first place, the references can show multi-dimensional relationships that are not visible in the classified file; secondly, the classified file remains to display an additional system of relationships.

(v) Clearly, as in any other system, the success of PRECIS will depend on the adequacy of the vocabularies of terms and the analysis of the relationships between them, both generic and compound. As the work is being undertaken by the staff of the BNB, and in particular by people who have been associated with the Classification Research Group and the work on the new general classification, there is reason to hope that it will be of high quality.

As a system PRECIS has undergone extensive tests at BNB and is still being modified in the light of experience. The publication referred to above is already out of date in certain respects. For example, the Relational Operators have been extended and modified. A further development is the increasing use of prepositions and phrases to reveal relationships between terms, as can be seen from the following example:

Document: The intervention of the League of Nations in the Greek invasion of Bulgaria in 1925.
Concept analysis: (4) Bulgaria, 1925 (3) Invasion – by – of (2) Greece
  [Sub 3 ↑] Greek invasion of Bulgaria, 1925 (3) Intervention – of
  – in (2) League of Nations
Index entries:
  Bulgaria, 1925
    Invasion by Greece. Intervention of League of Nations
  Invasion of Bulgaria, 1925
    By Greece. Intervention of League of Nations
  Greece. Invasion of Bulgaria, 1925
    Intervention of League of Nations
  League of Nations. Intervention in Greek invasion of Bulgaria,
    1925

Both chain indexing and PRECIS indexing force the reader to scan sequentially a set of index entries in order to make sure that no relevant compound is missed. Examine, for example,

the following index entries resulting from chain procedure in
BNB (1961):

Food: Agriculture: Economics	338.19
Food: Crops: Agriculture	633.[1]
Food: Dietetics	613.2
Food: Domestic economy	641
Food: Eating customs	394.1
Food: Lakes: Trout	597.55[1]
Food: Metabolism: Physiology: Medicine	612.392
Food: Processing and preservation	664
Food: Processing and preservation: Bibliographies	016.664
Food: Processing and preservation: Economics	338.47664
Food: Processing and preservation: Women: Labour: Economics	331.4864

Clearly a reader who wishes to discover all material on the
agricultural aspects of food and relies on the entry Food:
Agriculture will miss relevant entries in which the term Agriculture has been displaced by an intermediate term – e.g. Food:
Crops: Agriculture. A reader searching for economic aspects
of the food industries will not find an entry Food: Economics,
and only a full sequential search will guide him to the following
entries which may be relevant:

Food: Agriculture: Economics
Food: Processing and preservation. Economics
Food: Processing and preservation: Women: Labour: Economics

The following entries are taken from the sample PRECIS index
in the BNB publication referred to above:

BONES. Man	
Calcium. Metabolism. Diseases	616.71
Fractures	617.15
Marrow Diseases	616.15

Again, a person searching for Diseases of bones in man will
retrieve the two relevant entries only if he scans every entry at
BONES.

The problem is not too critical when a printed index is used,
for the printed page can be quickly scanned. Nor would there
be difficulties were the searching to be done by machine.

Sequential searching of cards is another matter: it is likely that relevant items will be missed by those with average time and patience.

The scatter is, of course, a result of the initial citation order which controls the sequence of terms in the linear display. Is there any way of generating a set of index entries giving alternative sequences other than the impracticable one of catering for all permutations? Sharp has analysed this problem by reference to the mathematics of combinations and has suggested that the number of necessary alternative orders can be reduced to manageable proportions. He shows how the 120 entries that would result from the straight permutation of five terms can be reduced to 16, and has devised a system of indexing based on his ideas which is referred to as SLIC (Selective Listing in Combination).[2] Even so, the number of entries would, of course, exceed the number produced by chain procedure – or the number acceptable to many librarians – and Sharp himself envisages the use of machines for this purpose.

Multiple Entry in the Classified File

However ingeniously index entries are manipulated to provide multiple approaches to the sequence of documents in the classified file, the fact remains that so long as each document is entered once only in the classified file the reader may be seriously inconvenienced. Whilst it is true that a good index will collocate for the reader all aspects of his subject, he may still have to search through several sequences in the classified file to discover the records of the actual documents. Thus a person specializing in the study of the novel will find, when using BNB, the following index entries:

Novels: American literature	813
Novels: Asian literature	890.[1]
Novels: Bibliographies	016.80883
Novels: Composition and general criticism	808.3
Novels: English literature	823
Novels: Hebrew literature	892.43

This follows from, among other things, the citation order in which language precedes form. The scatter would have been

7

greater had period taken precedence over form, for then we should have had such index entries as:

Novels: 18th century: English literature
Novels: 19th century: English literature
Novels: 18th century: German literature
  etc.

as well as those in the previous sequence.

Now there may be circumstances in which such scattering is intolerable – when two or more significant groups of users require different citation orders. Although the specialist in the literature of a particular language will find the D C citation order acceptable, the student of the novel as a literary form is not so well served. If we wish to provide the latter with the facilities given to the former then we must make added entries *in the classified file*. (Even then, of course, the reader will have to go to several places on the shelves – but no system can arrange documents in multiple orders.)

To achieve multiple entry in the classified file – i.e. the use of two or more citation orders – we require a notation that is expressive of compound relationships. U D C provides an example. An entry for a document the English Novel could be filed at

$$820 - 31 \quad \text{(Literature/English/Novel)}$$
$$\textit{and} \quad 8\text{--}31:820 \quad \text{(Literature/Novel/English)}$$

The first will relate it to other documents on English literature, grouped by forms; the second will relate it to documents on the novel, subdivided by languages.

The expense of multiple entry has to be considered. Every *document* on the English novel will require two entries. As the number of concepts in a compound subject increases so the possible number of entries will rise rapidly. A document on the 19th century English novel could be given six entries:

820–31"19"	(English/Novel/19th century)
820"19"–31	(English/19th century/Novel)
8–31:820"19"	(Novel/English/19th century)
8–31"19":820	(Novel/19th century/English)
8"19"–31:820	(19th century lit/Novel/English)
8"19":820–31	(19th century lit/English/Novel)

On the other hand, the number of *index* entries can be reduced. The two entries

> English literature 820
> Novels 8–31

will cover *all* entries for these two subjects. As all documents on the novel, no matter what the language, are collocated at 8–31, there will be no need for the kind of build-up that we find in the BNB index at the term 'Novels'. The saving effected by reductions in the number of index entries is, however, negligible when set against the consequent expansion in the classified file.

When multiple entry is practised – and it is frequently found in industrial libraries using UDC – the number of permutations is generally reduced to those representative of users' needs, and the system is standardized by means of 'rotation', each element in the compound being successively brought into the filing position:

> 820–31"19"
> 8–31"19":820
> 8"19":820–31

Such a system disturbs the sequence of concepts in the compound – i.e. the main sequence at which the document itself is shelved. An alternative that is often employed is to underline concepts to indicate the filing position:

> 820–31"19"
> 820–31"19"
> 820–31"19"

where the first will file at 820, the second at 8–31, and the third at 8"19".[3]

However, rotation of this kind will not bring each concept into juxtaposition with each of the others. If we rotate four elements – A, B, C and D – there is no way of juxtaposing C and A. The reader who wishes to relate these two concepts will have to scan *all* entries at A (or C). Here again, Sharp's SLIC indexing procedure provides a solution – though one that is prohibitively expensive for a conventional card file.

In such situations we reach the limits of what are known as pre-coordinate systems, i.e. systems which are based on headings summarizing the content of documents in terms co-ordinated according to a citation order. An alternative – post-coordinate systems – will be briefly discussed in Chapter 11.

A Brief Assessment of the Classified Catalogue

(i) By means of the classified file and the relative index, such a catalogue helps to collocate all the material on a given topic and *displays relationships* between subjects in a way more useful to the reader than does any other kind of catalogue.

(ii) Though to some extent indirect, in that its use often demands the prior use of an index, once the basic construction has been understood *it presents few difficulties to the reader.* Readers who use catalogues and bibliographies and indexes to books are hardly likely to be unduly disconcerted by it. In fact the separate files may well be more manageable than a single sequence as found in the dictionary catalogue, with all its attendant filing problems. It should be remembered that no catalogue is direct in all its approaches and a reader using catalogues which employ natural language will frequently have to follow up references.

(iii) Classified catalogues are *independent of language* to a large extent and where an international scheme of classification is used, especially UDC with its multi-lingual indexes, a literature search involving the discovery of foreign language materials is much more easily accomplished.

(iv) From the librarian's point of view the classified record has a number of special advantages:

(a) it is *simple to construct* because it utilizes work already done in classifying the document, and the indexing is a lessening task as the stock increases;

(b) it is *easy to maintain* – new terms for old subjects are easily accommodated by the addition of a new index card – the entries for the documents in the classified file remaining under the same class number (contrast the changing of headings in the dictionary catalogue);

(c) the *printing* of the sections of the catalogue is possible;

(d) *defects in stock are quickly seen* so from the stock editor's viewpoint classified catalogues are most valuable.

(v) *The effectiveness of the classified catalogue is limited by the defects of the classification scheme in use*, though judicious guiding and indexing can to some extent help to mitigate defects. In particular, the following defects have an adverse effect:

(a) *Lack of hospitality.* For examples see BNB where, under inhospitable sections of the classification such as 539.7, 645, 667.2, etc., many entries on different aspects of the subjects in question have to be accommodated at the same class number. The use in BNB of [1] and verbal extensions to subdivide such classes is of great assistance, but without these devices, the catalogue is much impaired. For example, 629.1388 in DC has to house all documents on Astronautics – documents on Instrumentation, Earth satellites, Monkeys in space, Manned flights, Control systems, and so on. If each of these topics is indexed to 629.1388 – as it must be if indexed at all, then the reader is faced with the job of looking through all the entries on Astronautics to find any particular one. A faceted scheme would have been able to accommodate most of these subjects simply by synthesizing existing elements (Instrumentation, etc.).

(b) *Lack of order or priority for facets.* This results in cross classification and consequent distribution of entries on the same subject in the classified file; e.g. in the Philosophy class in DC a book on Existentialism in Heidegger can be placed with books on Existentialism *or* Heidegger; similarly a book on Visual aids in Grammar schools can go with Visual aids *or* Grammar schools. Unless the cataloguer decides on an order and is consistent he will have books on the same subject at several places in the scheme.

(vi) Finally it can be said that many of the faults attributed to the classified catalogue are due not to the catalogue form itself but to the prevalence of poor examples. Catalogues without guiding, catalogues based on outdated classification schemes, catalogues without subject indexes or with indexes arbitrarily compiled can hardly be used fairly as ammunition in an attack on the classified catalogue as such. The lack of a clear understanding of the importance and function of the subject index is demonstrated in those libraries which substitute the printed index to the classification scheme for a self-made one. *Clearly the printed index cannot possibly index all the subjects in the library's classified file* – new subjects, compounds, new terms and synonyms; again, the printed index will contain many subjects which are not represented in the library and this can only discourage the reader from using the catalogue; finally, the printed index contains many notes for the classifier that cannot but confuse the reader.

READINGS

1. AUSTIN, D. *and* BUTCHER, P. *PRECIS*: *a rotated subject index system*. London, BNB, 1969.
2. SHARP, J. R. *Some fundamentals of information retrieval*. London, Deutsch, 1965. pp. 82–93.
3. This kind of rotation can be seen in the sequence of titles illustrating the London education classification: D.J. FOSKETT, *The London education classification*. London, University of London, Institute of Education, 1963. pp. 32–66.

The books by E. J. COATES and A. C. FOSKETT cited at the end of Chapter 6 are particularly relevant here.
DOUGHTY, D. W. 'Chain procedure, subject indexing and featuring in the classified catalogue'. *Library Association Record*, 57 (5), May 1955, 173–8.
JOLLEY, L. *The principles of cataloguing*. London, Lockwood, 1961. Chapter 4.
MILLS, J. 'Chain indexing and the classified catalogue'. *Library Association Record*, 57 (4), April 1955, 141–8.
RANGANATHAN, S. R. *Classified catalogue code*. 4th ed. Madras, Madras Library Association, 1958.
SHERA, J. H. *and* EGAN, M. E. *The classified catalogue*. Chicago, ALA, 1956.

Chapter 10
The Alphabetical Subject Catalogue

1. The Alphabetico-Direct Catalogue

Here we are concerned with subject headings of the kind found in Dictionary Catalogues (see also page 220). Traditionally the main feature of this kind of catalogue as we have seen (Chapter 6) is that it uses as subject headings terms in natural language using the natural form of phrase, e.g. ELECTRICAL ENGINEERING and CHILD PSYCHOLOGY rather than ENGINEERING, ELECTRICAL and PSYCHOLOGY, CHILD. The headings file alphabetically and there is some collocation of related headings – of *concretes* mainly, as opposed to the traditional disciplines and aspects (Economics, Engineering, Law, etc.) collocated by the classification scheme.

This is partly because in natural speech and in thought we tend to place the 'concrete' first, e.g. Pig breeding, Cotton industry, Theatre management, etc., and partly because, in their desire to avoid *class entries* like those in classified catalogues using the traditional schemes, dictionary cataloguers have deliberately collocated 'concretes' rather than disciplines. Cross references serve to guide the reader from a heading to a related heading, e.g. PHYSICS *see also* NUCLEAR PHYSICS, ECONOMICS *see also* FINANCE, MANAGEMENT *see also* THEATRE MANAGEMENT. The student should consult CBI under the traditional disciplines to discover the extent to which related headings are dispersed, and under 'concretes' (e.g. STEEL, UNITED STATES, RAILWAYS) to discover the extent of collocation.

There are thus two basic problems to be considered in the construction of the alphabetico-direct catalogue:
(i) The exact form of the heading;
(ii) The system of cross references.

The Creation of Headings and References through the Use of Classification Schemes

References in the alphabetico-direct catalogue are based on classification. Thus, references from a broad subject to a narrower one (e.g. ENGINEERING *see also* ELECTRICAL ENGINEERING) or from one coordinate subject to another (e.g. NOVEL *see also* SHORT STORY) and so on, involve classification whether overtly recognized as such or not. It may be that such references are not always made with explicit reference to a classification scheme, but then they are likely to be relatively unsystematic – classification is not thereby avoided. And quite apart from the reference structure, the creation of headings is itself classification: to accept as a heading the term BOOKS is to recognize a class, and the allocation of entries to that heading is classification. The question therefore arises: is it possible to make such headings and references by using a classification scheme in a manner analogous to the making of subject index entries? Ranganathan[1] and Coates,[2] among others, have suggested that this is possible – though modifications have to be made.

Suppose that headings and references were to be made for a document on Electrical engineering, classified by DC at 621.3. The chain for this would be:

> 600   Technology
> 620   Engineering
> 621.3   Electrical

Clearly the direct heading (one using the natural form of language) in an alphabetico-direct catalogue would be ELECTRICAL ENGINEERING. This document is also to some extent a document on Engineering and Technology; readers wanting documents on either of these subjects may be interested to know of its existence – just as those wanting documents on Electrical engineering may consult the catalogue under a broader heading like Engineering. Therefore the heading must be connected to related headings by the following references:

> ENGINEERING *see also* ELECTRICAL ENGINEERING
> TECHNOLOGY *see also* ENGINEERING

Note that references are made *one step at a time* – not, for example, from TECHNOLOGY directly to ELECTRICAL ENGINEERING, short-circuiting ENGINEERING. This is the only economic method. To jump steps would result in dozens and even hundreds of references from broad headings – if followed consistently a reference would have to be made from every class heading to every narrower heading; if not followed consistently, the reader would never be quite sure that he had not missed an important heading. This principle has unfortunately been ignored in practice.

Here is another example for a document on Inorganic chemistry, classified at 541:

Chain:

500	Science	
540		Chemistry
541		Inorganic

The direct heading for the document is clearly INORGANIC CHEMISTRY and the following references will be needed:

CHEMISTRY *see also* INORGANIC CHEMISTRY
SCIENCE *see also* CHEMISTRY

Note that references *down* the hierarchy are usual in alphabetico-direct catalogues; upward references (e.g. INORGANIC CHEMISTRY *see also* CHEMISTRY, CHEMISTRY *see also* SCIENCE) are less frequent. The practice stems from Cutter's Rule (187) – see page 216. There is little logical reason for it, and unless upward references are made, no one can claim that a reader can discover documents on all the ramifications of a subject to the same extent as by the classified catalogue.

From these examples it is possible now to frame a preliminary rule on the making of headings and references by chain procedure:

(a) *Construct the main heading by using the last term in the chain, qualifying it by such other terms from the superordinate links in the chain as are necessary* (e.g. in the above examples ENGINEERING and CHEMISTRY are added respectively to ELECTRICAL and INORGANIC to form a comprehensible heading).

(b) *Make reference to it from the next superordinate link in the chain and make reference to that link from its superior, and so on, thus constructing a chain of references modulating one step at a time.*

In this way the catalogue will answer requests for documents on a specific subject and at the same time reveal relationships between subjects; if desired, *upward references* can just as easily be made (CHEMISTRY *see also* SCIENCE).

Other references will also be needed:

(i) From *synonyms*, e.g. VERSE *see* POETRY; WIRELESS *see* RADIO.

(ii) From other *related headings* – in particular closely related coordinate subjects not found in the chain, e.g.:

> DRAWING *see also* PAINTING
> ECONOMICS *see also* COMMERCE
> COUNTERPOINT *see also* FUGUE

(such references are usually made in both directions, e.g. COMMERCE *see also* ECONOMICS, FUGUE *see also* COUNTERPOINT in addition to those above)

In practice *modifications* are necessary if the method is to prove successful, for there are times when the last term in the chain will not be the sought heading for the particular subject. Study the following chain for a document on the Birds of Britain:

> 590   Zoology
> 592/599   Systematic
> 598.2   Birds
> 598.2942   Great Britain

By strict adherence to the method outlined above, the heading would be:

> GREAT BRITAIN: BIRDS

– but this is not the sought order of terms; the term BIRDS is the significant one and the heading should be:

> BIRDS: GREAT BRITAIN

Notice that this problem does not arise in the case of subjects which can be stated in a single term (as CHEMISTRY) but only in the case of headings with several terms – and in particular in compounds where there is no 'natural' phrase in common use to guide us as to the order of terms (as there is in IN-ORGANIC CHEMISTRY). *Somehow modifications have to be made in such cases to bring the significant term into the main filing position.*

Can such modifications be made according to some pre-scribed method or must the determination of the final order of terms be a subjective judgement on the part of the cataloguer? Coates has outlined a possible method. He examines various compound subjects, for example: the manufacture of plastic toys; the design of concrete office blocks; heating in public libraries.

He suggests that the three most important elements in compound subjects can be called: Thing, Material, Action. These are the basic blocks from which compounds are built. In the first example, *toys* are Things, *plastic* is a Material, and *manufacture* is an Action. Each of the main elements of the above subjects can be analysed in this way. Coates suggests that in seeking compound subjects, readers automatically use the *significance order:*

Thing – Material – Action.

Thus the above subjects should be represented in the catalogue as follows if it is to meet the requirements of users:

TOYS : PLASTIC : MANUFACTURE
OFFICE BLOCKS : CONCRETE : DESIGN
PUBLIC LIBRARIES : HEATING

Other examples of headings conforming to this pattern are:

CHILDREN : PSYCHOLOGY
FLOWERS : FERTILIZATION
FACTORIES : INSPECTION
HOUSES : WOODEN : INSURANCE

Thus, whenever chain procedure results in an order which fails to reflect this significance pattern, *the chain must be modified accordingly.* Here are some examples of modification of this kind:

Chain:
669   Metallurgy
669.1   Iron, Steel
669.14   Production

Here the heading PRODUCTION : IRON AND STEEL would be modified to IRON AND STEEL : PRODUCTION in order to bring the Material before the Action and the result is a sought heading.

Chain:

636   Livestock, Domestic animals
636.7   Dogs
636.7082   Breeding

Again BREEDING: DOGS should give way to DOGS: BREEDING (i.e. THING: ACTION).

Further modification would be necessary if the last link in the chain were a Place, Period or Form division or a Form heading. Usually such links would be suppressed and used only as subdivisions in the heading (as in BIRDS: GREAT BRITAIN and SCIENCE: ENCYCLOPAEDIAS). However, an exception might be made for those subjects such as History and certain Social sciences where Place is a primary concept and should be retained as the main filing element, e.g. GREAT BRITAIN: HISTORY; GREAT BRITAIN: TRAVEL AND DESCRIPTION.

Thus chain procedure can be used for the creation of headings and references in the alphabetico-direct catalogue, though some modification will be necessary. The account of these modifications has been simplified here; other problems will undoubtedly arise, in particular when a compound contains two Things, or two Actions or two Materials. In this case an examination of the *relationships* between the terms might furnish a clue; Coates examines some twenty different types of relationship and sets out a relationship table, prescribing various solutions for each type.

It should be noted that this method does not always provide the traditional forms of heading: by and large phrases and sentences are avoided and the heading usually consists of terms separated by colons or some such device. Many cataloguers will object to them on the grounds that headings like TOYS: PLASTIC: MANUFACTURE; OFFICE BLOCKS: CONCRETE: DESIGN, etc., do not represent the 'public's habitual way of looking at things' and that they are not common phrases. But there are *no* common phrases for such subjects, and yet readers request material on such matters. What other solution is possible save a class entry under TOYS or OFFICE BLOCKS leaving the reader to search through all documents on such broad subjects for the specialized one required? The problems that arise from the use of phrases and sentences are insurmountable, and though the results of chain procedure might appear 'odd' it should also be remembered that modification has resulted in the key word being the main filing element. The reader will search for this element in the first place and once in that area of the catalogue should find the specific subject required without difficulty. References will of course be made from other terms in the compounds if not already covered.

The principles outlined by Coates have been put to good effect in *British technology index*, and students should examine this bibliography carefully as an illustration of some of the points made in this chapter.

It might be objected that the successful use of a classification scheme in this way will depend on the quality of the scheme, even when modifications are made. There is obviously a great deal of truth in this. Two basic weaknesses are possible. First, the *terms* used in the schedules may be unsatisfactory for the alphabetical catalogue. Schedule terms are not primarily chosen with indexing in mind and they may constitute an unsatisfactory basis for the job. We have already seen that references from synonyms will have to be made and other refinements may have to be introduced into the vocabulary. Take for example the following sequence from DC (17th ed.):

329	Practical politics
329.02	Political parties
329.022	Nomination of party candidates
329.0221	By convention
329.0222	By caucus
329.0223	By direct primary
329.0224	Boss dictation

Each of these will need modification before use with an alphabetical catalogue. In the first place, even supposing that we accept each division, the terms will have to be converted into a suitable set of nouns to represent the classes:

329	Politics, Practical
329.02	Parties
329.022	Candidates. Nomination

329.0221	Conventions
329.0222	Caucus
329.0223	Primary, Direct
329.0224	Boss direction

Again, a decision will have to be taken as to the acceptable generic level of the vocabulary: are we going to use every term in the schedules (even when revised) as a heading? In the above example we could decide to ignore all steps beyond 329.02, using PARTIES, POLITICAL as the heading for all documents on nomination, conventions, caucus, etc. If we do this, then we shall have to make references from the unused terms, e.g.

NOMINATION: POLITICAL PARTIES *see* PARTIES, POLITICAL

Such a step will avoid undue alphabetical scatter of closely related material. On the other hand, in a library with many documents on these subjects, it will lead to an undifferentiated build-up of entries at the broad heading. To avoid this we might use the divisions as subheadings:

PARTIES, POLITICAL: CANDIDATES: NOMINATION
PARTIES, POLITICAL: CANDIDATES: NOMINATION: CAUCUS
etc.

Apart from the terms themselves, a second disadvantage might arise through weakness in the classification *structure*. Enumerative schemes, as we have seen, very often consist of confused application of several characteristics of division. For example, in DC at 025, Library economy, division is primarily by function, giving rise to:

025.3   Cataloguing
025.4   Classification

Within 025.3 there is a division 025.33, Subject cataloguing. At 029, Indexing and documentation, we find 029.5, Indexing. It is clear that modifications of the kind already discussed will do nothing to provide a set of clear headings and references for a book on subject indexing when the basic structure of the scheme is as unsatisfactory as this. What is needed is wholesale re-casting of the schedules.

Lists of Subject Headings

If we were to conclude that classification schemes, in their present state, were inadequate as a basis for alphabetical subject cataloguing, we might try the alternative of creating a separate list of headings and references for the purpose. What are the essential features of such a list?

(i) It should list all acceptable terms representative of simple concepts.

(ii) It should make references to these terms from those that are unacceptable – e.g. synonyms and specific terms below the agreed generic level (as shown above). These are often referred to as lead-in terms.

(iii) It should reveal through a series of cross references the hierarchical relations between terms – e.g. LITERATURE *see also* POETRY.

(iv) Beyond this standardization of the basic vocabulary and relationships it should provide a citation order for the creation of compound headings consisting of terms from the list strung together. Such a citation order might be based on the standard order of Vickery, the significance order and relationship table of Coates, etc.

A list of subject headings is not, of course, a retreat from classification itself, but merely from strict adherence to any existing scheme. The determination of subject terms, the creation of references, and the analysis of categories and citation orders, are all familiar classificatory procedures. Indeed, an essential step prior to the alphabetical listing of acceptable terms would be the listing of categories of terms, and this would bear close resemblance to the sets compiled in the creation of a faceted classification. Only after such a step can the systematic network of references be made.

Perhaps the best example of a systematic list of this kind is the English Electric *Thesaurofacet*.[3] Terms are first presented in the form of a faceted classification which displays the generic relations between them and from which compound subjects can be synthesized. The thesaurus* part of the scheme acts as

---

* *Thesaurus:* a term commonly used for lists of subject headings, especially those compiled for use in post-coordinate systems and mainly restricted to simple subjects – rather than a mixture of simple and compound subjects.

an index to the classification schedules and displays further relationships between terms in the manner of a subject-heading list. The two parts of the *Thesaurofacet* can thus be regarded as complementary. It can be used in both pre- and post-coordinate systems.

A well-known engineering thesaurus is the *Thesaurus of engineering scientific terms* (Engineers Joint Council). Others are cited at the end of Chapter 11.

Traditionally, however, lists of subject headings are much more confused, enumerating simple and compound subjects in the manner of the older classification schemes, providing few rules for compounding subjects, and elaborating a network of references that all too often display little systematic organization. The most widely used general lists are Sears and Library of Congress.

SEARS LIST OF SUBJECT HEADINGS

First published in 1923, the 9th edition by B. M. Westby appeared in 1965. It is published by H. W. Wilson and modifications and additions in the successive editions are often based on the headings in the Wilson indexes. At the same time, it is founded on the Library of Congress list and avoids conflict with this larger code, its aim being to provide a list more suited to the needs of small and medium-sized libraries. Many specific headings found in Congress are rejected, with consequent recommendations for *class entry*, i.e. entry under broader subjects, e.g.:

> PLANE GEOMETRY *see* GEOMETRY
> PUBLIC LIBRARIES *see* LIBRARIES
> PUNCHED CARD SYSTEMS *see* INFORMATION STORAGE AND
>   RETRIEVAL SYSTEMS

The reason given for this is that smaller libraries will not require such specialized entries – in other words, if the library has only one or two books on Plane geometry, it is better to file entries for them with other books on Geometry, than to make the specific entry and refer: GEOMETRY *see also* PLANE GEOMETRY.

The same argument lies behind the frequent equation of nonsynonymous subjects, e.g. RELIGIOUS HISTORY *see* CHURCH HISTORY; though this is less excusable here for most medium libraries will have books on religious history other than Christian. The great danger behind this argument – as for all advocacy of broad headings or broad classification – is that all libraries, whatever their size, serve readers with specialized interests and their needs are not catered for.

The *scope* of the headings is stated to be 'the most commonly used scientific and technical subjects, names of chemicals and mineral substances . . . Most of the principal languages and literatures are included. Special names of other chemical substances (etc.) . . . should be added as needed.' Form headings are also included, e.g. ESSAYS, ENCYCLOPAEDIAS AND DICTIONARIES, etc.

Certain classes of headings are omitted: persons, places, systematic names in botany and zoology, names of individual battles, birds, fishes, flowers, fruits, treaties, trees, vegetables. Under JESUS CHRIST, SHAKESPEARE, UNITED STATES, CHICAGO, OHIO, are given the subdivisions that are to be used for other headings of the same type.

Headings usually take the *form* of plural nouns, though there are exceptions: the singular noun is occasionally used to differentiate between subject and form heading – SHORT STORY and SHORT STORIES; ESSAY and ESSAYS; and place may be used adjectivally for the arts, literature, religion and philosophy, e.g. ENGLISH LITERATURE; PAINTING, AMERICAN. (The adjectival form precedes subject only in the case of Literature headings.)

Compounds and phrases are included in the list, though further compounding is not recommended except by the use of some common and special subdivisions – ADDRESSES AND ESSAYS, BIBLIOGRAPHY, BIOGRAPHY, HISTORY, etc., which are separately listed at the beginning of the list and can be applied at any point. Period and place can also be added to any heading, though there are restrictions on the latter: in certain subjects place takes preference over subject, e.g. in travel and description, history, and some social sciences such as economic conditions, e.g. GREAT BRITAIN – ECONOMIC CONDITIONS, GREAT BRITAIN – HISTORY, etc.

The headings are essentially direct, but some manipulation

is found to give collocation (i.e. class headings), e.g. EDUCA-TION, ELEMENTARY; EDUCATION, HIGHER; LIBRARIES, CHURCH; LIBRARIES, COUNTY.

The headings have certain limitations:

(i) Arbitrary selection of compounds.

(ii) Inconsistencies in form: LIBRARIES, SPECIAL *but* MUSIC LIBRARIES; EDUCATION, HIGHER *but* PROFESSIONAL EDUCATION, TECHNICAL EDUCATION; EDUCATION OF WOMEN *but* NEGROES – EDUCATION.

(iii) Some headings are vague and without scope notes to define them: ROBBERS AND OUTLAWS; CRIME AND CRIMINALS; ROGUES AND VAGABONDS. (However scope notes are frequently found, e.g. ECONOMIC POLICY: *Use for works on the policy of governments towards economic problems.*)

(iv) The headings use American terminology – not, of course, a fault, but a limitation from the point of view of the British librarian, e.g. RAILROADS.

(v) There are some curiosities, e.g. RADICALS AND RADICALISM *see* ANARCHISM AND ANARCHISTS; RE-FORMERS; REVOLUTIONS. And MARXISM *see* COMMUNISM; SOCIALISM.

References. See and *see also* references are indicated. Under each heading the *see also* references away from that heading are listed first and these should be carefully studied as they might be preferable headings for the document in question. They are followed in turn by the *see* and *see also* references to the heading:

> HEAD
> > *see also* BRAIN; EAR; EYE; FACE; HAIR; NOSE; PHRENOLOGY
> > X   SKULL
> > XX BRAIN
> i.e. if an entry is made under HEAD
> > a *see* reference is required: SKULL *see* HEAD
> and a *see also* reference: BRAIN *see also* HEAD

These references are based on no easily observable principle and have the following *limitations:*

(i) There is little modulation, whole steps of division being short-circuited and an odd assembly of terms being frequently found: e.g.: LAW *see also* JURY, JUDGES. And MANNERS AND

CUSTOMS *see also* CASTE, DUELLING; SOCIAL CLASSES; TRAVEL; WOMAN – HISTORY AND CONDITIONS OF WOMEN. Under EDUCATION we find references to subjects taught, types of school, special methods, etc.

(ii) There are inconsistencies, e.g. under EDUCATION there is a reference to EDUCATION OF WOMEN, but none to EDUCATION OF PRISONERS or NEGROES – EDUCATION though such headings are to be found. Again under DISASTERS there are references to SHIPWRECKS; RAILROADS – ACCIDENTS, but not to AERONAUTICS – ACCIDENTS, though there is such a heading. Such inconsistencies are again the result of insufficient classification, and readers can never be sure that all headings relevant to their enquiries have been found.

In short, the structure, though vaguely based on classification – insofar as references are made from general to special subjects and between coordinates – is rudimentary.

LIBRARY OF CONGRESS. SUBJECT HEADINGS

A system for a particular library, but, like the Library of Congress Classification scheme, it has been widely adopted in other libraries. It follows Cutter's precepts in most important respects, and has headings and references similar to Sears (which is based on it) – it also has similar limitations. It is perhaps preferable to Sears for large general collections. The problems caused by enumeration of stock subjects are larger in scale – see, for example, the references under EDUCATION and INDIANS OF NORTH AMERICA. The layout is like Sears: headings being followed by references using the same symbols to indicate *see* and *see also* (x and xx). Supplements are issued every six months which indicate new headings and revisions.

AUTHORITY FILES

Lists of subject headings and, in fact, all index languages can be regarded as 'authority files'. By ticking off headings and references as used, the cataloguer can see at a glance when cataloguing a document which references need to be made and which are already in the catalogue.

Incidentally, authority files should also be made for all forms of catalogue; a file of cards may be used to record decisions made in author cataloguing, and in making a classified catalogue a file of cards showing what index entries have already been made for each class number will be invaluable, e.g.:

821(DC)
    Poetry: English literature
621.396 (UDC)
    Radio: Engineering
    Wireless *see* Radio

Cutter's Theories

Cutter's *Rules for a dictionary catalog* was first published in 1876, the 4th and last edition appearing in 1904. Though overtaken by more recent theory the rules still form the basis of much current practice, and for this reason – and because it cannot be said that all the problems Cutter deals with have been solved – they are still important.

Choice of heading

As we have seen there are two essential problems in the alphabetico-direct catalogue: choice of heading and the display of relationships between headings. Cutter was interested principally in the first of these and of the twenty-eight rules that are concerned with subject cataloguing, only two deal with the latter.

Cutter's main rule is 161: *enter a book under its specific subject (directly) and not under its containing class.* So far so good. The concept of direct specific entry is fundamental. But Cutter's definition of 'specific subject' is different from ours (page 97). For him it is a subject that can be *named*. In other words it does not include compounds tailor-made to fit the subject of the book. For example, he cites the subject: 'movement of fluid in plants' and states that as there is no recognized term for this subject, the document must be filed under the heading BOTANY (PHYSIOLOGICAL). Thus he dismisses the fundamental problem of compound subjects by ignoring it. No longer are there any great problems of term order in headings.

But note the cost: documents tend increasingly to be about these unnameable subjects, and to record them under their broad containing class – for despite the wording of the rule the definition of specific subject results in this – is of little help to the reader, who will be forced to search through many documents on the general subject in order to discover those on the specific subject sought. This will hardly do in any library today, but the more specialized the stock and the enquiries received the less satisfactory will it be. It is probably true to say that the reliance on nameable subjects as envisaged by this rule has led to the neglect of the overriding problem of term order by succeeding generations of cataloguers. Only comparatively recently, with the development of special libraries and the increasing chaos of catalogues based on this principle, has the problem been given the attention it deserves. In older textbooks on subject cataloguing the idea of nameable subjects is implicit and it is normal practice still in many libraries to avoid compound headings. A glance through the Library of Congress *Books – Subjects* will reveal that rather than formulate compound headings double or treble entry under each of the subjects in the compound or under a class heading is preferred. Thus in the July-Sept., 1963 volume we find:

(i) *The yeomen of Tudor and Stuart England*, by A. J. Schmidt, under:

    (a) COUNTRY LIFE – ENGLAND

    (b) ENGLAND – SOCIAL LIFE AND CUSTOMS

    (c) YEOMANRY (SOCIAL CLASS)

(but *not* GREAT BRITAIN – HISTORY – TUDOR, *or* GREAT BRITAIN – HISTORY – STUART, though these headings are in this volume).

(ii) *Bibliography on meteoric radio wave propagation*, by Meteorological and Geoastrophysical Abstracts, under:

    (a) METEORS – BIBLIOGRAPHY

    (b) RADIO WAVES – BIBLIOGRAPHY.

(iii) *Fatigue of aircraft structures*, by the Symposium on Fatigue of Aircraft Structures, Paris, 1961, under:

    (a) METALS – FATIGUE – CONGRESSES

    (b) AEROPLANES – CONGRESSES

(iv) *A photographic study of the origin and development of fatigue fractures in aircraft structures*, by J. Longson under:

(a) AEROPLANES – MATERIALS

(b) METALS – FATIGUE

Apart from the expense involved in this, as each of these headings is more general than the subject of the book, none is really satisfactory. The person wanting the compound will certainly find it under whatever element in the compound he looks up, but he will still have to search through many general books before coming to it, and the person seeking the general subject only will have to weed out many specialized entries. (Don't confuse this with the entry under two specific headings of a book on two specific subjects, such as Birds and Reptiles.)

Having thus avoided the fundamental problem of compound headings and citation order Cutter is left with the vague and unacceptable notion of nameable subjects. However, he recognizes that this will often demand headings consisting of more than a single term. In fact, in 174 he distinguishes the following forms of heading:

(a) *Single words*, e.g. Botany, Economics;

(b) *A noun preceded by an adjective*, e.g. Ancient history, Capital punishment, Moral philosophy;

(c) *A noun connected to another noun by a preposition*, e.g. Penalty of death, Fertilization of flowers;

(d) *A noun preceded by another noun used as an adjective*, e.g. Death penalty, Flower fertilization;

(e) *A noun connected with another by 'and'*, e.g. Church and State;

(f) *A phrase or a sentence*, e.g. Women as authors, Insects as carriers of plant disease. (Does Cutter here violate his rule for nameable subjects?)

Each of these may have *form and period subdivisions* – though in the case of country he makes a rule that country should never be used as a subdivision (165) – a rule that has been ignored in practice.

Now as these are acceptable 'definite' or 'nameable' subjects the rule should now be: enter under these words as they stand. But it is not so easy: some phrases and combinations of terms do not start with a significant filing word, so 175 makes the following qualification:

'Enter a compound subject-name by its first word, inverting

the phrase only when some other word is decidedly more significant or is often used alone with the same meaning as the whole name.'

Unfortunately, though he tries to pin down the meaning of 'significant' more closely, he fails to do so. He discusses the possibility of making a definite rule by always inverting to bring the noun* to the front but easily proves this not to be the significant term in every case (e.g. Canal, Alimentary). Prevost has much more recently accepted this on the grounds that at least it is a definite rule.

Thus Cutter opens the door to compounds and phrases of all kinds – so long as they are 'nameable' – and also opens the door to inversion, but gives no rule for this. The result is that catalogues based on these rules display a bewildering variety of forms of heading.

We said earlier that the problems arising from the use of phrases and sentences are insurmountable. Having now seen the nature of these we can ask whether the problems are less than those arising from the alternative use of simple terms in prescribed order such as result from the use of modified chain procedure. (It should be remembered that though the compounds may not be the kind of combinations used in real life, the significance order assures us of getting the sought term to the fore.) *The main disadvantages of phrases are:*

(i) *Filing:* where there are phrases, compounds, local divisions, and so on, there may be six or more separated sequences under one term.

(ii) The natural speech compounds have many almost *synonymous forms*, e.g.:

(a) Industrial relations; Capital and labour; Employer – employee relations; Labour relations;

(b) Electric distribution; Electric power transmission; Electric transmission; Electricity – Distribution; Power transmission, Electric; Transmission and power;

(c) Insects – injurious and beneficial; Diseases and pests; Economic entomology; Injurious insects – Pests, etc.

It is doubtful whether the enquirer's choice will correspond

---

* Cutter's attempt to solve cataloguing problems by grammatical methods (see also the forms of heading above) is interesting. Contrast Coates' prescription.

with that of the cataloguer on each occasion. Moreover when phrases like: Industrial relations; Arbitration, Industrial; Collective bargaining; Employers' representation in management; Labour contract; Personnel management; are used – as they frequently are (see Sears' *List of subject headings* for examples) – then the scattering of very closely related material is almost certain. Cutter may well have recognized this but avoided the use of terms separated by colons or dashes because he could find no satisfactory formula for arrangement by significance.

To sum up: Cutter introduced the idea of specific entry but in a limited sense, relying on nameable subjects. He advocated the use of a variety of forms of heading and allowed inversion but without giving a principle for inversion. Phrases present more problems than they solve; if inversion is also used the problems are multiplied. The chances of the reader finding the subject at the first attempt become remote. The only satisfactory solution is analysis into elementary elements and synthesis based on citation order using classification and significance formula.

The rules so far discussed – 161, 174, and 175 – are the main ones. Others should be noted by the student in particular: Language (167), Synonyms (168), Antonyms (171), and Country (164 and 165).

Related subjects (Rules 187 and 188)

Cutter stressed that the catalogue should be *syndetic*, that is, it should include a system of references relating the subjects scattered by the alphabetical arrangement.

Rule 187. Make references from general subjects to their various subordinate subjects and also to coordinate and illustrative subjects. Such references should be made one step at a time, though he qualifies this by saying that intermediate links may be jumped if no material exists on these in the library, thus opening the way for the chaotic reference pattern found in existing lists of subject headings (see below). Clearly this rule implies classification – for how else does one recognize subordinate and coordinate subjects? Cutter recognizes this for in 188 he suggests that a *synoptic table* of subjects could be constructed to present to the reader so that he might discover for himself related headings. He elaborates: 'In a way, this has been done already by the tables and indexes of two well-known schemes of classification – the "Decimal" and the "Expansive" which offer to the persistent enquirer – the only one who would ever use such tables – an opportunity to push his investigations into every ramification of his subject.'

Rule 188. Make references occasionally from specific to general subjects. This is not recommended by Cutter and cataloguers have followed his example and omitted to make references from, say, Physics to Science, though the arguments against this are vague and clearly such references would be most useful if made consistently and one step at a time according to a system of classification. In his examples Cutter goes well outside the normal chain and thus weights his argument by dubious examples.

The Alphabetico-Direct Catalogue: Summary

The use of verbal headings of any kind, under which entries for documents are filed, is immediately intelligible to the reader. If the headings are also direct, shaped according to everyday usage, an even greater advantage is apparently gained, for all information on the required subject will be found immediately by turning to the relevant heading. In practice two factors militate against this immediacy of access:

(i) Documents are published on subjects that cannot be expressed in a single word or accepted phrase;

(ii) Readers require documents on subjects that cannot be expressed in a single word or accepted phrase.

In such cases the chances of the heading chosen by the cataloguer coinciding with the one sought by the reader tend to become remote.

To reduce the effects of these two factors, cataloguers have used the following methods:

(i) *Multiple entry* under each term in the compound so that under whatever term the compound is sought the document will be found (see Library of Congress examples above, page 213). The disadvantages of this procedure are:

(a) it bulks the catalogue and thus reduces ease of use;

(b) it only reveals the precise compound indirectly because

the reader has to search through all documents catalogued under the particular term in order to find the one required;

(c) it does not help the person searching the catalogue not for the compound but for the subject under which the compound has been placed, because he will have to extract the general from the more specialized documents housed there.

(ii) *Entry under a more comprehensive term*, e.g. a document on Syncro-mesh gear-boxes in motor-cars would be entered under MOTOR VEHICLE ENGINEERING. This solution has the disadvantages associated with (i) plus the further disadvantage that it presupposes the reader will be able to name the relevant general head. Nevertheless it is a solution often adopted (see the headings in Sears' *List*) because it results in the collocation of documents on related subjects. In this, however, it has a further disadvantage: it is very difficult to decide when to adopt the broad heading. If number of entries on the subject in the catalogue under that heading is the criterion then the librarian must be prepared to re-catalogue regularly because the situation will change as the library grows.

(iii) Undoubtedly *specific entry* is more satisfactory than either of these solutions; the use of chain procedure and some kind of significance formula as described by Coates, will greatly assist in the production of sought headings. By the avoidance of phrases there is less confusion.

The problems associated with the linear arrangement of compound headings have already been discussed in terms of the classified catalogue (pp. 193ff). No matter how carefully the citation order is chosen some readers will be badly served. For example, the heading:

GEOGRAPHY: EXAMINATIONS

will suit the geography specialist, but not the person wanting information on examinations. For the latter a cross reference might be made:

EXAMINATIONS: GEOGRAPHY *see* GEOGRAPHY: EXAMINATIONS

Even so the search might be extensive if references to several headings had to be followed up.

A solution is full multiple entry of compounds (not to be confused with the partial kind referred to above) – e.g.:

GEOGRAPHY : EXAMINATIONS
and EXAMINATIONS : GEOGRAPHY

Complete *permutation* of terms is clearly too expensive; *rotation* is a possible answer, or *SLIC indexing* – but when compounds are made up of several terms expense will still be a deterrent. The earlier discussion of these matters on pp. 193ff is relevant here. The alternative offered by post-coordinate indexing will be considered in the next chapter.

Although the alphabetico-direct catalogue does not collocate the subjects collocated by the classification scheme, it does result in a degree of grouping – particularly of 'concretes' scattered by the classification. In this sense it offers a useful *supplementary order* to the one on the shelves and provides a useful basis for displays (see Chapter 17). The use of direct entry does, however, scatter much related material through the alphabet and only a good network of references can help the reader to find various aspects of his subject. Such references are also necessary because, as we have seen, readers look up the wrong terms.

References must be based on a classification scheme, modulating one step at a time, otherwise they will be too arbitrary and will multiply to such an extent that their value decreases rapidly (cf. the suggestions that references should be largely cut from the Library of Congress catalogues).

The production of an alphabetical catalogue may involve the cataloguer in additional work as compared with the classified catalogue because the selection of headings from a list is a separate and distinct task. Moreover, maintenance is likely to prove more onerous: changes in terminology are easily accommodated by the provision of new index entries in the classified catalogue, whereas in the alphabetical catalogue a change of subject heading may involve the alteration of many entries. Again, filing can become highly complex (see Chapter 16).

The *printing* of parts of the catalogue is less satisfactorily achieved than in the classified catalogue where homogeneous groups are ready-made.

Clearly catalogues destined for *international use* are more satisfactory if notation is used.

The Dictionary Catalogue

The dictionary catalogue is made up of author, title, subject, and form entries interfiled in one alphabetical sequence. In Chapters 1–4 we considered the problems of author entries, in Chapter 5, title entries, in this chapter we have considered subject entries (alphabetico-direct, the kind used in the dictionary catalogue) and in the next chapter we shall consider form entries. The comments made in these chapters are relevant to the dictionary catalogue – and the sections on the Alphabetico-direct catalogue are concerned with the problems that cause the dictionary cataloguer most trouble (textbooks on the dictionary catalogue invariably deal mainly with subject headings). Students considering the dictionary catalogue should in particular note the conclusions above.

Advocates of the dictionary catalogue claim that it is as simple as ABC – and certainly there is no preliminary psychological barrier against its use (as we are sometimes persuaded exists in the case of the classified catalogue). However, the subject approach has limitations arising from the use of natural language terms in alphabetical sequence, as we have seen. Given a more carefully planned procedure for dealing with subject headings and references, much could certainly be said in favour of the dictionary catalogue, for although it can never be as satisfactory a collocative record as the classified catalogue, it does offer a different subject arrangement from the one found on the shelves: concretes are collocated – and this includes the collocation of material by and about an author. (Note that in libraries which use the dictionary catalogue, classification is a matter of shelf arrangement only; this accounts for the neglect of classification in the USA where the dictionary catalogue predominates.)

Filing problems become increasingly significant as dictionary catalogues grow. The alphabet is not quite so simple as it may seem (see Chapter 16), and when in one sequence are found headings for all types of entry, the user is soon liable to lose his way – for an example, see the entries under, say, UNITED STATES in the five-year cumulation of the *Cumulative book index*, and imagine the difficulties that would arise if all the entries, headings and subheadings were transferred onto cards, where guiding is less easy. The problem of filing becomes particularly acute when one name can be used as author, title, subject (e.g. London, Birmingham, Liverpool, Hull, etc.) and it has been discovered in tests that readers frequently fail to distinguish between subject headings and title headings.

Because of the filing problems, there have been several experiments to divide the dictionary catalogue[4] into two or more sequences. The following methods have been tried:

  (i) Two sequences: (a) Author/Title (b) Subject/Form
 (ii) Three sequences: (a) Author (b) Title (c) Subject/Form
(iii) Three sequences: (a) Name catalogue* (b) Subject catalogue
      (c) Title catalogue

2. The Alphabetico-Classed Catalogue

On page 93 we gave an example of alphabetical headings which attempt to overcome the limitations of collocation in the alphabetico-direct catalogue without resorting to the use of notation in the manner of the classified catalogue. The alphabetico-classed catalogue is a compromise, and its weaknesses have led to its disuse in most libraries; an example can be seen in the *Subject indexes* of the London Library and the British Museum.

Its *limitations* can be summarized as follows (the examples refer to the list given on page 93):

* There are several versions of the *name catalogue*. In general, it contains all entries which have a proper name as the main filing element in the heading. Thus it can be viewed as an author catalogue to which have been added entries for documents about the authors (personal and corporate), as well as all material about other persons, and corporate bodies. Entries under place names (except when the name is the filing word for a corporate body, e.g. London University) are often excluded from the name catalogue and kept in the subject catalogue itself, though this practice is rarely understood by readers.

(i) *It collocates only through subordination* – coordinate classes must be arranged alphabetically according to natural language terms and inevitably related material is separated, e.g. as we have already pointed out, WIRING cannot be placed before INSULATION, MECHANICAL before ELECTRICAL, etc., given the subordination in the example.

(ii) *Moreover the limited collocation is achieved only at a price:*

(a) *Headings no longer reflect natural language order* (contrast the earlier headings for the alphabetico-direct catalogue) and so immediacy, one of the main advantages of using words as headings, is lost. An *index* of all subordinated terms, and *see also* references linking related coordinate subjects such as WIRING and INSULATION, will be needed.

Example of index entry:

SWITCHGEAR *see* ENGINEERING : ELECTRICAL : SWITCHGEAR

Example of reference in main sequence:

ENGINEERING : ELECTRICAL : INSULATION
   see also ENGINEERING : ELECTRICAL : WIRING

(b) *Headings are excessively cumbersome.* The above examples are simple subjects; compound subjects such as 'Wiring methods in prefabricated steel framed houses' would result in grotesque headings.

(iii) *Finally, choice of headings presents grave problems.* The cataloguer must make strict rules on the degree of subordination: e.g. whether all aspects of Engineering are to be subordinated to the heading ENGINEERING as in the example, or whether, in order to reduce the length of headings, ENGINEERING is to be used only for Engineering in general, a *see also* reference then being made to link this with the various sequences starting at ELECTRICAL ENGINEERING, MECHANICAL ENGINEERING, etc. Again, should a subheading EQUIPMENT be placed between ENGINEERING : ELECTRICAL and SWITCHGEAR? As we have stressed, a system of classification is vital.

READINGS

1. RANGANATHAN, S. R. *Dictionary catalogue code.* 2nd ed., Madras Library Association, 1952. Chapter 2.

2. COATES, E. J. *Subject catalogues: headings and structure.* London, Library Association, 1960. This book contains a basic examination of the alphabetico-direct catalogue. It is essential reading for the student.
3. AITCHISON, J. *ed. Thesaurofacet: a thesaurus and faceted classification for electrical engineering and related subjects.* Whetstone, Leics., English Electric Co. Ltd., 1969.
4. 'The divided dictionary catalog: a summary of the literature'. *Library Resources and Technical Services,* 2 (4), Fall 1958, 238–52.

COATES, E. J. 'The use of BNB in dictionary cataloguing'. *Library Association Record,* 59 (6), June 1957.

CUTTER, C. A. *Rules for a dictionary catalog.* Washington, GPO, 4th ed., 1904.

FOSKETT, A. C. *The subject approach to information.* London, Bingley, 1969. Much of Part I is of particular relevance to this chapter.

HAYKIN, D. J. *Subject headings: a practical guide.* Washington, GPO, 1951.

MOSTECKY, V. 'Study of the see also reference structure in relation to the subject of international law'. *American Documentation,* 7 (4), 1956, 294–314. Specialized but with general implications.

SEARS' *List of subject headings.* 9th ed., by B. M. WESTBY. New York, Wilson, 1965. pp. 13–29.

Chapter 11
Post-coordinate Systems

Traditional systems for the retrieval of documents on a subject basis – those using classification schemes, the classified catalogue and the alphabetical catalogue as described in this book – can be categorized as *pre-coordinate*. That is, they coordinate terms to form compound classes at the *indexing* stage. The subject heading is typically a summarization expressing the overall subject of the document, the terms comprising the summarization (where more than one is used) being strung together in a fixed order. Thus a document on school buildings will be assigned a heading in which the basic elements are coordinated: SCHOOLS – BUILDINGS or 371.62 (i.e. Education – Schools – Physical plant – Buildings). As in such circumstances a combination of elements can be placed in only one order in a single heading, index entries and references are used to assist the reader in locating the document when other elements in the compound are sought first. Clearly the order of elements is very important and, as we have seen, much attention has been directed to the problems of term order in the alphabetical catalogue and combination order of facets in the classified catalogue. Similarly, reference structure and indexing have also been the subject of much analysis and discussion.

However carefully we choose the combination order of elements, however methodically we make our indexes and references, the fact remains that our catalogue will serve some approaches better than others. Thus in the above example, the person interested in Schools is better served than the person interested in Buildings, for the latter will not find an entry for this document along with other entries on Buildings, and he must follow up references and index entries if he is to discover it. His search may well be extensive if he is interested in all aspects of Buildings, regardless of function, for entries will be scattered accordingly.

If we can say that one approach to a compound subject is primary, and all other approaches unlikely to be required, then this may be no great handicap to the vast majority of readers. If, however, many different approaches are likely and none has distinct priority – as frequently happens – then what is to be done to save the readers' time?

One solution is the *multiple entry of compounds*. (This is to be distinguished from the multiple entry of a compound under a series of broader headings – as practised, for example, in the L c *Catalog: Books: Subjects* and illustrated on p. 213.) There are several variants:

(i) *Permutation*. This is a possibility rarely, if ever, adopted because the total number of permutations of even a few coordinated terms soon reaches astronomical proportions.

(ii) *Rotation*. We have already seen that this is a common practice in the classified file in libraries using UDC (see p. 195). It may also be used in alphabetical catalogues (see p. 219). It allows the filing of entries having compound headings at each concept comprising the compound – either by bringing successively each term into the lead position, or by indicating (e.g. by underlining) the respective filing terms whilst retaining the original citation order. As noted earlier, no system of rotation can bring into juxtaposition each term in a compound consisting of three or more elements, and in a complex file the reader may still be forced into large-scale sequential scanning to coordinate the concepts in which he is interested. It is clear that rotation will increase the size of a file by a factor equal to the average number of elements in the compounds within it. An example of rotation can be found in the list of titles appended to the *London Education Classification*.

(iii) *Selective listing in combination*. A third system, put forward as an alternative to permutation, is that devised by Sharp, based on the mathematics of combination (SLIC). Though we noted this in the section on the subject index to the classified catalogue, it is obviously a principle that can be applied in any subject file. Again, it results in expense that would be considered excessive by most compilers of conventional manual catalogues.

Clearly there is no completely satisfactory remedy to the problem of providing multiple access to compounds in precoordinate systems. Post-coordinate systems tackle the problem

8

by shifting the process of coordination to the *search stage*. Characteristically the indexer deals with simple terms, e.g. SCHOOLS *and* BUILDINGS (rather than SCHOOL BUILDINGS): it is the user (or someone working on his behalf) who strings the terms together to create the compound subjects on which he wants material. Thus a person wanting materials on School buildings would search the file for those documents to which each concept had been assigned, disregarding those labelled with only one – or neither.

One method of achieving this would be to create a catalogue composed of a series of entries headed by simple concepts and listing under each the documents in the store relevant to that concept, as illustrated below:

SCHOOLS

0	1	2	3	4	5	6	7	8	9
20	11	142	73	194	95	86	7	88	19
110	31	262	113	204	105	116	97	118	119
	51	282	223	314	215	126	117	268	179
	121		293		275	236	237		219
	201					316	257		
	211								
	301								

BUILDINGS

0	1	2	3	4	5	6	7	8	9
30	21	142	53	64	75	66	17	88	39
110	41	272	123	74	115	76	107	128	129
140	51	302	243	204	205	106	157	158	179
	91	312	293	264	275	146	207	208	229
	291		303			226	317	298	309

Here the numbers are accession numbers representing documents. They are 'posted' in columns according to their final digits to facilitate searching. A reader seeking information on the compound School buildings would extract the two cards headed SCHOOLS and BUILDINGS and compare the items listed under each. Those common to both (i.e. 110, 51, 142, 293, 204, 275, 88, and 179) would be concerned with the topic in question.

The point is that such a file would satisfy the user equally well whether his primary approach were Buildings or Schools: as there is no pre-coordination of terms and thus no citation order for compounds, no approach is paramount. At any single entry the reader will find all material on the subject; beyond this he can reduce the scope by comparing additional entries to retrieve only the particular aspect he is interested in. Thus to the entry for SCHOOLS others headed SECONDARY, MATHEMATICS, and VISUAL AIDS could be added to search for common numbers representing documents on the compound subject, the use of visual aids in teaching mathematics in secondary schools. But, as we shall see, things are not in practice quite so simple as this.

This is the essence of such devices as *Uniterm*, developed in the United States by Mortimer Taube. *Optical coincidence* (*peek-a-boo*) devices, such as that developed in Britain by W. E. Batten (*Batten cards*), are closely related. In these each card is cross-ruled to provide several thousand individually numbered positions. Accession numbers are posted, not by writing the number on the card, but by punching a hole in the relevant numbered position. Entries are compared by holding the selected cards – representing the various elements of the sought compound – before a light source; the light will shine through where each card is punched in the same position. The numbers of these positions therefore represent the accession numbers of documents having information on each element in the compound represented by the particular selection of cards.

Such devices have immediately obvious practical limitations. A further step is required to convert the accession numbers into documents – though if used for searching offprints, pamphlets, and similar file collections (as is often the case), this step can be avoided by keeping the documents themselves in accession number order. There is also a limit to the number of documents that can be entered on one card. (Some optical coincidence cards allow 10,000 different positions for punching.) Of course, cards can be added to supplement those that become full but this increases the difficulty of the search because of the increase in the number of cards that have to be matched. It is generally accepted that as the collection of documents grows beyond 8,000, so the efficiency of the device is reduced. Some libraries have partly overcome this by starting new files at regular intervals (say, yearly). This again extends the search time but may not be a decisive factor where the stock soon dates, rendering older catalogues largely unused. For these reasons, and because they are less satisfactory tools than conventional catalogues for the general public, they are used mainly with highly specialized collections of limited size serving a restricted clientele.

Edge-notched cards may also be used in post-coordinate systems. There is, however, a difference in structure here; any single card will usually carry bibliographical information for only one document, each concept relevant to the subject matter of that document being represented in code form by a series of notches punched out from holes along the margin. For example, entries for documents on nineteenth-century German poetry might appear thus (the detail is deliberately over-simplified to illustrate the principle):

The first position is the code for Poetry, the eighth for Nineteenth century, and the twelfth for German. To find what the library has on a given topic, the searcher must first ascertain which code position represents that topic. He must then extract the cards which have that position notched to the edge. He can do this by a process of *needling*. A needle is put through the pack of cards (which may be kept in random order) at the relevant hole position. As the cards are raised on the needle, those which are notched to the edge at that position will drop away from the pack. If the compound Nineteenth-century German literature were required, three needles put through the pack at the positions noted above would result in the dropping of cards punched for those three concepts.

As all four edges of the cards are likely to be used, needling may have to be done up to four times, each successive operation being performed on the cards dropped by the previous one. For example, if the three concepts in our example were distributed along three edges of the cards concerned, then documents on Poetry would be dropped if the pack were needled at the appropriate place along one edge; if the dropped cards were then needled at the appropriate position along a second edge, cards on Nineteenth-century poetry would be dropped; and if documents on Nineteenth-century German poetry were required, then *these* cards must be needled at the code position representing German along the third edge.

As much information may be punched into the card as space allows. Though there are limits to the space available for punching, much more information can be coded than is suggested by the simplified diagram given above. Students should study the readings given at the end of this chapter as a necessary corrective to the dangers inherent in the extreme simplification here.

Besides the general advantages associated with post-coordinate systems, punched cards have several advantages over the other devices noted so far. In particular, cards can be kept in random order, and full bibliographical descriptions are available without recourse to an accession file. But again, there are limits to the size of catalogue that can be handled in this way, and their use is largely confined to special collections.

With the use of data-processing machines and computers many of the practical disadvantages of post-coordinate systems disappear; large files can be searched, and searched rapidly – though the present limited accessibility of machines remains a problem. Body-punched cards, paper tape, magnetic tape, magnetic discs, microfilm, etc., can be used to store information, be it bibliographical entries, abstracts, or full texts. The matching of demands and documents is achieved through the intermediary of a coded language capable of expressing the concepts inherent in both. The demands may be for a total (or partial) print-out of the store to produce published catalogues, or for the extraction of bibliographical data in response to requests.

Although machines, in common with other post-coordinate devices, can be searched directly on behalf of a reader, providing multiple access to compound subjects and so satisfying all approaches equally well, it should be remembered that in the case of printed catalogues produced by computers, etc., the economics of permuted entries apply, and the machine will usually be programmed to a specific citation order. An alternative that is being increasingly adopted is the production of numbered lists of items arranged by author, title, or broad subject groups, with indexes made up of simple subjects under

2.0 INSTITUTIONAL INDEX
(TYPICAL ROLE)
This category indicates major social institutions and structures
that are subjects of the research,
or the characteristic role that an
individual subject or group of subjects of study take.

2.1 Family. 16, 25, 64, 80, 88, ˙441,
502, 568, 587, 684, 828, 946, 1045,
1047, 1063, 1223, 1298, 1308, 1407,
1485, 1494, 1522, 1567, 1636, 1909,
1913, 1932, 2031, 2062, 2125, 2193,
2256, 2295, 2311, 2424, 2630, 2671,
2698, 2699, 2726, 2864, 2865, 2982,
3004, 3035, 3151, 3158, 3174, 3244,
3343, 3471, 3478, 3490, 3502, 3584,
3649, 3786, 3791, 3931, 4190, 4286,
4303, 4310, 4327, 4524, 4529, 4530,
4543, 4581, 4582, 5155, 5263, 5393,
5405, 5566, 5630, 5654, 5781, 5834,
5986, 6096, 6279, 6380, 6393, 6401,
6438, 6512, 6595, 6651

2.2 Kinship (except nuclear family),
clan, tribe (a group comprising a
set of families, clans, or generations tied together by myths of
blood community and common origin). 361, 889, 1134, 1743, 2427,
2672, 2673, 3966, 4007, 4174, 5639,
6229, 6351, 6422

2.3 Neighborhood: a group whose relations are based upon geographical
propinquity in a larger urban setting. 98, 99, 355, 787, 1035, 1542,
1796, 2006, 2007, 2079, 2526, 3664,
4148, 4771, 6608

2.4 Acquaintance group: voluntary
group based on face-to-face association. 92, 594, 713, 1184, 1542,
1679, 1696, 1759, 2745, 2976, 3719,
4052, 4560, 4561, 5188, 5374, 5656,
5699, 6032, 6119, 6128, 6496, 6502,
6619, 6648

2.5 Small company: 50 employees or
less, 90, 192, 291, 856, 1139, 1193,
1544, 3529, 4214, 4465, 4828, 5402,
5510, 5597, 6484, 6639

2.6 Middle-sized or large company:
more than 50 employees. 293, 393,
401, 402, 667, 707, 730, 1491, 1560,
1603, 1606, 1608, 1654, 1751, 1780,
1790, 1859, 1870, 2108, 2538, 2686,
3659, 3934, 3935, 4023, 4236, 4331,
4337, 4705, 4716, 4806, 4917, 4953,
5037, 5093, 5349, 5442, 5648, 5854,
5921, 6057, 6200, 6415, 6416, 6477

2.7 Industry: a grouping of all companies engaged in a basically similar kind of business. 12, 14, 63,

2. An extract from *ABS guide to recent publications in the social and behavioral sciences*[1].

each of which are 'posted' the numbers of the documents to
which that 'descriptor' has been assigned. An example of this
type of bibliography is the *ABS Guide*[1] (see figure 2). They are,
in general, inadequate retrieval tools; though easily (all too
easily) produced, the use of a post-coordinate style of indexing
vocabulary without corresponding means of coordination on
the part of the searcher prevents any convenient access to
compound subjects. The *dual dictionary* (see, for example the
ERIC *Catalog of selected documents on the disadvantaged: subject
index*[2]), a computer-produced bibliography consisting of a
numbered list of items with a duplicated index in book form
allowing the matching, page by page, of document numbers
printed out under sets of simple terms (cf. such devices as
Uniterm), is an attempt to overcome this defect (see figure 3).

ABILITY

0	1	2	3	4	5	6	7	8	9
1180		1122	1883	(1234)	1285	2146	1177	1168	1839
1540		1192	1913	1404	1425		1307	1198	(2678)
2340		1522	2563	1574	2555		1637	2008	
		1702	2573	(2454)					
		2372	(2733)						

ABILITY GROUPING

0	1	2	3	4	5	6	7	8	9
1870	1111	1202	1883	1214	1175	1886	1177	1198	
2320	2101	1372		2304	1215		1207		
		1452			1315		1227		
		1692							
		1882							

ABILITY IDENTIFICATION

0	1	2	3	4	5	6	7	8	9
1760	1621	1222	1193	1344	1215	1226	1757	1308	1199
		1752	1233		1225		1967	1648	1209
		1303			1885		2177	1758	1309

ABLE STUDENTS

0	1	2	3	4	5	6	7	8	9
				1164	2135		1287		
				1204					
				2184					

ACADEMIC ABILITY

0	1	2	3	4	5	6	7	8	9
	1621		1423	1114		1496	2547		
	2271					2376			
	2561								

ACADEMIC ACHIEVEMENT

0	1	2	3	4	5	6	7	8	9
1130	1241	2042	1883	1194	1235	1216	1587	1578	1369
1590	1611	2552	2623	1764	1275	1486	2257	2628	1459
1621	2562			2054	1615	1616	2377		2229
1921				2484		1966			2429
2101						2146			2569
2561									

EVALUATION

0	1	2	3	4	5	6	7	8	9
1710	1111	1002	1453	(1234)	1105	1056	1217	1208	1599
1860	1171	1182	1563	1274	1165	1146	1347	1318	2299
1900	1711	1472	2533	1384	1445	1166	1457	2388	2579
2290	1841	1542	2593	1774	1455	1196	1667	2598	(2679)
2490	1861	1842	(2703)	1784	1595	1886	1677	2708	
2730	2591	1862	(2733)	1864	1845	2496	1897		
		2512		1874	2195		2467		
		2592		1884	2275		2477		
				2104	2345				
				2344	2435				
				(2454)	2695				
				2604					
				2674					
				2714					

EVALUATION METHODS

0	1	2	3	4	5	6	7	8	9
1100						1146			

EVALUATION NEEDS

0	1	2	3	4	5	6	7	8	9
2140									

EVALUATION TECHNIQUES

0	1	2	3	4	5	6	7	8	9
	1191	1002		1004	1015	1796	1787		1169
									1179
									1869
									2459

EVENING COUNSELING PROGRAMS

0	1	2	3	4	5	6	7	8	9
			1453				1457		

EVENING PROGRAMS

0	1	2	3	4	5	6	7	8	9
1050	1871								

EXCEPTIONAL (ATYPICAL)

0	1	2	3	4	5	6	7	8	9
	1242			1265					
				2065					

3. Two pages from the parallel sequences of a dual dictionary. The numbers ringed refer to documents having in common the two concepts of Ability and Evaluation.

So far in this chapter we have done no more than examine a few examples of post-coordinate devices, pointing to certain practical difficulties. The whole account has avoided the real problems that arise from the very idea of post-coordination. It has been assumed that the mere compounding of simple terms, assigned by the indexer without regard for such compounding, will result in the satisfactory retrieval of documents. This assumption – whether we are thinking in terms of manual or machine systems – is clearly open to question. Unless we devise further controls it is likely that we shall retrieve both too many documents and too few.

Too many documents. Terms which summarize the subject content of a document or a reader's request are always terms in a relationship. Change the relationship and you change the subject; the Philosophy of history is not the History of philosophy. The mere compounding of the simple index terms Philosophy and History will retrieve documents on both subjects. To give a more complex example: the conjunction of Teaching, English, Nineteenth century, and History will result in the retrieval of documents on (a) History of English teaching in the nineteenth century; (b) History of the teaching of English in the nineteenth century; (c) Teaching of English history in the nineteenth century; and (d) Teaching of nine-teenth-century English history. Furthermore, every one of these documents will also be retrieved by someone wanting materials on the Teaching of English, the History of teaching, etc., or simply on Teaching or History. Similarly, a document on the Development of child psychology and its effects on teaching will be retrieved when what is wanted is information on the Psychology of teaching. The confusion is multiplied when exhaustive indexing is practised, i.e. when terms are assigned to documents not merely on the basis of a summarization of its content but according to key concepts and terms in the text.

Most of these examples illustrate how unwanted items may result from *false coordination*. (Such items are often referred to as *false drops*.) To correct this we need a way of limiting the extent of retrieval – a means of allowing the recall of items on the Philosophy of history *but not* the History of philosophy. It could be argued, however, that the retrieval of documents (a)–(d) in response to a request for information on Teaching is justified insofar as all of them are on various aspects of teaching. True, but there still remains the problem of differentiating between these subjects – and between these and documents on teaching in general. If we aim to give the reader systematically organized information on documents something more than mere co-ordination is required.

Too few documents. Apart from compound relationships there are generic relations between concepts. A document on Teaching is a document on Education; one on the Teaching of English is related to one on the Teaching of history, both belonging to the Curriculum facet. A retrieval system which consists solely of simple terms fails to provide the searcher with what is often a major clue in the discovery of information. Moreover, it is a common fact that users searching for specific subjects frequently fail to identify the correct specific terms –

and here the display of generic relationships is an essential aid. From this point of view it can be seen that the uncontrolled post-coordinate index is likely to yield only a fraction of the relevant materials.

However, it should be borne in mind that generic relationships can be 'programmed' into the search or 'output' stage through the use of the vocabulary of the system – e.g. the thesaurus. Thus, even when the relationships between Education, Teaching, and History teaching are absent from the device itself, they can be discovered by the user through the intermediary of the thesaurus.

There is another reason why comprehensiveness is likely to suffer. Without controls related materials will be scattered under synonyms or partially synonymous terms.

It is through the expression of relationships – by means of structure, citation order, and relationship symbols – that *pre-coordinate* systems largely avoid the kinds of problems outlined above.

Although in the early days of post-coordinate indexing there was a marked reluctance to introduce controls, because it was naively thought that an untrained clerk could cope with the job of making entries under simple terms, over the years much attention has been devoted to this question and the following forms of control have been developed:

(i) *Pre-coordination.* A certain measure of pre-coordination is common, especially for compounds frequently required. For example, in the *Thesaurus of metallurgical terms*[3] we find: High frequency induction furnaces, High speed steel tools, High temperature tests, etc.

(ii) *Links.* Links are a common form of 'interlocking' device: the use of a code symbol to indicate an association between two concepts and so reduce false coordination. They are commonly used when indexing exhaustively multi-topical documents. Suppose, to take a simple example, that an article on teaching in primary schools made special reference to the language of children. The terms Teaching, Primary schools, Language, and Children may be assigned to it in the index. To prevent the retrieval of this article in response to any enquiry on Language teaching, we might attach a common symbol (A) to the terms Language and Children, and another (B) to

Teaching and Primary schools. In this way false coordination of Language and Teaching will be avoided.

(iii) *Role indicators*. Links will obviously not enable us to distinguish between the Philosophy of history and the History of philosophy. Here it is not a matter of indicating that the terms are associated; only by showing the *nature* of the association can we avoid confusion. This is the function of the 'role indicator' – a symbol which is added to a term to make explicit its role in the compound relationship. If, for example, we had a symbol, e.g. (B), to indicate 'approach' or 'point of view', then a search for the Philosophy of history would entail the coordination of Philosophy (B) and History; conversely, History (B) and Philosophy would be the relevant terms to search for the History of philosophy. Again, the terms Violence and Children may be used in indexing documents on Violence committed by children and Violence to children: only by the use of indicators meaning, respectively, 'agent', or 'source of action', and 'patient', or 'subject of action', shall we be able to distinguish between the two categories.

Roles used in the *Chemical engineering thesaurus*[4] are as follows:

A Input to a chemical reaction, etc.
B Product
C Waste, contaminant, impurity
D Special agent, catalyst, accelerator, stabilizer
E Solvent, media, environment, support
F Independent variable studied for how it is affected
G Dependent variable studied for how it is affected
H Active concept, subject of study
I Passive concept, object of study
J Device, material, or method for accomplishment
—Modifiers, adjectives, proper names, companies, persons

The use of roles has been the subject of investigation and controversy in recent years. When used with exhaustive indexing (which is common) there are practical difficulties because in any one document a concept may be treated from the point of view of a number of roles. In such cases to indicate all of them is tantamount to indexing none – and the latter is obviously the easier course.

(iv) *Weights*. This is a form of control of a rather different character from those listed above. As exhaustive indexing is common in post-coordinate systems, it being not unusual to assign twenty or thirty terms, or even more, to a document, the degree of recall in the system is likely to be high. However, documents retrieved in response to any particular term are unlikely to have an equivalent degree of significance in relation to the concept concerned; in some documents it will be central, in others marginal. *Weights* are symbols – often numbers – added to terms by the indexer to indicate their relative importance in the document. They enable the searcher to select first the documents with the required weighting of terms; only if these do not satisfy him need he examine others on the subject.

Pre-coordination, links, role indicators, and weights are devices which enable us to reduce the number of unwanted items retrieved in response to requests. If we are to go beyond this and create facilities for generic searching, some system of cross referencing or, in the case of machine systems, hierarchical coding, may be necessary. This – and synonym control – can only be achieved through a list of terms in which such relationships are shown. Such a list is often referred to as a *thesaurus*. Those familiar with conventional lists of subject headings will have no difficulty in finding their way around a typical thesaurus. One is tempted to say that the enthusiasts for post-coordinate systems, being forced to admit reluctantly that control was necessary, couldn't bear to use the old-fashioned term 'list of subject headings'. At any rate, a thesaurus in this context is a list of simple (or partially pre-coordinated) terms, often referred to as *descriptors*, alphabetically arranged and indicating unused, broader, narrower, and related terms. They differ from other lists of subject headings in being confined largely to simple terms suitable for post-coordinate systems, and in being (though not in all cases) rather more systematically compiled. In the example reproduced here (see figure 4), the meaning of the symbols is as follows:

UF Use for (synonyms, etc.)
NT Narrower terms
BT Broader terms
RT Related terms

These symbols are used in most thesauri.

The thesaurus is a tool for use by the indexer when selecting

```
H—IRON PROCESS·                    HOLDING FURNACES                    ORIFICES
   BT   FLUIDIZED BED REDUCTION       UF   FOREHEARTHS                    OUTLETS
        REDUCTION (CHEMICAL)               SETTLERS (FOREHEARTHS)         PINHOLES
        THERMAL REDUCTION             BT   FURNACES                       POROUS MATERIALS
                                           METALLURGICAL FURNACES         VOIDS
HOBBING                               RT   BATCH-TYPE FURNACES
   USE GEAR HOBBING                        BLAST FURNACES              HOLES (ELECTRON DEFICIENCIES)
                                           CUPOLAS                        RT   ACCEPTORS (ELECTRONIC)
HOBBING CUTTERS                            ELECTRIC FURNACES                   BAND THEORY
   UF   HOBS                               GAS-FIRED FURNACES                  CARRIER LIFE
   BT   CUTTING TOOLS                      HEATING FURNACES                    CONDUCTION BAND
        MILLING CUTTERS                    OIL-FIRED FURNACES                  CURRENT CARRIERS
   RT   GEAR CUTTERS                       OPEN FLAME FURNACES                 ELECTRICITY
                                                                              ELECTRONS
HOBS                               HOLE CONDUCTIVITY                          ENERGY GAP
   USE HOBBING CUTTERS                UF   P CONDUCTIVITY                      HOLE CONDUCTIVITY
                                      BT   CONDUCTIVITY                       HOLE DENSITY
HOISTING                                   ELECTRICAL PROPERTIES              HOLE MOBILITY
   UF   LIFTING                            PHYSICAL PROPERTIES                HOLE TRAPS
   RT   BULK TRANSPORTERS                  RESISTIVITY
        CRANES                        RT   ELECTRON CONDUCTIVITY         HOLE SIZE
        LOADING                            HOLE DENSITY                     UF   BORE
        MATERIALS HANDLING                 HOLE MOBILITY                     RT   CALIBRATION
        SHAFTS (EXCAVATIONS)               HOLES (ELECTRON DEFICIENCIES)          DIAMETERS
        SKIPS
                                   HOLE DENSITY                         HOLE TRAPS
HOISTS                                BT   CARRIER DENSITY                 RT   CARRIER DENSITY
     USE SKIPS                             ELECTRICAL PROPERTIES               CARRIER LIFE
                                           PHYSICAL PROPERTIES                 HOLE DENSITY
HOLDERS                               RT   ELECTRON DENSITY                    HOLES (ELECTRON DEFICIENCIES)
   (EXCLUDES FLAME HOLDERS)                HOLE CONDUCTIVITY                   RESISTIVITY
   NT   TOOL HOLDERS                       HOLE MOBILITY
   RT   ANCHORS                            HOLES (ELECTRON DEFICIENCIES) HOLMIUM
        BANDS                              HOLE TRAPS                       BT   CHEMICAL ELEMENTS
        BOLTS                                                                   METALS
        BRACKETS                     HOLE MOBILITY                              NONFERROUS METALS
        CHUCKS                          BT   CARRIER MOBILITY                   RARE EARTH METALS
        CLAMPS                              ELECTRICAL PROPERTIES
        CLEVIS                         RT   ELECTRON MOBILITY            HOLMIUM COMPOUNDS
        CLIPS                              HOLE CONDUCTIVITY                BT   METALLIC COMPOUNDS
        FASTENERS                          HOLE DENSITY                        METALLOID COMPOUNDS
        JIGS                               HOLES  ELECTRON DEFICIENCIES        RARE EARTH COMPOUNDS
        NAILS
        NUTS (FASTENERS)             HOLES                              HOMOGENEITY
        PINS                            UF   BORES                         RT   CLUSTERING
        RETAINING RINGS                    CAVITIES                            COEFFICIENT OF VARIATION
        RIVETS                             PERFORATIONS                        DISPERSION
        SPIKES                        RT   LASTING DEFECTS                     HETEROGENEITY
        SPLINES                            CRACKS                              HETEROGENEOUS STRUCTURE
        STAPLES                            DEFECTS                             HOMOGENEOUS STRUCTURE
        STRAPS                             DIE CAVITIES                        SAMPLING
        STUDS                              HOLES (ELECTRON DEFICIENCIES)       STANDARD DEVIATION
                                           HOLE SIZE                           STANDARD ERROR
HOLDING (RETAINING)                        LEAKAGE                             VARIABILITY
   USE RETAINING                           OPENINGS                            VARIANCE
```

4. An extract from *ASM Thesaurus of metallurgical terms*[3].

acceptable terms. He may also use it to create a network of
references or a system of coding expressive of generic relationships. But perhaps its main use, as already indicated, is as an
aid in searching. An unusual example, and one well worth
study, is the English Electric *Thesaurofacet* already referred to;
it is a two-part system consisting of a classification scheme for
electrical engineering and a thesaurus, the two complementing
each other in the display of terms and relationships. A thesaurus
is a reminder that in post-coordinate systems no less than in
pre-coordinate, classification is fundamental. Not only is it
essential to the delineation of synonyms and generic relationships of the kind illustrated: it is the basis for the analysis of
roles and links and decisions as to the extent and nature of
pre-coordination. Beyond this, it need hardly be said, the adop-

tion of a post-coordinate system in no way affects the need for classification in both the conceptual analysis of the subject content of documents and the requests of readers, and the translation of these concepts into the terms used in the system.

From this brief survey of post-coordinate systems it can be seen that while they provide an alternative means of tackling the problems arising from pre-coordination, they too have their weaknesses and many of the difficulties remain unresolved. The early enthusiasm with which they were advocated has been tempered in the light of experience.

Having examined various forms of pre- and post-coordinate systems, we can now classify them as follows:

A. Systems distinguished according to coordination stage.
   1. Those in which co-ordination occurs at the input or indexing stage: *Pre-coordinate systems*. (Summarization is the norm.)
   2. Those in which coordination occurs at the output or search stage: *Post-coordinate systems*. (Exhaustive indexing is the norm.)
B. Systems distinguished according to search procedure.
   1. Those in which terms (simple or compound) are searched for entries (items), e.g. pre-coordinate devices, *Uniterm*, optical incidence devices: *Term entry systems*.
   2. Those in which entries (items) are searched for those having relevant terms assigned to them, e.g. edge-notched card systems: *Item entry systems*.
   (Machine systems can fall into either category.)

READINGS

1. *ABS guide to recent publications in the social and behavioral sciences.* New York, American Behavioral Scientist, 1965.
2. EDUCATIONAL RESEARCH INFORMATION CENTER. *Catalog of selected documents on the disadvantaged: subject index.* Washington, GPO, 1966.
3. AMERICAN SOCIETY FOR METALS. *Thesaurus of metallurgical terms.* Metals Park, Ohio, ASM, 1968.

4. AMERICAN INSTITUTE OF CHEMICAL ENGINEERS. *Chemical engineering thesaurus.* New York, AICE, 1961.

The student will find the following books valuable not only in relation to this chapter, but to the whole of Part Two of this book:

LANCASTER, F. W. *Information retrieval systems: characteristics, testing and evaluation.* New York, Wiley, 1968.

SHARP, J. S. *Some fundamentals of information retrieval.* London, Deutsch, 1965.

VICKERY, B. C. *On retrieval system theory.* 2nd ed. London, Butterworths, 1965.

VICKERY, B. C. *Techniques of information retrieval.* London, Butterworths, 1970.

Students requiring further information on the mechanized retrieval systems may find the following useful (though this is not to say that they deal only with the mechanics):

ARTANDI. S. *An introduction to computers in information science.* Metuchen, N. J., Scarecrow Press, 1968.

BOURNE, C. P. *Methods of information handling.* New York, Wiley, 1966.

HARRISON, J. *and* LASLETT, P. *The Brasenose conference on the automation of libraries.* London, Mansell, 1967.

KENT, A. *Textbook of mechanized information retrieval.* 2nd ed. New York, Wiley, 1966.

KIMBER, R. T. *Automation in libraries.* Oxford, Pergamon Press, 1968.

MARKUSON, B. E. *ed. Libraries and automation.* Washington, Library of Congress, 1964.

See also the readings cited in Chapter 12.

Chapter 12
Index Languages

Any retrieval system consists of a set of devices for ensuring that demands and documents can be effectively matched. A subject system provides for such matching in terms of the subjects expressed in demands and documents; somehow we have to ensure that when a reader makes a request for, say, material on Anglo-Saxon architecture, then the documents containing relevant information are retrieved.

One matching device is shelf arrangement, a device which, in a library of any size will require a classification scheme complete with a set of notational symbols representing in a convenient shorthand form classes in the scheme and allowing a preferred order to be maintained. Whether in conventional or other form, the catalogue is another device. We have seen that two basic forms of organization are possible; entries representing documents – sometimes referred to as 'surrogates' – can be arranged according to their subjects by means of terms or class symbols, and so retrieved in response to demands for documents on these subjects (term entry systems); alternatively, surrogates can be coded with the subjects relevant to each and the whole file searched for items matching the code required by the reader (item entry systems). We may use an index in which subjects are represented by simple terms to be compounded by the searcher (a post-coordinate system), or one with built-in compounds (a pre-coordinate system). Bibliographies in general are also retrieval devices; the difference here is that the bibliography is not coextensive with the stock of the library – it may omit items in stock and include others not in stock. The use of bibliographies therefore requires further devices – e.g. author catalogues – for matching items retrieved against the stock of the library. Finally, the librarian and reader must be regarded as 'devices' in the system, and an important decision that must be made by those organizing retrieval systems is how much can be left to the searcher – a decision that must be based on such matters as the economics of staffing and knowledge of users and their needs.

A common element of all subject retrieval systems, no matter what the devices used, is *language*. Both demands and documents are expressed in terms of language and any matching of the two must therefore involve its use. Basically language consists of *vocabulary* and *syntax*. When Samuel Beckett writes:

> Ruins true refuge long last towards which so many false time out of mind. All sides endlessness earth sky as one no sound no stir. Grey face two pale blue little body heart beating only upright. Blacked out fallen open four walls over backwards true refuge issueless.[1]

we recognize the vocabulary – the difficulty in understanding arises from the lack of conventional syntax; the normal rules governing the construction of sentences have been ignored or modified. These rules are concerned basically with word order and the use of relators – prepositions, conjunctions, relational pronouns, etc. While allowing that Beckett's use of language might inspire a degree of insight unattainable through conventional usage, for common purposes meaning resides in the use of terms with accepted definitions organized by accepted syntactic rules.

The adequate representation of subjects in a retrieval system cannot rely solely on the use of common language. Modifications of both vocabulary and syntax are required; a controlled language, i.e. an index language, has to be created. Such languages are commonly presented in the form of classification schedules or lists of subject headings and thesauri. The process of matching documents and demands is then essentially one of translating the language they use into the artificial language of the system.

We need such a controlled language because our concern is with concepts, with language *and* meaning, rather than with language alone. We cannot take the language of the document and the language of the reader and match them satisfactorily without regard to the concepts being expressed. From our point of view language is a vehicle for meaning, and the greatest difficulties in information retrieval arise in those cases – all too frequent – when the relation between term and concept is loose. (Of course, we *can* index on the basis of terms only – as in KWIC and similar devices – but the limitations are obvious.)

The distinction between vocabulary and syntax can be usefully applied to the study of index languages. Each needs to be controlled, and in the next sections of this chapter we shall examine several of the controls that have been commonly applied.

The Control of Vocabulary

The vocabulary of an index language has to be controlled in a number of ways. *Synonyms*, for example, have usually to be eliminated; the indexer cannot, except perhaps in special circumstances, accept both Wireless *and* Radio, Chironomidae *and* Midges, for any such acceptance will scatter material on identical subjects. The problem is not just one of simple synonyms. From the indexer's point of view language is full of *quasi-synonyms* – terms which are not sufficiently distinct in meaning to warrant acceptance of each. Such terms are usually 'confounded'. In the 'single-term dictionary' given in one of the *Cranfield Reports*[2] we find Circularity an accepted term, standing also for Roundness; Component standing for Element and Part; Estimate standing for Prediction and Assessment. In the *London education classification*, Accidents and Illnesses are treated as synonyms, as are Learning and Memory.

There are whole areas of study which, though hardly differentiated, are known by two or more labels – as, for example, Educational psychology and the Psychology of education. (And the difficulties are multiplied in practice by the fact that individual documents use terms with individual meanings: *The political sciences* may in fact be a book about the Social sciences rather than Political science.) The *Introduction* to BC is full of examples of the problems that arise as soon as we try to cater for meaning rather than words alone. In some areas of study, notably the social sciences, the problems of vocabulary are acute. Basically it is a matter of deciding how far we can impose conceptual order on the chaos of terminology, how far we can establish meanings and use terms to accord with our conceptual analysis. And, of course, as indexers, we are not autonomous.

There are obvious constraints within which we have to work, and any modifications of vocabulary must be judged with reference to users. Decisions must be spelled out in the form of 'scope notes' and references made from the terms we have discarded.

Related to synonyms and quasi-synonyms are word-forms. These are often confounded in index languages. Classification schemes, for example, usually confound adjectival and noun forms in country divisions. Alphabetical lists of terms frequently confound word-endings: Measurement stands for measuring, Mixture stands for mixed and mixing, etc. Great care has to be taken over this to ensure that the result is not too great a lack of specificity in the language. For example, if in a classification scheme we have a place for 'Teachers and teaching' but no distinct place for either, then in any compound formed from this class we are likely to have several distinct concepts housed together without differentiation – e.g. the Psychology of teachers and the Psychology of teaching.

The confounding of opposites is also common – though, again, care has to be taken to see that we do not confound two subjects on which extensive literature exists. Cutter (171): 'Of two subjects exactly opposite choose one and refer from the other, e.g. Temperance and Intemperance, Free Trade and Protection.' And in the *London education classification* we find:

Jah   Aptitude, ability (includes lack of aptitude, ability)
Jak   Interest (includes lack of interest)

In each of the situations described so far the central problem has arisen through the existence of several terms conveying one meaning so far as the needs of the indexer are concerned. The converse – one term/many meanings – gives rise to further controls. Simple homonyms like 'china' are easily dealt with. More diffuse and difficult to control are those terms which are capable of various interpretations. 'Bibliography', for example, may stand for a series of very different subjects. Perhaps the most notorious example is the word 'culture'. In his book, *Classification and indexing in the social sciences*[3] Foskett used 'democracy' to illustrate the point. We can, of course, ignore this problem – indeed Foskett makes a case for collocating all books on democracy regardless of the very different concepts treated within them. And there is obviously a limit to the extent to which we can interfere in the language used by writers and their readers. In many such cases, however, the addition of qualifiers or subdivisions may give the required precision: Bibliography, Enumerative; Bibliography, Historical, etc. Scope notes should be included in the language wherever decisions are made regarding the meaning of terms used, and a supporting network of references (or index entries) must be carefully devised.

Another decision will concern the extent of the vocabulary. We might, for example, decide to place a numerical limit on the number of terms to be included. Such an extreme form of control would achieve an index language which, like pidgin English, would be capable of being easily learned and used, but just as pidgin English is inadequate for the expression of fine shades of meaning, so a limited index vocabulary may not be able to do justice to the subjects encountered in documents or required by readers, and it may result in the burden of the search being undertaken by the reader *after* the index language had done its work. This is not necessarily a defect; in a subject where language and meaning are confused beyond redemption it may be the only answer. How far vocabulary restrictions can be used as a form of control will depend ultimately on the nature of the collection and the kinds of demands likely to be made upon it.

A particular form of restriction commonly employed is the use of a generic term to represent the species subsumed under it. (The converse – the use of a particular to house the general – is found in practice but is largely unintentional, forced on the indexer by the inadequate definition of categories.) In *The abridged Bliss classification* we find:

GWL Reptiles
      Tortoises, Lizards, Snakes, Crocodiles, Alligators

and further examples have already been cited in the section on specificity (pp. 97ff.).

Indeed, the generic level of an index language is one of the fundamental problems facing the maker (and user) of a retrieval system. Languages operating at a high level of generality will be relatively insensitive. If, for example, a classification scheme contained terms for only such broad operations and types of libraries as Cataloguing and Academic, then documents on LC or university libraries would be outside its range. However, it should be recognized that a language of such limited capacity may, by forcing the reader to scan a wide range of entries, ensure that items are not overlooked. Thus, whoever wants information on university libraries will be forced to scan all entries with the heading academic libraries. In this way he may retrieve items which, though not entirely about university libraries, are highly relevant to his needs. In contrast, the user of a system employing a highly specific language may be tempted to rest content with the items retrieved at the specific heading. Some have argued for generality on these grounds. Taken to its extreme limits the argument would result in the abolition of all forms of subject organization – on the grounds that the only way a person may be certain of not overlooking an item is to search every document in the library.

A fair degree of specificity is usually considered to be essential in an index language – sufficient, at any rate, to differentiate between the concepts represented in the documents in the collection. In other words, 'literary warrant' is a basic determinant of degree of specificity. The needs of users is obviously the other major factor to be taken into account. Because literary warrant and user needs vary we find index languages of varying sensitivity. CC operates at one level, Ranganathan's depth schedules at another.

All the above forms of control depend on a systematic analysis of terms and meanings. One particular form of systematization that has yielded a high degree of control in the production of index vocabularies is the analysis of terms and concepts by reference to fundamental categories – PMEST, Thing-Material-Action, etc. Quite apart from the use of such categories as a determinant of syntax (see below), they have been of immeasurable value in the identification and definition of terms, and in the clarification of index languages generally.

Terms in the vocabulary of an index language can often be broken down into basic components or 'semantic factors'. For example, 'bus' is a simple term in the vocabulary of transport, but it can be 'factorized' into an assembly of more simple elements – conveyance, public, road, petrol driven, etc. 'Taxis' in biology is a shorthand term for expressing the idea of 'locomotory movement of an organism or cell in response to a directional stimulus. . . .' An important decision facing the maker of an index language is the extent to which he accepts terms as they stand or reduces them to the basic constituents comprising their definition (and, perhaps, their extension as well as their intension). On this decision will rest, in part, the quality of retrieval. Thus, if taxis is accepted as a term in the language without further analysis, the chances of retrieving related material on stimulus-response are reduced.

Traditionally classification schemes have provided a partial answer to this problem by means of hierarchical arrangement. To put 'murder' in the following sequence: Crime – crimes of violence – crimes of violence to persons – murder, means that, within the limits of linear arrangement, material on murder will be juxtaposed with its basic constituents. This kind of structuring is also achieved by hierarchical linkage in alphabetical lists of terms.

As a result of these and other forms of vocabulary control, we shall arrive at a set of terms which can be categorized as code terms (basic terms used in indexing) and lead-in terms (terms not used but likely to be sought by users).[4] Clear directions must be included to guide the reader from lead-in terms to code terms.

The Control of Syntax

The range of an index language, its sensitivity to concepts, is not simply a matter of vocabulary. Provision must also be made for syntax, i.e. for the expression of relationships between the terms comprising the vocabulary. These relationships are, as we have seen, of two kinds: generic (or paradigmatic) and compound (or syntagmatic). *Generic relations* usually find expression in the organization of the vocabulary itself. Thus in classification schedules it is through the successive degrees of subordination that such relations are made explicit. To give an example from cc:

N	Fine arts
NA	Architecture
NA,3	Dwelling
NA,37	Castle

In alphabetical lists of terms the relationships are expressed through a series of hierarchical cross references:

Arts *see also* Architecture
Architecture *see also* Dwellings
Dwellings *see also* Castles

It is also important to direct the reader from terms that are not accepted because they fall below the generic level of the vocabulary to those that are. For example, to refer back to the illustration in the previous section: University libraries *see* Academic libraries. Similarly in a classification schedule we might find, as in UDC (abridged ed.):

371.9   Education of special categories of pupils:
Handicapped, blind, deaf and dumb, etc.

In such cases the terms Handicapped, blind, deaf and dumb, are below the generic level of that particular schedule. Nevertheless they must be included both in the schedules and in the index to the scheme as lead-in terms. (Of course this could be taken to extreme lengths – the criterion in establishing such lead-in terms is whether they are likely to be sought by users.)

The display of generic relationships allows the reader to broaden or narrow the scope of his search at will; he can, in other words, improve either the recall or the precision according to his needs.

In addition to the expression of generic relationships, rules and facilities must be provided for the *compounding of terms* from the vocabulary in order to express more complex meanings. It is the inadequacy of such syntactic devices that is responsible for the weaknesses of many commonly used languages – the traditional classification schemes and lists of subject headings. Even those languages that enumerate compounds must, if they are to be satisfactory, base their enumeration on syntactic principles and rules – a necessary condition all too often ignored; whilst it is obvious that analytico-synthetic languages such as CC, languages in which the vocabulary is largely composed of simple elements hierarchically organized, must provide clear rules for the creation of compounds. (Where such rules are not provided – as, for example, in UDC – there is a gain of flexibility, but in the end the classifier has to invent his own rules if consistency is to be achieved.) And in the case of post-coordinate systems, as has been shown in the previous chapter, the completely free coordination of simple elements at the search stage has proved to be an insufficient basis for a retrieval system.

Two major syntactic devices in common language are word order and relators or linking mechanisms. In the English language, for example, there are acknowledged patterns of words for the expression of statements, exclamations, questions, etc. When we read the statement 'Sparrow killed Cock Robin', the order of words contributes significantly to our understanding of who did what to whom. It is the order of words that helps us to distinguish between 'office post' and 'post office' – or, to quote the hackneyed example, 'blind Venetian' and 'Venetian blind'. Relators – prepositions, conjunctions, relational pronouns, etc. – give further aid. Thus the use of 'and' and 'in' make explicit the relationships between science, classification, and indexing in Vickery's title, *Classification and indexing in science*. No one will be misled into thinking that this is a book on, say, science in classification and indexing. And words like 'influence', 'effect', 'consequence', 'cause', are often essential elements in the expression of relationships between words – as in the following title: *The influence of social class on the language of the child, and its consequences in education.*

In index languages the use of word or term order and relators as syntactic devices is also common. Ranganathan's PMEST, Coates's Thing-Material-Action and relationship table, Vickery's 'standard' citation order, are some of the examples of formulae for determining term order already referred to in earlier pages of this book. These can be regarded as attempts at standardizing and controlling syntax – as were earlier rules by Cutter, the Thing-Process sequence of Kaiser, the grammatical approach of Prevost, etc. We find partial examples in lists of subject headings; for although they have tried to maintain common language forms and to avoid specification of compounds, they are not without their syntactic rules – as, for example, in the instruction to give Place priority over Subject in certain circumstances.

However, we should not overlook a major distinction between the functions of term order in common language and its function in index languages. Whilst it may in the latter case as in the former be used to clarify meaning, its main function is the manipulation of classes to effect the retrieval of documents in response to demands; it is by the manipulation of classes represented by terms that documents and demands are matched. Term order, whether in the form of classification symbols or words, facilitates the arrangement, and hence the subsequent location, of classes in a sequence. When in an alphabetical index we debate whether to use the heading CHILDREN-PSYCHOLOGY or PSYCHOLOGY-CHILDREN, or whether in a classification sequence to put a document on three-colour processes in lithography with lithography or colour-processing, our concern is not primarily with meaning. What we are doing is trying to find a unique slot to house a class of documents and to label it in such a way as to maximize retrieval – both of it and related classes. It is to this end that such standard orders as PMEST have been devised. Those who claim that compound terms in an index should reflect word order in common language are ignoring this difference in function, and it is hard to see how common syntax could yield satisfactory retrieval when its aims are so different.

The main aim of term order, then, is arrangement. Though not entirely absent from post-coordinate systems, it is mainly a problem in pre-coordinate ones (and, of course, in printed indexes of a pre-coordinate kind resulting from post-coordinate systems). A major principle underlying term order is significance. Whenever a compound is of a kind that can be expressed in more than one way the question of order arises and can be answered, at least initially, by reference to significance – that is, by an analysis of the relative importance to the searcher of the concepts concerned. The result of such analysis is to bring into prominence key concepts.

Although in specific instances and situations it may be quite easy to establish an order of priority, to state such orders in general terms is far more difficult. Bliss left it at the 'general educational and scientific consensus'. Ranganathan postulated five major categories and arranged them in the significance order PMEST, though, as the definition of Personality is obscure, (it appears to mean 'the most significant facet'), this still leaves an open question. Coates, with particular reference to the alphabetical catalogue suggests Thing-Material-Action as a general order of categories, but again a difficulty arises over the definition of Thing. The same goes for Vickery's citation order: Thing-Part-Constituent-Property-Measure-Patient-Process/Action/Operation-Agent, though in terms of the scientific materials for which it was intended this may introduce relatively little ambiguity. In any case, such citation orders of fundamental categories are by their nature highly abstract and are intended for general rather than precise guidance.

One important clue to significance is the kinds of relationships existing between the terms of a compound. The study of these relationships led Coates to suggest the extension and modification of his basic significance order by the application of a set of rules expressed in a 'relationship table'. And Vickery's order is clearly a statement of relationships. To recognize that two terms are in a Whole/Part, Property/Constituent, Agent/Patient relationship, etc., is a step towards determining the relative significance of each and hence the most generally useful order to adopt.

It is important to recognize that there is no essential connection between individual terms in the vocabulary of an index language and the categories used to express citation order. For example, the term 'trade unions' is an Agent and 'government policy' a Patient in the following compound subject: 'The influence of the trade unions in the shaping of government policy.' The categories are reversed in a document on 'The influence of government policies on the trade unions'. This fact gives rise to particular problems in the construction of classification schedules, problems which are still far from being solved. The recent work of Ranganathan, his attempt to create a 'freely-faceted' scheme in the seventh edition of cc, is particularly interesting in this connection.

Term order, determined by reference to fundamental categories, their significance and relationships, is a major syntactic device in index languages designed for use in pre-coordinate systems, no matter whether the presentation of the language is in the form of an alphabetical list of terms or a classification schedule. Although this has not always been admitted, the most cursory study of recent writings in the field of information retrieval will reveal the close affinities that exist between what have been traditionally regarded as distinct modes of operation.

Although the primary purpose of term order is arrangement, it is true that order usually reveals meaning. Quite complex strings of terms in BTI, for example, are meaningful without any further indication of the relationships between them:

ENZYMES: Reactions: Rate: Measurement: Spectrophotometry: Stirrers.

HYDROGEN: Townsend discharge: Magnetic fields, crossed: Electron drift: Velocity

The structure of a classification schedule allows us to read the successive steps of division as a 'sentence'; any individual term can be unambiguously defined by its context. There is no difficulty, for example, in understanding that the last step of division in the following chain (from the *London education classification*) can refer only to the place of science in the curriculum of primary schools:

R—S   Educands and schools
Ral   Schools and schoolchildren, generally.
Rav   Primary, elementary
M—P   Curriculum
Mob   Sciences

With the exception of phase relationships (influencing, bias, etc.) there has been little need to identify by means of a set of *relators* the kinds of relationships existing between terms in a pre-coordinate language. The coordination itself has been sufficient. However, schemes which list each concept once and once only – as in the new general classification – *must* provide a set of Relational Operators to specify relationships between concepts and any compound. See for example, the class number cited in the section on the new general classification – p. 123.

In post-coordinate systems, however, where we are dealing with terms out of context – simple terms, the coordination of which is left to the search stage – it is necessary to use relators to specify relationships and so avoid false coordination. Various kinds of linking symbols and, in particular, role indicators, have in recent years been developed to a degree of sophistication that was hardly foreshadowed in the more simplistic theories propounded by certain pioneers of post-coordination. The

Relational Operators used in PRECIS indexing (p. 187) are an example of the kind of thing commonly found in such systems. See also p. 234.

To sum up: an index language comprises a vocabulary and syntax. Each needs to be controlled. In the case of vocabulary decisions have to be made regarding synonyms, generic level, categories, semantic factoring, etc. The expression of generic and compound relationships can be regarded as syntax. Classification schedules, lists of subject headings, thesauri, are ways of presenting the vocabulary and displaying the basic generic relations for use in both pre- and post-coordinate systems; term order and relators are used to express compound relationships, the emphasis in pre-coordinate systems being on term order, in post-coordinate systems on relators.

The Effects of Controls

We have, from time to time, noted the effects produced by particular forms of control as used in index languages. These effects, along with other factors influencing the performance of retrieval systems, have been the subject of much investigation and controversy in recent years. A major investigation, undertaken in the sixties, is the Aslib Cranfield Research Project, which was supported by the American National Science Foundation.[5] Although some of the measurements used in the investigation have been criticized, a number of extremely valuable fundamental concepts have emerged and been given wide currency as a result of this work – and in particular the notions of Recall and Precision as the basic parameters of a retrieval system.

Recall. The whole purpose of a retrieval system is to recall documents relevant to readers' needs. If in any collection there are fifty documents relevant to a particular need and all are retrieved, we can say that the recall ratio is 100 per cent. *Recall ratio* is the ratio between the total number of documents in a collection judged to be relevant to a request and the number actually retrieved through the system. If only twenty-five of the fifty documents had been retrieved the recall ratio would have been 50 per cent.

Now, of course, it would be possible to provide 100 per cent recall by examining every document in the collection every time a request is made. And so we have to add to the recall ratio another measure if we are to establish the relative efficiency of the system. This is the *precision ratio*: the ratio between the total number of *relevant* documents retrieved by the system and the sum total of documents retrieved in the search. Suppose, for example, that we have a personal file of 1000 photocopies of periodical articles and that we arrange this file in alphabetical author order. Now let us imagine that we want to retrieve all photocopies concerned with a particular topic. In order to be quite sure that nothing is missed we may have to go through the 1000 items from A–Z extracting the ones that are relevant. Let us say that there are ten such items. At the end of the operation we shall have 100 per cent recall. But note the cost; to achieve that figure we shall have scanned every document in the collection. In such a case the precision ratio would be 10:1000, or 1 per cent. (In a collection of any size the percentage would be virtually zero.) If we now arrange the photocopies into, say, fifty subject areas so that we need search only twenty documents to get the same recall figure, then we shall have clearly improved the precision ratio; it will now be 10:20, or 50 per cent.

Any grouping of documents, or surrogates, whether by classification schedules or alphabetical headings, acts as a filter, enabling us to find the documents we want while at the same time avoiding the retrieval of unwanted documents. In the above example the division of the collection into fifty groups meant that we could avoid searching through 980 of the 1000 photocopies and still achieve 100 per cent recall. Ideally, of course, we should like to be able so to group items that we retrieve all the relevant documents *and no others* – i.e. 100 per cent recall and 100 per cent precision. However, a retrieval system in practice always operates at a certain balance between recall and precision. This is because the more precise the filter is the more likely it is to act as a barrier to a relevant document. In the end we have to accept a compromise.

Now as measures of operational efficiency these ratios are hard to handle – largely because of the difficulties of defining and measuring relevance. Since the Cranfield investigations much has been written on this subject. From our point of view, however, their value lies in the fact that they enable us to categorize according to their probable effects the various forms of control used in an index language.

On the one hand there are the controls that are likely to improve the recall ratio of a system. If, for example, we control synonyms so as to avoid the scatter that results from uncontrolled terminology, then we shall improve the recall ratio. As synonyms are rarely exactly synonymous and as we extend such control by confounding quasi-synonyms, word-forms, etc., we may at the same time be reducing the precision ratio. To treat educational psychology and the psychology of education as synonymous is to ensure that a reader does not miss relevant items even when he has a particular conception of one or the other of these terms; though he may have to search through a series of documents that from his point of view are irrelevant.

A most important factor affecting the recall/precision ratio is the generic level of the index language. As we have already shown, languages operating at a high level of generality will be relatively insensitive, i.e. they will lack precision. On the other hand, in terms of their recall ratio they may be quite successful. If, for example, in using the *London education classification*, we simply allocate all documents on History as a curriculum subject to the class number Nig, then there will be no differentiation in the system between documents on various kinds of history – economic, social, political, local, etc. A person interested in the teaching of economic history will now have to search through all documents classified at Nig. In the end he will recall not only materials on the precise subject of his search, but also those which, though relevant, are not on the specific subject – documents on history in general, and others which draw parallels between the teaching of, say, social history and economic history and those on local history which make important reference to economic factors, etc. If we had a special slot for Economic history we should have improved the precision ratio, but only at the probable expense of reducing recall.

The provision of hierarchical links such as those displayed in classification schedules or through the reference structure in an alphabetical language, and the breaking down of terms into their semantic factors, can similarly be seen as devices for improving the recall potential of a system.

The net result, in short, of all these forms of control is to increase the size of the classes into which documents or their surrogates are grouped (i.e. to reduce the specificity of the language), and hence to increase the recall potential of the system, whilst at the same time tending to reduce its precision.

On the other hand, devices which help us to reduce the size of classes – i.e. which increase its specificity – can be regarded as precision devices. If we differentiate between homonyms and the like, or generally increase the size of the vocabulary to allow more precise specification, then these measures are obviously precision devices. So are all devices which allow the coordination of classes (whether at the indexing or search stage), for by this means we reduce the size of a class and achieve a more restricted search. Thus facilities for compounding, links, and roles are all designed to the same end, namely, the reduction of 'noise', of unwanted items. Weights, though not a coordinating device, serve the same general purpose.

Although a major determinant of the performance of a retrieval system is the index language used – and in particular the degree of specificity it allows – this is not the only factor. Although this chapter is concerned with index language it would be misleading to conclude without a word on the other major determinant of a system's performance, namely, *exhaustivity* of indexing. In essence, although very exhaustive indexing requires an extensive vocabulary, exhaustivity can be distinguished from the language of the system; it is a matter of the quantity of the input. It is basically a matter for policy decision.

Exhaustivity, as we have seen, refers to the extent to which we take account of the various topics or themes within a document. It will always be relative, but 'complete' exhaustivity would mean the indexing of every topic of significance in a document. For example, we might say that Noam Chomsky's *American power and the new mandarins* has the following major themes: (i) American involvement in Vietnam, (ii) Objectivity in the social sciences and liberal scholarship, (iii) Intellectuals and responsibility, (iv) Political resistance; as well as a host of less extensive but not unimportant comments on the Russian Revolution, the Spanish Civil War, etc. Where exhaustive indexing is practised the book would be assigned to each of these subjects. Traditionally analytical entries have been used, though sparingly, for this purpose; and very useful such analyticals might prove to the user of the catalogue. Made with care they obviously improve the recall ratio of the system.

With the development of post-coordinate indexing it has been much more common (because it is so much easier) to go through a document picking out key terms and assigning the document to each. At this level of exhaustivity precision begins to suffer. In the first place many of the 'key' concepts are in fact treated relatively scantily and the result is that the searcher retrieves a mass of documents in response to any enquiry, many of which have little or no relevance to his needs. (Weights are a way of trying to remedy this weakness.) In the second place, such practice in a post-coordinate system greatly increases the chances of false coordination, once again raising the number of irrelevant documents retrieved.

The rapidity with which significant developments occur in the field of information retrieval is such that even an introductory textbook is liable to date quickly. It is not simply that a few new systems are introduced; the changes are of a kind that affect basic theory. With recent work on *automatic indexing*, for example, many of our basic concepts and theories may soon stand in need of radical reappraisal. It is particularly important in this field that the student consult current journals and the books listed below and in other sections of this book.

READINGS

1. BECKETT, SAMUEL. 'Lessness'. *New Statesman*, 79 (2042), 1 May 1970, 635.
2. CLEVERDON, C. W., MILLS, J. *and* KEEN, M. *Factors determining the performance of indexing systems*. Cranfield, Aslib Cranfield Research Project, 1966. 2v. in 3. Volume 1, Part 1. 'Text' contains the dictionaries referred to.
3. FOSKETT, D. J. *Classification and indexing in the social sciences*. London, Butterworths, 1963.
4. These terms are used in the Aslib Cranfield Research Project— see p. 7 of the volume referred to in 2 above.
5. See 2 above. Also:
   CLEVERDON, C. W. *Report on the first stage of an investigation into*

the comparative efficiency of indexing systems. Cranfield, Aslib Cranfield Research Project, 1960.

CLEVERDON, C. W. *Report on the testing and analysis of an investigation into the comparative efficiency of indexing systems.* Cranfield, Aslib Cranfield Research Project, 1962.

This research has excited much comment and controversy. An article summarizing early work is:

LANCASTER, F. W. *and* MILLS, J. 'Testing indexes and index language devices: the Aslib Cranfield Project'. *American Documentation*, 15 (1), January 1964, 4–13.

See also: CLEVERDON, C. W. 'The Cranfield tests on index language devices.' *Aslib Proceedings*, 19 (6), June 1967, 173–194.

Two extensive reviews by B. C. VICKERY can be found in *Journal of Documentation*, 22(3), September 1966, 247–249, and 23(4), December 1967, 338–340.

Many of the arguments have centred around the concept of 'relevance'. An interesting article on this subject is:

REES, A. M. 'The relevance of relevance to the testing and evaluation of document retrieval systems'. *Aslib Proceedings*, 18(11), November 1966, 316–24.

The standard work on automatic indexing referred to above is:

SALTON, G. *Automatic information organization and retrieval.* N.Y., McGraw-Hill, 1968.

A useful series of articles surveying developments in information retrieval is being published in *Journal of Documentation* under the series title 'Progress in documentation'– e.g.

BATTY, C. D. 'The automatic generation of index languages'. *Journal of Documentation*, 25 (2), June 1969, 142–51.

MILLS, J. 'Library classification.' *Journal of Documentation*, 26 (2), June 1970, 120–60.

Chapter 13
Subjects and Forms

There is some confusion as to what is meant by the term 'form'. Basically it refers to the form in which material is presented – hence the phrase *form of presentation*. For example, information on, say, Engineering, can be presented in the form of an encyclopaedia, or handbook, or periodical, or essays, or lectures, etc.

Sayers,[1] and others, have distinguished another category, which has been called *inner form*, and includes bibliography, theory, law, geography, history, biography, statistics, among many others. These are certainly pervasive, they can be found in all subjects, but they are quite different from the form of presentation as distinguished above. In fact they are, strictly, not forms at all, but *common subjects*. In the case of form of presentation, the information to be communicated is not radically affected by the form; a certain piece of information in Engineering may be communicated as a periodical article, a lecture, an essay, or arranged in the form of an encyclopaedia. *Inner form represents a restriction in terms of the subject:* thus a book on the *theory* of librarianship will not include information on such matters as issue methods, library buildings, reference methods, and so on (except in so far as they are expressions of the theory); but a textbook or a periodical or an encyclopaedia of librarianship in general may include information on all of these things. The one restricts the subject content, the other does not.

The fact that both form of presentation and inner form are pervasive has led to their being confused. Thus in classification schemes, they are often found intermingled in a table of *common subdivisions* the class numbers for which can be applied throughout the scheme. For example, in UDC (01) represents Theory, (02) Handbooks, outlines, (03) Encyclopaedias, (09) Historical treatment, (092) Biographical treatment, and so on;

9

these can be compounded, e.g. 5(03) Encyclopaedia of Science, 5(092) Biography of Scientists. Again, in lists of subject headings there is usually a table of common subdivisions which can be added to a subject heading in the list – in Sears for example, we find: Addresses, Bibliography, Biography, Finance, Laws and regulations, Periodicals, Study and teaching, Tables; and these also can be compounded, e.g. SCIENCE – HISTORY, EDUCATION – STATISTICS, etc., as required. Clearly all these elements are common and should be so listed separately to avoid repetition in the schedules, but the two types must be distinguished in a classification scheme; and in a scheme that attempts to arrange general before special, the form of presentation should have a notation that allows it to precede the inner form because the latter unlike the former are specialized divisions of the subject.

In 1960, BNB,[2] dissatisfied with the confused common subdivisions in DC, introduced a new system using letters, as follows:

a Form of presentation subdivisions, e.g. ab Periodicals, ap Anecdotes.

b Common subject subdivisions, e.g. bd Law, bg Biography.

c Common time subdivisions, e.g. cc Ancient history, ct Nineteenth century.

d Common place subdivisions, e.g. d1 Great Britain, d4 Europe.

Example of their application:

620	Engineering
620ab	Periodicals
620bd	Law
620bg	Biography
620ct	History: Nineteenth century
620d1	Great Britain

Form is usually a *secondary* approach; if a reader wants a specific encyclopaedia of a subject, he will expect to find it with the subject; if he wants a specific piece of information on a subject he may need to search through periodicals, encyclopaedias, textbooks, and so on before finding it and will therefore be glad to find all such documents together with the subject. Hence the common *subdivisions*.

On occasions, however, the subject content is general. The *Encyclopaedia Britannica*, for instance, cannot be classified by subject; neither can *The Listener*. *In such cases form takes priority*. All classification schemes have a place for such general works – often called the *Generalia class*. However, in most schemes the Generalia class also houses miscellaneous classes that should be placed elsewhere in the scheme. In DC for example, Class 000 is used for Generalia: 010 Bibliography, 020 Librarianship, 030 General encyclopaedias, 040 General collected essays, 050 General periodicals, 060 General societies, miscellanies, 070 Journalism, newspapers, 080 Polygraphy, 090 Book rarities. Librarianship, Journalism, and Bibliography, and Book rarities ought to be found accommodation in proximity with the Literature class (as in BC); Newspapers ought to be collocated with Periodicals.

Again, in SC we find A000 General encyclopaedias, A001 General collections, A004 General concordances, and so on. Brown extends the meaning of Generalia to include subjects with general application, e.g. Education, Mathematics.

Similarly in lists of subject headings there are headings for such forms, e.g. ENCYCLOPAEDIAS AND DICTIONARIES, PERIODICALS, etc. These headings accommodate:

(a) general works written in such forms;
(b) documents *about* the forms.

In a classification scheme the Generalia class is sometimes called a *Form class*, to distinguish it from the list of form sub-divisions. There are other examples of Form classes: those which cater for *artistic form*. Artistic forms – painting, sculpture, symphony, novel, etc., – are closely allied to form of presentation; they are forms by which an imaginative vision is presented. Here, however, the form obviously vitally affects the vision and rightly becomes an important element in the classification: hence such form classes as found in the 700's and 800's in DC. In these form classes are accommodated documents which are in the particular form as well as documents about the form (i.e. where form is the subject). Within the broad classes the particular form divisions may not take precedence however – thus in Literature, language and period may take precedence over form, as is possible in UDC, e.g. 820"15"-2 Sixteenth-century English drama (where 820 stands for English literature, "15" for sixteenth century, and –2 for drama). In DC language takes precedence, but form has priority over period – thus the same subject would here be expressed as 822.3 (where 82 stands for English literature, 2 for drama and .3 for Sixteenth century).

In the lists of subject headings there are also headings for artistic forms. However literary form headings traditionally accommodate only:

(a) documents *about* the form;

(b) *collections* of works in the form.

Example: SHORT STORY in Sears is used for documents on the short story, and SHORT STORIES for collections of stories by various authors; POETRY is used for works on the appreciation, etc., of poetry, POETRY – COLLECTIONS is used for anthologies of poetry by various authors. It is left to the shelf classification to show what individual novels, books of poetry, etc., are in the library, and the author entries must be used to find what documents there are by particular authors. In this respect the dictionary catalogue is less satisfactory than the classified.

Obviously, some clarification of these matters is needed. First, we ought to omit common subjects from any treatment of forms. *Space* and *time*, though common, are certainly not forms. Nor are the various more or less common *approaches* to a subject – Philosophical, Historical, Biographical, etc. Many subjects can be used as an approach to another: there is an ethical approach to medicine, an economic approach to art, a philosophical approach to history and a historical approach to philosophy, a psychological approach to religion, and a sociological approach to almost any form of human activity. Within these approaches there can be particular viewpoints – an ethical approach to medicine may be in terms of Christianity (or Catholicism), an economic approach may be Marxist in character, and so on – right down to an individual author viewpoint. It is probably best to leave such approaches and viewpoints to some sort of relationship device so that to any subject may be added the particular viewpoint selected from the relevant area of the index language – otherwise we shall be forced to try to enumerate all possible viewpoints in a common table.

Closely allied to approach, in this sense, are those terms which concern *technical approaches* (e.g. case-study, statistical study, linguistic analysis, etc.), and the comprehensive idea of 'research in . . .' Many, though not all, of these are pervasive, and again it could be left to a relationship device to link such terms to subjects – for literature will exist on all of them and some provision for them will be found in most general index languages. They are closer to common subjects than forms, clearly affecting the content of a work.

Artistic forms can hardly be called pervasive and are best dealt with as they arise in the analysis of categories within particular arts.

This leaves us with a heterogenous group of terms – periodical, encyclopaedia, primer, etc. – which are more accurately described as forms of publication than are the above. However, it would perhaps, in view of their varied character, be best to refer to them as *specifications subsidiary to subject*. Several sub-groups can be distinguished: *bibliographical forms* (e.g. encyclopaedia, dictionary, bibliography); *physical forms* (e.g. book, periodical, recording, film); and *level of presentation* (e.g. primer, intermediate textbook, advanced monograph). Even then the divisions are hardly clear-cut, and many sub-groupings are possible. One might ask, for example, where 'government publications' might fit – a group based on a publisher limitation.

The important thing to remember is that specifications of this kind are always to be regarded (except for the sake of convenience in a particular organization) as secondary to subject. There are circumstances in which it hardly seems worth the effort to include them in the input to a retrieval system, and careful judgement is necessary when making decisions as to whether or not to use them. Certainly they must be regarded as secondary to the other elements traditionally regarded as 'forms' and broadly analysed as common subjects and approaches in this chapter. In many instances they are of less significance than the authorship of the document – an element they displace when included.

READINGS

1. SAYERS, W. C. B. *A manual of classification.* 3rd ed. rev. London, Grafton, 1955. p. 54.
2. BNB *Supplementary classification schedules.* London, BNB, 1963.

For several of the categories of approach mentioned in this chapter I am indebted to my colleague Derek Langridge.

Part Three
Description

Chapter 14
Description

Descriptive cataloguing is concerned with the information given in the body of the entry as distinct from the heading (see page 16).

There are two main questions to be answered in a consideration of descriptive cataloguing:

(a) What information should be given?

(b) In what order should the information be given?

Purpose

Our answers to these questions will depend to a large extent on what we regard as being the purpose of the description. Basically there are three possible purposes:

(i) *to identify or individualize the document* being catalogued, i.e. to give sufficient information for the reader to be able to distinguish one edition of a document from another;

(ii) *to characterize the document*, i.e. to give information that will assist in the choice of a document – information as to its character (subject, level, authorship, etc.);

(iii) *to place the entry* in its most useful position within the chosen heading.

AACR prefaces its rules on descriptive cataloguing with the following statement of principles:

The following principles provide a common basis for the rules for the description in a catalogue of all library materials.

Object of descriptive cataloguing. The object of description is consistently to describe each item as an item, to distinguish it from other items (especially from other items in the library), and to show its bibliographical relationship with other items.

Description of a perfect copy. When possible the description should be that of a perfect copy. Imperfections in a particular copy are indicated.

Extent of description. The item is described as fully as is necessary to achieve the object stated above, but with economy of data and expression.

Terms of description. The information presented by the author, publisher, or other issuing authority in or on the item generally forms the basis of the catalogue description; the wording of the description is partly a transcription of the printed statements, partly conventional. Explanations are given of ambiguous or unintelligible statements transcribed from the book, and obvious errors are indicated.

Style. The parts of the description are given so far as possible in a consistent order and a uniform style. No specific recommendations are here made, however, for a standard lay-out of the entry, since an appropriate presentation depends on the form of the catalogue and the physical means used to produce it.

Sources of the Description

The basic information in any description must be derived from the document – in the form of a perfect copy. This is not to say, however, that other information may not be added, particularly in the form of notes.

In any book the *title page* is the primary means of identification and has always, therefore, been considered especially important as a source of information in descriptive cataloguing. It should not, however, be regarded as sacrosanct in every detail. Although a full transcription of the title page is often essential for the proper identification of an edition and even, possibly, a particular copy of an early printed work (and indeed is sometimes employed in detailed bibliographies of modern authors), for the vast majority of works catalogued in libraries such treatment would be inappropriate. 'Fullness of transcription of the title page is not necessary for the identification of editions or issues.'[1] Not only do cataloguers *select* the information that they need from the title page, frequently omitting certain items, they also *reorganize* that information. Clearly the cataloguer is out to produce a description in a standard order, and that order is rarely reflected in the title pages of documents. Although much of the information in the description will certainly be taken from the title page, the description itself will reproduce the title page only insofar as the two are identical in terms of content and layout.

That the information on the title page will seldom be fully reproduced in a catalogue entry is not, however, an invitation to the cataloguer to tamper indiscriminately. Indiscriminate selection and reorganization will soon reduce the accuracy and reliability of the catalogue. In particular, care should be taken to ensure that the title itself is fully transcribed in the form given on the title page. Failure to do so is liable to cause difficulties in the subsequent identification of the documents recorded. (There may be occasions when this basic rule has to be modified but, as we shall see, great caution must be exercised when making such modifications.) And even when items are omitted from, or added to, the title, it is customary to indicate such alterations by the use of, respectively, omission marks (. . .) and square brackets.

Of the older codes, AA is the one that most clearly displays unqualified veneration of the title page and it has often been accused of fussiness in its rules for descriptive cataloguing. Doubtless its compilers were influenced by the rapid growth of historical and critical bibliography at the turn of the century. And caught thus between an influential and related – though distinct – discipline on the one hand, and the needs of libraries on the other, their rules are so prickly with inconsistencies that many of them are impossible to apply with any degree of assurance.

In 1948 the Library of Congress published a report entitled *Studies in descriptive cataloging*[2] which is still of value as an analysis of problems in descriptive cataloguing. The following year the Library of Congress *Rules for descriptive cataloging*[3] appeared. In general these rules are simpler and more consistently worked out than those of earlier codes, and although they were never widely adopted in this country, their influence through the Library of Congress catalogues and printed card service has been considerable. Indeed, the chapters on descriptive cataloguing in AACR are, to a large extent, based on the Library of Congress *Rules*.

In the notes that follow reference is made to certain basic AACR rulings, though no attempt to summarize the code has been undertaken. It should be recognized that in this section of the code there are several differences between the North American and British texts. Reference here is to the latter.

Title

All codes agree that title should be given first, because this is the most useful filing element within the author heading. Readers consulting the author catalogue expect to find a title sequence within any individual heading; similarly, readers consulting the subject catalogue expect to find within any subject heading first an author sequence, and within the author sequence titles filing alphabetically. This is because title is the primary individualizing element for a particular document – it distinguishes it from other documents by the same author.*

However, this is not always straightforward in practice, because a work may appear under different titles in different editions – for example, Hemingway's *Fiesta*, otherwise known as *The sun also rises*. Whenever a work is published under more than one title the cataloguer is bound to choose between them – *and the occasions when a choice arises are the same as those for title (main) entry*, i.e. the title differs in the several volumes of a work; the title of the work varies in the different editions; the work is known in various countries under different titles. The student should refer to Chapter 5 for a discussion of these problems and their treatment in the codes.

Whether the cataloguer chooses to file the entry by the title in the particular document he is cataloguing, and so in the majority of cases satisfy the needs of readers seeking that document; or whether he chooses a uniform title – say, the original title in the case of a translation – whatever the title of the particular document, so satisfying readers who want to see all editions of a work together – will depend on whether his aim is to produce a direct or collocative catalogue.[4] If his aim in making the *heading* has been collocation, then collocation should, if he is to be consistent in this, be continued in the title element in the description. *Example:*

---

* *Note:* Examples of bibliographical references in which *date* precedes title are not uncommon, thus allowing a chronological display of a writer's works.

Direct (using the title as found in the document)
    (i) Camus, Albert
        L'étranger . . .
    (ii) Camus, Albert
        The outsider; translated by Stuart Gilbert . . .

In a large catalogue cross references would also be made:

    Camus, Albert
    L'étranger
        For an English translation see: Camus, Albert. The outsider

– thus relating editions scattered by direct entry.

Collocative (using a uniform title)
    (i) Camus, Albert
        L'étranger . . .
    (ii) Camus, Albert
        [L'étranger. English]
            The outsider; translated by Stuart Gilbert . . .

Here again, references may be needed, e.g.:

    Camus, Albert
    The outsider
        see his L'étranger. English.
        where all editions and translations will be found.

Note that the uniform title is placed in brackets to indicate that it is a filing title only – the title of the document in hand follows in the normal way:

Shakespeare, William
    [Richard II]
        The tragedy of Richard II . . .

As in the case of title entry there is one occasion when a uniform heading will usually result in both collocation and the sought entry for a particular document; that is when a recognized classic is in question, e.g.:

Virgil
    [Aeneid. English. Selections.]
        The story of Pallas; edited by Bertha Tilly, from Virgil's 'Aeneid' books 8, 10, 11, and 12 . . .

Some account of AACR's approach to this issue has been given in Chapter 5. Generally speaking uniform title is preferred – a major exception being revised editions of a work. Chapter 4 of the code (Uniform titles) synthesizes rules for title as main entry and title as part of description and is, without doubt, the most systematic attempt so far at codification in this area.

The older codes are neither comprehensive nor consistent. AA (143) prefers a direct style for title as part of the description, though frequently advocating collocative *headings* – whether for authors or titles. This is shown in the example in the rule for Epitomes (17):

Malory, Sir Thomas
    The boy's King Arthur . . .

where, although the original author is selected as the heading rather than Lanier (the writer of the epitome), the document will not file with the original document (*Morte d'Arthur*) within the author heading.

Thus objective (iii) above will be achieved in different ways according to the main purpose of the catalogue.

As already indicated, whether a uniform title is used or not the cataloguer must make an exact transcript of the title on the title page. AACR (133A) states: 'The title proper is transcribed exactly as to order, wording, and spelling . . .' However, some modifications are allowed. In particular:

(i) 'Long titles are *abridged* if this can be done without loss of essential information. The first words of the title are always included in the transcription. All omissions from the title are indicated by a mark of omission.' (133 B).

(ii) '*Additions* to the title required for reasons of grammar or intelligibility may be made in English, or in the language of the title. Short explanatory additions may be taken from the book itself or supplied by the cataloguer. All additions must be enclosed in square brackets.' (133D).

(iii) 'The *subtitle* is considered a part of the title and transcribed in the entry in the same manner as the title proper, except that a long subtitle which is separable from the title may be omitted and quoted in a supplementary note, if this increases the clarity of the entry. A subtitle preceding the title on the title page is transposed to the position determined by the general pattern of the catalogue entry . . .' (133 F).

[Clearly it is important that the subtitle be thus transposed in order to create a proper filing order. The emphasis on preserving subtitles is justified; not only do they help to characterize books but they may also individualize them – e.g. at least two of Sabartés books on Picasso are called *Picasso* and are distinguishable only by their subtitles.]

Features Apart from the Title Frequently Found in the Description

(i) *Author*. It could be argued that as the author is given in the heading, repetition of the author's name after the title in the description serves no useful purpose. Indeed, the Library of Congress *Rules for descriptive cataloging* (1949) did not require it, though it had been called for in AA. AACR returns to the earlier practice: 'The statement of authorship appearing in a work is transcribed in the body of the entry, whether the author is personal or corporate' (134A). R. O. Linden explains: 'It appears that, as the *Rules for descriptive cataloging in the Library of Congress* did not require the author statement, cataloguers were spending a great deal of time checking books already catalogued to find out how the author's name appeared on his books.'[5]

Obviously there will be many occasions when the author statement will be a straight repetition of the author heading, and AACR allows the cataloguer to omit it in such cases. However, when there are discrepancies between the heading adopted and the author as shown on the title page, author must be cited – for example, when a work entered under a corporate body also has a personal author. Again, where there are additional authors, translators, editors, illustrators, etc., they should be given (after the title or in a Note below the main description) especially if added entries are made under their names, otherwise the reason for the added entry will not always be apparent.

(ii) *Edition*. Although the statement of edition is no guarantee of revision (this is often more clearly revealed by pagination) the statement should be given because readers ask for particular editions according to the publisher's statement. *Impression*, on the other hand, can be ignored.

'The edition is always stated if given in the book. The terms of the statement are those of the book. Provided that the edition is formally presented in the book, even if not on the title page, it may be written without square brackets.' (AACR 135A).

Additionally, 'the names of editors, compilers, translators, illustrators, etc., are transcribed when the work may be characterized or cited by their names'. (AACR 136).

(iii) *Imprint* (i.e. place of publication, publisher, date – usually in this order). 'The imprint as recorded in the catalogue entry shows the place of publication . . . the name of the publisher . . . and the date of publication . . . in that order. It is given in the language of the book, except that in the date Roman numerals are replaced by Arabic numerals. If the imprint particulars are formally presented in the book, but not necessarily on the title page, they are transcribed without square brackets.' (AACR 139A).

Date is most important as it helps to individualize a document, especially in the case of a new edition that is not numbered (2nd, 3rd, etc.) by the publisher. Libraries often give the date of the document in hand, information regarding previous dates of publication being given in the subsequent Notes. However, AACR (142) states that 'the date to be given is the date of the edition, which may be followed by the date of the imprint where the difference is important, or by the copyright date' – e.g. 1960 (1962 reprint). But a footnote adds: 'In libraries where separate cataloguing is accorded to copies of books on the basis of differences in the publishers' imprint dates, the date to be given is that of the publishers' imprint. The relation of this date to the edition is explained, where necessary, in a note.' Date also helps to characterize a document – documents on certain subjects published in certain years may be judged to be out of date, biased, etc.

Publisher is of little individualizing importance, though it may help to characterize a document in so far as certain publishers are reputed to be reliable in certain subjects. AACR (141) moves away from the older practice of detailed transcription of publisher's name: 'The publisher's name is given in the briefest form in which it can be understood and identified without ambiguity.'

Place of Publication is again of value only in so far as it reveals to the perceptive reader possible biases, differences in terminology likely to be found in the document, etc. The relevant AACR rule here is (140).

(iv) *Collation* (i.e. statement of pagination or number of volumes, illustrations, size). 'The general aims of a collation statement are (i) to present a picture of the physical characteristics of the work to the reader, so as to assist him in identifying it, and to tell him something of its nature; (ii) to assist in showing how various editions of a work differ from each other; and (iii) to ensure that all those parts of a work are described which would be retained in binding or rebinding it. The terms used are those for which accepted definitions are available rather than those of the author and publisher, if there is any conflict between the two.' (AACR 143A).

Pagination is an important guide to the amount of revision in a new edition; a well-revised book, particularly one on a rapidly expanding subject, will rarely have the same number of pages as the original. AACR (143B) requires the various sequences of pages to be given – e.g. xxi, 209p. – but many libraries give only the last numbered page, introductory sequences, etc., being ignored unless exceptionally lengthy. Such pagination statements also help to characterize documents in that it is useful when making a selection to know whether the document has six volumes, 600 pages, or a mere twenty pages. Where a work is in several volumes it is usual to give only the number of volumes, omitting the pagination for each.

One of the interesting features of AACR is that it treats plates, including frontispieces, as a part of the pagination statement – an improvement on AA which confused plates (a type of page) with illustrations. One of the examples in rule (143B4) reads: x,32,73p., 12 plates.

Illustrations. There are occasions when it is especially useful to know whether a book contains *illustrations* (e.g. art books, travel descriptions, and so on) and occasions when it would be useful to know the *type* of illustration (portraits in biographies, maps in geography books, etc.). Though AACR (143D) allows the use of the term *illus* to cover all forms of illustration, it also sets out the types of illustrations which may be specified: 'When particular types are important they are designated by the following terms in alphabetical order: charts, coats of arms, facsimiles, forms, genealogical tables, maps, music, plans, portraits (or group portraits but not both), samples.' (Abbreviations of these terms are given in Appendix III of AACR.) Gone are some of the older AA types – diagrams, photographs, and tables. The number of 'illustrations, portraits, maps, etc., may be specified in the collation if it can be readily ascertained or verified from the work itself (e.g. when the illustrations are listed or their number stated), but only if the work or illustration warrants such description' (AACR 143D3). The statement of illustrations is separated from the pagination statement by a semi-colon: vii, 31p., 12 plates; illus., maps.

In general the illustration statement has little bearing on individualization; it is of interest mainly in helping to indicate the character of the book.

Size (usually given in centimetres) is of importance mainly as an indication of shelving (outsize sequence) and this will usually be indicated in any case by a location symbol following the class number. Measurements are of little significance except in certain categories such as atlases. AACR (143E) states: 'The height of a book is normally given in centimetres, exact to within one centimetre. . . . Books, however, which are ten centimetres or less in height are described in millimetres. . . .'

(v) *Series* is often useful as an indication of style and level of the document, e.g. *Nutshell series* (Sweet and Maxwell), *Monographs on physical subjects* (Methuen), etc. Amorphous series such as *World classics* are less usefully noted, though many such series are of a high general standard and inclusion of a work is some indication of level; format too is also revealed to anyone familiar with the series. The value of the series statement is thus purely for characterization – though there are cases, certain sequences of research reports and government publications for example, where precise statement of series (e.g. AWRE NR 2/63) may be essential to identification; and AACR (144A3) – 'In making series statements for official publications the form used in official citations is preferred' – ought to be more strongly worded.

AACR follows the traditional practice of placing the series

statement in brackets after the collation. 'The series statement consists of the title of the series and the number within the series of the part being catalogued. The title of the series may also include the name of the author of the series if all parts are by the same author, or of the editor of the series, especially if the name is required to explain a heading. The series statement is made in the language in which the indication of series is given in the part being catalogued' (144A2).

(vi) *Notes/Annotation/Abstracts*. See below.

The order of descriptive items is usually that followed in the notes above: title, edition, imprint, collation, notes, annotation (or abstract). Apart from the title as filing element the order of the rest is less significant; however, the most important items should be placed first as readers tend to read only the first few lines of the entry!

Notes. Annotation. Abstracts

The information provided by the description as outlined above is limited; it follows a set pattern and has a narrow range. Therefore further information may be given in the form of notes, annotation or abstract in order to:

(i) *elucidate or develop the existing description* (e.g. a note on the history of the document – its date of original publication for instance; a note on the illustrations – that they are woodcuts printed from the original blocks for example; and so on). Such notes should be kept to a minimum, the information whenever possible, i.e. when sufficiently brief, being incorporated into the primary description so as not to scatter information on the same point through several parts of the entry.

(ii) *characterize the document more fully* by adding information on the author (qualifications, etc.) or subject matter (level, etc.) and possibly the document's relationship to other documents.

Notes, annotations and abstracts are found mainly in what Cutter would call Full catalogues[6] – those which aim at characterization.

NOTES

The number of notes will, of course, vary from entry to entry and so may their arrangement – according to their relative importance. AACR (145) defines their purpose as follows: 'Notes are made to assist in identifying a publication, to record information about the library's own copies of it, or to present any other information that may be useful to those consulting catalogue entries for the publication. Notes amplify or qualify formal description when the rules for the body of the entry do not permit the inclusion of the needed information in any other form than a note, or when the incorporation of the information in the body of the entry would be misleading, cumbersome or inappropriate. They may explain a heading when the explanation is not apparent elsewhere in the description. They may also indicate the nature and scope of a work, and its literary form.'

Though noting that variations to suit a particular publication or library are inevitable, AACR suggests an order conforming to the order of descriptive items:

(1) *Notes on the title,* such as variations in title through editions, spine title, caption title.

(2) *Notes on author statement (or heading), editor, etc.,* e.g. Chairman: Sir Sydney Roberts.

(3) *Notes on the edition,* e.g. Text of the 2nd edition (1872) with a new introduction.

(4) *Notes on the imprint,* e.g. Originally published in England by Routledge and Kegan Paul; 'Published for the British Council' – a quotation from a source other than the title page.

(5) *Notes on the collation,* e.g. Collotype plates; Steel engravings specially prepared for this edition by the author; Bound with Ryan, Mary. Our Lady's hours [New York, 1945?].

(6) *Notes on the series,* e.g. Also issued without the series statement.

(7) *Relationship to other publications and other bibliographical history,* e.g. Based on the novel of the same title by Herman Melville; PhD thesis, Columbia University; Offprint from the Library Association Record, v. 71, no. 5, May 1969.

(8) *Nature, scope, language or literary form of the work,* e.g. Essays; Text in Arabic; Play in 3 acts.

(9) *Contents* (or partial contents). 'Contents are noted, selectively or fully, to show the presence of material not necessarily implied in the title, to stress an item of particular interest, or to itemize a collective title.' (145 Cq) Lists of chapter headings are generally to be avoided, but such lists may be necessary where each chapter is by a different author and analytical entries (see Chapter 15) are to be made. Partial contents notes may be made for such things as especially significant sections of a collection or bibliographies included in the document. It is better to summarize the contents as an annotation than to list chapter headings indiscriminately.

ANNOTATION

Students may quibble about the study of annotation when so few library catalogues contain any. But most librarians will at some time have to annotate a reading list and those who prepare abstracts, reviews, and literature reports will, despite the differences between these forms, gain useful experience through the practice of annotation.

Any or all of the following points may be covered:

(a) *Authorship.* Academic qualifications and experience might be mentioned, the latter being the more important. Details should be relevant to the subject of the book, and not simply biographical; the fact that a man is, say, director of an observatory, does not mean that he will be qualified to write on eighteenth-century furniture. Such notes will help the reader to select between one document and another.

(b) *Subject.* A subject annotation may be limited to the elucidation of an obscure title such as *My eyes have a cold nose*, or *Organization man.* It may be an extension of the title, pointing out features in the document that one would not expect to find; conversely it might limit the title, e.g. a note to the effect that only terms in the biological sciences are included in Henderson's *Dictionary of scientific terms.*

Purpose of the book, treatment of the subject. Where a specific grade of reader is envisaged this might usefully be noted (e.g. 'for City and Guilds electrical technicians' course', 'assumes a knowledge of A-level physics', etc.).

Viewpoint. Where the document reviews a subject from a

particular angle, this might be noted – though great care has to be exercised and only viewpoints which are quite definite and not merely suppositions on the librarian's part should be mentioned, e.g. 'Roman Catholic interpretation of existentialism', 'a Marxist view of history'.

(c) *Relationship to other publications.* Any specific relationships should be mentioned – for example, if the document is a reply to another, or a sequel. In booklists, etc., where the librarian may be trying to stimulate or guide reading, it would be legitimate to go further and suggest an order of reading (elementary before advanced, general before specialized works, etc.). Savage advocated this ('reading courses') in his book on annotation and there is evidence to suggest that in some libraries at any rate (e.g. in technical colleges) it might be welcomed by readers. It should be restricted to booklists.

Evaluation in annotation.[7] There is inevitably a personal element in any evaluation; moreover, it is frequently a temporary matter and liable to date (see E. A. Baker's comments on *Ulysses* in his *Guide to the best fiction*). Again, the writer has to be well-practised in the art if he is not to sound naïve – a kind of amateur critic. Above all, unless he is well acquainted with the subject, his comments are likely to be misinformed. For these reasons alone, evaluation should never be included in the catalogue itself, even such modest comments as 'the standard work' are liable to sound foolish in a very short time. In booklists which are ephemeral and where the librarian is trying to stimulate reading, some kind of evaluation may be practised, e.g. a comparison between one title and another in the list. Some librarians substitute quotations from reviews for personal evaluation.

Finally, a word of warning: annotations should be concise – about fifty words, say; few people have time to read verbose statements. And *beware of stating the obvious* – in many cases the title will be explicit. Students should study very carefully examples of annotation in booklists and bibliographies.

Some Factors Affecting the Nature and Amount of Annotation in Libraries

(a) *Kind of library.* The various kinds of library have different attitudes to annotation – for example, *university librarians* rarely include annotation in their catalogues or produce annotated booklists (though the latter are frequently prepared for students by members of the teaching staff); *special librarians* with a small, known clientele are able effectively to restrict annotation to notes on those sections of documents that are of particular concern to their needs, and many prepare abstracts and literature reports as a regular duty; *public librarians* with a large and varied clientele and a missionary outlook frequently restrict annotation in catalogues but are comparatively prolific producers of annotated booklists. Students should note that all such comments are generalizations; they should collect and study samples of library publications.

(b) *Kind of literature.* For example, titles of documents in *Science and technology* are often explicit and the annotator can concentrate on such matters as author's background, research involved, level and knowledge required, where these can be stated precisely, theories advanced. In the literature of the *Social sciences*, terminology being in a fluid state, it will often be necessary to state the exact scope of the work; and as there are many amateurs in certain areas of the social sciences the degree of original work and the method of investigation may be referred to; also the school of thought reflected in the work, such being frequently found (e.g. 'A Keynesian approach to economics'). Other special considerations apply to *Fiction*, *Children's books*, and so on – even to special classes of material like *Government publications*, where terms of reference, etc., may be noted.

(c) *Catalogue/Booklist.* We have already shown that annotation may differ according to whether it is designed for the permanent catalogue or ephemeral booklist.

(d) *Availability of published annotated lists.* Duplication is to be avoided as far as possible, and references may be made to the relevant publication for an annotation (e.g. *British Standards Year book, British book news, Guide to the best fiction*).

(e) *Access.* Where much stock is in closed access and where, as a consequence, great reliance is placed on the catalogue as a selection tool, annotation is particularly desirable.

(f) *Age.* Older books which have become classics need annotation only in special circumstances (e.g. in a children's list). An annotation for Plato's *Republic*, for example, is likely to appear pretentious.

The student should consider these factors when discussing annotation and use them to qualify general statements on the subject.

ABSTRACTS

Whereas an annotation is a third-person comment on a publication, indicating not merely the content but the level, author's qualifications, etc., an abstract is typically a straight summary of a work written from the standpoint of the original writer. The extent to which an abstract can adequately summarize a document is partly determined by the length of the original: most abstracts are of strictly limited length and although there are instances of abstracts running to 2,000 words, the average is nearer 100–200. Consequently, while abstracting services often include brief summaries of lengthy works – books, reports, etc. – discussion of the nature of abstracts commonly refers to periodical articles and other relatively short pieces, especially when full summaries are being considered. Another factor affecting length is the character of the original; longer abstracts are more easily accepted for foreign works, documents with a high density of factual information, those not easily accessible, etc. Again, where the abstractor has a particular clientele in mind it may be that he can cover the original adequately but selectively, drawing attention only to those features of the original which are of particular relevance to his readers. Length is also a function of style and most abstracts, though avoiding clipped telegraphese, have certain stylistic features which help to keep wordage to a minimum. Outlet may also affect length; a printed abstracting service will usually force a greater degree of reduction than, say, a duplicated library bulletin or even a series of catalogue cards.

A very important determinant of length is the intention of the abstractor – or, more generally, the policy of the abstracting service. In particular, a distinction is often made between those abstracts which aim at simply alerting the reader to the existence of an item that may be of interest, and those which attempt to include all significant information from the original and thus present the reader with – at least in many cases – a substitute for the original. The former are often referred to as *indicative* abstracts, the latter as *informative*. Whereas the indicative abstract is often little more than a broad statement of content, an extension of the title, the informative abstract will give the principal ideas, methods, findings and conclusions of the original. The indicative abstract can thus be seen as occupying a place midway between the usual form of entries in an indexing service on the one hand and a fully developed abstracting service on the other. However, 'indicative' and 'informative' denote 'ideal types' – in practice it is a matter of degree. Moreover, few published services are 'pure' in this respect; individual services offer a mixture of types although each may show a dominant tendency towards one or the other. Thus the *Bulletin signalétique* may be viewed as a service consisting primarily of indicative abstracts, whereas in *Chemical abstracts*, *Psychological abstracts*, and *Sociological abstracts* the informative abstract predominates. The indicative abstract may often resemble an annotation in its use of third-person style.

Although abstracting services are not unknown in the humanities, they are most frequently found in science and technology, and detailed discussion of the nature of abstracts tends to be in the context of scientific research reports, etc. Thus, at the end of their article on the subject, Borko and Chatman[8] give the following *Criteria for an adequate abstract*:

Content
    Purpose: A statement of the goals, objectives, and aims of the research or reasons why the article was written. This statement should be included in both the informative and indicative abstracts.
    Method: A statement about the experimental techniques used or the means by which the previously stated purpose was to be achieved. If the techniques are original or unusual, or if the abstract is informative, more detail should be included.
    Results: A statement of the findings. The informative abstract tends to be more quantitative than the descriptive abstract.
    Conclusions: A statement dealing with the interpretation or significance of the results.

Specialized content: Certain subject-matter fields require that the abstract contain specialized information. Medical journals, for example, require that the abstract contain details of diagnosis and treatment, drug dosages, etc., where applicable. In writing or evaluating abstracts in these fields, the specialized requirements must be considered.

The abstract is to be brief (100–500 words) and non-repetitive.

Form

More variation is possible in the form of the abstract. Therefore, form criteria must be applied judiciously and cautiously. The major criteria are clarity of content and conciseness of expression. Having recognized the existence of great variation in form, we can nevertheless specify general differences between the informative and indicative abstract.

Informative	*Indicative*
1. Active voice	Passive
2. Past tense	Present
3. Discusses the research	Discusses the article which describes the research.

One advantage of including abstracts in catalogues is that more detailed indexing is possible; index entries may be made not only for the terms used in the headings but for significant terms in the abstract also. *Chemical abstracts*, for example may, on occasion, include well over a hundred index entries for a single abstract.

Example of an informative abstract:

Meakin, A. O. 'A survey of library users in Southampton'. *Libr. Ass. Rec.*, 71 (5), May 1969, 144–148. Maps.

The object of this survey was to provide data for (a) a comparison with a 1963 survey; (b) measuring the effect of a new branch library; (c) correlation with Broady's ecological survey of Southampton. Library use, expressed as the ratio (appropriately adjusted) between those eligible to vote and those registered as adult readers, was related to such factors as class (using Broady's categories), topography, location of libraries, communications, and parking facilities. 22.9% of the population aged 14 and over were registered readers, predominantly middle class areas having the highest readership (over 40%), even where there was no library nearby. There have been no significant changes since 1963. The continuing growth in the use of Eastern Library, opened in 1961, can be attributed to the branch's location in a busy shopping centre with a large catchment area and a good system of public transport and parking facilities; that use is not still more extensive is because those living on the townward side are cut off by an intersecting main road and gravitate naturally to the city centre. Use of Woolston Library has declined slightly: the area is isolated by the River Itchen, a busy main road, and a natural escarpment; the library is poorly sited outside the shopping centre and on the brow of a hill, and faces competition from adjoining libraries. Despite certain weaknesses – the exclusion of children, the unsuitability of polling districts as a survey basis, and the neglect of information in the 1966 Sample Census – the survey has stimulated publicity and assisted in formulating policy and identifying areas for future investigation.

An *indicative abstract* for the above might read as follows:

An attempt to relate library use to such factors as class, topography, location of libraries, and communications. The methods and general findings of the survey (1968) are outlined, the detailed results being illustrated by reference to two branch libraries.

The length of the first of these examples demonstrates the difficulty of giving in a few words an informative abstract of even a short research article. Yet, compared with many such articles in scientific journals, Meakin's contribution is lightweight. It is not surprising to discover that policy statements by the editors of abstracting services frequently attempt to define kinds of information that may be *excluded*. As examples Borko and Chatman cite: detailed descriptions, particularly of experiments, organisms, or methodology; facts already well established; speculation by the author or general conclusions which do not follow immediately from the results, etc. Clearly an element of evaluation will creep in when such recommendations are applied, and detailed subject knowledge on the part of the abstractor may be called for. Inevitably significant data will, on occasion, be omitted. Nevertheless, compromise is required if the reader is not to be overwhelmed and if the economics of the operation are to remain realistic.

How Much Description?

A cataloguer who wishes to restrict descriptive items to a bare minimum will choose only those which assist individualization, leaving out characterization completely. Therefore his entry will have title, edition, date. Cataloguers who want further information will add the other elements as they think fit – probably the most useful (apart from notes and annotation) after the above-mentioned minimum will be pagination, publisher and series, with illustrations in special cases.

Cutter divides catalogues into three categories: *Short, Medium,* and *Full*:

> I shall use the three words Short, Medium, and Full as proper names, with the preliminary caution that the Short family are not all of the same size, that there is more than one Medium, and that Full may be Fuller and Fullest. Short, if single columned, [Cutter is here envisaging a printed catalogue], is generally a title-a-liner; if printed in double columns, it allows the title occasionally to exceed one line, but not, if possible, two; Medium does not limit itself in this way, but it seldom exceeds four lines, and gets many titles into a single line. Full usually fills three or four lines, and often takes six or seven for a title.[9]

British Standard 1629: 1950 *Bibliographical references* suggests Author, Title, Date and Series as the bare minimum.

The extent of description will be affected by:

(i) *Economic factors* in the particular library.

(ii) *The nature of the document* – for example, a rare work will usually get fuller treatment than an everyday publication of the book trade; again, art books may have relatively full collation, and so on (see *Special Materials* below).

(iii) *The nature of the catalogue* – for example, a printed catalogue is likely to be more restrictive than a sheaf catalogue; again, booklists produced by the library may vary the style of entry considerably (thus some are arranged primarily by title rather than by author, detailed collation is rarely given though special details may be noted in the annotations, which are often lengthier than those in the main catalogue, etc.). Students should examine as many catalogues, bibliographies and booklists as possible, from this point of view. Developments in computer catalogues are giving rise to new assessments of the detail and sequence of catalogue entries.

Added entries when shortened (i.e. when not unit entries, see page 21) usually contain only the information necessary for individualization as stated above – title, edition, date.

Example of Description

Main Entry – Full

Miller, H   C
   The ageing countryman: a socio-medical report on old age in a country practice. London: The National Corporation for the Care of Old People, 1963.
   191p. 22 cm.
   Includes reading list.
   The author, a general practitioner in Cressage, Shropshire, analyses conditions for the aged in his practice. Observations based on experience are supported by records of interviews and detailed statistics.
   Accession no.   362.6

Comment. The annotation might be extended in a booklist to indicate that the statistics were gathered between October 1958 and September 1959, and that a form devised by the Department of Social Medicine of Birmingham University was used, as this indicates added authority in the work.

Added Entry, or Short/Medium

   The ageing countryman
      Miller, H   C
         The ageing countryman: a socio-medical report on old age in a country practice. 1963.
      Accession no.   362.6

Comment. In a truly Short catalogue even the sub-title would be omitted unless necessary to distinguish it from another work of the same title by the same author.

Description of Special Categories of Materials

In this chapter we have been concerned in broad general terms with the description of monographs. Special categories of materials require special treatment, but in a book of this size there is space to do no more than demonstrate this point through a few examples.

Following the publication of AACR with its sections on special materials, the situation regarding the cataloguing of such materials has changed. Rules are now widely accessible where before they were scattered through numerous special, and often elaborate, codes. Although these special codes, in many cases originating in specialized libraries, will still be used – both on account of their merits and the detail they present – the presence of special rules in a general code ought in time to effect a measure of standardization and improved practice in those libraries which, having relatively few examples of these materials, tended previously to give them scant attention. It ought also to be easier for students to study the problems involved now that rules have thus been brought together.

In the following notes reference is made only to AACR. Some examples of other codes are listed in the references at the end of this chapter.[10]

PERIODICALS

A periodical, unlike a book, appears at intervals over an indefinite span of time. During its life it may undergo numerous changes – of title, editor, imprint, numbering, size, etc. These characteristics give rise to major problems in descriptive cataloguing – to quote G. E. Hamilton: 'The description of a serial which is prepared by a cataloguer is therefore not a static thing, as is the description of a monograph, but is dynamic, a statement of things as they have been and as they are, but with a question mark always just beyond the entry, representing the future issues.'[11] In addition the cataloguer may, on many occasions, be dealing with incomplete holdings of particular titles in his library.

AACR begins its chapter on serials – which covers 'periodicals, continuations, and works published frequently or regularly in new editions (such as guide books, who's whos)' – with an outline of the aims of serials description: '(1) to present an adequate account of the whole published set of each serial; (2) to indicate and describe the library's holdings, and (3) to construct entries which need the minimum of alteration because of changes during the course of publication of serials.'

The elements to be covered in the description are – in AACR order: title and (if required) subtitle, volume designation and dating of the serial as published, place of publication, publisher, date (if required), collation, and series statement (if any). 'All further information that is necessary (including an indication of the library's holdings) is given in notes after the series statement.'

To give a simple example:

The Assistant librarian. Vol. 46–   Jan. 1953–
   London: Association of Assistant Librarians.
   v.   cm.
   Monthly.
   Continues The library assistant, v.1–45, 1898–1952.
   Library has: v. 50–   , Jan. 1957–

An obvious difference between this and an entry for a monograph is the 'open' style of entry: volume numbers, dates, etc., being left open so long as the periodical remains alive.

Note that the code recommends that the catalogue entry represent the full serial – the 'whole published set' – even though the library's holdings may be incomplete, the holdings themselves being subsequently indicated in the notes. In practice many libraries adopt the reverse procedure – or simply restrict information to their own holdings. As holdings change with the purchase of back-files, etc., economy lies with AACR. On the other hand, AACR procedure may well cause the cataloguer more work. Moreover, where the catalogue is for public use (in place of, or in addition to, a visible index), as not all clients bother to read detailed notes, the reference librarian will frequently be asked for issues that are discovered to be not in stock only after a further inspection of the catalogue.

AACR, following its rules for each part of the entry, outlines fourteen topics that could be the subject of Notes. They include changes of title, editors, issuing body, duration and suspension of publication, bibliographical history and relationships, supplements, holdings, indexes.

Hamilton has criticized these rules for their excessive detail, among other things:

I do not for a moment dispute the importance in a large research library's catalogue of almost every piece of information, and in certain circumstances any bit of it may be extremely valuable. Nevertheless, unless the rules are applied in individual libraries with a good deal of discretion, directed towards tailoring the entries to meet the needs of the staff and users of the library, the consequence will be the provision of entries in catalogues which will in many cases be far more detailed than is necessary, and the expenditure of a great deal of cataloguers' time and library money in ascertaining details which cannot be discovered from the publication in hand.[12]

However, it should be recognized that the code makes it clear that discrimination is to be exercised. After the outline of aims quoted above, the following statement is made: 'The proportionate value which a library attaches to each of these aims depends partly on the number and nature of its serials holdings, and partly on what other records of serials it maintains.' As Hamilton himself remarks: 'We should recognise that the rules for descriptive cataloguing are guides and not mandatory instructions.'[13]

PHOTOGRAPHIC AND OTHER REPRODUCTIONS OF DOCUMENTS

The rules in AACR relating to the cataloguing of works produced by photographic techniques (other than reissues by the same publisher, reprint editions, etc.) vary according to the following categories:

(a) *Facsimile editions* (i.e. 'editions the chief purpose of which is to provide replicas that reproduce as closely as possible the original publication, manuscript, etc., that has been copied' – rule 190). If a new title page is provided, this forms the basis of the catalogue entry, otherwise the original title page as reproduced is used. 'In the latter case the original imprint is followed by the imprint of the reproduction, supplied in brackets if necessary: London, 1783 [London: N. Douglas, 1926.]' Collation follows the general rules for collation. Notes should clearly indicate that the entry refers to a facsimile, and should provide the information necessary to the proper identification of the original work – for example, the original title page details where this has not been used in the body of the entry.

(b) *Photoreproductions to be described as such* (191). With the exception of original editions in microfilm (see below) the entry should, in such cases, describe the *original* work reproduced. The details referring to the *reproduction* are to be given in notes indicating: (i) type of reproduction (microfilm, photocopy, etc.); (ii) imprint details for the organization responsible for the reproduction; (iii) physical description (in the case of microreproductions, the number of pieces – cards, reels, etc. – and height and/or width). In the case of a macroreproduction (a photocopy, for example) the physical description need be given only when it differs significantly from the description of the original. The following example is provided:

Shirley, James
 The gentleman of Venice, a tragi-comedy presented at the house in Salisbury Court by Her Majesties servants. London: Printed for H. Moseley, 1655.
  78p. 18cm.
  Micro-opaque. New York: Readex Microprint, 1953. 1 card. 23 x 15 cm. (Three centuries of drama: English, 1642–1700)

If the copy is an *original edition in microfilm* (191C) it is 'catalogued according to its own indicia of identification':

American periodical series: eighteenth century. 1–33. Ann Arbor, Mich.: University Microfilms, [1942?]
 33 reels. 35mm.
 Microfilm.

MAPS

As maps are without conventional title pages the cataloguer has to determine the source of his information. AACR (212A) states: 'The whole face of a sheet map is considered as the source of cataloguing information' – but this needs to be qualified, for the face of the map may present varied information and alternative forms. Thus AACR (212B) has to give a priority order for choice of *title* in those cases where the face of the map presents more than one: 'Preference over a margin title is given to the title within the border of the map, or within a cartouche, which, on early maps, includes author, title, imprint, etc. If a base map has been overprinted, the overprinted title is used for the body of the entry. The dedication, in whole or in part, may be used as the title for early maps.' Again, in the choice of *author heading* a decision has often to be made between carto-grapher, editor, and corporate body – and AACR (211A) states: 'A map, series or set of maps, or an atlas, etc., the content of which is mainly confined to geographic information, is entered under the person or corporate body that is explicitly indicated as primarily responsible for its geographic content. The ap-pearance on a map of the phrase "compiled by" or its equivalent in a foreign language is ordinarily understood to indicate primary responsibility.' (As a result, a map may – as in the example given for the rule – be entered under National Geographic Society, even though an editor and cartographer are named.) As responsibility is not always explicit, AACR has to provide a priority order for the various possibilities (211B).

The title may be followed by the *author statement* (in this case cartographer, engraver, editor, etc.) in conformity with (134). An additional item of information of particular significance is *scale* – and this (by 212D) is given after the author statement and is normally expressed as a ratio, e.g. 1:90,000.

Other elements in the description (212 E–H) follow the usual pattern: *edition* (which may combine a standard series designa-tion); *imprint*; *collation* (in which size includes height and width – of the sheet or of the map itself if the difference is significant); *series*.

Information on certain other features peculiar to maps may form the basis of *notes* – e.g. projection (212 J 5) and insets and additional features (212 J 10). Notes may also give some indica-tion of content (e.g. the precise area covered by the map) and sources and bibliographical history.

Finally, where a map contains additional material (e.g. an inset) AACR stresses the importance of providing analytical entries (212 L).

Example:

John Bartholomew and Son.
  Norfolk. Scale: 1:126,720. Edinburgh: Bartholomew, 1965.
  Map 52 x 81 cm. fold. to 22 x 11 cm. (Half-inch contoured Great Britain.)
  Reduced from Ordnance Survey with local revision to date of publication.

MOTION PICTURES AND FILMSTRIPS

The authorship of films being normally diffuse and of slight significance so far as retrieval is concerned, main entry is by *title* (220A). Difficulties arise from the fact that there are often variations in titles and AACR rules that entry should be 'under the title under which it is released, whether or not it is the title of the original release, followed, after any alternative title or subtitle, by the designation (*Motion picture*) or (*Filmstrip*)'.

Producer and distributor (when the film is distributed by a company other than the one responsible for production) take the place of the normal *author/imprint* statement. The names of the companies follow the title and designation and are in turn followed by the date of release (223 B–D). 'For identification purposes, the city or country in which the main office of a foreign producing company is located is also given when known.'

The *collation* statement (224) indicates length (running-time or number of frames); whether sound or silent, in colour, sepia, or black and white; and the width of the film in millimetres. It is followed by *series* note (225).

As with all special materials *notes* may be extensive. AACR (226–9) suggests, *inter alia*, variant titles, credits and cast, and summary of content.

Particular problems arise in the cataloguing of 'films issued in a series or as continuations (e.g. a newsreel)'. By (229A) these are treated as collections. In such cases the collation indicates the total number of reels and notes analyse the contents. Other films 'prepared for release in chapters' are treated as serials (229B).

Example:

> The Specialist (Motion picture). Heald-Samson Productions. Ritz Film Distributors, 1967.
>
> 20 mins. sd. b&w. 35mm.
>
> Based on the novel The specialist, by Charles Sale.
>
> *Credits:* Producer, Sybil Samson; director, James Hill; music, Alan Clare; film editor, John Bloom. *Cast:* Bernard Miles.
>
> The exploits of a country carpenter who specializes in building privies.

(This example is a modified version of an entry in the *British film catalogue.*)

MUSIC

Although superficially more closely related to conventional book form than some of the other materials treated in this section, music presents the cataloguer with unique and complex problems which demand specialist attention.

In the first place, arrangements, transcriptions, collections and works of mixed authorship call for special extensions of the general cataloguing rules for determining appropriate headings, and AACR (230–232) provides for a number of such cases. Added entries and analyticals are common.

Then again, many title pages are unsatisfactory bases for descriptive cataloguing; they frequently omit information necessary for the proper identification of works. In addition, the information may not be presented in an order suitable for straight transcription. Even the following examples of simple title pages will demonstrate the point:

> Schubert/String Quartet/Cuarteto/'The Death and the Maiden'/ 'La Muerte y la Doncella'/D Minor. Re Menor/Op. posth.
>
> Quartet/No 17/F Major/for 2 Violins, Viola and Violoncello/by Ludwig van Beethoven/op. 135
>
> Brahms/Quartet/für Klavier, Violine/Viola und Violoncello/opus 26

Add to this the international nature of music publishing and the consequent range of languages likely to be met in a music library, and it is easy to understand why the use of *uniform titles* is commonplace. Such titles assist both identification and collocation.

AACR (233) states: 'A uniform title is established to bring together all editions and arrangements of a work that would not otherwise be brought together. It consists essentially of the title with which the work was originally issued or, alternatively, of the title or designation by which the work is cited in standard musical literature.' The following example is provided:

> Wagner, Richard.
>   [Meistersinger von Nürnberg]
>   The mastersingers of Nuremburg.

Rules (234–43) deal with the construction of a uniform title –

in particular one consisting of 'conventional terms describing the form of the composition and its instrumentation (e.g. sonata for piano, symphony, concerto for violin and orchestra, string quartet), together with its position in a sequence of the composer's works, its key, and possibly a popular name . . .' In such instances the order of elements in the uniform title is standardized: 'form and instrumentation, number (if any) within an established sequence of the form, key, opus (or equivalent) number, descriptive title or sobriquet'. The example given is as follows:

Sonata, piano, no. 14, C sharp minor, op. 27, no. 2 (Moonlight)

These rules also prescribe the style of uniform title for collections, excerpts, arrangements, reductions, etc.

The description proper follows the uniform title, and the appropriate rules here are (244–8). As the cover of a musical work often contains more information than the title page itself, AACR suggests that the description be based on 'data presented by the title page, cover or caption, whichever gives the fullest information'. It should consist of *title; imprint* (in which the plate number or publisher's number may be used as a substitute for date when the latter is not available); *collation* (where pagination may be complicated by the necessity for specifying score and parts); *series. Notes* may cover such matters as form of composition, medium of performance, text, notation, contents.

Examples:

Vitali, Giovanni Battista.
   [Sonata, violins 2, bass viol or cello, and organ or harpsichord or piano, F major, op. 5, no. 8 (La Guidoni)]
   Sonata, op. 5, no. 8, in F major: 'La Guidoni'; for two violins, bass viol or cello, and organ or harpsichord (or piano); newly edited by Michael Tilmouth. London: Stainer and Bell, 1960.
   Score (25p.) and 4 parts. 30cm.

Mussorgsky, Modeste.
   [Boris Godunov. Vocal score. English]
   Boris Godunov: an opera in four acts with a prologue, the subject taken from Pushkin's dramatic chronicle of the same name, and Karamazin's History of the Russian Empire. The complete and original text edited in accordance with the

autograph manuscripts by Paul Lamn; English translation by David Lloyd-Jones. London: Oxford University Press, 1968.

418p.   30cm.

Duration: about 3 hours.

PHONORECORDS

Phonorecords (a term used to cover a variety of recording media), being different from other works (books, music, etc.) in form rather than content, the general cataloguing rules apply with certain modifications. First, the *title* (or uniform title) is followed by 'a statement of physical medium . . . to distinguish the aural from the visual forms of the same work' (252A). *Imprint* (252C) may include place, record publisher, date and serial number of the recording. *Collation* (252D) will vary in detail according to the particular form of the medium (disc, tape, etc.). The collation for the general run of records specifies number of volumes or sides, diameter of the record, speed, and the term 'microgroove' or 'stereophonic' as appropriate. Information as to participant, performer, medium; language; date and details of original recording; supplementary materials; etc., are provided in the *Notes* (252F). As with music it is often necessary to make added entries and analyticals.

Example:

Schubert, Franz

[Quintet, violins 2, viola, violoncellos 2, C major, D.956] *Phonodisc.*

String quintet in C major, D.956 (opus 163). Saga XID 5266. 1966.

2s. 12 in. 33⅓ r.p.m. microgroove.

Aeolian String Quartet, with Bruno Schrecker, 2nd. violoncello.

PICTURES

Chapter 15 of AACR covers 'pictures, designs, and other two-dimensional representations'. Although the code recognizes that such materials are often catalogued in special collections by 'subject or other category', rules are frequently needed for author/title headings, and (260–4) provide such rules under two headings; single works and collections. In general, the latter may be entered under author (artist, etc.), collector or title according to circumstances; the former under the author or, if anonymous, under title.

Difficulties may arise in the provision of a *title* statement when the work is known by a title (or titles) attributed to it; when the work contains variant titles; and when the work is without a title. (265) caters for these conditions, indicating how a form of title is to be arrived at. *Author statement* (266) may cover 'all persons or firms [excluding publisher] mentioned as having contributed to the production of the picture'. *Imprint* details for reproductions (267–8) correspond to those for books – though the information is often much less certain. *Collation* includes a statement of the physical medium or form, (269 1c) providing a list of commonly used terms; a statement of colour; and size. *Series* (270) and supplementary *notes* (271) follow, the latter providing further information on such matters as authorship, alternative titles, physical description, provenance, and – for reproductions – location of the original.

Example:

> Constable, John.
> Wivenhoe Park, Essex. Greenwich, Connecticut, New York Graphic Society, [19– ?]
> col collotype.   50 × 92cm.
> Reproduction of the original (oil on canvas) in the Widener Collection, National Gallery of Art, Washington, DC.
> Printer: Arthur Jaffé Heliochrome Company.

READING

1. LIBRARY OF CONGRESS. *Studies in descriptive cataloging.* Washington, GPO, 1948.
2. LIBRARY OF CONGRESS. op. cit.
3. LIBRARY OF CONGRESS. *Rules for descriptive cataloging.* Washington, GPO, 1949. Supplement, 1952.
4. For an interesting discussion of this see: VERONA, S. 'Literary unit versus bibliographical unit'. *Libri*, 9 (2), 1959, 79–104.
5. LINDEN, R. O. 'Chapter 6: Separately published monographs and other non-serial publications (rules 130–156)'. (In *Seminar on the Anglo-American cataloguing rules (1967)* ... London, Library Association, 1969. pp. 45–54.)
6. CUTTER, C. A. *Rules for a dictionary catalog.* 4th ed. Washington, GPO, 1904. p. 11.

7. A plea for evaluation in annotation and abstracts is made by D. G. MACRAE, Professor of Sociology, London School of Economics, in an article entitled 'Information services and literature currently available to research workers and librarians' (In *Information methods of research workers in the social sciences*. London, Library Association, Reference, Special and Information Section, 1961).

8. BORKO, HAROLD *and* CHATMAN, SEYMOUR. 'Criteria for acceptable abstracts: a survey of abstracters' instructions'. *American Documentation*, 14 (2), April 1963, 149–60.

9. CUTTER. op. cit. p. 11.

10. Examples of books and codes covering special categories of material include:

DAVINSON, D. E. *The periodicals collection: its purpose and uses in libraries*. London, Deutsch, 1969.

GRENFELL, D. *Periodicals and serials*. 2nd ed. London, Aslib, 1965.

OSBORN, A. D. *Serial publications*. Chicago, ALA, 1955.

REDFERN, BRIAN. *Organizing music in libraries*. London, Bingley, 1966.

MUSIC LIBRARY ASSOCIATION *and* AMERICAN LIBRARY ASSOCIATION. *Code for cataloging music and phonorecords*. Chicago, ALA, 1958.

INTERNATIONAL ASSOCIATION OF MUSIC LIBRARIES. *International cataloguing code for music*. Peters, 1957 – (vol. 1, 1957; vol. 2, 1961).

NATIONAL FILM ARCHIVE. *Rules for use in the cataloguing department of the NFA*. 5th rev. ed. London, British Film Institute, 1960.

ASLIB. FILM PRODUCTION LIBRARIANS' GROUP. *Film cataloguing rules*. London, Aslib, 1963.

11. HAMILTON, G. E. 'Chapter 7: Serials (rules 160–168)'. (In *Seminar on the Anglo-American cataloguing rules (1967)* ... London, Library Association, 1969. pp. 55–66.) An article which, apart from its analysis of the code rules, raises a number of basic points on the cataloguing of serials in such a way as to make it a valuable general reading for students.

12. HAMILTON, G. E. op. cit. p. 60.

13. HAMILTON, G. E. op. cit. p. 61.

TAIT, JAMES A. *and* ANDERSON, F. DOUGLAS. *Descriptive cataloguing: a student's introduction to the Anglo-American cataloguing rules 1967*. London, Bingley, 1969.

Part Four
Policy and Organization

Chapter 15
Analytical Cataloguing

Analytical cataloguing is a term used to refer to the cataloguing of parts of documents – articles in periodicals, contributions to symposia, proceedings, etc. 'An analytical entry is an entry for a part, or a number of parts, of a publication for which a comprehensive main entry has already been made. Its purpose is to describe those parts of a publication that cannot be treated adequately (by either author or subject approach) in the entry for the whole publication' (AACR 156).

In libraries which use unit entries in their catalogues, added entries might be used to serve the purpose of analyticals, so long as information given in the unit clearly indicates the reason for the added entry heading. The advantage of this method is economy. On the other hand separate analyticals have the advantage of clarity; the reader has no need to scan the body of the unit entry and the notes to discover the information required. However, analytical entries are not to be confused with added entries for secondary subjects, joint authors, etc. They are for specific parts of documents, often distinguished from the containing document by having a different author.

AACR (156) prescribes slightly differing treatment for analyticals according to whether they refer to parts with separate title pages and separate paging, parts with separate title pages and continuous paging, or parts without special title pages. But basically the 'analytical entry consists of a description of the part analysed, followed by a short citation (known as the "analytical note") of the whole publication in which the part occurs'.

Analytical entries can be made under author, title or subject as illustrated below:

(i) *Author analytical*

Jonson, Ben
    Volpone, or The fox.

(*In* Morrell, J. M. Four English comedies of the 17th and 18th centuries. Harmondsworth, Middlesex, 1950. 18cm. p. 11–129)

(ii) *Title analytical*

Arden of Feversham
The lamentable and true tragedie of M. Arden of Feversham in Kent ... (*In* McIlwraith, A. K. ed. Five Elizabethan tragedies. London, 1938 (1936 reprint). 15 cm. p. 241–324)

(iii) *Subject analytical (alphabetical heading)*

TECHNICAL EDUCATION—SPAIN
McSweeny, J   H
Craftsmen and technicians in Spain.
(*In* Technical education, v. 5, no. 2, Feb. 1963, p. 60–63)

(iv) *Subject analytical (classified catalogue – UDC)*

378.962(46)
McSweeny, J   H
Craftsmen ... (as in (iii) above)

AACR suggested layout for analyticals appears clumsy by comparison with the practice of indexing and abstracting services. Here, for example, are typical entries from (a) *Sociological abstracts*, (b) *Psychological abstracts*, and (c) *British technology index*:

(a) Laskin, Richard (Illinois Institute of Technology, Chicago), A MASTER'S DEGREE PROGRAM IN SOCIOLOGY, American Sociologist, 1968, 3, 1, Feb, 16–18.

(b) **Arkin, Arthur M.** (Montefiore Hosp., Bronx, N.Y.) **Sleeptalking: A review.** *Journal of Nervous & Mental Disease,* 1966. **143**(2), 101–122.

(c) Holland's lifting equipment industry. M. Corper. Dock & Harbour Authority, 49 (Dec. 68) p. 228–90. il.

There is no generally accepted standard for such citations and AACR, with its different objectives, is unlikely to effect an improvement in the situation. As can be seen from the above examples there are variations in both content and order of items. One frequently met variant not illustrated here is the placing of year of publication immediately after the author's name – sometimes referred to as the Harvard System.

In 1951 the British Standards Institution (1629: 1950) suggested the following layout for analytical entries:

Articles in Books
Ramsbottom, John. 1931. Fungi pathogenic to man. MEDICAL RESEARCH COUNCIL. A system of bacteriology in relation to medicine. Vol. 8. London, H.M. Stationery Office, 1931. pp. 11–70.

(Note the position of the date after the author's name in order to give a filing sequence in chronological order within an author heading.)

Abridged:
Ramsbottom, John. Fungi pathogenic to man. MEDICAL RESEARCH COUNCIL, A system of bacteriology in relation to medicine. Vol. 8. 1931. pp. 11–70.

Articles in Periodicals
Caunter, C. F. 1947. The possibilities of light engine development. Aeronautics. Vol. 16, part 6, June, 1947. pp. 35–41.

Abridged:
Caunter, C. F. The possibilities of light engine development. Aeronautics. Vol. 16, 1947. pp. 35–41.

This style is less streamlined than it might be and for this and other reasons the standard has not been widely accepted. At the present time (1971) a revised standard is in preparation.

When are Analytical Entries Required?

In general terms, whenever a part of a document is significant on account of its author, title, or subject. Subject analyticals are easily the most widely used type, but author analyticals may be useful when a complete work which is likely to be required is included in a collection (see the example in (i) above) – for even if the library has copies of the work separately published it may be useful to know of the existence of another. The author analytical may also be useful if the library has a particular interest in an author, e.g. public libraries may index all writings of local authors; college libraries may index the writings of members of staff: in such cases even short articles in periodicals and contributions to books may warrant an entry. The title analytical will be valuable for those works which have no author (as in the example (ii) above), otherwise title analyticals will not usually be made, a reference to author being more satisfactory. Subject analyticals may be needed to discover articles which provide information not readily available in the library in book form – especially when the subject is of special interest in that library. In libraries concerned with rapidly developing subjects where periodical articles and contributions to collections, transactions, etc., contain some of the most up-to-date information available in print, and where readers frequently demand comprehensive lists of the literature on a subject, the catalogue may be mainly composed of such analytical entries.

The Cost of Analytical Cataloguing

(i) *Amount*. Jolley writes: 'There is clearly no end to the proliferation of these entries. After all, each item in the index to each book is a potential analytical subject entry. Black has stated: "We index twenty periodicals. The index, which contains some 35,000 cards, grows at the rate of 5,000 a year." '[1]

(ii) And it is not just a matter of amount; periodicals, articles, etc., present specific *cataloguing problems*: for example, whereas the cataloguer can frequently get a fair impression of the subject content of a book by glancing at the contents list, introduction, etc., in the case of an article he has often to scan the whole. Moreover, the subject may well be a piece of research into a 'new' subject presenting problems of classification, subject headings, indexing; for this and other reasons, many articles will be concerned with highly complex subjects rarely, if ever, met in books, e.g. the action of certain carcinogenic and inactive hydrocarbons on the mitochondira of liver cells. Such subjects present special problems to the subject cataloguer.

(iii) Further expense arises from the fact that analytical entries, being often for ephemeral subjects, need constant *weeding* (the use of different coloured cards or slips to distinguish analyticals from other entries is of value here).

(iv) Such entries bulk the catalogue, making its *use* increasingly difficult and time-consuming – and if they are kept in a separate sequence the danger is that they may be overlooked by users.

Substitutes

It may be that the use of computers will at least save a certain amount of effort; though the initial analysis and coding is likely to remain outside the realm of automation, at least for some time to come, the filing and cumulation of entries and the production of print-out may be left to the machine. Again, for certain purposes, *contents lists* may be used as a substitute: these are simply lists of articles arranged under the titles of the containing journals. Their production is amenable to computers, or they may be duplicated for users from typed copy or photocopies of title pages. Of course, they fail to provide an adequate basis for retrospective searching (even when they are computer-produced and complemented with author and keyword indexes), but they can supply a valuable current awareness service and may fill the gap between publication date and the appearance of published indexes, abstracts, etc. There are also published contents lists – notably the weekly *Current contents* (Institute of Scientific Information, Philadelphia), a service made up of several bulletins covering science and technology and the social sciences.

Published bibliographical tools – keyword indexes, conventional indexes, abstracts, etc. – are the usual substitutes adopted by librarians. As the literature of subjects expands so such tools as *British technology index, British humanities index, Chemical abstracts,* etc., act as substitutes for the librarian's own catalogue. Although they are not a perfect solution, librarians using these aids have been able to make great savings – and indeed to do work otherwise impossible. In particular, when the coverage of such services exceeds that of the library, the reader's attention is drawn to items he would otherwise overlook – and with the development of the National Lending Library's services the interlending that such discoveries necessitate has been made very much easier.

The limitations of published services (as substitutes) are, very briefly, as follows:

(i) They may not reflect the special needs of the library – thus the indexing may be selective and omit 'minor' articles or items of correspondence which though of limited general interest are of concern to a particular library; or an abstract may omit to bring out a point in an article which, though minor, is of great value in a particular library. In the same way an index may give a subject heading that covers the general theme but not the section of the article of special interest; or the bibliography itself may have a special viewpoint – thus, for example, *Printing abstracts*, being produced for the trade, is not geared to the requirements of librarians studying printing methods.

(ii) They may cover only a limited selection of periodicals, others taken in the library thus remaining unanalysed.

(iii) They may be seriously out of date.

(iv) They may be poorly organized – e.g. poor headings and cross references, unsatisfactory indexes (in the case of abstracts), infrequent cumulation. (However, it could be argued that many published services, being produced by specialists who have applied themselves to the problems of indexing, are superior in organization to the typical home-made catalogue.)

(v) Their use necessitates, even with the best systems of cumulation, a search through several sequences (weeks, months, years). To this should be added the fact that the librarian, having discovered material in these bibliographies, must often search his own catalogues to see whether the documents referred to are in the library.

(vi) Whilst periodicals coverage might be satisfactory, composite works may not be included, and so the librarian is still faced with the analysis of such documents. Remember too that many subjects lack any published indexing or abstracting services, and many more lack really efficient ones, though the situation improves each year.

Policy

Thus the policy of any library regarding analytical cataloguing will be affected by the following considerations:

(i) The number of periodicals, proceedings, etc. taken. In a library which takes only a few works the librarian may find it practicable to do his own indexing – and this may be more economic than buying the frequently expensive published bibliographies. But his service will be limited accordingly.

(ii) The availability of published bibliographies in the subject(s) covered in the library, and their effectiveness according to the considerations mentioned above. The librarian may need only to supplement the existing bibliographies to compensate for their defects.

(iii) The extent to which readers require comprehensive literature searches.

(iv) The nature of the subject(s) – rapidly developing (in which periodicals, articles, etc., are the main source of information) or comparatively static.

(v) The nature of the periodicals, etc. Where articles are of an ephemeral nature they may not warrant extensive analysis. In some libraries, e.g. those in certain commercial subjects, much of the stock is of an ephemeral nature. Self-indexing cuttings files may then be made, rather than analytical catalogues.

In *public libraries* analytical cataloguing is often found in certain special collections, e.g. the local history collection – though too rarely are the local newspapers indexed at all. The commercial and technical departments frequently have special indexes of articles of local concern – and note the cooperative or centralized indexing in technical services like Sinto, Ladsirlac, Hertis, etc. Catalogues of drama and music collections frequently contain analytical entries. Too often, however, periodicals are taken and bound but not indexed – and too often the published indexes are not available either. In small libraries there is perhaps an even greater case for the use of analyticals to make up for the deficiencies of the book stock.

University libraries usually take large numbers of periodicals and rely to a very great extent on the published indexes. In any case, their subject catalogues are, with some notable exceptions, rudimentary.

In *special libraries* – especially industrial libraries – the situation varies, often according to the availability of specialized published indexes. In general, however, much subject analysis of periodicals and other composite material is usual, because of the inadequacy of books and the demands of readers for comprehensive surveys of the literature. The indexing can be selective and yet remain efficient because users' requirements can often be clearly defined.

READING

1. JOLLEY. Quoted in Osborn, A. D. *Serial publications*. Chicago, ALA, 1955. p. 179.

———

PEARSON, J. D. 'The analytical cataloguing of periodicals in a specialized field'. *Library Association Record*, 57 (1), January 1955, 1–7.

TAUBER, M. *The subject analysis of library materials*. New York, Columbia University, School of Library Service, 1953. Includes several chapters of relevance here and elsewhere in this book.
See also the readings on periodicals noted in Chapter 14 and the many articles on published indexing and abstracting services. The services themselves should also be examined – and note particularly the introductions to the various cumulations of the *British technology index*.

Chapter 16
Order in Catalogues: Filing

Once catalogue entries are made, they have to be filed in order – and this is not always as simple an operation as it may at first appear to be. Indeed there are several elaborate codes of rules for filing, and unless the cataloguer uses a code he is bound to mis-file entries – then all his cataloguing will have been in vain. The bigger the catalogue the greater the problems – but size is not the only factor; certain types of catalogue present more difficulties than others.

In a classified sequence the order is determined by the notation and filing is an automatic process except where symbols having no ordinal value are used (brackets, dashes, strokes, etc.). In such cases the filer has to observe very carefully the filing order laid down for such symbols. The real filing problems arise in alphabetical sequences, and in particular those sequences where several types of entry (author, subject, title, form, analyticals) are interfiled – as in the dictionary catalogue.

In this chapter we shall examine some of the problems as set out in the ALA *Rules for filing catalog cards*.[1] Although a second edition of these rules appeared in 1968, the original rules of 1942 are still widely used and reference will be made to both editions in the following notes.* The aim here is to identify some of the more important problems and to indicate briefly solutions offered by this code. Several other codes exist[2] but I have made no attempt at a comparative analysis – nor, I think, should the student try to do so (at least, not until familiarity with one set of rules has been achieved). Comparison at this stage is likely to lead only to confusion.

The second edition begins with notes establishing a Basic Principle and a Basic Order:

---

* The numbers in brackets refer to the ALA rules and the dates indicate edition where this is not obvious.

Basic Principle: Filing should be straightforward, item by item through the entry, not disregarding or transposing any of the elements, nor mentally inserting designations. In the following rules there are only a few situations where this principle is not applied: these are usually due to the structure of the heading.

Basic Order: 1) The basic order is alphabetical, word by word, except in certain areas where a numerical or chronological arrangement is preferable.

2) When the same word, or combination of words, is used as the heading of different kinds of entry, the entries are arranged alphabetically word by word, disregarding kind of entry, form of heading, and punctuation, except that personal surname entries are arranged before other entries beginning with the same word or combination of words.

These initial statements reflect a trend towards simplification and consistency, a trend that is noted in the Preface: 'Because of the difficulties encountered in using that [1942] edition, and the many pleas for simpler rules that were received, it was decided that the new edition should be a consistent code of rules derived from one basic principle, with as few exceptions as possible.'

Where the 1942 code had either accepted the traditional complexities of 'classed arrangement' (i.e. the filing of different categories of entries as groups), or retained them in alternative rules, the new code makes a significant move towards single-alphabet orders. For example, there is now no longer provision for separate sequences under such a heading as Wells, according to category of entry (person, place, subject, title): with the exception of personal surname entries all file in a single alphabetical sequence.

Another important feature of the 1968 code is its relation to AACR; the committees responsible for these two codes worked in cooperation and the filing rules are now consistent with the main code. Clearly there is a relationship between choice of heading and filing. The initial choice is, in fact, partly a response to the question: with what other entries shall the entry for this document be collocated? When AACR recommends the use of structured uniform titles – e.g. Bible. *N.T. Mathew. English. Revised* . . . or Sonata, piano, no. 14, C sharp minor, op. 27, no. 2 – an elaborate filing order is being created. If filing rules are developed in the context of a general cataloguing code there are obvious gains in consistency and standardization.

The 1968 code is divided into two parts. 'Part One, Alphabetical Arrangement', contains four basic rules for alphabetization and special rules for the alphabetization of abbreviated forms, variant forms, and names. 'Part Two, Order of Entries', is concerned with the problems that arise in the arrangement of particular sequences (authors, subjects, titles, etc.).

Alphabetical Arrangement

BASIC RULES

The 1968 code (as 1942) advocates 'word by word' order rather than 'letter by letter' (1968: 1, 1942: 1). For example:

> I met a man
> Im Wandel der Jahre
> Image books
> Image of America
> Images of America
> Imaginary conversations
> In an unknown land
> In the days of the giants
> Inca

Initial articles (1968: 4) are generally to be disregarded. (An appendix gives a list of such articles in various languages.)

> A apple pie
> A travers la France
> Apache
> An April after
> Aquarium
> L'art des jardins
> Artists

ABBREVIATED FORMS

Initials are to be regarded as one-letter words. They are to precede longer words beginning with the same initial letter. Entries consisting of initials plus words are to be interfiled with those consisting of initials only (1968: 5).

> A.
> A.A.
> AAAA
> AAA Foundation for Traffic Safety
> AAAS Conference on Science Teaching
> AACE
> A., A.J.G.
> AAUN news
> 'A' and 'B' mandates
> A., André C. H., *see* . . .
> A apple pie
> A.B.
> The ABC about collecting
> ABC and XYZ
> A.B.C. programs
> A., J
> A was an archer
> Aa, Pieter van der
> Aabel, Marie

Acronyms (1968: 5) are treated as words rather than as initials unless they are 'written in all capitals with a space or period between the letters (e.g. UNESCO; U.N.E.S.C.O.), which forms are to be filed as initials'.

Abbreviations. Both editions – (1942: 5) and (1968: 6) – specify arrangement 'as if spelled in full in the language of the entry' (Dr as Doctor, Mr as Mister, Vt as Vermont, Va as Virginia, etc.). An exception is made for Mrs, which is filed as written. Note also that initials standing for names of organizations are treated as initials not abbreviations (1968: 5).

Numerals. Arrange as if spelled out in the language of the entry (1968: 9, 1942: 9). Round thousands are filed as if expressed as hundreds, e.g. 1100 as eleven hundred, but 1001 as one thousand and one. The 1968 code also notes certain 'special usages'. Example:

> 10 ans de politique sociale en Poland (i.e. dix)
> 1915; revue de guerre en deux actes (i.e. dix neuf cent quinze)
> Henry V, King of England, 1387–1433 (i.e. Henry, King of England, 5)
> Henry VIII, King of England, 1491–1547 (i.e. Henry, King of England, 8)
> Henry VIII and his wives (i.e. Henry the Eighth)

Henry V: a facsimile of the first folio ... (i.e. Henry the Fifth)
1918, the last act (i.e. nineteen eighteen)
100 American poems (i.e. one hundred)
112 Elm Street (i.e. one twelve)
2400 business books (i.e. twenty four hundred)

Note: by (1968: 25) given names are arranged by designation and then numerically – as in the examples above.

VARIANT FORMS

There are two main categories here: (i) variations in *spelling*, and (ii) variations in the citing of *compounds*. In general the 1968 code recommends the 'interfiling of the same words spelled differently and of the same compound words written differently, when more than one form appears in the catalog'.

Words spelled in different ways (1968: 10). 'When different entries, including corporate names, begin with or contain the same word spelled in different ways (e.g. Color and Colour), choose one spelling ... and file all entries under that spelling.' Certain criteria for making a choice among various spellings are given – e.g. commonly accepted current usage, American spelling, modern rather than archaic. References are to be made from variant forms. (A choice need be made only when more than one form appears in the catalogue.)

Words written in different ways (1968: 11). When a compound word appears in the catalogue in only one form, the form found in the document is to be adhered to: 'Arrange as two words compound words that are written as two separate words', and 'Arrange as one word compound words that are written as one'. Hyphened words are arranged 'as separate words when the parts are complete words, i.e. when each part can stand alone as a word in the context of the combined word (e.g. Epoch-making, but not Co-operative)'.

However, when the compound appears in different forms in the catalogue (as one word, hyphened, or as two words), entries are to be interfiled under the one-word form and appropriate references made – e.g. Homecoming, with reference from Home-coming or Home coming.

These rules correspond in general terms with the 1942 rules, though there are specific differences – e.g. whether to use the single-word form or the hyphened form for words that could be written in both ways was left to the cataloguer (1942: 11).

NAMES – ALPHABETIZATION

Apart from the problems that arise in the arrangement of entries for proper names (see below), there are difficulties of alphabetization in certain cases – for example, compound names, names with prefixes, etc. Rules 13–18 (1968) provide for such cases. *Compounds* (1968: 13, 1942: 12) are to be treated as separate words (e.g. Hall-Edwards, Hall Williams); *names with prefixes* (1968: 14, 1942: 13) are treated as one word (e.g. De la Roche). Differences in *spelling* (1968: 18, 1942: 15) are, of course, to be maintained (e.g. Anderson, Anderssen, etc.).

Order of Entries

The provision of the kinds of rules we have been examining so far – rules relating to alphabetization – is only one of the functions of a filing code. Beyond this there is the need for rules dictating the order of (or within) the various kinds of entries. The problem can be seen most clearly in the case of the dictionary catalogue: here one has to consider the arrangement of author, title, subject, and place entries in relation to each other. One heading – London, for example – may be each in turn. In such instances are we to distinguish between the different Londons or file all entries in one alphabetical sequence regardless of their nature? Even when a dictionary sequence is not employed there are problems of order within the different categories of headings. For example, in a personal name sequence there is the question of how to file those entries that have the same heading distinguished by designation, those that refer to a family or clan, those that are corporate bodies (firms, etc.); within any one author heading there are problems relating to the order of items – editions of a work, critical studies, added analytical entries, etc.; in an alphabetical subject sequence there are various kinds of subheadings (periods, places, subjects, etc.) which may be arranged in separate sequences or in straight alphabetical order. In a catalogue of any size these problems soon become acute and it is hardly surprising that

complex rules have resulted. In general, however, the trend
has been towards simplification: whereas earlier codes tended
to create elaborate classifications according to types of entries,
there is now a distinct preference for single alphabetical
sequences.

BASIC RULE

The basic rule for order of entries (1968:19) states:

A. When the same word, or combination of words, is used as the
heading of different kinds of entry, arrange the entries in two
main groups as follows:
   (1) Single surname entries, arranged alphabetically by forenames.
   (2) All other entries, arranged alphabetically word by word,
   disregarding kind of entry, form of heading, and punctuation.
B. Arrange subject entries under a personal or corporate name
immediately after the author entries for the same name.
C. Interfile title added entries and subject entries that are identical
and subarrange alphabetically by their main entries.

Example:
Love, John L.
LOVE, JOHN L.
Love, William
Love
Bowen, Elizabeth } (i.e. title added entry)
LOVE
Magoun, F. Alexander } (i.e. subject entry)
Love
Mamis, Justin } (i.e. title added entry)
Love and beauty
LOVE, MATERNAL
LOVE POETRY
LOVE – QUOTATIONS, MAXIMS, ETC.
Love songs, old and new
LOVE (THEOLOGY)
Love your neighbor

Note: the headings in capitals are subject headings.
   By contrast, the corresponding rule in the 1942 code (24)
allows 'classed order', i.e. arrangement by categories of entries

in four sequences: person, place, subject (when neither person nor place), title. An alternative provides for alphabetical arrangement, though even here when title and subject headings are identical, title entries are to follow the subject entries – thus the book by Bowen would file after the one by Magoun in the above example. The argument advanced for this segregation is that it facilitates a search for a title, especially when the author is not known. However, several studies of users of catalogues have shown that this distinction is not understood and it has been finally abandoned in the 1968 rules.

The rest of the code is largely concerned with the problems that arise in filing particular categories of headings. A brief summary will indicate their scope.

PERSONAL NAME ENTRY ARRANGEMENT

The main rule here (20B) prescribes that the order of entries under the same personal name shall be: (1) Surname alone with nothing following it; (2) Surname alone followed only by dates; (3) Surname followed by designation, forenames, or initials (in straight alphabetical sequence).

Example:
Smith,
Smith,   fl. 1641
Smith, Adam
Smith, Captain
Smith, J
Smith, John
Smith, Mr.

This rule alters the provisions of the 1942 code where, by rule 19, surnames alone or those followed by appellatives, designations, etc., preceded the same name with initials or forenames.

Other rules in this section cover special types of surname entries: names of clans, families, etc. (22); corporate name entries beginning with a surname (23); place names followed by a personal name or title (24); and given name entries, where the special problems which arise in filing forenames and similar headings for kings, dukes, etc., are considered.

AUTHOR ENTRY ARRANGEMENT

This section deals with the arrangement of entries within an author heading. The basic rule (26A) states that such entries should be arranged in three sequences: (1) Works *by* the author, subarranged alphabetically by their titles; (2) Works *about* the author, without subdivision, subarranged alphabetically by their main entries; except subject entries for individual works, which are arranged in Group 1 immediately after the author entries for the same work; (3) Works *about* the author, with subdivisions, subarranged alphabetically by the subdivisions.

The remaining rules cover such matters as translations, editions, author/title added entries, analytical entries, etc. Special consideration is given in rule 27 to 'organized author arrangement' using uniform headings.

These rules, though relatively complex, are simple compared with the rules – and alternative rules – in the 1942 code: (25) and (26).

CORPORATE ENTRY ARRANGEMENT

Rule 28 (1968) stipulates that corporate entries are to be arranged 'in their alphabetical places like titles', and that where there are different kinds of entries under the same corporate name they are to be arranged in groups: (1) author without subheading; (2) subject without subdivision, and identical title added entries interfiled; (3) name with subdivisions interfiled alphabetically with titles, etc.

Example:

United Nations
UNITED NATIONS
United Nations and how it works (i.e. title)
UNITED NATIONS – BIOGRAPHY
United Nations. Economic Commission for Europe
UNITED NATIONS. ECONOMIC COMMISSION FOR EUROPE
UNITED NATIONS – EGYPT
United Nations forces (i.e. title)

ANONYMOUS CLASSIC ENTRY ARRANGEMENT

Rules 29 and 31 (1968) cover anonymous classics (Bible, etc.), giving examples of the arrangement of entries arrived at by AACR.

PLACE ARRANGEMENT

Entries beginning with a place name may be authors, titles, or subjects; they may have corporate body, subject, or geographical qualifiers. London. Greater London Council; LONDON – WHARVES; London, Ont. Rule 31c (1968) states that where there are different kinds of entries under the same geographical heading the basic order shall be: (1) Author without sub-heading; (2) Subject without subdivision, and identical title added entries interfiled; (3) Headings with corporate and/or subject subdivisions interfiled with each other and titles.

Example:

London, Jack
London (i.e. place as author)
LONDON
London and Londoners (i.e. title)
London. Central Criminal Court
LONDON – DESCRIPTION
London, Ont. Council
LONDON, ONT. – HISTORY
London scene (i.e. title)
LONDON – WHARVES

(In studying the examples in this section of the 1968 code, students should note that some of the headings – e.g. London. National Gallery – would exist only as references if the British text of AACR were being used.)

Once again the 1968 code follows the simpler of the 1942 alternatives – see rules 31 and 32 in that code, where various degrees of grouping according to types of entries are allowed.

SUBJECT ARRANGEMENT

The 1942 code had also given alternative patterns for subject arrangement. One of these was a classified arrangement using eight types of headings – e.g. subject alone, as SCIENCE; subject with form or subject subdivisions, as SCIENCE – PERIODICALS; subject with period subdivisions, as SCIENCE –

HISTORY – 1600–1800; etc. The other was a simplified arrangement which, except in its placing of period divisions, closely resembles the order adopted in the 1968 code. The latter (32c) outlines the basic order as follows: (1) Subject without subdivision, interfiled with identical title entries; (2) period divisions, arranged chronologically; (3) alphabetical extensions of the main subject heading, interfiled in one alphabet with titles and other headings beginning with the same word.

Example:

EDUCATION
EDUCATION –1945–
EDUCATION – AFRICA
EDUCATION – AIMS AND OBJECTIVES
Education and American civilization (i.e. title)
EDUCATION - U.S.
EDUCATION – U.S. – 1945 –
EDUCATION – U.S. – BIBLIOGRAPHY

TITLE ENTRY ARRANGEMENT

As already demonstrated, titles are interfiled with other kinds of headings, after surname entries under the same word. Rule 33 (1968) provides for such problems as identical title added entries, arrangement of different editions of the same title, etc. It also specifies details of subarrangement under title main entries for periodicals and newspapers (33D).

The rest of the code deals with Added Entry Arrangement (34); Cross-Reference Arrangement (35) – 'a reference or explanatory note precedes all other entries under the same word or words'; Numerical and Chronological Arrangement (36); and Non-Book Materials Arrangement (37) – an extension of the 1942 code, covering music, phonorecords, motion pictures and filmstrips, and radio and television programmes.

Computers and Filing Rules

The following statement appears in the *Preface* to the 1968 code: 'These filing rules are basically for . . . manual filing. It may well be that the development of machine methods of filing will result in changes both in the form of entries and in their arrangement, in the not too distant future.'

The production of catalogues and bibliographies by computers is now a well-established procedure. And, of course, as a part of the process the computer has to be given instructions regarding the filing order of elements for the final print-out: it has to 'learn' alphabetical and numerical order, to recognize spaces between elements in the headings, etc. The need for relative simplicity in programming and operation requires that such instructions be kept to a minimum. Although the 1968 code shows a marked trend towards simplification, it is not without its complexities. There are several rules which oblige the filer to read the heading 'as if . . .' – for example, (9) which tells the filer to arrange numerals in titles 'as if spelled out in the language of the entry'. The simplest way of dealing with such a situation when using a computer is to spell out the numerical form so as to avoid the necessity of providing further instructions. Again, the rule for order of entries (19) states that when the same word is used for various categories of entries, personal surname entries are to precede all others. But the computer cannot file London, Jack before London unless given additional instructions. Rule 6, stipulating that abbreviations (Dr., Mr., etc.) shall be 'filed as if spelled out in full in the language of the entry', is another such example; so is rule 4 which calls on the filer to disregard initial articles.

The maker of a code for computer filing can resolve these difficulties in several ways:

(1) He may ignore the problem and accept a change in the final order. For example, he may decide to forego differentiation between personal surname entries and other categories, allowing the computer to print out the arrangement: London; London, Jack.

(2) He may devise a programme of instructions in order to ensure a predetermined order. For example, if it were considered desirable to file period subdivisions of a subject before other subdivisions, coding must be such as to allow the computer to differentiate between these two types of subdivision and to give priority in filing to the former.

(3) He may modify the heading itself so as to achieve the desired result. For example, titles beginning with numerals

can be coded as written out; initial articles can be omitted; abbreviations can be spelled out. In this way no additional instructions will be necessary.

An example of a code for computer filing that demonstrates these procedures and gives comparisons with the 1942 code, can be found in *Computer filing of index, bibliographic and catalog entries*,[3] by Hines and Harris. And the Birmingham School of Librarianship is at present undertaking a research programme to test basic principles established by a Library Association Filing Rules Working Party before a new code is formulated for computerized filing. Section 4 of the *MARC record service proposals*[4] affords valuable insights into some of the filing problems facing BNB as they prepare to computerize their operations.

READINGS

1. ALA. *Rules for filing catalog cards*. 2nd ed. Chicago, ALA, 1968. (An abridged edition is also available.)
2. For example: LIBRARY OF CONGRESS. *Filing rules in the dictionary catalogs*. Washington, Library of Congress, 1956.
   CUTTER, A. C. *Rules for a dictionary catalog*. 4th ed. Washington, GPO, 1904.
   BRITISH STANDARDS INSTITUTION. *Alphabetical arrangement*. London, BSI, 1951. (B.S. 1749: 1951.)
3. HINES, THEODORE C. *and* HARRIS, JESSICA L. *Computer filing of index, bibliographic and catalog entries*. Newark, N. J., Bro-Dart Foundation, 1966.
4. BNB. *MARC record service proposals*. London, BNB, 1968. (BNB/ MARC documentation service publications, no. 1.)

The close relationship between filing problems and choice of heading is evident in: DEWEY, H. *Specialized cataloging and classification*. Wisconsin, College Typing Co., 1956. v. 2. Chapter 46: 'The Bible as an example of complex organization problems in the card catalog'.

An interesting article on this subject is:

PERREAULT, J. M. 'Approaches to library filing by computer'. (In *Proceedings of the 1966 clinic on library applications of data processing*; ed. by H. Goldhor. Champaign, Illinois, University of Illinois Graduate School of Library Science, 1966.)

Chapter 17
Order on the Shelves.
Guides for the Reader

We have seen that the majority of documents are normally arranged according to subjects, using notational symbols representing those subjects in classification schemes. We have also seen that no matter how carefully constructed the scheme, it will separate as well as collocate related material. Catalogues help to compensate for this deficiency, by added entries or references or index entries: thus the book on two distinct subjects can only be shelved at one place but in the catalogue two entries can be made (either in the classified file or under two headings in the alphabetical catalogue); a book on a compound subject may have only one entry in the catalogue, but references or index entries will help to bring it to the attention of readers of those other elements of the compound which the class number failed to bring to the fore.

The limitations of shelf arrangement coupled with other disadvantages of *close classification* on the shelves (long class numbers, possible confusion for the reader, expense of alterations as new editions of schemes are produced) have led some cataloguers – especially those used to dictionary catalogues, where classification is a matter of shelf arrangement only – to deny the value of close classification of documents.[1] (The arguments are weaker where a classified catalogue is in operation and correspondence of shelf numbers with those used in the classified file is desirable – for, as we have stressed throughout this book, specific or 'close' classification in the classified catalogue is essential.)

However, it should be remembered that many of the objections to close classification are founded on classification schemes which have the faults associated with enumeration and many of the disadvantages (e.g. length of class numbers) would be largely overcome by the use of a faceted scheme with carefully apportioned notation. Again, there is no denying that close classification which distinguishes documents on one subject from those on another must be an aid to readers and staff, e.g. if twenty books on Industrial administration are classified at the same broad number, regardless of the specialized topics dealt with, then the reader who wants a document on say Work study or Quality control, will have to look through all these documents before he can be sure that a relevant one has not been missed – which would not be true if each of these specialized subjects had distinct class numbers. And it should be remembered that such a search will have to be made whenever documents on subjects more specific than that represented by the class number are required. Thus close classification enables the reference librarian to deal quickly with readers' enquiries. And there are other advantages which should not be lightly overlooked: (a) stock editing is greatly assisted; (b) stocktaking is facilitated; (c) records and statistics of issues, stock, etc., can be made in detail as required.

Reader interest arrangement[2] in public libraries is the outcome of the adverse attitude to shelf classification in its most extreme form. Instead of the usual classes, documents are arranged according to interests of casual readers. Such classes as the following are found: Current Affairs (or Everyman's business world or World today), People and Places (subheadings: Interesting people, Famous and History, Adventurous lives, War, Our country, Exploring nature, etc.); The Bright Side (Fiction, Plays, Essays, etc., of a chatty nature); Group Activities (Public speaking, Amateur theatricals); Your Family (Child care, The later years, Pets); and so on. It is suggested for small collections only.

Whilst close classification certainly has its limitations, such a solution to the problem is too drastic, alienating, as it does, the serious reader (and most readers are interested in particular subjects, even if they are 'general readers', i.e. even if their particular interest is temporary). Pandering to a 'mass public' (which, as Raymond Williams has pointed out, only exists in the mind – and especially the minds of certain journalists, film producers, etc.) can hardly do anything to support claims for more of the public's money for public libraries. Nevertheless there is no need to stick at the other extreme and suppose that once documents are closely classified the rest is up to the reader.

Limitations of shelf classification should be overcome by:

(i) *Displays:*[3] and especially displays that take as their theme attributes scattered by the classification – a country or a period or such 'concretes' as ships, children, etc. This is equally true for all kinds of library, for even in a special library concerned with a very limited field, the classification will still scatter related material. A relative index is a good guide to useful display subjects. This kind of display is particularly useful in a highly departmentalized library system, where the tendency to regard each department as quite separate from the others must be overcome by displays which collocate material from several. (An interesting example of a department which does itself cut across the traditional classes is the International Library in Liverpool, where documents on many aspects of various countries are housed.)

(ii) *Publications:* booklists which also cut across the traditional classes. Booklists which reflect the traditional classes are useful too, in that they are more attractive to the reader than the library catalogue. Again, published guides can help the reader to understand the arrangement and use of the library.

(iii) *Guiding:* classification will certainly present major difficulties to the reader if the shelves are not adequately guided. If departmental stores dealing with simple products need notices, how much more they are needed in libraries dealing with highly complex products. This is not to say that the library should be cluttered with ugly signs; all notices should be carefully contrived and aesthetically pleasing. There should be:

(a) a diagrammatic presentation of the layout of the collections conveniently placed, e.g. near the entrance;

(b) large guides to the various tiers of shelving (cf. the notices in some departmental stores). These guides will be composed mainly of one word (Engineering, Chemistry, etc.) and near by, where necessary, there should be further notices showing the breakdown of these main classes;

(c) guides to individual shelves, placed on the edge of the shelves themselves;

(d) cross references to indicate major separations, e.g. in a library using DC a reference from the Economics section to the Commerce and Business sections, and vice versa; also to parallel sequences where this is thought to be necessary.

An interesting development in shelf arrangement is seen at

Tottenham. Here the librarian, dissatisfied with the traditional breakdown into 'lending' and 'reference', and yet not convinced that subject departmentalization provided the answer, has arranged his stock according to a concept he calls *service in depth*.[4] In essence, the library is divided into several sections – counter, information and quick reference, general fiction, history, travel, biography, etc., in such a way that popular subjects are near to the counter and the less popular, 'student's subjects' are in the quietest part of the room; all books, periodicals, etc., reference or lending, are shelved together in the appropriate subject bay where provision is made for study as well as browsing. Classification remains, but, with the division of stock, the librarian hopes to cater for the general reader and the student more satisfactorily than with the traditional arrangements.

Guides to the Catalogues

The catalogues are themselves the chief guide to the stock and the most important single way of breaking down the barriers erected by the classification of books. Whatever the type of catalogue the distributed relatives are collocated and the deficiency of the original classification is remedied. However they are never simple tools – no precision instrument ever is. Therefore, if the most is to be made of them, they need themselves to be carefully guided. There are several possibilities.

GUIDING IN THE CATALOGUE

(a) *Colour.* We have already mentioned the value of colour in the classified catalogue; it would also be of undoubted value in the dictionary catalogue. For example, all author entries might be in white, subject entries in red, title entries in blue, and so on. In this way the reader is less likely to confuse the various types of entries. If only reference cards were in a different colour from the entries themselves something would have been achieved. Colour means that the instructions to the public (see below) can be very much more easily stated (e.g. 'If you want a book on a particular subject consult the catalogue under the heading for that subject: all subject entries are on blue cards').

(b) *Cross references*. The cataloguer should never hesitate to make cross references. Even an entry filing very close to another is often missed unless the reader's attention is directed to it; this is especially true in the classified file and in the more complicated sections of the dictionary catalogue.

(c) *Tabs*. Tabs should be used in card or sheaf catalogues, and thumb holes in the latter where possible.

(d) *Guide cards*. Every opportunity should be taken to ensure that guide cards are filed in appropriate places: e.g. at the main classes in the classified file, and at the beginning of complex sequences under country, etc., in the dictionary catalogue.

Guides Outside the Catalogue

(i) NOTICES

By the side of the catalogue there should be a clear notice giving basic instructions on the use of the catalogue. Such instructions should be brief, precise, non-pedantic, and well laid out (note the best examples of instructions issued by manufacturers on the use of their products). Remember that the reader is not interested in the catalogue, but only in answering an enquiry. The question and answer form or a modification of this, as shown below, is one method.

Example:

Classified catalogue

This catalogue contains entries for all books in the library, arranged in three sequences: (a) the classified section, where entries are arranged by class numbers representing the subjects of the books – as on the shelves; (b) the index of authors and titles; (c) the index of subjects.

To discover what books the library has by a certain AUTHOR consult the *author/title index*.

To discover whether the library has a book with a certain TITLE consult the *author/title index*. Not all books are entered under their titles, and if you cannot find the one you are looking for ask a member of staff to help.

To discover what books the library has on a certain SUBJECT, consult the *subject index* – this will give the class number at which entries for books on that subject will be found in the *classified section*.

THE NUMBER AT THE BOTTOM RIGHT OF THE CARD IS THE NUMBER AT WHICH THE BOOK WILL BE FOUND ON THE SHELVES. IF YOU CANNOT FIND THE ANSWER TO YOUR ENQUIRY PLEASE ASK A MEMBER OF STAFF TO HELP.

Dictionary catalogue

This catalogue contains entries for all books in the library, arranged alphabetically under their authors, titles, and subjects.

To discover what books the library has by a certain AUTHOR consult the catalogue under his name.

To discover whether the library has a book with a certain TITLE consult the catalogue under the title. Not all books are entered under their titles, and if you cannot find the one you are looking for ask a member of staff to help.

To discover what books the library has on a certain SUBJECT consult the catalogue under the name of that subject. For the best results the specific subject required should be sought; thus if you want books on Chemistry, look up Chemistry, not Science; if you want books on English poetry, look up English poetry, not Poetry or Literature.

THE NUMBER AT THE BOTTOM RIGHT OF THE CARD IS THE NUMBER AT WHICH THE BOOK WILL BE FOUND ON THE SHELVES. IF YOU CANNOT FIND THE ANSWER TO YOUR ENQUIRY PLEASE ASK A MEMBER OF STAFF TO HELP.

Instructions, as already pointed out, can be more effective if colour is used in the catalogue.

(ii) PRINTED GUIDES TO THE CATALOGUE

These might be issued separately or as part of a general guide to the library. In the case of special libraries, academic libraries, or special departments of public libraries – wherever readers frequently undertake extensive literature searches – the guide to the use of the catalogue might be combined with a pamphlet outlining the use of bibliographies, etc., in the literature search.

Again, over-elaboration is to be avoided, but there may be space for diagrammatic presentation; the use of colour in the diagram itself would assist comprehension.

Example:

Dictionary catalogue

(a) The catalogue contains entries for all books, pamphlets, and certain periodical articles, etc., arranged in one alphabetical sequence under author, title, and subject headings:

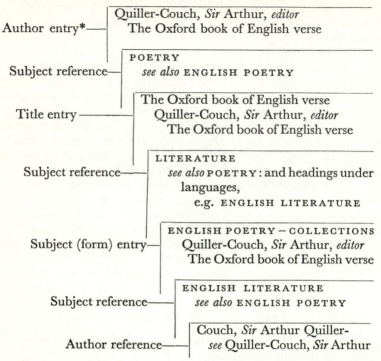

Author entry*———
> Quiller-Couch, *Sir* Arthur, *editor*
> The Oxford book of English verse

Subject reference———
> POETRY
> *see also* ENGLISH POETRY

Title entry —————
> The Oxford book of English verse
> Quiller-Couch, *Sir* Arthur, *editor*
> The Oxford book of English verse

Subject reference———
> LITERATURE
> *see also* POETRY : and headings under languages,
> e.g. ENGLISH LITERATURE

Subject (form) entry———
> ENGLISH POETRY – COLLECTIONS
> Quiller-Couch, *Sir* Arthur, *editor*
> The Oxford book of English verse

Subject reference———
> ENGLISH LITERATURE
> *see also* ENGLISH POETRY

Author reference———
> Couch, *Sir* Arthur Quiller-
> *see* Quiller-Couch, *Sir* Arthur

(b) The catalogue will thus tell you what material the library has:
by a certain author
with a particular title
on a certain subject

(c) *Author and title entries:* Author entries are made for all books, except for anonymous works which are entered under title. Title entries are also made for certain other titles, but as these are selective, you should consult the librarian if a particular title cannot be found, rather than assume that the book is not in stock.

(d) *Subject entries:* Books are entered under their specific subjects and therefore for the best results you should first look up the subject required under its precise heading, rather than under more general headings – e.g. if you want material on Chemistry look up Chemistry, not Science; if you want English poetry, look up English poetry, not Poetry or Literature.

* Again, where coloured cards are used to differentiate the various kinds of entry this should be indicated here.

(e) *References:* There are two kinds of references: *see references* from an unused heading, e.g. Couch, in the above example; *see also references* from a used heading to related headings, e.g. LITERATURE *see also* POETRY. *See also references,* which file after the entries under that heading, should always be checked as they may indicate headings more likely to have material on the subject of your enquiry than the headings first consulted.

(f) *Description:* The fullest description of a document is found under the author entry. Details include: title, edition, place of publication, publisher, date, number of pages (or volumes), illustrations, size.

(g) *Arrangement:* The general arrangement is word by word, not letter by letter:

New Amsterdam	NOT	New Amsterdam
New England		Newark
New wives for old		New England
Newark		Newman
Newman		New wives for old

When the same word can be an author, title, or subject, personal author files first and is followed by all other entries in a straight alphabetical sequence, e.g.:

Wells, H. G. ....Author (personal)
WELLS ....Subject
Wells of despair ....Title
WELLS, OIL ....Subject
Wells (Somerset) UDC ....Author (corporate)

THE NUMBER AT THE BOTTOM RIGHT OF THE CARD IS THE CLASS NUMBER AT WHICH THE BOOK WILL BE FOUND ON THE SHELVES. IF YOU CANNOT FIND THE ANSWER TO YOUR ENQUIRY PLEASE ASK A MEMBER OF STAFF TO HELP.

The amount of detail here will depend on the clientele. Several items might be usefully expanded if warranted – for example, the section on the author entry might mention the use of headings for corporate authors; the section on arrangement might mention arrangement under a prolific author particularly if the library has an extensive Literature collection. The librarian should at all times try to place himself in the position of the reader and ask just how much information will be useful without becoming overpowering, and he should remember that the catalogue itself contains – or ought to contain – guiding and references to assist the user.

READINGS

1. Some limitations of classification are listed in Chapter 4 of the following book. It should be noted, however, that the author has modified some of her views since. KELLY, G. O. *The classification of books.* New York, H. W. Wilson, 1938.

2. ØRVIG, M. 'The reader interest arrangement, an American shelving system with a future'. *Libri,* 5 (3), 1955, 223–32.

3. SAVAGE, E. A. *Manual of book classification and display.* London, Allen and Unwin and the Library Association, 1946.

4. MCCLELLAN, A. W. 'Service in depth'. *Library World,* 52, April 1950, 183–5.

Chapter 18
Physical Forms of
Catalogues

Qualities

Catalogues should be:

(i) *Flexible* – they should allow entries to be withdrawn and inserted easily so that the catalogue can be kept up to date.

(ii) *Easy to use* – to handle and consult (and preferably by more than one reader at a time). They should be equally accessible to staff and public.

(iii) *Easily guided* – to enable the user to find the relevant entry with the minimum of trouble.

(iv) *Economic* – both to produce and maintain. They should wear well.

(v) *Capable of being produced by some reproduction process* – so that duplicate catalogues can easily be made or entries produced centrally for branch libraries, etc. Alternatively, they should be capable of taking unit entries produced by a central agency like BNB.

(vi) *Compact.*

(vii) *Portable* – within the library or outside.

No single form of catalogue has all these qualities. The most widely used forms are card and sheaf. Several libraries produce printed book catalogues, and some still have guard book catalogues.

The Card Catalogue

Comprises a set of cards, usually 5×3 in. (122×72 cm.) each entry being on a separate card, the whole filed in a series of drawers together forming a catalogue cabinet. In the standard size cabinets on the market, each drawer holds about 1,000 cards.

QUALITIES

(i) *Completely flexible* – insertion and withdrawal of entries easier than with any other form.

(ii) *Easily handled* – and although in the past it has been said that readers have a psychological aversion to the form, its present widespread use in offices and business and industry invalidates this argument. It can be used by several readers at once, though one reader tends to block several drawers when using it. However, difficulties of filing and use increase with the growth in size and complexity of card catalogues – a factor that lends weight to arguments for the use of some of the newer forms of catalogue such as those produced by computers.

(iii) Though perhaps not so easily guided as the printed page in a book, the judicious use of *guide cards* of different colours and with various sized tabs can greatly facilitate use (see Chapter 17).

(iv) It is *economic* to produce and the cards wear well. The card form is the one most frequently adopted by centralized cataloguing agencies.

(v) Various methods are available for the *reproduction* of cards – spirit duplicators, addressing machines, etc. More recently automatic typewriters have been employed. Both the LA and the ALA have produced surveys of methods.[1]

(vi) It is relatively *compact*, but *not portable* of course – unless a stand on wheels is adopted, but this is a practicable proposition for small catalogues only, and there are obvious disadvantages.

The Sheaf Catalogue

Comprised of sets of slips held in specially manufactured loose-leaf binders. The size of slips varies, a standard size being $7\frac{3}{4} \times 4$ in., though one corresponding approximately to the 5×3 in. card size is available. Each binder holds some 500–650 slips in the standard sizes, and they are filed in a series of pigeon-holes forming a catalogue cabinet.

QUALITIES

(i) Where each slip carries a separate entry – as is normal –

the catalogue is *completely flexible* allowing easy insertion and withdrawal. However, it must be acknowledged that slips are inserted and removed a little less easily than cards because they are flimsy.

(ii) As this catalogue is in book form it is *easily handled*, and the fact that (a) each binder contains fewer entries than a drawer in a card catalogue and (b) each sheaf is *portable*, means that there is less likelihood of one reader monopolizing the catalogue.

(iii) It is *not so easily guided* as the card catalogue and this especially reduces its effectiveness where the arrangement is complex – as for example in a specialized subject.

(iv) It is more *economic* than the card catalogue because (a) the slips are cheaper – though against this must be offset their limited durability as compared with cards; (b) it takes less space; (c) duplicate entries can be made (up to a certain number) by the cheapest of all reproduction methods – carbon paper.

(v) Because of the ease of duplication and the fact that standard-sized slips are larger than the standard cards, it has been used in many *union catalogues* (e.g. by many of the Regional Bureaux) – it being more easy to accommodate a grid showing the location of the document concerned.

The sheaf catalogue is specially useful therefore (a) for union catalogues, (b) whenever detailed entries are normal, and (c) when economy is a pre-eminent consideration.

The Guard (Book) Catalogue

A book catalogue, having several entries on each page, but made by hand – by pasting slips (often cut out from printed accession lists) to the stout manilla pages of the book. The form is still used in some academic libraries; the British Museum has a guard book catalogue of some 1,250 volumes. Strict order is difficult to maintain, and it is not suited to a library where books are being regularly withdrawn from stock. In the British Museum, where obviously much pasting is required at least two copies are necessary so that volumes will not be out of circulation when amendments are being made.

The Conventionally Printed (Book) Catalogue

Open access, a bigger turnover of book stock, and the costs of printing after the first world war account in part for the decline of the printed catalogue. Some libraries have continued to produce them, either for the whole stock or substantial sections, e.g. Glasgow, Edinburgh, Liverpool; others – e.g. Bristol and Westminster – have started printed catalogues since the second world war, Westminster claiming[2] that theirs represents an actual saving in costs when weighed against the fact that filing time (using the old sheaf catalogue) was the equivalent of one full-time assistant's work.

Some libraries – national libraries and those with unique special stocks – have a duty to print their catalogues, which are clearly major bibliographies. Librarians would be very much poorer without such catalogues as those produced by the RIBA, the London Library, and the Library of the LSE and others cooperating in the *London bibliography of the social sciences*. The use of photography and lithographic printing techniques has allowed the Library of Congress to produce a series of invaluable catalogues since the last war,[3] and the British Museum has similarly been able to complete the *General catalogue of printed books*[4] which, by normal methods it would have taken until the end of the century to finish. Many librarians produce printed catalogues for *parts* of their stock, e.g. the catalogues of local history and genealogy published by Manchester Central Library, the music catalogue of Liverpool, and so on.

QUALITIES

(i) It is *inflexible*. There are various methods in use for keeping it up to date:

(a) new editions, regularly produced,

(b) printed supplements, with subsequent cumulations (either of the supplements or the whole work),

(c) supplements on card or other flexible form – useful in the library itself, but not outside it.

Note that supplements cannot amend the original catalogue – the problem of indicating *withdrawals* remains. For this reason alone, the printed catalogue is not ideally suited to a rapidly changing stock.

(ii) It is, of course, *easy to use*; there is no form of catalogue offering greater clarity than a printed catalogue, where by various typographical and layout devices the *arrangement can be clearly understood* and many entries seen at a glance. Against this should be set the inconvenience of supplements.

(iii) Generally speaking it is *uneconomic* as compared with the other forms, though where there are many service points the total cost of producing and filing other forms of entry (e.g. cards) must be recognized. Sales may help to offset costs.

(iv) A major advantage is *portability*. Not only may the whole stock of the system be seen at any service point, but the readers may take copies home, and, apart from the convenience of this, additional *publicity* is thus indirectly obtained. Direct publicity may be achieved by sending a copy to important organizations.

The attractions of the book form of catalogue have stimulated numerous attempts to make it a viable proposition. For example, various forms of reproduction methods have been used in an attempt to reduce costs. But although these have been partially successful, the basic problems of frequent resetting (or retyping) for cumulation and reprinting have remained. The use of computers may well provide an answer to these problems.

The Computer (Book) Catalogue

The library catalog in card form is a comparatively recent phenomenon and is the result of the growth of library work beyond the bounds of technology. Sixty years ago the rate of growth of library collections had outpaced the ability of the book-form catalog to cope with the input; the solution to this problem was the card catalog. Technology, however, is catching up with the growth of library work, and through such devices as high-speed, graphic arts quality automatic typesetting, the library profession may one day be able to consider the reinstatement of the book-form catalog as a feasible working tool.[5]

Recent developments in automatic data processing are revolutionizing the production of library catalogues. In particular, the use of computers has resulted in a revival of the book catalogue. Cataloguing data may be fed into the computer in the form of punched cards or paper tape, etc., and from this basic information lists organized in a variety of orders (author, title, subject, etc.) can be printed out. If multiple copies are required, several reproduction methods, including computer typesetting, are available.

Many examples of computer book catalogues can now be seen. The earliest experiments took place in the United States in the 'fifties, but British librarians have not been slow in following this lead, as the pages of *Program*[6] demonstrate. Examples include general catalogues (as in the London Boroughs of Barnet, Camden, Greenwich); periodicals lists (Aston University, Loughborough University of Technology, City University); subject indexes (Aston University, Loughborough University of Technology); indexes of reports, bibliographies, bulletins, etc. (ICI Mond Division Organization, UKAE-AWRE Aldermaston); special collections (Newcastle-upon-Tyne University); etc.

QUALITIES

Book catalogues produced by these methods retain many of the advantages of the conventionally printed forms without the attendant disadvantages.

(i) There is the wide appeal of the book form itself and, as computer technology improves, the appearance of the printed page, so often marred at present by the use of undifferentiated block capitals and the compression of information, will undoubtedly improve. The revival of this ancient but, for many purposes, unsurpassed form of catalogue by the use of the most modern of techniques is the subject of an interesting article by Jesse Shera.[7]

(ii) Though limitations of programming, the capacity of line-printers, and general economic considerations, have sometimes – as in the London Borough catalogues – restricted the *amount of information* in individual entries, this is again, no doubt, a feature of early development. (It has been argued that the restrictions, insofar as they compel a close analysis of the make-up of entries, may not be entirely a matter for distress. One of the advantages of adopting new methods is that old habits have to be reviewed.)

(iii) One of the strongest arguments advanced for this form of catalogue is that *multiple copies* can be readily produced, and in a variety of arrangements, without any additional filing effort. Thus each branch of a large system can have a record, usually with locations indicated, of the total stock; and copies may be sold or distributed outside the library – especially in the case of catalogues of special collections or materials.

(iv) Although no catalogue can surpass the card or sheaf forms in *flexibility* – where, at least in theory, a new entry can be added or an old one withdrawn in a matter of seconds – the computer book catalogue, when compared with the conventionally printed form, is remarkably flexible. The speed with which data can be fed into the computer and new or amended catalogues printed out is determined by economic rather than technical factors. Accessions lists for the Camden and Barnet catalogues appear fortnightly, each cumulating up to a period of four months, at which point the cumulations are integrated with the basic catalogue.[8,9] (However, it should be noted that the fortnightly lists are arranged by author only – the classified arrangement and indexes appearing only at the four-monthly stage of cumulation.) And it should be remembered, when making comparisons, that card catalogues, especially in large library systems, become so complex that flexibility is affected: in particular, the speed with which updating is effected may be considerably reduced. Filing in many libraries constitutes a serious bottleneck in the cataloguing process.

(v) One of the major problems in computerized cataloguing is the *older stock*: to produce cumulating catalogues of accessions is one thing, to catalogue the complete stock of the library in this way is another matter. Present practice frequently results in three catalogues: the basic card catalogue, the cumulated printed catalogue of accessions, and the current accessions list. The problem will tend to diminish in most libraries with time, but it is unlikely to disappear, and sooner or later the question of integrating older materials will have to be faced.

(vi) *Costs* of computer book catalogues appear to be higher than traditional card or sheaf forms. However, comparative costs are difficult to assess in view of the various factors that have to be taken into account. Moreover, costs are likely to diminish as the use of computers becomes more widespread.

(vii) *Equipment* is clearly a factor of a different order here. It is unlikely that any but the largest libraries will be in a position to acquire for their own use the large computer systems necessary for library work. But as centralized computer facilities become more generally available, this is unlikely to prove a major obstacle.

The scale of computerization lends new force to the arguments in favour of centralized cataloguing. If the duplication of cataloguing by conventional forms in libraries up and down the land is wasteful, how much more so is such duplication when computers are used? (The case for the production of machine-readable cataloguing data by a centralized agency such as BNB will be discussed in Chapter 20.)

Other Forms of Catalogues

(i) *Visible indexes.* There are two types in general use and the student should endeavour to examine them at first hand: (a) those holding cards with only a certain depth of edge visible, and (b) those made up of narrow strips about $\frac{1}{4}$ in. wide which are mounted one below the other in a frame, the finished appearance being like a number of lines on a printed page. The latter are mainly used for short (title-a-line) periodicals catalogues; a reader can see at a glance what periodicals are in the library – and colour may be used to indicate the department in which the periodical is housed. They have also been used for subject indexes to classified catalogues. The former are in regular use as periodicals accession registers: they usually hold a large card and as both back and front can be used, offer much-needed space for recording receipts, holdings, location of copies, etc. They also allow the use of coloured indicators filing along the edge of the cards, indicating frequency and non-arrival of an issue.

(ii) *Punched cards, computers, etc.* We have noted above the use of computers in the creation of book catalogues. (They can also be used to produce individual entries in card or sheaf form.) But the computer may itself be used *as a catalogue*; that is, the information may be stored within the computer and called for as required – by author, title, subject, etc. This direct interrogation of the computer has been the subject of much research and several systems have been developed, though so far their use is limited to specialized collections.

READINGS

1. PARGETER, PHILIP S. *The reproduction of catalogue cards*. London, Library Association, 1960 (LA pamphlets, no. 20).
   AMERICAN LIBRARY ASSOCIATION. Library Technology Project. *Catalog card reproduction*. Chicago, ALA, 1965 (LTP publications, no. 9).
2. VOLLANS, R. F. 'The published booklist and the exploitation of stock: 1. Printed catalogues'. (In Library Association. London and Home Counties Branch. Annual Weekend Conference, 1954. *Bibliography and the bookshop*. pp. 25–33.)
3. The most extensive development is the printing of the massive National Union Catalog – Pre-1956 Imprints, a task that is likely to take ten years. Several accounts of this project appeared in the press at the time of its announcement – e.g. *Bookseller*, 18 March 1967, pp. 1594–8.
   See also: COMMANDER, JOHN. 'Filming the National Union Catalog'. *Catalogue and Index*, no. 17, January 1970, 4–6.
   For a general account of the bibliographic work of the Library of Congress see: MUMFORD, L. QUINCY. 'Bibliographic developments at the Library of Congress'. *Libri*, 17 (4), 1967, 294–304.
4. FRANCIS, F. C. 'The new British Museum catalogue'. *Times Literary Supplement*, 6 October 1966, p. 928.
5. SPARKS, DAVID E. *and others*. 'Output printing for library mechanization'. (In *Libraries and automation: proceedings of the conference on libraries and automation held at Airlie Foundation, Warrenton, Virginia, May 26–30, 1963*, edited by Barbara Evans Markuson. Washington, Library of Congress, 1964. p. 155.)
6. *Program*—v. 1–8 subtitled *News of computers in British university libraries;* v. 9– *News of computers in British libraries*. University of Belfast, School of Library Studies. 4 p.a.
7. SHERA, JESSE H. 'The book catalog and the scholar'. *Library Resources and Technical Services*, 6(3), Summer 1962, 210–16.
8. MAIDMENT, WM. R. 'The computer catalogue in Camden'. *Library World*, 67(782), August 1965, 40.
9. MEAKIN, A. O. 'The production of a printed catalogue by computer'. *Library Association Record*, 67(9), September 1965, 311–316.

Chapter 19
Limited Cataloguing

Limited cataloguing is a term used to refer to any reductions in the amount of cataloguing. Two types are possible:

(i) reduction in the number of entries per document – even, perhaps, total omission of certain entries (*selective cataloguing*),

(ii) reduction in the descriptive cataloguing – including simplification of the heading (*simplified cataloguing*).

Its main purpose is economy. Limited cataloguing is usually a result of a realization of cataloguing costs (note the interest in this in the 1930s when economy was in the air); today, as literature increases in amount and complexity, librarians are bound to ask whether all their cataloguing is really necessary and whether indeed over-elaboration is not resulting in difficulties for cataloguers, reference librarians, and readers. On the other hand, the interests of users – and this includes staff – must not be prejudiced: no real economy is achieved if the cataloguer, by such reductions, passes the buck to the reference librarian, as, for example, broad subject cataloguing and classification often does. Also, cuts may result in re-ordering material already in stock. Any cuts should be based on a careful assessment of needs – actual and potential.

Moreover, it should be remembered that limited cataloguing is not the only method of achieving economies.

(i) *Inefficient codes and classification schemes* are responsible for much over-elaboration and waste. The ease with which codes and schemes based on defined principles and careful analysis of basic problems and elements can be used and understood, results in a saving in the initial cataloguing; and the fact that a pattern will be more clearly discernible will result in ease of reference by staff and readers.

(ii) Analysis of *method* too will help: for example, we have noted the economies resulting from the use of chain indexing as against the more haphazard methods – an economy that also benefits the user because searching can be more systematic. In cataloguing departments much time can be saved by the use of forms with blanks for author, title, imprint, and collation details from which the typist can produce all the necessary entries. Again, flow of work in the department should be carefully organized if full efficiency is to be achieved.

(iii) Economy can be achieved if catalogue entries are based on *information found in the document*, thus reducing the need for bibliographical and biographical checking. This will also, as we have seen, usually result in headings sought by readers. The idea is found in BM (4); more recently, as 'no conflict' cataloguing, it has been adopted in the Library of Congress (see below). The general tendency can also be found in AACR.

The use of computers will undoubtedly affect the amount of cataloguing. For example, where book catalogues for individual library systems have been produced by this method (see Chapter 18) there is evidence of reduction in descriptive detail. On the other hand, the catalogue entries produced by large-scale centralized computer systems (those, for example, now being developed by national bibliographical services) may well provide an extensive range of data from which the user can select the required details. (See Chapter 20 for an account of centralized cataloguing – a major objective of which is, of course, economy of effort.)

To return to limited cataloguing as defined above. Clearly it is *relative*, being governed by the amount of cataloguing normally done, which varies from library to library; thus, one library might, in the normal course of things, omit collation altogether, and for such a library another's plans for limiting collation to pagination could hardly be applied in the interests of economy. For this reason it is difficult to generalize; we have to assume a standard of cataloguing based on existing codes and classification schemes in general use and then ask what reductions might be made.

Simplified Cataloguing

In fact we have already done this so far as simplified cataloguing is concerned. In Chapter 14 we saw how description could be limited to those items necessary for the *identification* of particular editions of documents (the prime duty of description); we showed how other information desirable for the *characterization* might be added and suggested an order of priority for this. One form of simplified cataloguing might, therefore, be to limit description to items of information necessary for identification, omitting further characterization.

In the past much of the discussion on simplified cataloguing has taken place in the context of the AA code. Students should glance at AA (137–74) and the associated Library of Congress rules (e.g. those on pages 51–3): they will then see why simplified cataloguing has been regularly practised since 1908. Although, in general, detail has been reduced in AACR, there is no doubt that many libraries will consider it unnecessary to give all the information suggested in the descriptive rules.

Selective Cataloguing

(i) In general, note the possibility of using *tools other than the catalogue* for the retrieval of documents, thus helping to reduce cataloguing. For example, *shelf arrangement* of general place directories may obviate the need for entries under place for these works in the catalogue; other materials may be 'self-indexing' in this way. Or *bibliographies* may be used to effect economies, e.g. a library having all or most British Standards or government publications, say, may make a catalogue only to supplement the official bibliographies of these, providing approaches not otherwise catered for; again, a gramophone record library might simply make a brief catalogue of contents, relying on makers' lists, and other bibliographies for reference work. Cranshaw[1] suggests that on occasion the *shelf list* might be used as a substitute for the catalogue. Today few librarians maintain shelf lists (i.e. records of stock filed in shelf order and used particularly for stocktaking), it being considered more satisfactory to use such time as would be spent on their compilation on a catalogue instead.

(ii) *Author/title entries.* Author may sometimes be dispensed with in favour of some other entry, e.g. title or subject; too often by older codes author entry duplicated subject or form entry – see, for example, AA rules for concordances, thematic catalogues, directories, statutes, and treaties. *Author/title analyticals* are seldom needed, as compared with subject. *Author added entries or references* should also be limited. In general an added entry or reference should be made:

(a) if that particular document is likely to be sought under the secondary author, and

(b) if the secondary author is sufficiently well known for a reader to want all his writings.

Thus joint author entry can frequently be omitted, as can entries under secondary editors, translators, illustrators, etc. *Title added entries or references*[2] should be made if more likely to be remembered than author or editor (as in some collections, e.g. *Oxford book of . . .*); other distinctive titles may deserve an entry – but note the value of bibliographies such as *British books in print* for this. Added entries and references should not be made for undistinguished titles, subtitles, etc., or for inversions of titles – and they should never be made as a substitute for subject entry or when the subject entry will lead easily to the document remembered only for its title, e.g. *Physics for sixth forms*. *Series entry* might be limited to subject series; again publishers' lists such as Dent's list of titles in the *Everyman series* can be used.

(iii) *Subject entries.* Although subject entries may be restricted in particular cases, such restrictions are not to be generally recommended. However, we have already noted certain practices that may be less economical than others:

(a) *Multiple entry for compound subjects* – rather than specific entry, e.g. a document on Control devices for ventilation should, except in special circumstances, be entered under the specific heading VENTILATION – CONTROL DEVICES (or the specific class number) rather than double entered under VENTILATION *and* CONTROL DEVICES (or the appropriate class numbers for these subjects). References and index entries should be used to cater for readers who look up other terms in the compound (i.e., in this instance, Control devices).

(b) *Multiple entry for books on several subjects when these can be expressed by a more general heading*, e.g. a book on Leatherwork, basketry and metalwork may best be entered under the general class of Handicrafts, relying on classification and references to draw the reader's attention to the book.

(c) *Uncontrolled references in the alphabetico-direct catalogue* – rectified by using a classification structure. See Sears or Library of Congress lists of subject headings under broad headings such as EDUCATION for examples of uncontrolled references.

(d) *Uncontrolled indexing in the classified catalogue* – rectified by chain procedure.

Suggestions have been made that the classified *shelf arrangement* be relied on to show what documents are available in certain *popular subjects*, the catalogue then simply giving a reference, e.g. '635 Gardening: for books on gardening see the shelves at 635'. This is particularly unsatisfactory in lending libraries where a considerable proportion of the stock might be on loan, and indeed wherever there are several sequences on the shelves necessitated by size, display, and so on. Moreover it cannot ever be really satisfactory because of course added entries cannot be made on the shelves for books on more than one subject, little detailed guiding can be undertaken, and none but the broadest of references can be made. Even with popular subjects these may be useful.

Finally, *Subject analyticals* should not duplicate published indexes unnecessarily.

Factors Affecting the Amount of Cataloguing

So far we have been considering economies in general terms. However, in practice, there will be a number of variable factors affecting the amount of cataloguing. The following are the chief of these.

(a) *Type of material.* Librarians have long recognized that not all categories of material demand the same amount of cataloguing. One doesn't spend the same time over a firm's brochures as over incunabula. For example:

(i) *Fiction.* Simplified cataloguing is universal and rarely is any entry made under the class number in the classified file or the form heading in the dictionary catalogue. Some librarians have even suggested cutting out the cataloguing of ephemeral fiction altogether, but this seems too drastic – as much time would be spent distinguishing between the ephemeral and the non-ephemeral as would be spent on the simplified cataloguing itself, not to mention the reduction in reader service and the waste of staff time. A minority consider that fiction deserves the same attention as non-fiction, on the grounds that *The brothers Karamazov* is quite as meritorious as, say, *The little Madeleine*.

(ii) *Children's books*. Again, simplification is usual – though certain descriptive items, in particular series note and annotation, are very useful and in certain circumstances might be retained. It is desirable to simplify classification and headings. It is sometimes said that a good children's librarian will obviate the need for a catalogue, but even in ideal conditions where the librarian has adequate time to assist all readers, children will lose valuable experience in the use of the catalogue – nor is it certain that the children's librarian will never need a catalogue.

(iii) *Pamphlets*, etc. It must be stressed that physical form of material alone is not a reliable guide – a pamphlet may often be more valuable than a book; but in practice circumstances often force such distinctions. Often the cataloguer has so many pamphlets that only by limited cataloguing can he get them on the shelves at all. Though by no means ideal, in such circumstances individual subject cataloguing may be abandoned and a reference such as the following made in the catalogue under the appropriate heading:

> 373   Secondary schools
>   For pamphlet material on Secondary schools
>   *see* pamphlet box at 373

Alternatively, individual author cataloguing may be abandoned leaving only individual subject cataloguing. Again, pamphlets in series may be classified and catalogued as a whole; for example, all pamphlets in the *Writers and their work series* may be classified at 820 and catalogued as a series, not as individual pamphlets – but note that this puts the burden of responsibility for remembering the series, when a reader asks for information on a writer, on the reference librarian.

(b) *The degree of accessibility and lending:* where stock is freely accessible and available for loan – or, alternatively, where the stock is held in closed access – the catalogue is likely to be the basic source of information.

(c) *Physical form of catalogue and possibilities for the mechanical reproduction of entries or the use of centralized services:* printed catalogues are likely to result in relatively limited cataloguing because of their expense; and where entries have to be made by hand reductions are also likely. As already noted, the use of computers is likely to affect the amount of cataloguing.

(d) *Availability of substitutes* such as bibliographies and the possibilities of using them rather than the catalogue.

(e) Possibilities of *self-indexing methods*.

(f) *Degree of permanence of stock* – the more ephemeral the material the less detailed is the cataloguing likely to be.

(g) *Needs of users* – types of enquiry: the more detailed the enquiries, the greater the need for detailed cataloguing.

(h) *Needs of staff* – the extent to which they are called upon to supply specific information.

Obviously these factors will differ from library to library – a library of commerce is likely to have more ephemeral material than a library of the fine arts; demands for comprehensive literature surveys are likely to be fewer in general departments of public libraries than they are in research libraries, and so on. In practice each cataloguer has to weigh the various factors one against the other and try to achieve as satisfactory a compromise as possible. And students, when considering limited cataloguing in libraries of a particular kind should use the factors listed above as a basis for their analysis, the special requirements of the libraries concerned being used to modify the general points made in this chapter.

Limited Cataloguing in the Library of Congress

Since 1947 the pressure of work in the Library of Congress has been enforcing limited cataloguing. It is interesting to note the form that this has taken, bearing in mind that this is, with the possible exception of the Lenin Library, the largest library in the world.

Broadly speaking, policy is as follows:

(i) All documents are catalogued from information found in the document itself. Thus the name found on the title page is accepted as the author of the document and only if there is a clear indication of a relationship between that name and another already used as a heading in the catalogue is the matter investigated further. Hence the term *no conflict cataloguing*. Thus biographical and bibliographical checking is severely curtailed. Added entries are, in general, restricted to those that may be useful for finding purposes.

(ii) All documents are, on receipt, allocated to the following categories:

Group 1: basic reference books, research materials. These receive full cataloguing according to the published rules.

Group 2: general trade publications, e.g. biography, history, drama, poetry, textbooks, fiction, children's books, etc. Many of the publications of corporate bodies, including governments, are placed in this group too. In the cataloguing of such materials, no added entries are made at all, except for occasional added title entry, and in cases of conflict between personal and corporate author. Descriptive cataloguing is also much simplified, e.g. last numbered page suffices for pagination and kinds of illustrations are not specified; notes are restricted.

Group 3: groups of documents considered primarily as a group. Here the collection is catalogued as a group and the individual items comprising that group are listed in the notes.

Group 4: minor materials, catalogued collectively. Here there is no recording of individual items; instead a 'form card' is made under the appropriate author or subject to the effect that 'miscellaneous publications including reports and other minor material not separately catalogued can be found classified at . . .'

Clearly the sorting of documents into these categories is itself no light task and has necessitated the designation of staff for the purpose.

READINGS

1. CRANSHAW, J. *Cutting catalogue costs 50 per cent.* London, AAL, 1950. (AAL reprints, no. 4.)
2. LUBETZKY, S. 'Titles: fifth column of the catalog'. *Library Quarterly*, 11(4), October 1941, 412–30.

The problems of cataloguing in a large library are perhaps seen in their most acute form in the Library of Congress. For this reason I have included in this chapter the section on Congress practice. The extent of the problem can be seen by scanning *Annual reports* of the Librarian of Congress. For example, in the report for 1952, he writes: 'We have not been able to catalog each year all the books we receive, nor have we been able to provide a subject approach to three fourths of the books we did catalog . . .' (p. xviii). See also the article by Taube, noted in Chapter 4, where, on p. 4, we find: 'In the 1947 estimates (Library of Congress) the average time required to perform descriptive cataloging is given as two hours twenty minutes per title or three books per cataloger in seven hour day.' Such facts as these should be remembered when considering simplified cataloguing.

A useful article on Library of Congress practice is:

JOLLEY, L. 'A note on "limited" and "simplified" cataloguing in the Library of Congress'. *Journal of Documentation*, 8 (2), 1952, 99–105.

The astonishingly short-sighted reactions on the part of some librarians to the proposals for simplification can be read in the various American journals at the time of the *Studies in descriptive cataloging* report (already noted in Chapter 14), and in the report itself.

Chapter 20
Centralized Cataloguing

Centralized cataloguing is the cataloguing of documents by some central organization such as BNB or the Library of Congress, its main purpose, from a cataloguing point of view, being to save duplication of effort in the cataloguing departments of numerous independent libraries. (The term is not used in this chapter to refer to centralization within one library system.)

Forms of Centralization

(i) *Card (or sheaf) service,* i.e. the production of the actual physical entries (unit entries) which individual libraries can buy and, after adding the appropriate headings to the basic unit, file in their catalogues. BNB card/sheaf service is an example of this.

(ii) MARC *service,* i.e. the production of cataloguing data in machine-readable form (e.g. magnetic tape), which libraries can then search directly or use as a basis for the creation of conventional forms of catalogues and bibliographies.

(iii) *Information service,* i.e. the production of a bibliography from which libraries then construct their own catalogues either by cutting out the entries and pasting them on cards, etc., or using the information provided as a guide in their own cataloguing – or, possibly, by using the bibliography as a substitute for a catalogue. The BNB service was solely of this nature prior to the establishment of the card service in 1956. Such bibliographies do, of course, serve important functions other than cataloguing – book selection and acquisition, identification and location.

Some services today combine (i), (ii) and (iii) – e.g. BNB and the Library of Congress.

(iv) *Cataloguing-in-source,* i.e. the cataloguing of books by a central organization, in association with the publishers, before publication, the catalogue entries being then printed in the books themselves.

Coverage

Area. In Britain we tend to think of centralized cataloguing in national terms: the BNB service covers only materials published in the United Kingdom (though the picture is changing with the advent of cooperative MARC services – see below). The BM has never undertaken a centralized cataloguing service, and its published catalogues, though covering materials from many countries, have, on account of their slowness in appearing and their idiosyncratic cataloguing, been unsuitable for this purpose. The Library of Congress service, being a product of the national library, covers an increasing proportion of the world's literature and is used by many libraries outside the United States.

Period. Centralized services normally cover current materials, though they may maintain backfiles of cataloguing data – for example, it is still possible to buy BNB cards for books covered by the service in earlier years. Even when such backfiles are not kept, the published bibliographies may serve to provide the individual libraries with information from which they can construct their own entries. However, it must be remembered that cataloguing and classification must change with the times and, as a basis for cataloguing, the data provided years ago is likely to be limited.

Materials. Large-scale organizations frequently omit certain categories of materials (e.g. maps, sheet music, government publications, etc.) and rarely include analytical entries for articles in periodicals, etc. Partly for this reason special services may be found, e.g. *British catalogue of music*, HMSO card service, *Engineering index, International bibliography of education*, and so on.

Ideally a centralized agency would provide – and provide promptly – in a variety of forms, cataloguing data for all kinds of materials published throughout the world, current or retrospective. Such an ideal poses many problems, and is unlikely to be achieved – if it is to be achieved at all – without a large measure of international cooperation. Recent developments, to be noted later in this chapter and Chapter 21, have brought the dream a little closer to reality.

Prior Requirements

The success of a system of centralized cataloguing depends on:

(i) *Uniformity of cataloguing and classification in a sufficient number of libraries.* Of course uniformity tends to follow in the wake of centralization, but there must at least be prior agreement as to the scheme (or schemes) of classification, the cataloguing code to be used and, where physical entries are to be provided, agreement as to the physical form of catalogue. Centralized agencies can, especially when computers are used, make some provision for local needs, but if too many libraries believe their requirements to be unique, centralization can have only limited success, and may become quite impracticable.

(ii) *Duplication of stocks in libraries.* If all library stocks were identical centralization of cataloguing would be relatively simple. The theory behind centralized cataloguing rests upon the assumption that libraries are duplicating cataloguing. But duplication occurs substantially for relatively few titles – and in particular for books published in the country concerned, or in the language of that country. A centralized agency gets its biggest returns on such books; its returns diminish as it ventures beyond them into foreign and special materials. One answer to this problem is to limit coverage – as BNB has, until recently, limited its service to British materials. The result will be that those libraries taking a high proportion of special and foreign materials will tend not to use the system. Another answer is to base the service on the national and foreign accessions of a large national library, for then the centralized service will be a by-product of its own cataloguing: but even large libraries like the Library of Congress cannot, alone, meet the needs of the country's research libraries, as several American studies have proved. A more satisfactory solution, assuming that it were practicable, would be to enlist the cooperation of other centralized agencies throughout the world in order to increase coverage without pricing the service out of the market: such cooperation – referred to as shared cataloguing – is now, as we shall see, being initiated. Even so, no attempt is so far being made to cover periodical articles and similar 'hidden' items in these centralized/cooperative schemes: for the bibliographic control of such items, abstracting and indexing services exist, with varying degrees of success, in many subjects.

(iii) *The existence or establishment of some machinery by which new documents can be seen by the central agency or agencies* – either immediately after publication or even prior to publication. Speed is essential – entries must be available as soon as the librarian receives the document, otherwise cataloguing delays may result in his abandoning the scheme. Usually the central organization is based on a national library or copyright office, where by law publishers may be forced to send at least one copy of every book published. This is more successful than reliance on the goodwill and cooperation of publishers.

(iv) *Financial backing to establish the service* – though it may pay its way later.

(v) *An economic and technologically sophisticated method for producing the bibliography and/or cards, tapes, etc.*

Advantages and Disadvantages

(i) *Economy.* Foremost advantage is the great saving in labour; the uneconomic duplication of cataloguing effort in hundreds of libraries can be avoided. There is also the saving in reproduction equipment when actual physical entries are provided. (Note that some libraries which had installed expensive equipment before BNB card/sheaf service continue to duplicate their own entries, using the BNB entry as a master copy: they claim that the method is cheaper.) Against this economy must be set the work involved in ordering cards, etc. though this is relatively slight.

(ii) *Generally superior cataloguing:* cataloguers whose full-time job it is to catalogue the country's literature are likely to be better at it than those librarians for whom cataloguing is just one of many tasks. On the other hand, special local requirements of individual libraries cannot be foreseen – though these are not, except in certain highly specialized libraries, likely to constitute an overwhelming drawback and, in any case, the local cataloguer can usually modify entries to suit his needs.

(iii) The resulting *uniformity of cataloguing* in many libraries is of great help to librarians, readers, bibliographers. More-over it makes possible schemes of cooperative book acquisition and storage, because each participating library can be made responsible for buying and storing all books placed at specified class numbers by the central cataloguing organization.

(iv) On the whole, although there may be examples of delays, cataloguing is probably more *prompt* than if left to individual libraries, where arrears in cataloguing are certainly not unknown.

Some Examples of Centralized Cataloguing (Card Services)

(i) BRITISH NATIONAL BIBLIOGRAPHY

(a) A self-supporting organization, controlled by a Council representing among others the Library Association, the British Museum, the Publishers' Association, and the Booksellers' Association. The documents are seen as they arrive at the Copyright Office. The first issue of the bibliography itself appeared in 1950; the card service began in 1956; and the *British catalogue of music* (BCM), for entries recorded in which cards are not available, started in 1957. Entries for sheaf catalogues are also provided. BNB appears weekly (classified with an author/title index); the index cumulates monthly and subject index entries are added; the whole cumulates quarterly (4-monthly from 1971) to the annual volume and there are further cumulations every five years. BCM (classified with index) appears quarterly and there are annual cumulations. Cards are ordered by quoting the BNB entry number for the item required.

(b) BNB includes all British books, with a few exceptions, the most important of which is maps; sheet music is covered by BCM and books about music are found in both. BNB is particu-larly useful for its coverage of government publications, research reports, and publications of organizations, for although it is not exhaustive, it is far more comprehensive than any of the trade bibliographies.

(c) Classification is basically by DC; cataloguing is now by AACR. (BCM uses a faceted scheme specially designed for the bibliography.) BNB has used a modified version of DC for the last twenty years in its main arrangement. The 14th edition has formed the basis, though certain changes from subsequent editions have been assimilated. More important, in using and interpreting the schedules consistency has been maintained by means of citation orders established by the classifiers. Four features have been particularly significant.

(i) The use of 'featuring', i.e. the verbal translation of class numbers in the classified file, demonstrating steps of division in the classified arrangement.

(ii) The extension of the schedules where necessary in order to create specific headings – such extensions being verbally expressed after the symbol [1], e.g.:

530.1	PHYSICAL THEORY
530.1 [1]	Causality
530.1 [1]	Space
530.11	Relativity

Such verbal extensions have allowed indexing of key concepts by chain procedure regardless of the limitations of the classification scheme.

(iii) The introduction, after 1960, of a lettered notation for common and certain special subdivisions – compare, for example, the divisions at class 656 in the 1961 cumulation with those of previous years.

(iv) The use of chain indexing to produce an alphabetical subject index of outstanding quality.

More recently 17th edition Dewey numbers have been given in addition to the BNB/DC numbers. Plans for the near future include the full adoption of standard DC as the basis for the classified arrangement (18th edition from January 1971), supplemented by detailed PRECIS indexing.

(d) BNB is used by an increasing number of libraries – especially since the card service was established. (Before that libraries could use it only as a master for their own card production, though some tried using marked copies of the bibliography for branch library catalogues.) It is relatively cheap and has certainly raised standards of cataloguing in this country.[1]

(e) At the time of writing extensive developments are in progress at BNB. Some of these developments, e.g. PRECIS indexing, have already been noted (Chapter 9); others will be discussed later in this chapter in the section on MARC, and in Chapter 21 where shared cataloguing programmes are examined. Computer-assisted techniques are being rapidly adopted and these are likely to facilitate improvements in indexing and in the speed of cumulation.

Particularly interesting is the *Books in English* bibliography. This is produced by a technique evolved by the National Cash Register Company and known as PCMI (Photo Chromic Micro Image). By this technique data can be transferred, at a reduction of 150:1, from microfilm to a transparency approximately 4″ × 6″ in size. The microfilm is in turn produced by a technique referred to as COM (Computer Output Microfilming), by which data from magnetic tape is transferred at high speed on to microfilm. As a result of these two processes it is possible to accommodate on approximately six transparencies a bibliography of all books in English published in one year throughout the world, as recorded by BNB and LC for the UK and US MARC tapes. Such transparencies are now being produced and a 'reader' is available. It is estimated that this, the most comprehensive bibliography of books in English yet produced, will list over 70,000 items each year with a total of 300,000 entries. The arrangement is by standard DC and, in addition to full bibliographic description, entries carry LC card numbers, Standard Book Numbers, LC class numbers and LC subject headings. There is a separate alphabetical sequence indexing authors, added authors, and titles. A serious omission is the lack of a subject index, and for the present the index to the DC schedules has to be used as a substitute: however, a scheme for introducing subject index data is being tested by BNB. During the early trial period of the system cumulation will occur every two months to the annual 'volume'. To quote the BNB publicity handout on PCMI: 'In a few years' time a file of transparencies an inch or so thick will contain more information in a more accessible form than a whole shelf of bibliographies.'

(ii) LIBRARY OF CONGRESS

(a) Although Edward Edwards had suggested in the 1840s that centralized cataloguing be carried out in Britain the idea

12

was very slow in coming to fruition – a hundred years in fact. In the United States on the other hand, the Library of Congress has supplied a card service since 1901 – and there had been several predecessors even then. Note that the card service is a product of the Library of Congress – not a separate organization – and the cards are in fact simply an extension of the library's cataloguing. Each item catalogued by the Library is given a serial number ('card number') and these numbers are noted in the *Cumulative book index* through which the cards are ordered. Today, as the Library of Congress catalogue is being printed regularly in the *National union catalog*, cards can also be ordered through that – but the service existed for years without its own printed bibliography, just as BNB existed as a bibliography without the printed cards.

(b) Being a national library catalogue – unlike BNB, which is purely a national bibliography – it is possible to acquire cards for foreign books via the Library of Congress, and the numbers of such items have substantially increased since the introduction of the Shared Cataloging Program (see Chapter 21). Coverage and cataloguing details are now restricted according to the limited cataloguing practices briefly outlined in Chapter 19.

(c) The author/title headings are based on the 1908 Code with modifications from the ALA code; descriptive cataloguing follows Library of Congress *Rules for descriptive cataloguing*. Library of Congress class numbers and DC numbers are given as well as subject headings from the Library of Congress List.

Author/title and descriptive cataloguing at LC is at present under review. With the development of shared cataloguing and MARC, pressure for international standardization is growing, and it would obviously be a general advantage if LC were to adopt AACR (though even here there are significant differences between the British and American rules, particularly over rule 98 – concerning the entry of corporate bodies under place – and the descriptive rules generally). It has been suggested by Sumner Spalding that the present LC catalogues be 'wound up' by a specified date and a new catalogue, based on AACR, be started.[2] Whether such a solution would be agreed by users, and in particular the users of the Library of Congress itself, is still an open question.

(iii) H. W. WILSON

H. W. Wilson, American publishers of many indexes and bibliographies (including the *Cumulative book index*) provide a card service also. It differs from that of the Library of Congress in the following features:

(a) It is selective – based on an assessment of the needs of medium-sized libraries.

(b) Classification is by D C only and the subject headings are chosen according to Sears' List. (N.b. neither this nor the L C service give any assistance in the making of a subject index for a classified catalogue – a reminder of the status of this form of catalogue in the U S.)

(c) Annotations are frequently given.

(d) The cards are sold in sets – so many per title according to the number of entries considered necessary for that particular document, the assessment being based upon the manufacturer's conception of the needs of medium-sized libraries.

(iv) TWO EXAMPLES OF SPECIALIZED SERVICES

(a) H M S O *cards:* cards are supplied as required for all government publications. The cataloguing is unorthodox (e.g. there are such headings as *House of Commons papers, Command papers,* etc.) and there is a fair amount of inversion of titles, as in the published lists. However, they can be amended by the librarian. Some libraries that buy most government publications take a full set (they are relatively cheap) to make subject catalogues of government publications to offset the inadequacy of the published lists.

(b) *Engineering index.* A periodicals indexing service on cards. The cards are published in special groups covering various engineering topics and these groups can be separately acquired. Cards are sent on a subscription basis and are not applied for independently. The cost is high but they enable a library to create a catalogue of articles on any of a wide range of engineering subjects. Naturally the coverage of American periodicals is fullest.

The Cataloguing-in-source Experiment

Between June 1958 and February 1959, the Library of Congress carried out an experiment to find out whether the pre-publication cataloguing of books was a practicable proposition.[3] 1,200 books were catalogued from publishers' proofs so that a catalogue entry could be printed on the verso of each title page. *The advantages were considered to be:*

(a) *Immediate availability* in the book itself of a full catalogue entry, with the consequent possibility of getting the book into the readers' hands earlier than when other cataloguing methods were used.

(b) *Saving in costs* in libraries through elimination of certain operations, e.g. the ordering of Library of Congress cards would be simplified as there would be no need to check bibliographies for card numbers.

(c) *Bibliographic standardization.* The national bibliographies and others would tend to use the cataloguing style of the entry in the book.

Two of the questions which the experiment sought to answer were:

(a) Would all publishers be willing to send proof copies?

(b) Could adequate cataloguing be carried out from proof copies?

The conclusion was that due to:

(a) the cataloguing discrepancies that arose through alterations in the book after cataloguing,

(b) costs (it would cost the Library of Congress some three-quarters of a million dollars each year),

(c) dissatisfaction of publishers whose time sheets were delayed, and

(d) the dissatisfaction of some librarians,

cataloguing-in-source was not a feasible proposition at the time. However, many have argued about the results and there is still a body of opinion that would like to see further tests made.

MARC

Earlier in this chapter we indicated that the centralized production of entries in machine-readable form such as magnetic tape was a possibility. And as local computer facilities multiply and become increasingly accessible to librarians, so the prospects for this form of centralized cataloguing improve. Basically it would mean that the centralized agency would catalogue the materials, record the data on magnetic tapes, and supply libraries with copies of the tapes from which, using a computer, they could then produce printed catalogues of their stock – or card entries. In addition, the tapes would allow added facilities for the manipulation of data, thus forming a valuable base of information from which various kinds of bibliographies could be produced. (Theoretically it would be possible for an individual library to maintain its catalogue solely in machine-readable form, interrogating the computer directly to answer enquiries. Whether such a form of catalogue would, alone, satisfy all user needs is open to question. In any case it would require permanent access to the computer, and although the future may well lie with such 'on-line' operations, for the present at least we can say that it is hardly a practicable proposition for the majority of libraries.) Developments in computer cataloguing are occurring with such rapidity that any detailed account of the changes now taking place will quickly date. In this section we shall restrict ourselves to a broad survey.

Following the King Report on automation in the Library of Congress,[4] a programme aimed at the eventual production of cataloguing data in machine-readable form, i.e. MARC (MAchine-Readable Cataloguing), was established. It was decided that weekly tapes should be produced and, in the initial experimental period, issued to a small number of co-operating libraries, each tape covering the weekly batch of American publications catalogued by the Library of Congress. The first tapes were issued in October 1966, and at that stage only sixteen libraries were involved in the project. But tapes can be duplicated at speeds of up to 30,000 characters a second, and it was not long before the number of cooperating libraries was substantially augmented. The experimental project (now referred to as MARC I) came to an end in 1968 and was followed by the establishment of a permanent subscription service embodying modifications in format, etc. (MARC II), based on the findings of the experiment. By subscribing to this service it is now possible to acquire in machine-readable form cataloguing data for American publications and, increasingly, for foreign publications acquired under the Shared Cataloging Program (a US government-financed scheme for the acquisition by the Library of Congress of publications on a world-wide basis – see Chapter 21).

Information provided in the MARC record includes, among other things: the descriptive data, author/title headings, subject headings (Library of Congress), a series of class numbers (LC, DC, National Library of Medicine, National Agriculture Library subject category number), and identification numbers – e.g. the Library of Congress card number.

BNB and MARC

Whilst these developments were taking place at the Library of Congress, other national bibliographical services were experimenting with the use of computers. West Germany began to produce its current national bibliography by computer in 1966: since January 1st of that year the weekly lists, supplements, and cumulations have been type-set by a Linoquick machine controlled by paper tape. There has been as a result a marked improvement in the speed of cumulation, the half-yearly list which previously took over a year to produce now being completed in under three months.[5]

Similar systems were being considered at the BNB in the mid-sixties. Plans were, however, substantially influenced by the American developments. As Coward puts it: 'If any two schemes looked like being complementary to each other they were the MARC project and the BNB computer project.'[6] Investigations began into the feasibility of producing a British MARC record, the idea being that such a record could then be available to libraries with computer facilities, and at the same time would serve as the basis for the production of the national bibliography and card service.

The prospects for such a development were greatly improved by the introduction in 1967 of a system of Standard Book Numbers, by which British publications could be identified, from the publicity stage to the publication itself, by a unique number. Such a system is a necessary prerequisite for the effective manipulation of records in machine-readable form, and although in the US the Library of Congress card number served the purpose in the first instance (it being, unlike the BNB number, printed in the book, etc.), a similar system of standard numbers has now been adopted, and indeed is rapidly spreading throughout the world.

That the BNB has not proceeded to develop a purely national MARC system can be understood by reference to (a) the capacity of computers, (b) the needs of British libraries, and (c) the establishment of the Library of Congress system. As regards the first, it should be recognized that the processing capacity of MARC systems is well beyond the current book production of any one country: so to limit the input would be to disregard the potential services that might be offered. Again, as current British publications form only a part of the total acquisitions of many libraries, it would clearly be an advantage if the machine-readable record were to contain foreign publications also. Finally, in view of the fact that the Library of Congress was already producing MARC data for a great many documents originating in countries throughout the world, and as that library was willing to duplicate tapes for others to use, it appeared wasteful to duplicate such effort in other countries.

It is as a result of such considerations that the BNB/MARC project has been developed in close cooperation with the Library of Congress. Agreement has been reached on many aspects of format (i.e. the bibliographic format and the general design of the machine system). In August 1968 the first of the BNB/MARC weekly tapes was issued to a small group of libraries in this country, and although initially these tapes covered current British publications only, by 1969 data from the American MARC tapes were being added. In return – and in connection with the Shared Cataloging Program of the Library of Congress – BNB supplies the Library of Congress with tapes for the publications catalogued in London.

It is impossible to give any idea of the complexity of this operation in a brief summary such as this. Certain problems still evade solution, and although it can be claimed that many of these are matters of detail, they should not be minimized on that account. A factor which cannot, of course, be regarded as a mere detail is that of standardization. The use of MARC tapes underlines the need for standardization of descriptive cataloguing, for although modifications can be made by individual libraries (just as modifications have always been made to cards produced by a central agency), such modifications are costly. 'The extent to which a library feels able to accept a standardized record from a central agency is certainly critical as far as MARC is concerned. Modification costs are high. There is, I would suggest, a minimum packet of data on the MARC record which a user must be prepared to accept. I have called this the "primary data packet". It can be defined as those fields in a catalogue entry which can be manipulated and organized in different contexts, but which are not altered in any way by the systems in which they are placed. These fields – from title line to note – are the descriptive core of the entry, and, if you cannot take them over more or less as they stand, then you are stuck with your own cataloguing.'[7] Modifications of headings – whether of author, title, or subject (within the range offered on the tapes) – *can* be programmed by individual libraries, as Linford has pointed out,[8] but again they cannot be lightly undertaken – if only because the costs of such modifications are more obvious than similar modifications in manual systems.

However, it must not be assumed that the use of computers by centralized agencies must result in restrictions. On the contrary, it could be persuasively argued that the capacity of automated systems to produce catalogues arranged according to a wide variety of characteristics – especially when several classification schemes are incorporated into the record – allows freedom of choice beyond anything that manual systems can achieve. Certain forms of standardization would seem to be a relatively small price to pay for such flexibility. Additionally, in the process of automation the BNB is revising its indexing procedures and it may well be that in PRECIS we shall have a more effective index than hitherto.

Other objections to MARC that have been raised represent opposing views. On the one hand there have been those who have pointed out that the data will not cover a sufficiently high proportion of the materials catalogued in their libraries – and this, of course, may well remain so for many years in those libraries which undertake analytical cataloguing of periodicals, etc. (though there is no reason to suppose that such data will not in due course be disseminated in machine-readable form from central indexing agencies). However, so far as individually published items are concerned the cooperation between BNB and the Library of Congress, with its Shared Cataloging Program, must result in an increasingly comprehensive record of the world's publications. At the other extreme are those who see the full tapes as being cumbersome for those with limited collections. The production of selective tapes for such libraries would seem to be the answer, but such editing will probably be left to the individual library: it would not be difficult to programme local computers to create such selective tapes from the full record.[9]

A further problem is that of older books. MARC records are at present available only for current materials. Although in time the demand for older materials will decline, the problem cannot be ignored. In large national libraries we have huge potential data files of such materials, and the translation of such files into machine-readable form is a matter that will, no doubt, receive greater attention once the recording of current publications is satisfactorily settled.[10] After recognizing the British Museum's plans for computerized catalogues, the Dainton Committee Report states:

The direct benefits to the British Museum Library of a computerized catalogue are large and obvious. Further benefits would accrue from the application of the same basic information in other ways. For example, a central computer programmed to carry out the bibliographical services of the cataloguing division of the Department of Printed Books and the routine documentation of the BML's Copyright Receipt Office, could also be used to generate BNB's card and list services. Already the BNB is well advanced towards automatic production techniques based upon magnetic tapes containing, in MARC format, information about new British publications. However, at the present time, there appears to us to be a possibility of the BNB and the BML establishing separate and mutually incompatible computer facilities which would result in considerable duplication of effort and capital expenditure. We, therefore, consider it urgent to investigate the possibility of developing a single computerized system for carrying out both operations.[11]

A factor that will clearly affect the success of MARC is the speed with which materials are recorded. Doubts have been expressed on this point by a number of librarians. How far these doubts are justified remains to be seen. One can only point to the efforts being made in the Shared Cataloging Program and at BNB to produce cataloguing records as quickly as possible – from proof copies if at all feasible.

Whatever the initial reactions, there is little doubt that the use of computers by centralized agencies is bound to increase. The implications – not only for cataloguing, but for book ordering, acquisitions, circulation control, interlending systems, dissemination of information, etc. – are extensive. Some of these will be noted in other chapters. Whilst allowing that technological developments will result in reappraisals of service, the important thing is to ensure that they do not determine our priorities.

READINGS

1. LEWIS, P. R. 'British National Bibliography provision in public libraries'. *Library Association Record*, 70(1), January 1968, 14–16. Also: 'The demand for the British National Bibliography: a survey . . .' *Journal of Librarianship*, 1 (2), April 1969, 88–106.
2. See *Catalogue and Index* for progress reports.
3. LIBRARY OF CONGRESS. *The cataloging-in-source experiment.* Washington, Library of Congress, 1960.
4. KING, G. W. *and others. Automation and the Library of Congress.* Washington, Library of Congress, 1963.
5. KÖSTER, K. 'The use of computers in compiling national bibliographies, illustrated by the example of the *Deutsche Bibliographie*'. *Libri*, 16(4), 1966, 269–81.
6. COWARD, R. E. 'BNB and computers'. *Library Association Record*, 70(8), August 1968, 198–202.
   See also the *BNB/MARC Documentation Service Publications*, no. 1 – June 1968 –. London, BNB, 1968 –.
7. COWARD, R. E. 'The United Kingdom MARC service' (In COX, N. S. M. *and* GROSE, M. W. *ed. The organization and handling of bibliographic records by computer.* Newcastle-upon-Tyne, Oriel Press, 1967. pp. 105–17).
8. LINFORD, J. E. commenting on HALL, A. T. 'Some questions about the MARC project'. *Library Association Record*, 71(9), September 1969, 275–8.
9. COX, N. S. M. *and* GROSE, M. W. op. cit. p. 116.
10. COWARD, R. E. op. cit. (6) p. 199.
11. Report of the National Libraries Committee (Dainton). London, HMSO, 1969 (Cmnd 4028). para 373.

Chapter 21
Cooperative and Shared Cataloguing

Traditionally a clear distinction has been drawn between co-operative and centralized cataloguing. Whereas the latter, as we have seen, refers to the production of cataloguing data by a centralized agency, the former has been used to refer to the situation where a number of independent libraries share the work of producing a catalogue for their mutual benefit. The distinction is clear if we consider the role of the BNB on the one hand and that of the National Central Library and the Regional Bureaux on the other. The one produces, in various forms, catalogue entries for new British publications which can be used by any library subscribing to the service; the other is concerned with the creation of a series of union catalogues based on data supplied by individual libraries, the primary purpose being to enable the location of items and hence, through a cooperative system, the fuller utilization of the documentary resources of an area.

This traditional distinction is gradually being eroded. However, before elaborating on this point, we shall examine cooperative cataloguing as conventionally understood, with particular reference to the British scene.

As we have indicated, a central feature of cooperative cataloguing is the *union catalogue*, defined by Larsen as follows: 'a catalogue listing in one sequence the holdings or part of the holdings of two or more libraries'.[1] The location of all copies of the documents catalogued may be indicated or location may be only partial – as in the *World list of scientific periodicals* or the *Short-title catalogue* of Pollard and Redgrave.

The Basic Functions of Union Catalogues

(i) *To reveal the total document resources of an area*, so enabling readers' requests to be satisfied, and allowing systematic book selection. The union catalogue will be a major bibliography in its own right, e.g. BUCOP, our fullest single list of world periodicals. But note that it is usually limited in its approach – normally providing only an author/title finding approach.

(ii) *To assist in the location of items.* Without union catalogues this can be done only by (a) consulting all the catalogues of all the libraries concerned, (b) circulating 'wants lists', or (c) writing to the library most likely to have the required document. In certain circumstances – e.g. when the request is for a specialized document and a specialized loan collection is accessible, or when a large national lending library such as the NLL is in operation – this last method might be a real alternative to the union catalogue.

Factors to be Considered in Compiling a Union Catalogue

(i) *Purpose and relation to existing union catalogues.* Duplication is to be avoided, especially when, as today, there are still many types of material that cannot be located through union catalogues. A careful statement of purpose will be the touchstone by which the compiler will consider the factors listed below.

(ii) *Area.* This must obviously be carefully defined. *Local catalogues,* though limited, are of great value in showing at a glance the contents of libraries within easy reach; they can be kept up to date more easily than national lists; there is more chance of their being published – and so they may facilitate direct borrowing between libraries as against the more time-consuming process of borrowing through a central clearing house. *National catalogues,* or those covering a large region having many libraries, are bound to be so much more unwieldy and difficult to maintain – note the present arrears in the regional union catalogues of this country. It is doubtful whether national catalogues of *books* showing all locations in the country are a practicable proposition today. (The problem is tackled in the UK by having a series of regional catalogues which aim at including all locations within the region, and a national catalogue showing which regions have a particular title; in the US the national catalogue shows locations in particular libraries but is highly selective in the number of locations shown.)

(iii) *Material.* Limitations based on materials must be very carefully calculated and should be clearly indicated for the users' sake. Examples of limitations:

(a) *Form*, e.g. BUCOP is limited to periodicals and the term is very closely defined (for example, it excludes newspapers first published after 1799, annual reports of organizations, but includes yearbooks, proceedings, and so on).

(b) *Subject*, e.g. *The World list of scientific periodicals*.

(c) *Period*, e.g. *British union catalogue of early music printed before 1801*, *Gesamtkatalog der Wiegendrucke*, Pollard and Redgrave's *Short-title catalogue*.

(d) *Language*, e.g. the union catalogue of Russian books housed at NCL.

As can be seen from the examples listed above many union catalogues have several specified forms of limitation.

(iv) *Arrangement*. As union catalogues are used most frequently to assist in identifying and locating documents some particulars of which are already known, an alphabetical author or title arrangement is to be preferred. Other tools should be used in the initial selection of material. Subject arrangement would certainly have its uses, but in most catalogues it would present insurmountable problems of maintenance and filing. The use of punched cards and other mechanical and electronic devices may result in multiple arrangements of union catalogues: for example, *New serial titles*, the American equivalent of BUCOP, appears in a classified version in addition to the basic title list. In the Library of Congress a trained filer can handle some 250 cards an hour in a catalogue of a quarter of a million cards, but the speed is down to fifty an hour in the main catalogue with its millions of entries. In some catalogues where location is the sole purpose no account is taken of forenames in filing – entries under, say, Jones, being filed by title; it is claimed that greater speed in both filing and searching is achieved in this way. Simplification of cataloguing through the use of AACR – for example, the reduced specification of degrees of subordination in headings for corporate bodies – should be of particular value in large union catalogues.

(v) *Description*. All that is strictly necessary is the minimum of detail for the identification of an edition of a document (author, title, edition, date). More may be given but this is all that is needed for identification. Published union lists of periodicals frequently give little more than brief title – see, for example, LULOP. On the other hand, some lists attempt to show the relationships between titles; indeed BUCOP provides a very full record of such matters. Locations should, in the case of periodicals, show the holdings of each library that has not a full file of a particular title and should indicate for how long the title is filed. Symbols are often found to indicate the availability for loan of each title and whether photocopies can be made if required.

Rules for headings and description must be laid down by the compiler, and cooperating libraries will have to amend their usual style of cataloguing accordingly. Such amendments may be left to the compiler but this is less satisfactory. Clearly, standardization of cataloguing is as important in cooperative as in centralized cataloguing.

(vi) *Compilation and revision.* There are several possible methods:

(a) The largest library may make a catalogue of its collection for circulation to the other cooperating libraries. These in turn will indicate which of the documents listed are in stock and will add further titles not so far listed.

(b) The above method may take too much time. An alternative is to have several copies made of the basic catalogue, thus allowing a number of libraries to be working on the project simultaneously. Eventually the catalogue will be reassembled and unified.

(c) Each library may, for the purpose, make a catalogue of its own holdings. These catalogues are then assembled centrally.

Photography has been used successfully since the war for the compilation of union catalogues, particularly in Canada and Germany. The catalogues of cooperating libraries are photographed and catalogue entries made from the film by some suitable method of reproduction. There are various methods. Much labour is saved in this way, but its success depends on cooperating libraries having very similar cataloguing practices, for, as we have mentioned, headings and descriptions must be consistent. Undoubtedly *computers* will be increasingly used in cooperative cataloguing, and several examples of printed catalogues produced by computer can be seen today – as a glance through the pages of *Program* will reveal.[2]

Compilation is not the end, of course. There must be provision for adequate revision – and this means continuous revision. This is not always recognized in the case of printed union catalogues. Someone, or some organization, should be regularly notified of amendments and additions and a file of these should be maintained so that new editions can easily be brought out when justified.

(vii) *Physical form of catalogue.* The standard 5 × 3-in. card is not suitable for union catalogues where many locations have to be shown, which is the reason why all the catalogues (except the London union catalogue and the Welsh regional catalogue) in the national interlending scheme in this country are in *sheaf* form. There are many examples of *printed* union catalogues of a limited kind (catalogues of periodicals, incunabula, music, and so on) but for obvious reasons few large-scale union catalogues of books get into print. An exception is the *National union catalogue* of the Library of Congress (see below). Print allows a union catalogue to become a valuable bibliographical tool in any library that can afford it; it also allows direct borrowing between libraries rather than through a central agency – though this may result in one library, because of its size, location, or fame, being overloaded with requests. It is also possible, of course, to store a union catalogue in the form of *magnetic tape,* etc., whether or not the catalogue is to be printed out. If printing were not envisaged then the library holding the tapes would have to serve as an information centre for requests.

Examples (Great Britain)

The national system of library cooperation – comprising the National Central Library, the Regional Bureaux, and the Outlier Libraries – is largely dependent on the various union catalogues that have been built up over the years. The National Union Catalogue at the NCL, which indicates in which region a particular document can be found, is in sheaf form, as are all the union catalogues of the Regional Bureaux (except, as already mentioned, those of the London Region and Wales). The Regional Bureaux union catalogues indicate the whereabouts of a particular document in the region concerned. The NCL also maintains a selective union catalogue of the Outlier

Libraries (i.e. non-public libraries cooperating in the national system). Altogether the National Union Catalogue, the London Union Catalogue (which is housed in the NCL) and the Outlier Catalogue contain over five million entries. At the NCL there are also several special union catalogues, e.g. the union catalogues of Russian and German books.

Since January 1959, the National Union Catalogue has excluded books listed in BNB; the regions now aim to be self-sufficient in BNB books. Thus the NCL can concentrate on remedying defects in the stock of older materials, foreign works, and so on.

Not all the union catalogues in the national system are up to date and the Roberts Report (1959)[3] and the Working Party (1962)[4] recommended as a matter of urgency that money be spent in making up arrears. The Dainton Report (1969) takes up the old cry:

> The UGC report on libraries (paragraphs 107–9) has shown how far the incompleteness of the NCL's union catalogues has contributed to the overall delays in its services. This is partly because the union catalogues have, through lack of manpower, not been kept up to date and partly because some cooperating libraries for whatever reason have been unable to provide the NCL with records of their acquisitions and disposals in the most appropriate form or as quickly as desired. The very large arrears in entering details of items available for inter-library lending must seriously reduce the effectiveness of the union catalogues. Unless a substantial effort is devoted to correcting this situation there will be little hope of decreasing the present substantial proportion of cases in which resort has to be made to the slow, costly and relatively ineffectual speculative search. We, therefore, recommend that the highest priority be given to this work on the union catalogues, if necessary at the expense of other activities. Even with the development of computerized cataloguing, which we believe offers the most hopeful long-term prospect for a rapid locating service, the satisfaction of the needs of users will depend on maintaining the primary locating tool as nearly up to date as possible.[5]

And, further in the Report, the Committee has this to say on computerized catalogues:

> The union catalogues of the NCL contain entries for items, a high

proportion of which must also be recorded in the British Museum
Library catalogue and some of which will be included in the BNB.
We have already urged the need to take immediate steps to
remedy the arrears in the NCL's union catalogues as a first step
towards improving inter-library lending. But, if the stretched
services of the NCL are not to break down in the course of the
next few years under the continually increasing load of international book publishing and heavier demands on its inter-
library lending services, computerization will be essential. The
conversion of the union catalogues alone into machine-readable
form would be very costly, but if this could be achieved as part
of a larger project which also embraced computerization of the
services of the BNB and the BML, considerable economies should
be effected.[6]

In addition to these limitations, the national system has two
major defects:

(i) Many non-public libraries do not participate. Thus a
truly national system of book selection, storage, and document
retrieval, is not possible.

(ii) Partly as a result of (i), whilst coverage of modern British
trade publications is now generally adequate, many gaps still
exist in the coverage of specialized, older, and non-trade
materials.

To a certain extent it is because of the deficiencies in the
national system that many other examples of cooperation exist
in this country today, only a few of which can be mentioned
here. A major development has been the *National Lending
Library for Science and Technology*, based originally on the old
library of the Science Museum, which had for years been a
major outlier library of the NCL. The basic aim of NLL was to
create a collection of materials in science and technology which
could be borrowed on direct application by libraries which had
themselves attained certain standards of stock provision. Since
moving to its headquarters at Boston Spa in the 1960s, the
library has extended its scope to include materials in the social
sciences. Its Director, D. J. Urquhart states:

At the NLL we have given a very wide interpretation to the term
'social sciences'. For instance, it includes 'Legal studies' and
'education'. Moreover, in selecting periodicals we have tried to
obtain all those which contain some social science material. This

inevitably means that we are now receiving a number of periodicals which contain material in the humanities. We find, for instance, that we are now receiving about half of the current periodicals covered by *Historical abstracts*. In fact, the NLL may well be receiving more 'history' periodicals than any other library in the UK.[7]

It is estimated that requests made to this library will top a million in 1970. Publications include the list of serials received, the *NLL Translations bulletin*, the quarterly *Index of conference proceedings*, and the monthly *British research and development reports*. The library maintains few catalogues. The establishment of a central lending library on this scale represents a shift from the philosophy of mutual cooperation embodied in the Regional Bureaux. The effectiveness of the library's services, in terms of coverage, availability, and speed of provision, account for the rapid growth in its use.

Since the 1930s there has been a measure of cooperation between *university libraries* – witness the *Union catalogue of the periodical publications in the university libraries of the British Isles* (1937) and the recent work of SCONUL (Standing Conference on National and University Libraries). The latter organization, with the NCL, has compiled a union catalogue of books published before 1800. Some cooperation is also seen amongst special departments of universities, e.g. the libraries of the Institutes of Education.

Aslib has also initiated much cooperation between special libraries, though its policy has not been primarily aimed at the creation of union catalogues. However, some union catalogues of periodicals in certain fields have been produced by special groups, e.g. *Union list of periodicals on aeronautics and allied subjects*, 1953.

Since 1945 many public libraries have tried to organize *special services for local industry*, following the example of Sheffield whose service (SINTO) was started in the 1930s. Union catalogues are to be found in many of these services – thus in CICRIS (West London Commercial and Technical Library Service), the scheme based on Acton and involving many public and special libraries in west London, there are union catalogues of, amongst other things, periodicals and directories.

Again, at a regional level are the useful lists of periodicals produced at the instigation of the LA Branches.

An important published union catalogue facilitating direct interlending is the *British union catalogue of periodicals*. Since 1962 this catalogue has been maintained at the NCL and a quarterly supplement with annual cumulations is produced. BUCOP and the *World list of scientific periodicals* are now amalgamated at the NCL and a separate annual cumulation for scientific and technical titles is published.

The various systems of library cooperation in Britain have been subjected to close scrutiny over the years. One of the most recent surveys to include this subject, the Dainton Report, has already been quoted. A particularly significant proposal in that report was that the loan stocks of the NCL should be moved to the NLL at Boston Spa to create a 'National Loan Locating Centre'.[8] The Committee also favoured the transfer of the union catalogues. These proposals have to be set against the Committee's wider recommendations for the creation of a coordinated National Bibliographic Service.

Such recommendations can be viewed as attempts to short-circuit a system which has creaked more noticeably with the passage of time. A major cause of delays is the state of the union catalogues, both regional and national. Another is the hierarchical system whereby requests go through a series of searches at regional, national, and possibly international levels. By recommending a more extensive national loan service the Dainton Committee is suggesting a way of overcoming the latter defect. But it is not at the same time abandoning the concept of either regional or national union catalogues – indeed, it has stressed the need to keep them up to date. It is not, in other words, recommending a unilateral approach.

There have been more outspoken critics. Esterquest, for example, in a survey of library cooperation in Britain,[9] questioned the Regional Bureaux/NCL structure, favouring a more direct national loan service. More recently Urquhart[10] has made his position clear in a series of articles pointing to the costs and deficiencies of the existing system and recommending, among other things, the establishment of large-scale loan centres to which direct access could be made nationally or internationally. Buckland,[11] after comparing costs of a centralized system and one based on regional union catalogues, concludes that 'a system of multiple union catalogues is likely to be more expensive in terms of editing and searching than a single union catalogue system'. The author goes on to assert that studies have indicated that 'at any given level of demand and satisfaction, fewer loanable copies of an item are needed if provision is made on a national rather than a regional basis and that this difference increases sharply as the level of demand rises. This remains true whether stock for loan or locations in a union catalogue are considered . . . It seems unlikely that interlibrary cooperation would seriously suffer if the Regional Library Bureaux were to concentrate on other forms of co-operation than the maintenance of union catalogues.'

Clearly the trend would appear to be away from multiple union catalogue systems. It is a trend that seems likely to be accelerated if ever the computerization of large central union catalogues becomes a reality.

Examples (USA)

A very different pattern of library cooperation exists in the United States. There is no equivalent to the Regional Bureaux network, though there are several centres for regional co-operation, such as the one at Philadelphia and the Midwest Storage Center in Chicago. These regional centres often maintain selective union catalogues of the libraries in their area.

The most striking feature, however, is the central role of the Library of Congress. It cannot be too strongly emphasized that this library combines the functions of the BM, the NCL and the BNB. Only when one recognizes the degree of centralization can the system of library cooperation in the United States, and particularly recent developments there, be understood. The Library of Congress is the national library *and* it is the agency for centralized cataloguing. At the same time it is responsible for maintaining not only its own catalogues but also the huge National Union Catalog, now containing over sixteen million entries. This catalogue is composed partly of its own cards, on which some locations are shown, and partly of cards supplied by cooperating libraries in the United States. Although the locations are selective, all major research libraries, including the National Library of Medicine and the National Agriculture Library, cooperate closely with the Library of Congress. The NLM and the NAL publish their own catalogues also. And if Buckland's calculations, noted above, are correct, then selective location on a national scale may be an adequate substitute for more comprehensive systems of regional union catalogues. Moreover, the National Union Catalog also appears in published form: since 1957 accessions have been published monthly, with cumulations up to five-year periods; and at present the whole backfile for pre-1956 imprints is being produced in book form, completion – in over 600 volumes – being forecast for the end of the decade. The US thus has a union catalogue which gives locations immediately, albeit selectively, and which can be examined in any library which can afford to buy it. As the nearest thing we have to a current international catalogue of books, it is one of the world's major bibliographies.

The Library of Congress is also responsible for the union catalogue of periodicals – published as the *Union list of serials*, with regular supplements in title and classified order, the former being cumulated annually.

An interesting development which occurred in the 'fifties was the Farmington Plan, a decentralized cooperative scheme involving a number of large libraries in the States and aiming at improving the acquisition of foreign materials. Catalogue entries for the materials acquired under this scheme are forwarded to the Library of Congress for inclusion in the National Union Catalog. However, this development has been largely overshadowed recently by the more spectacular Shared Cataloging Program.

The Shared Cataloging Program

Though an American development, the Shared Cataloging Program has international implications and is of such importance that it merits separate consideration here.

The Higher Education Act, passed by Congress in 1965, contained a section – Title II C – which authorized the Library of Congress (i) to establish a comprehensive collection of scholarly materials published throughout the world; (ii) to create adequate bibliographical records of these materials within three to four weeks of receipt; and (iii) to distribute such records as required, either as catalogue cards or in machine-readable form.

Substantial funds were made available, and since 1965 the Library of Congress has undertaken its new responsibilities with remarkable energy. It quickly established a global network of national and regional offices as the basis for a vast exercise in international cooperation. Each office is now responsible for the selection, acquisition and despatch of local materials – selection being done in many cases from advance printer's copy of the national bibliography. Speed is further effected by transporting the materials by air. Coverage includes trade and non-trade materials – monographs, proceedings, transactions, atlases, etc. Certain categories – e.g. maps, non-book materials, periodicals, and dissertations – are excluded. (Channels for the acquisition of some of these excluded categories had already been established.)

In addition, the overseas offices supply bibliographic data as a basis for LC cataloguing. In many cases the Library of Congress accepts the cataloguing undertaken for the national bibliographies in the countries concerned, adding only the supplementary information required for the LC system. (In Britain, for example, the office is located with the bookseller Stevens and Brown, and the bibliographic information is supplied by BNB – now in the form of MARC tapes.) The programme can thus be seen as reducing duplication in cataloguing on an international scale. Apart from the economy of this procedure, a higher degree of accuracy is achieved through the use of local personnel. This last advantage becomes particularly significant when one remembers the difficulties that face cataloguers dealing with materials in lesser known languages.

The Shared Cataloging Program (also referred to as the National Program for Acquisitions and Cataloging) involves the National Library of Medicine and the National Agricultural Library as well as other libraries in the United States.

As a result of these activities – the complexity of which can be appreciated only through a study of the readings given at the end of this chapter – the coverage of the Library of Congress card service has increased dramatically. It has been stated that a number of large research libraries in the US have found that

the cards are now available for 77 per cent of their book pur-
chases – an increase of 25 per cent – and that they are available
four months earlier than before.[12] And as the service improves,
more foreign libraries are beginning to use it. The number of
cards sold in 1968 was over seventy-eight million. One should
also remember that an ever-increasing amount of the bibliographic information resulting from the Shared Cataloging
Program is available in machine-readable form, and in the
near future we shall, no doubt, see an expansion of the kind of
cooperation now taking place between BNB and LC under the
MARC programme. It is also likely, as Coward[13] has pointed
out, that the exchange of machine-readable cataloguing data
between various national centres will be a feature of the
cataloguing scene during the next few years. Indeed, there are
many good reasons for avoiding too heavy a reliance on one
national library, even one on the scale of the Library of
Congress, and the budget cuts to the Shared Cataloging
Program (1969) are a warning.

In view of some of the current British arguments about the
degree of centralization desirable in a cooperative cataloguing
scheme, it is interesting to note that the Americans, after
attempting, with only limited success, decentralized cooperation under the Farmington Plan, have now reverted to their
more usual mode of operation: centralization under the Library
of Congress. It is worth noting too that the 1965 Act came only
after the cooperative efforts of the libraries involved in that
scheme had been boosted by a programme known as the
Public Law 480 Program – by which the Library of Congress
established offices in certain countries (mainly those with an
underdeveloped book trade) in order to procure books for the
libraries in the scheme. This can be seen as a forerunner of the
Shared Cataloging Program: in itself it had only limited
success, funds being inadequate to support either the international network of offices required or the efficient cataloguing
of the materials.

The Future

In this and the preceding chapter we have been examining
various systems of centralized and cooperative cataloguing.

We have noted that the distinction between the two is less clear-cut today than it used to be. More precisely, we can say that whilst the functional distinction remains – the one aiming at reducing cataloguing effort by the provision of centralized services, the other at facilitating the full use of existing library resources, the *systems* by which these functions are carried out are hardly likely to remain (at least in Britain) as distinct as they have been so far.

With the development of cooperation between centralized cataloguing agencies, seen in the BNB/MARC programme and the programme of Shared Cataloging, the capacity of such services is greatly increased. As the world's literature is increasingly brought under control in this way, so the use of such services by libraries of all kinds is likely to grow. Just as union catalogues in a single library system are effectively produced as a by-product of its centralized cataloguing, so it would seem likely that a selective national union catalogue in conventional or machine-readable form might be produced as a by-product of the work of a centralized national cataloguing agency. For some years the BNB has, on a limited scale, been able to notify the NCL of locations as a result of its card service. As BNB's coverage widens the cooperation between BNB and NCL to produce a national union catalogue on lines similar to that of the Library of [Congress may well emerge. Such cooperation would not, in itself, be sufficient, but it would undoubtedly create a firm basis for other supplementary forms of cooperation.

The probability of such a development is increased by the failings of the present system of cooperation based on multiple union catalogues. As noted above, there has been much discussion of these failings in recent years, and the tendency of recent writings seems to be in favour of a more centralized system: the centralization of union catalogues as distinct from a series of union catalogues, and the centralization of loan services such as provided by the NLL and as recommended by the Dainton Report.

There may, then, in Britain emerge a system of national cooperation based on central loan collections and a central union catalogue created in part through the cooperation of a centralized cataloguing agency, itself cooperating with other national agencies. None of this will, however, obviate the need for certain additional local and special union catalogues.

While such a system could gradually be developed for current books, the problem of older books remains. Many requests satisfied by cooperative schemes are for such older materials. Here again a new pattern may emerge in British librarianship, for, undoubtedly, the basic stocks of older books are housed in the national libraries that have so far stood outside the cooperative system. The recommendations of the Dainton Report for a national bibliographic system and developments within the national libraries themselves suggest that the situation may be about to change.

But a textbook is not the place for crystal-gazing. Tentative prognostications of the kind made here depend for their realization on agreement on principles and techniques, financial support, etc. Though there are signs that considerable efforts are now being made to rationalize centralized and cooperative cataloguing – witness, for example, the measure of agreement on cataloguing reached by the joint Copyright Libraries/BNB Working Party – there are also many problems and areas of disagreement. The point is that although the nature of any new developments remains unpredictable, substantial – and possibly rapid – changes are likely.

READINGS

1. LARSEN, K. *National bibliographical services* ... Paris, Unesco, 1953. p. 56.
   See also: BRUMMEL, L. *Union catalogues* ... Paris, Unesco, 1956.
2. *Program* – see reference no. 6 at the end of Chapter 18.
   See also: DEWS, J. D. 'The union list of periodicals in the Institute of Education libraries'. (*In* COX, N. S. M. *and* GROSE, M. W. ed. *The organization and handling of bibliographic records by computer*. Newcastle-upon-Tyne, Oriel Press, 1967. pp. 22–9.)
3. The structure of public library services in England and Wales (ROBERTS). London, HMSO, 1959 (Cmnd. 660).
4. Inter-Library Cooperation in England and Wales. London, HMSO, 1962.
5. Report of the National Libraries Committee (Dainton). London, HMSO, 1969 (Cmnd 4028). para. 264.

6. Dainton Report, para. 374.
7. URQUHART, D. J. 'The regional bureaux and the NLL'. *Library Association Record*, 72(1), January 1970, 11–14.
8. Dainton Report, para. 423–31.
9. ESTERQUEST, R. T. *Library cooperation in Great Britain*. Chicago, Association of College and Research Libraries, 1955.
10. For example: URQUHART, D. J. op. cit. and: URQUHART, D. J. 'Cooperation – local, regional or national?' *Library Association Record*, 71(7), July 1969, 197–201.
11. BUCKLAND, M. K. 'The quantitative evaluation of regional union catalogues'. *Journal of Documentation*, 23(1), March 1967, 20–7.
12. WESTBY, B. M. *Shared cataloguing*. Dublin, University College, 1969. p. 7.
13. COWARD, R. E. 'BNB and computers'. *Library Association Record*, 70(8), August 1968, 198–202.

See also: *Libri*, 17(4), 1967, 270–313 – for several articles on the Shared Cataloging Program and the Library of Congress.
WELLS, A. J. 'Shared cataloguing: a new look at an old problem'. *Aslib Proceedings*, 20(12), December 1968, 534–41.
BATTY, C. D. 'Cooperation in cataloguing'. *Aslib Proceedings*, 21(12), December 1969, 488–97.

Chapter 22
The Process of Cataloguing

There are two reasons why I have deliberately avoided calling this chapter 'the organization of the cataloguing department'. In the first place, it would be a pretentious title for the notes that follow. To discuss realistically the organization of the cataloguing department would demand recourse to case studies; departments of various sizes and in different types of libraries would have to be examined. This would require an amount of space quite disproportionate in a book of this nature. In the second place, such a title presupposes that a cataloguing department is necessary, and this is manifestly unjustified – many libraries exist without one; this book is not written with any single type of library in mind. Students should not accept without at least a momentary critical glance the assumption that cataloguing departments as we know them today are necessary in any kind of library. The functional division of libraries into such departments as Lending, Reference, Cataloguing, etc., has been criticized for years – though few public librarians in this country have in practice reorganized their libraries on other lines even when new buildings have presented new opportunities. It may well be that the cataloguing of books is best done by subject librarians for whom cataloguing is but one of many tasks (selection, reader service, etc.). At Tottenham this was tried with, I understand, some success.[1]

The Operations Involved

In all types of libraries, documents are ordered, accessioned, catalogued, processed, shelved, and so on – and although the organization of these operations varies enormously to suit special conditions, the basic operations and the factors that have to be considered in planning the organization remain to a large extent the same. It is hoped that the notes which follow will help the student to assess the work of the cataloguer when visiting libraries as part of his course.

(i) *Ancillary operations.* Although the following go beyond what can strictly be called cataloguing, they must be remembered because they are closely connected with cataloguing, not only in the sequence of events, but also, more fundamentally, in overall organization. For example, it is important to see that records made for these processes are coordinated with the records made in cataloguing.

(a) Ordering.

(b) Receipt.

(c) Accessioning.

(d) Processing (e.g. labelling, pocketing, numbering).

(e) Assignment to shelves (possibly including departments and branches).

(ii) *Cataloguing operations.*

(a) Deciding author/title headings.

(b) Descriptive cataloguing.

(c) Classification.

(d) Deciding alphabetical subject headings, or index entries.

(e) Production of catalogue entries, i.e. the physical entries themselves.

(f) Filing entries.

(g) Making records (e.g. authority files, statistical records).

(h) Revision of entries. Re-cataloguing.

(iii) *Occasional duties associated with cataloguing.*

(a) Production of lists of new additions.

(b) Production of bulletins, special subject lists, etc.

ORGANIZING THE OPERATIONS

(i) *Who is to be responsible?*

As already indicated, the cataloguing may be the sole function of one person or department, or it may be shared by various subject librarians (i.e. specialists in the bibliography of the subjects, not necessarily subject specialists as such) as part of their job, only the processing being undertaken by the functional department. (In a small library the problem hardly arises.)

The main advantages of sharing the work are:

(a) The cataloguing is never out of touch with the needs of the reference service because the cataloguers will also be the reference librarians.

(b) The knowledge of books which cataloguers inevitably acquire will be utilized directly in the service to readers.

(c) No cataloguer can be conversant with the whole field of knowledge; where subject specialists are used the work is likely to be better performed.

A disadvantage is that the final catalogue may lack overall uniformity as a result of its being produced by several librarians on a subject basis. But well-formulated rules and procedures should minimize this. In a large system, someone may be responsible for the final coordination.

It is interesting to note that even where a functional division exists, some special subjects (e.g. music, children's literature) are frequently catalogued by the librarians directly concerned with the librarianship of these subjects, thus introducing to some extent a non-functional element.

In a large library system with many branches and departments a further problem arises: *is the cataloguing to be done centrally (by a central cataloguing department or by subject specialists working at the central library) or by individual departments or branches?* Where only special subject departments are concerned – as, for example, in a university or a large central public library employing subject librarians – it would seem best to let the departments do their own cataloguing, but according to an overall framework of rules and procedures to allow the compilation of a union catalogue and, possibly, the centralization of the processing. On the other hand, less can be said in favour of decentralization among the branches of a public library system where there are great similarities of stocks and services – for then there are all the administrative difficulties associated with decentralization, without the advantages of having subject librarians on the job; in this case, the uniformity in the system's catalogues and the central union catalogue, coupled with the economies resulting from bulk processing and the mechanization of card reproduction, make centralization worth while.

To summarize: cataloguing may best be done by subject librarians as a part of their duties, rather than by a functional cataloguing department – though a functional department may exist for the processing and for the coordination of cataloguing. In a large library system cataloguing is best done centrally except where the components of the system are subject departments whose librarians may then catalogue the books in their subjects as part of their duties.

At this point we should also consider to what extent the operations involved in cataloguing require the use of professional staff, but this matter is treated in the next section.

(ii) *The flow of work*

In deciding on the order of cataloguing operations, two factors must be borne in mind:

(a) *The need to sort the stock* initially into groups demanding different treatment – such groups as: BNB and non-BNB; new (further divided into 'rush' and 'routine', subject groups, materials for limited cataloguing, and so on) and replacements, second copies, new editions, etc., where reference will have to be made to previous treatment. Without this initial sorting of the stock the efficiency of the cataloguing process will be much reduced.

(b) *The need to divide the cataloguing process itself.* Certain operations have greater affinities than others, and they should be grouped. The traditional distinction between classification and cataloguing should not be allowed to determine the order of operations in the flow of work; the basic divisions are:

1. Author/title work.
2. Description.
3. Classification, indexing or subject headings.

The flow of work might therefore be something like this:

1. *Accessioning* (non-professional).
2. *Sorting* the stock into such groups as suggested above (professional).
3. *Author/title work* (professional). Will obviously demand a knowledge of the cataloguing code and the library's modifications as well as the basic principles of cataloguing. Care must be taken to ensure that decisions are consistent with previous work and an authority file may be maintained for this purpose.
4. *Description* (professional). This should be done by whoever

is responsible for 3. Decisions regarding title transcript are, as we have seen, related to choice of heading, and some other features of the description (e.g. a note as to the chairman of a committee report) may be included to explain to the enquirer the reason for the heading, whether main, secondary or reference.

5. *Subject work* (professional). Clearly the business of classification is closely related to subject indexing in the case of the classified catalogue and to the choice of headings and references in the dictionary catalogue. To have two people involved in the subject work for one document is to duplicate intellectual effort unnecessarily.

It has already been noted that much time is saved if a pre-printed form (say, 5×8 in.) is used in the cataloguing process. This form might be the original order form, one side being used as the order record, the other for cataloguing. It should have space for author, title, edition, date, collation, notes, class number, index entries (or subject headings and references), accession number. The form might be filed, after use, as a stock record. The use of a pre-printed form helps the cataloguer by reducing his task to essentials: he no longer has to think of the *possible* types of information that might be included – the form reminds him of them. It is particularly useful when a new member of staff is appointed.

6. *Processing* (non-professional). To occupy for any length of time professional or pre-professional staff with processing is not only to create dissatisfaction but also to waste manpower at a time when it can least be afforded. Processing is now increasingly performed by book suppliers.

7. *Typing* of catalogue entries or the master copy or some reproduction process (non-professional).

8. *Checking* the typing and processing (professional).

9. *Production of unit entries* from the master copy (non-professional).

10. *Addition of heading to unit entries* as indicated by the cataloguer (non-professional).

11. *Distribution of documents* to their respective departments and branches (non-professional).

12. *Shelving* of documents (non-professional).

13. *Filing* of catalogue entries (non-professional). Clearly,

many of the tasks labelled non-professional demand training – but this is not to say the training of a professional librarian.

The above order of operations refers, of course, to new documents. After the sorting stage, replacements, second copies, etc., will have separate treatment. Figure 5 might help the student to visualize the flow of work.

When BNB cards are taken, many books will fall into a separate category. The cataloguing will be reduced to a decision as to how many entries are needed for a particular title, their headings, and the construction of a subject index. A matter of some importance is the timing of the operations, and in the flow of work the following categories might be established:

(a) books received, not yet in BNB (an ever-decreasing number in general libraries and no longer substantial),

(b) books received, cards on order,

(c) BNB cards received, books awaited.

It is important to make sure that there is close liaison with the order department, otherwise cards are liable to be ordered twice or in insufficient quantity to meet the total demand.

The pattern outlined here bears the same resemblance to any particular cataloguing department as does a map to the country it represents. The general outline is, I believe, correct, but it is highly simplified. Students should visit as many libraries as possible and examine the cataloguing processes found there. In their attempts to perceive the pattern, this simplified account may be useful.

The Cataloguing Staff Manual

In a cataloguing department of any size, a loose-leaf staff manual may save much misunderstanding and inconsistency. Its main purpose is to enable each member of staff to define his job, to see the part in relation to the whole, to answer queries on details of the cataloguing style. It will be particularly useful to new members of staff – especially to new heads of the department.

OUTLINE OF THE CONTENTS

1. *Flow of work* – the overall picture. Relationships with other

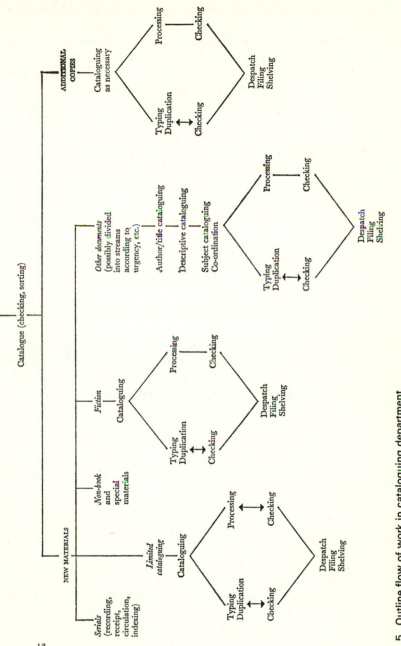

5. Outline flow of work in cataloguing department.

departments, especially the order department, should be carefully indicated.

2. *Number and type of catalogues in the system* – union catalogues, staff catalogues, branch and departmental catalogues.

3. *Author/title cataloguing and description* – deviations from the code in use (headings, description), annotation policy.

4. *Subject cataloguing* – level of classification, deviations from the scheme (major examples), and facet orders for various classes where they need establishing.

Indexing procedure, guiding and featuring used. In the case of a dictionary catalogue, where a standard list of subject headings is used, major modification might be indicated (e.g. the limitation of place entry); procedure regarding new headings, compounds, etc. Where chain procedure is used in subject work, the process should be outlined and modifications such as the suppression of form divisions, abstract terms, etc., noted.

5. *Analytical cataloguing* – policy and practice.

6. *Limited cataloguing policy.*

7. *Production of catalogue entries* – methods of card reproduction, the use of BNB cards.

8. *Maintenance of catalogues* – policy for regular inspection.

9. *Staff duties* – it is very important that the duties of all members of staff, professional and non-professional, be noted.

10. *Examples of the various kinds of entries.*

READINGS

1. MCCLELLAN, A. W. 'The organisation of a public library for subject specialisation'. *Library Association Record*, 57 (8), August 1955, 296–303.

––––––––––

MANN, M. *Introduction to the cataloging and classification of books.* 2nd ed., Chicago, ALA, 1943. Chapters 13–14.

TAUBER, M. F. *and others. Technical services in libraries.* NY, Columbia University Press, 1955. Chapter 14.

These two readings represent a useful introduction to the main organization problems.

An interesting but more specialized paper is:

SWANK, R. C. 'Cataloging cost factors' (*In* STROUT, R. F., *ed. Towards a better cataloging code.* University of Chicago, Graduate Library School, 1956, pp. 53–67.)

On BNB cards in libraries *see*:

HARPER, S. F. 'BNB cards at Willesden'. *Library Association Record,* 59 (8), August 1957, 269–71.

HILL, G. 'The use of BNB cards at Manchester College of Science and Technology'. *Librarian,* 47 (10), October 1957, 192–5.

The periodical *Library Resources and Technical Services* frequently has interesting articles on organization problems in cataloguing departments.

On the problems of reclassification *see*:

PERREAULT, J. M. *ed. Reclassification – rationale and problems* . . . College Park, Md., University of Maryland School of Library and Information Services, 1968.

Part Five

Examples of Practical Cataloguing

Chapter 23
Examples of Practical Cataloguing

Example 1

Title-page transcript. Economic Development/for/Latin America/ Proceedings of a Conference/held by the International Economic Association/Edited By/Howard S. Ellis/Assisted by/ Henry C. Wallich/London/Macmillan & Co Ltd/New York. St Martin's Press/1961

Notes. Back of the title page: *Copyright by the International Economic Association, 1961.* The Introduction states: *The present volume embraces papers, critical comments prepared in advance, and the informal discussions of a roundtable of the International Economic Association held at Rio de Janeiro, August 19–28, 1957.* Although the emphasis of the book is on 'issues involved with the supply of capital, and with international economic relations', and despite the fact that many of the papers concern theoretical problems that have universal interest, the book is essentially about economic conditions in Latin America. There are some tables. The book has ten pages (roman numerals) followed by 478 (arabic) and one unnumbered. Height: $22\frac{1}{2}$ cm.

Classified Catalogue

CLASSIFIED FILE (USING DC 16th ed.; AACR)

330.98000631
>   International Economic Association. *Conference, Rio de Janeiro, 1957.*
>   Economic development for Latin America: proceedings of a conference held by the International Economic Association; edited by Howard S. Ellis, assisted by Henry C. Wallich. London: Macmillan; New York: St. Martin's Press, 1961.
>   x, 478 p. 23 cm.
>   Although primarily concerned with economic conditions in

Latin America, the book is also useful for its general theoretical emphasis and, in particular, its studies of capital and international economic relations.

AUTHOR/TITLE INDEX

(i) International Economic Association. *Conference, Rio de Janeiro, 1957.*

Economic development for Latin America: proceedings of a conference held by the International Economic Association: edited by Howard S. Ellis, assisted by Henry C. Wallich. 1961.

330.98000631

(ii) Economic development for Latin America
International Economic Association. *Conference. Rio de Janeiro, 1957.*
Economic development . . . (*as in* (i) *above*)

(iii) Rio de Janeiro. International Economic Association Conference, 1957.
see International Economic Association. *Conference, Rio de Janeiro, 1957.*

(iv) Ellis, Howard S , *ed.*
International Economic Association. *Conference, Rio de Janeiro, 1957.*
Economic development . . . (*continue as* (i) *above*)

(v) Wallich, Henry C , *ed.*
International Economic Association. *Conference, Rio de Janeiro, 1957.*
Economic development . . . (*continue as* (i) *above*)

SUBJECT INDEX

(*Chain:* 300   Social sciences
330   Economics
330.9   History. Geography. Conditions
330.97/989   The Americas
330·98   Latin America. South America
330.9800063   Conferences. Congresses
330.98000631   International
Proceedings)

Index :

(i) Proceedings

for conference proceedings on a subject *see* subject. Or *see* the name of the conference in the Author/title index.

(ii) International conferences

for proceedings of international conferences on a subject *see* subject. Or *see* the name of the conference in the Author/title index.

(iii) Congresses

for proceedings . . . (*as above*)

(iv) Latin America: Economic conditions   330.98

(v) South America: Economic conditions   330.98

(vi) Americas, The: Economic conditions   330.97/.989

(vii) Conditions, Economic   330·9

(viii) History, Economic   330.9

(ix) Geography, Economic   330.9

(x) Economics   330

(xi) Social sciences   300

COMMENTS

(i) *Classification.* In D C, as in most other schemes, Economic history, geography, and conditions are subordinated to the subject Economics, rather than place.

(ii) *Classified file.* If it were considered that questions of Capital and International relations were especially important in this book, added entries might be made at the class numbers for these subjects. They would then be separately indexed in the Subject index.

Author heading. AACR 69C(1) applies here, this being a conference organized by and restricted to a society.

Description. More detailed than found in many libraries where repetition of author's name and parts of the collation and annotation would be omitted. Author statement can be omitted by AACR 134. Capitals are kept to a minimum; in general terms they are restricted to corporate bodies.

(iii) *Author/title index.* The description in each entry should include sufficient detail to explain the added entry heading or reference. However, repetition of main author may be omitted. In these examples I have regarded the added entry description as a unit, hence all the details are found in each entry. A title entry is given here because many people may remember this as the name of the conference, rather than the organizing body. Similarly, a reference is made under place, Rio, though this is not called for by AACR, as conferences are frequently remembered by place.

(iv) *Subject index*. The chain is given here showing how each step of division is reduced to single words, not phrases. The single words indicate only the particular step of division. In particular, phrases like Economic history are avoided because they will give rise to faulty indexing and open the way to endless permutations. The success of the indexing depends on this initial analysis. Any synonyms of the terms listed will also be included, as well as keywords (see below). Indexing can now proceed, each step being qualified by relevant superordinate steps.

Form divisions are given blanket references. Some of these may seem of marginal importance but they may be sought by readers on occasion – and, once made, they will stand for all future occasions.

Entries (iv), (v) and (vi) : here the qualifiers do not follow the strict order which would be: Latin America: Conditions: Economics, etc. Transposition of terms *after* the filing word is to be very carefully regulated, but there are occasions when it gives a more meaningful order. Transposition of *primary* filing terms (to give, e.g. Economic conditions) is never to be practised, for reasons already given in Chapter 9.

In DC, South America and Latin America are given the same number. The cataloguer could choose one of the terms and refer from the other.

Note the absence in DC of a place for the Americas. In indexing we can show the range of the schedules as in entry no. (vi) but in most libraries a document on the Americas would be given the number 970, though then the documents on America and North America would be indistinguishable (cf. 385 Railway transport which has to be used to accommodate documents on Transport in general).

For reasons of economy, the entry no. (vi) might be omitted altogether, its use being reserved for documents specifically on The Americas only. But then a reference would be needed: America *see* Americas, The; North America, United States of America, South America, Latin America, etc. Without such a reference people seeking information on America would not be served.

Entries (vii)–(ix) break the normal pattern of nouns separated by colons, a pattern usually to be preferred. The adjectival form of qualifier is necessary because the entries History: Economics, etc., would be ambiguous, and in (viii) misleading. The entry History: Economics would mean History of economics – but this has a distinct place at 330.1.

Keywords, i.e. terms representing concepts of major significance in the title and summarization of the content of a document. Students should make sure that all keywords are indexed, though this may be impossible if the terms represent concepts narrower than the subject of the document. In this case, the main keywords are: Economics, Conditions, America, Latin America, and all are fitted into the chain *before* indexing. They must be indexed, as the reader may approach this book via any of these terms; again, he may be glad to know of the existence of this book if he is interested in any of these subjects.

Indexing by Other Schemes

(i) UDC. $338(8 = 6) (063)$

(*Chain*:
3	Social sciences	
33	Economics	
338	Conditions. History	
338(7/8)	The Americas	
338(8)	South America	
338(8=6)	Latin America	
338(8=6) (063)	Conference documents)	

Index: (Form divisions as for DC)
Latin America: Economic conditions $338(8=6)$
South America: Economic conditions $338 (8)$
Americas, The: Economic conditions $338(7/8)$
Conditions, Economic   338

History, Economic   338
Economics   33
Social sciences   3

(ii) BLISS. T4C5

(Chain: T   Economics
            T4   Conditions. Geography
            T4a   The Americas
            T4c   Latin America
            T4c5   Conference proceedings)

Index: (Form divisions as for D C)
           Latin America: Economic conditions   T4c
           Americas, The: Economic conditions   T4a
           Conditions, Economic   T4
           Geography, Economic   T4
           Economics

Note. Bliss differentiates between Economic history (T9) and Economic geography (T4) and equates Economic conditions with the latter. The country subdivisions are taken from Schedule 2. South America is not in the chain. The form division 5 (which is not, unfortunately, specific), is from the divisions enumerated under T.

(iii) LIBRARY OF CONGRESS. HC 161

(Chain: H   Social sciences
            HB/HJ   Economics
            HC/HD   Conditions. History
            HC 95   The Americas
            HC 161/170   Latin America. South America
            HC 161   Collections. Conference
                                                  proceedings)

Index: (Form divisions as for D C)
           Latin America: Economic conditions   HC 161/170
           South America: Economic conditions   HC 161/170
           Americas, The: Economic conditions   HC 95
           Conditions, Economic   HC/HD
           History, Economic   HC/HD
           Economics   HB/HJ
           Social sciences   H

Note. When dealing with a non-expressive notation, the full extent of the schedules for the specific subject being indexed should be shown (e.g. Economics HB/HJ) where there is no one number representing that subject (as there is, for example, in America: Economic conditions HC 95). In the latter case, only the one number should be shown, as this is the number representing that specific subject and will be used on the spines of books; good guiding in the classified file should indicate the full range of the schedules.

(iv) BROWN. L 100.10 W 7.705.786

(*Chain:* L   Social sciences
      L 100   Economics
      L 100.10   History. Conditions.
      L 100.10 W   The Americas
      L 100.10 W 7   Latin America
      L 100.10 W 7.705   Conferences
      L 100.10 W 7.705.786   Proceedings)

Index: (Form divisions as DC)
      Latin America: Economic conditions   L 100.10 W 7
      Americas, The: Economic conditions   L 100.10 W
      History, Economic   L 100.10
      Conditions, Economic   L 100.10
      Economics   L 100
      Social sciences   L

Note. Brown gives no indication of the placing of Economic history and conditions. To avoid confusion with History of economics, the latter could be given the number L 100.5.10 (i.e. Economics – Theories – History). The clumsy form divisions would probably be omitted. It would be possible to place such a book in Brown at the country number – W 700, treating country as concrete, though Brown does not advocate this. Note that when a composite number is created by adding a further number from the schedules, the three-figure base in the second number can be modified (W 7 instead of W 700).

(v) COLON (6th ed.) X.791p

(*Chain:* X   Economics

x.1/.9 Economic situation by country
x.7   The Americas
x.791   South America. Latin America
x.791p   Conference proceedings)

Index: (Form divisions as for DC)
Latin America: Economic conditions x.791
South America: Economic conditions x.791
Americas, The: Economic conditions x.7
History, Economic x.1/.9
Conditions, Economic x.1/.9
Economics x

Note. The form division p is an anteriorizing common isolate and should precede Time and Space divisions according to Ranganathan's instructions; however, whilst this may be satisfactory in the majority of cases, it seems here hardly to give the best order and I have therefore attached the form division *after* the Space facet.

Example II

Title page transcript. Facing the title page: The/Sayers/Memorial/Volume/Edited by D J Foskett and B I Palmer/The Library Association/ *Title page:* Essays in/Librarianship/in memory of/William Charles/Berwick Sayers/Edited by/D J Foskett B I Palmer/for the Classification Research Group (London)/London 1961

Notes. Six unnumbered pages followed by pages 7–218. There is a frontispiece – a portrait. Height: 25½ cm. This *festschrift* was originally planned to coincide with Sayers' eightieth birthday; his death occurred just before the book was completed. A series of essays by different authors, ranging over a wide field of librarianship, e.g. classification, education, and children's libraries, with emphasis on the first.

Classified Catalogue

CLASSIFIED FILE (USING UDC; AACR)

02(04)
    Classification Research Group (London)
        The Sayers memorial volume: essays in librarianship in memory

of William Charles Berwick Sayers; edited by D. J. Foskett and B. I. Palmer for the Classification Research Group (London). London: The Library Association, 1961.

218 p.; port. 26 cm.

Essays by a number of writers on various aspects of librarianship, with the emphasis on classification.

AUTHOR/TITLE INDEX

(i) Classification Research Group (London)
The Sayers memorial volume: essays in librarianship in memory of William Charles Berwick Sayers; edited by D. J. Foskett and B. I. Palmer for the Classification Research Group. 1961.

02(04)

(ii) Foskett, D   J   , *ed.*
Classification Research Group (London)
The Sayers . . . (*continue as* (i) *above*)

(iii) Palmer, B   I   , *ed.*
Classification Research Group (London)
The Sayers . . . (*continue as* (i) *above*)

(iv) The Sayers memorial volume
Classification Research Group (London)
The Sayers . . . (*continue as* (i) *above*)

(v) Sayers, William Charles Berwick
Classification Research Group (London)
The Sayers . . . (*continue as* (i) *above*)

(vi) Berwick Sayers, William Charles
see Sayers, William Charles Berwick

SUBJECT INDEX

(*Chain:* 0   Generalities
02   Libraries. Librarianship
02(04)   Essays)
Index:
(i) Essays
for essays on a particular subject *see* subject
(ii) Libraries   02
(iii) Librarianship   02
(iv) Books
see also Librarianship

COMMENTS

(i) *Classified file*. Again, if the book is to be considered especially valuable for its contribution to classification, an added entry might be made at the relevant class number and this would be separately indexed.

Author heading. There is some doubt that this should be entered under the CRG. By AACR 17A (1) the document should be 'a work that is by its nature necessarily the expression of the corporate thought or activity of the body.' AACR 17B seems more relevant – in which case it ought to be entered under Foskett. Form of heading for the CRG is by AACR 60.

Description. The layout of the double title page shows quite clearly that the title is The Sayers memorial volume, the second title page consisting of the sub-title.

(ii) *Author/title index* is by AACR 60. There is no necessity for an index entry under Sayers – and except in a large catalogue the title entry would suffice. Though Sayers cannot be considered an author, neither is he the subject.

(iii) *Subject index*. Note the equation of Libraries and Librarianship, not found in all other schemes. *See also* references are rare in the subject index, but a link between Books and Libraries must be made. An entry Books: Librarianship would be misleading.

Indexing by Other Schemes

(i) DC (17th ed.) 020.8

Chain and index as for UDC.

(ii) BLISS. ZN 7

(*Chain:* z   Bibliology. Books. Bibliography. Documentation
                 Libraries
      ZN   Libraries. Librarianship
      ZN 7   Essays)

Index: Essays
         for essays on a particular subject *see* subject
         Libraries   ZN

Librarianship   z n
Bibliology   z
Books   z

Note. The class number for Libraries is selected, rather than Librarianship at z p, as the latter is concerned exclusively with Librarians, i.e. the career of librarianship. Librarianship is normally understood to be more than this and therefore it seems better to use z n as the general number for Libraries and Librarianship. z p would then be indexed as Librarians. Only Bibliology and Books can be indexed to z because each of the other terms in the schedules at that number is subsequently specified more precisely. As the major aspects of Books (Bibliography, Libraries, etc.) are collocated at z it is possible to index Books to z (contrast d c and u d c).

(iii) LIBRARY OF CONGRESS. z 665

(*Chain:* z   Bibliography and Library science. Books
          z 662/1000.5   Libraries
          z 665   Librarianship
                              Essays)

Index: Essays
          for essays on a particular subject *see* subject
          Librarianship   z 665
          Libraries   z 662/1000.5
          Books   z

(iv) BROWN. M 950.954

(*Chain:* M 700/999   Books
          M 900   Library history and economy. Libraries
          M 950   Library economy. Librarianship
          M 950.954   Essays)

Index: Essays
          for essays on a particular subject *see* subject
          Librarianship   M 950
          Libraries   M 900
          Books   M 700/999

Note. As in the case of Bliss and Library of Congress, Brown collocates various aspects of Books at M 700/999 and it is possible to make an index entry for this. M 950 was chosen for Librarianship rather than M 952, the latter being reserved for its more specialized meaning – the profession of librarianship (cf. Bliss).

(v) COLON (6th ed.) 2 p7

(*Chain:*   2   Library science. Librarianship
            p7   Symposia. Essays)

Index: Essays
               for essays on a particular subject *see* subject
           Librarianship 2
           Books
               see also Librarianship

Note. The book number p7 seems the nearest thing in the schedules to Essays. The *see also* reference is made again because Books as a concept is scattered in the classification.

Analytical Entry

A composite work of this nature may give rise to a number of analytical entries. These would be best entered under subject in the classified file, e.g.:

372.8:168.2
   Kyle, Barbara
      Classification in the school curriculum (*In* Classification Research Group (London). The Sayers memorial volume. London. 1961. p. 194–202)

Shelved at: 02(04)

This article is concerned predominantly with elementary schools. This would be indexed in the *Subject index* as follows:

(*Chain:*   3   Social sciences
            37   Education. Schools
            372   Pre-School and Elementary
            372.22   Elementary
            372.4/.8   Curriculum
            372.8   Other subjects
            372.8:168.2   Classification)

Index: (i) Classification: Curriculum: Elementary Education
372.8:168.2
 (ii) Curriculum: Elementary education   372.4/.8
 (iii) Elementary education   372.22
 (iv) Education   37
 (v) Schools   37
 (vi) Social sciences   3

(An entry might also be made in the *author index* as follows if it is considered that a reader may want this article, remembering only the author, or might want to discover all material by Barbara Kyle:

Kyle, Barbara
     Classification in the school curriculum (*In* Classification Research Group (London). The Sayers memorial volume. London, 1961. pp. 194–202)

Shelved at: 02(04)

COMMENTS

(i) *Classification.* The enumeration at 372 in UDC clearly shows that the curriculum in elementary schools is collocated at 372 rather than at 371.214 – the number for curriculum generally. Within class 372, .4/.8 is devoted to the curriculum and therefore this is a hidden step of division which should be brought out in the index. It is better to use 372.4/.8 to stand for curriculum rather than 372.22:371.214 which is not only cumbersome but also leads to a less satisfactory filing order.

(ii) *Indexing.* The major keywords: Schools, Curriculum, and Classification are covered. Two links – at 372 and 372.8 – are not indexed, the latter being unsought, the former being simply a guide to the classifier. (Each of the terms (Pre-School and Elementary) is enumerated (at 372.21 and 372.22) and therefore cannot be indexed to 372.) The grouping at a general class number of terms which are specifically catered for within the class is a hazard that the indexer must be aware of; it is frequently met in DC and other enumerative schemes. Synonyms need not be indexed as secondary filing terms, i.e. there is no need for an entry: Elementary schools *as well as* entry no. (iii).

Example III

Title page transcript. The New Whitehall Series/No. 11/The Ministry of/Agriculture, Fisheries and Food/Sir John Winnifrith/κcв/Permanent Secretary to the Ministry/London. George Allen and Unwin Ltd/New York. Oxford University Press Inc. *Notes.* First published 1962 (indicated on back of title page). 12 unnumbered pages followed by 13–271. The book is 22½ cm. high and there are some diagrams. The New Whitehall Series is prepared under the auspices of the Royal Institute of Public Administration and is edited by Sir Robert Fraser, oвe. 'The purpose of the series is to provide authoritative descriptions of the present work of the major Departments of Central Government.' There are, apart from chapters on the organization of the Ministry, chapters on farm subsidies, agricultural guarantees, farming, the agricultural worker, statistics and economics, and so on - all from the point of view of the work of the Ministry.

Dictionary Catalogue

MAIN ENTRY (USING DC 17th ed.; AACR)

Winnifrith, *Sir* John
   The Ministry of Agriculture, Fisheries and Food. London: George Allen and Unwin; New York: Oxford University Press, 1962.
      271 p.; illus. 23 cm. (New Whitehall series, no. 11)
      Describes the organization of the Ministry and outlines its work in the various aspects of British agriculture.

354.420682

ADDED ENTRIES AND REFERENCES (AUTHOR/TITLE)

   (i) New Whitehall series—no. 11
         Winnifrith, *Sir* John
            The Ministry of Agriculture, Fisheries and Food. 1962
                                                      354.420682
   (ii) Fraser, *Sir* Robert, *ed.*
         see also New Whitehall series

(iii) Royal Institute of Public Administration
　　　see also New Whitehall series

ADDED ENTRIES AND REFERENCES (SUBJECT) – USING
SEARS (9th ed.)

　(i) GREAT BRITAIN. *MINISTRY OF AGRICULTURE, FISHERIES AND FOOD*
　　　Winnifrith, *Sir* John
　　　　　The Ministry . . . (*continue as in entry no.* (i) *in the author
　　　　section above*)

　(ii) Agriculture, Fisheries and Food, *Ministry of*
　　　see
　　　Great Britain. *Ministry of Agriculture, Fisheries and Food*

(iii) Ministry of . . .
　　　for the various Government Ministries, Departments, etc., *see*
　　　the name of the country with the subdivision *Ministry of,*
　　　Department of, etc., e.g.
　　　Great Britain. *Ministry of Agriculture, Fisheries and Food.*

(iv) GREAT BRITAIN—POLITICS AND GOVERNMENT
　　　see also subject entries under GREAT BRITAIN followed by
　　　names of Departments, Ministries, etc., e.g. GREAT
　　　BRITAIN. *MINISTRY OF AGRICULTURE, FISHERIES AND FOOD*

　(v) ADMINISTRATION
　　　see names of countries, cities, etc., with the subdivision
　　　POLITICS AND GOVERNMENT, e.g. GREAT BRITAIN –
　　　POLITICS AND GOVERNMENT

(vi) CIVICS
　　　see names of . . . (*continue as in* (v) *above*)

(vii) CIVIL GOVERNMENT
　　　see names of . . . (*continue as in* (v) *above*)

(viii) GOVERNMENT
　　　see names of . . . (*continue as in* (v) *above*)

(ix) POLITICS
　　　see names of . . . (*continue as in* (v) *above*)

　(x) GREAT BRITAIN – GOVERNMENT
　　　see GREAT BRITAIN – POLITICS AND GOVERNMENT

(xi) POLITICAL SCIENCE
　　　see also names of countries, cities, etc., with the subdivision
　　　POLITICS AND GOVERNMENT, e.g. GREAT BRITAIN –
　　　POLITICS AND GOVERNMENT

(xii) POLITICS, PRACTICAL
　　　see also names of . . . (*continue as in* (xi) *above*)

(xiii) PUBLIC ADMINISTRATION
　　　see also names of . . . (*continue as in* (xi) *above*)
(xiv) AGRICULTURAL ADMINISTRATION
　　　see also subject entries under names of government depart-
　　　ments concerned, filed under country, e.g. GREAT BRITAIN.
　　　MINISTRY OF AGRICULTURE, FISHERIES AND FOOD
　(xv) ADMINISTRATION, AGRICULTURAL
　　　see AGRICULTURAL ADMINISTRATION
(xvi) AGRICULTURE AND STATE
　　　see also AGRICULTURAL ADMINISTRATION

COMMENTS

(i) *Author/title work.* The references under Fraser and the
Royal Institute of Public Administration are *see also* references
because each of these may be the author of a book and therefore used as a heading. By AACR 33N, a series entry should
specify in the heading only the title and number of the volume
in the series. If the cross references from Fraser and the Royal
Institute were made there would therefore have to be a note –
at the beginning of the series entries, say – indicating their
respective roles.

(ii) *Description.* It is most unlikely that in general practice
both publishers would be mentioned – unless the first were a
foreign imprint and the second English.

(iii) *Subject work.* A document about a person or corporate
body should be entered under the heading appropriate for
that person or body, using AACR (or whatever code is in use)
to ensure that the documents by and about an author file side
by side in the catalogue. References from alternative forms are
made – and these will stand for both the author and subject
headings.

Naturally a specific heading of this kind is not to be found in
Sears and therefore, as with all other cases of newly created
headings, it has to be related to the nearest heading in Sears.
Two headings are closely related:

　　GREAT BRITAIN – GOVERNMENT AND POLITICS (by
　　analogy with Sears' US – GOVERNMENT AND POLITICS)
　　and: AGRICULTURAL ADMINISTRATION

References to the chosen heading are therefore made from
each of these and then the relevant references to the Sears

headings in each case, thus ensuring that, within the framework of Sears, references are made one step at a time. The style of the blanket references can be discovered by checking the relevant headings and noting the method Sears uses. Blanket references are usually made for countries in this way in preference to direct references which would have to be made for every country and would quickly bulk the catalogue.

In fact Sears fails to relate AGRICULTURAL ADMINISTRATION to the relevant headings for PUBLIC ADMINISTRATION. This is why it is necessary to relate our chosen heading to *two* headings in Sears – headings which should be in chain: PUBLIC ADMINISTRATION *see also* AGRICULTURAL ADMINISTRATION *see also* names of countries subdivided by the relevant Ministry, Department, etc., e.g. GREAT BRITAIN. *MINISTRY OF AGRICULTURE, FISHERIES AND FOOD*

As in indexing for the classified catalogue it is very important to see that all *keywords* are covered by the headings and references.

SUBJECT HEADINGS BY CHAIN PROCEDURE (USING DC)

(*Chain:* 300   Social sciences
350   Public administration. Government. Politics
354   Central government (outside US)
354.42   Great Britain
354.420682   Ministry of Agriculture, Fisheries and Food)

Subject heading:
   GREAT BRITAIN. *MINISTRY OF AGRICULTURE, FISHERIES AND FOOD*

References: (references from the alternative forms for Ministry would be made as in Sears above).

(i) GREAT BRITAIN – CENTRAL ADMINISTRATION
see also names of Departments, Ministries, etc., arranged under countries, e.g. GREAT BRITAIN. *MINISTRY OF AGRICULTURE, FISHERIES AND FOOD*

(ii) CENTRAL GOVERNMENT ADMINISTRATION
see also names of countries with the subheading CENTRAL ADMINISTRATION, e.g. GREAT BRITAIN – CENTRAL ADMINISTRATION

(iii) PUBLIC ADMINISTRATION
see also CENTRAL GOVERNMENT ADMINISTRATION

(iv) GOVERNMENT – PUBLIC ADMINISTRATION
    see PUBLIC ADMINISTRATION
(v) POLITICS – PUBLIC ADMINISTRATION
    see PUBLIC ADMINISTRATION
(vi) ADMINISTRATION, PUBLIC
    see PUBLIC ADMINISTRATION
(vii) SOCIAL SCIENCES
    see also PUBLIC ADMINISTRATION

COMMENTS

The heading remains as by Sears – the book is about a government department and the heading must follow AACR no matter what order the chain gives. In fact this means that the final link in the chain is suppressed and references must be made from the suppressed terms – Ministry, and its inverted forms.

Another question that arises is whether to suppress the term Great Britain in relation to Central administration, i.e. whether the heading from which the first reference is made ought to be CENTRAL ADMINISTRATION – GREAT BRITAIN rather than GREAT BRITAIN – CENTRAL ADMINISTRATION. Country is normally suppressed but in certain fields, e.g. government, economic conditions, or history, country is so crucial a factor that it is traditionally given precedence over subject.

Then there is the heading CENTRAL ADMINISTRATION* – ought this to be inverted to give ADMINISTRATION, CENTRAL? This is a matter of opinion – I have preferred to keep to chain order and this will result in documents on Public administration in general being at PUBLIC ADMINISTRATION with documents on Central and Local government being under their respective headings. This is certainly the sought pattern for Local government, and consistency is achieved.

A check of keywords will reveal that the chain procedure here fails to relate the book to the headings for Agriculture, except by the reference from the inverted form of the Ministry. This could be remedied by intercalating in the chain a logical step between the last two links:

* CENTRAL GOVERNMENT would be equally acceptable.

354.42 Great Britain
354.420681 Agriculture. Ministry of Agriculture, Fisheries and Food

which would give the reference:

AGRICULTURE — GREAT BRITAIN — CENTRAL ADMINISTRATION
see also GREAT BRITAIN. *MINISTRY OF AGRICULTURE, FISHERIES AND FOOD*

(or a *see* reference might be used if it were considered that the two headings were virtually synonymous in the literature). Other references would be modified accordingly.

Example IV

Title-page transcript. Facing the title page: [Frontispiece with the words:] A review of the graphic arts edited by Allan Delafons
Title page: penrose/annual/volume 56/Nineteen Sixty-two/ Published by Lund Humphries 12 Bedford Square London WC 1
Notes. The text consists mainly of articles by different writers reporting developments in various aspects of printing, e.g. paper, inks, design and layout of books, posters, packaging, etc. It is profusely illustrated, many of the plates being in colour; many illustrations consist of actual samples of printing on a variety of papers. 168 pages of text. Diagrams, tables. Height: 29 cm.

Dictionary Catalogue

MAIN ENTRY (USING DC 16th ed.; AACR)

Penrose annual: a review of the graphic arts; edited by Allan Delafons. v.56. London, Lund Humphries, 1962.
   168 p., plates; illus. (some col.). 29 cm.
   Articles on various aspects of printing, e.g. paper, inks, design and layout of books, posters, packaging, etc. The illustrations include many actual samples of paper and printing.

655.058

ADDED ENTRIES AND REFERENCES (AUTHOR/TITLE)

Delafons, Allan, *ed.*
  Penrose annual: a review of the graphic arts; edited by Allan
    Delafons. v.56. 1962.

655.058

ADDED ENTRIES AND REFERENCES (SUBJECT) – USING
SEARS (9th ed.)

  (i) PRINTING – YEARBOOKS
        Penrose annual . . . (*continue as in the author added entry*)
  (ii) INDUSTRIAL ARTS
        see PRINTING
  (iii) LAYOUT AND TYPOGRAPHY
        see PRINTING
  (iv) TYPOGRAPHY
        see PRINTING
  (v) BIBLIOGRAPHY
        see also PRINTING
  (vi) BOOK INDUSTRIES AND TRADE
        see also PRINTING
  (vii) BOOKS
        see also PRINTING
  (viii) GRAPHIC ARTS
        see also PRINTING
  (ix) PUBLISHERS AND PUBLISHING
        see also PRINTING
  (x) TYPESETTING
        see also PRINTING
  (xi) YEARBOOKS
        for yearbooks of a subject *see* subject with the subdivision
        YEARBOOKS, e.g. PRINTING – YEARBOOKS

COMMENTS

  (i) *Author/title work and description.* An example of title main
entry style – the hanging indentation referred to on page 73.
Entry is under title because the book is a serial, treated
according to the basic rule AACR 6A. Added entry is made for
the editor.

  However, as a periodical, 'open entry' style could have been
adopted – and indeed would have been in any library taking
the annual regularly, e.g.

Penrose annual: a review of the graphic
  arts . . . Vol. 1 – 1895 – London,
  Lund Humphries, 1895 –
     v., plates; illus. (some col.). 29 cm.

             655·058

(There would be further notes recording changes of editors, title, etc. An annotation might be included.)

 (ii) *Subject work.* Straightforward. The reference from INDUSTRIAL ARTS despite its appearance does not equate these terms with Printing – there are similar references to other 'industrial arts' which would be made when appropriate. References nos. (iii), (iv) and (x) are upward references from narrower headings; as two of them are *see* references they illustrate the limited specificity in Sears. The other references are examples of collateral links. The subdivision YEAR-BOOKS is from Sears list of subdivisions which precedes the main list of headings.

SUBJECT HEADINGS BY CHAIN PROCEDURE (USING DC)

(*Chain:* 655 Printing. Publishing. Book trade
       Printing
  655·058   Yearbooks)

Subject heading:
    PRINTING – YEARBOOKS

References
 (i) YEARBOOKS
    for yearbooks of a subject *see* subject with the subdivision YEARBOOKS
 (ii) BOOK TRADE
    see also PRINTING
 (iii) PUBLISHING
    see also PRINTING

COMMENTS

A keyword: Graphic arts, is missing and as there is a place for Graphic arts in DC at 74/76, this must be regarded as a collateral *see also* reference:

(iv) GRAPHIC ARTS
  see also PRINTING

A similar reference may be made from Bibliography:

(v) BIBLIOGRAPHY
  see also PRINTING

Such collaterals are not automatically arrived at by chain procedure (just as there is no automatic way of acquiring them in the making of subject heading lists). Keywords will usually help to remind the cataloguer of them; for the rest he must rely on subject knowledge and, of course, his knowledge of the scheme.

ANALYTICAL ENTRY (SUBJECT)

The following heading and references are constructed by chain procedure from the DC number 016.655:

(*Chain:* 01   Bibliography
   011/019 Bibliographies
   016   Subject
   016.655   Printing)

Subject heading and analytical entry:
  PRINTING – BIBLIOGRAPHIES
   Mosley, James
    A graphic arts booklist: 1959–61 (*In* Penrose annual,
    London. 1962. Vol. 56)

              655·058

References:
 (i) BIBLIOGRAPHIES – SUBJECT
   see also names of subjects with the subheading BIBLIO-
   GRAPHIES, e.g. PRINTING – BIBLIOGRAPHIES
 (ii) SUBJECT BIBLIOGRAPHIES
   see BIBLIOGRAPHIES – SUBJECT
 (iii) BIBLIOGRAPHY
   see also BIBLIOGRAPHIES

Note. The intermediate link BIBLIOGRAPHIES *see also* BIBLIOGRAPHIES – SUBJECT has been omitted as the two headings will file in close proximity. 'Subject' is suppressed in (ii) as being an unsought term.

Appendix
Dewey Decimal
Classification*

There are, of course, many criteria by which we can assess the relative merits of the various classification schemes: order, notation, revision facilities, use in other libraries, bibliographies, card services, and so on. The fundamental concern however must be that of subject order; this is surely what classification is about: the grouping of things by degree of likeness so that each subject has its 'address' either on the shelves or in the classified catalogue. A scheme whose order fails to meet the requirements of a particular clientele, or which demonstrates little order at all beyond, say, rudimentary grouping by period, geography, or physical form, is clearly unsatisfactory – no matter how attractive the after-sales service. And this applies, as I shall hope to show, even in libraries which use dictionary catalogues as an additional retrieval device.

The basic order in Dewey as in all schemes in general use today rests on a framework of conventional disciplines – literature, history, physics, sociology, and so on. These form what we traditionally call the *main classes*. A satisfactory order of this kind requires:

(i) that the major disciplines should be presented;

(ii) that they should be given space relative to their size;

(iii) that the order of classes should show 'gradation', bringing related fields into proximity (as far as possible within the confines of linear order); and

(iv) that there should be provision for major changes to meet the inevitable fluidity of disciplines – i.e. there must be flexibility to allow:

(a) extension of developing disciplines,

* I am glad to acknowledge permission to reprint this conference paper which was first published in: PERREAULT, J. M. *ed. Reclassification: rationale and problems.* College Park, University of Maryland School of Library and Information Services, 1968.

(b) reduction of contracting disciplines

(c) movement of disciplines or parts of disciplines from one section of the scheme to another to express developing relationships.

Table I shows in outline the main class order of Dewey and Congress. It can be seen that the general order of the sciences and technologies is similar: both begin with mathematics and work through the physical to the biological sciences, graduating into medicine and applied sciences. Here Congress improves on Dewey by relating agriculture to the biological sciences and medicine; a further improvement is the juxtaposition of engineering and building. Both separate the particular sciences from the derived technologies – chemistry is apart from chemical technology, and so on.

In both schemes philosophy, psychology, and religion are clustered together, a grouping explicable in terms of their nineteenth-century origins: a particular weakness today is the separation of psychology from the social sciences, and from sociology in particular. Another similarity can be seen in the grouping of the arts (including music and architecture) in close proximity to literature, though of course Congress also includes language at this point. Whether the juxtaposition of language with literature is as weighty an advantage as has on occasion been claimed is, I think, debatable. (And we should remember – at least in the case of modern European languages – it is only juxtaposition, not integration.)

To place the social sciences alongside geography and history as in Congress is clearly more satisfactory than the broad scatter we find in Dewey. And again the Library of Congress arrangement of the individual social sciences is more coherent than Dewey's with its inexplicable scattering of economics and commerce, political science and administration, and so on. Had Congress placed the classes running from economics to finance *after* law, and statistics at the end, thus relating sociology to history, geography, and anthropology, and placing it with anthropology at the head of the social sciences – a position it ought to have by virtue of its content, theory, and methodology – then the order would have been better still.

All main class orders are bound to be only relatively

satisfactory as the linear sequence does violence to the complex relationships. Bliss, by providing alternative locations – for bibliography and social psychology, for example – partly overcomes the problem by allowing libraries to select the relationships they wish to emphasize. There are few alternatives of this kind in Congress or Dewey and from this point of view there is little to choose between them.

To sum up: in both schemes the major disciplines are represented (though the absence of a law schedule in the latter is a weakness*), and because both are constantly being revised the balance between disciplines reflects changing needs (though this is not evident in the apportionment of notation). Gradation at this broad level is rather better in Congress, but both schemes are hampered by their nineteenth-century origins – as, for example, in the treatment of anthropology and psychology. Both are reluctant to make major relocations of disciplines.

But how important is main class order as a criterion when evaluating schemes that use roughly the same conventional disciplines as a framework? It is possibly less important in small or large general libraries than in those of medium size: in small libraries users soon learn to find their way around, in large ones subject departments (complete or partial) collocate scattered relatives. In all libraries signposting and printed guides can assist the reader. In the classified catalogue poor main class order is a handicap, but again catalogues may be divided between departments and in the non-divided catalogue the index and references in the classified sequence can substantially reduce the worst effects.

More significant is the order *within* main classes. The requirements here are that:

First, there should be a clear place for each of the *simple elements* generally regarded as falling within the province of that discipline and found in the literature. This is less straightforward than it sounds once the whole field of knowledge has been divided into broad disciplines – particularly when we come to deal with simple subjects that recur in several areas without undergoing any great transformation: thus a group is a group whether you happen to be a

* The Law schedule is now available.

psychologist, a sociologist, or a social psychologist. The only way round this is to allocate such topics to *one* of the disciplines concerned.

Second, in addition to the provision of places for simple subjects, each class should also provide clear places for the *complex subjects* which result from the fusion of the elements. For example, not only should there be places for the simple elements *poetry* and *19th Century literature*, but also for the complex subject *19th Century poetry;* and while there should be a slot for *John Donne*, another for *20th Century literature*, a third for *poetry*, and a fourth for *English literature*, there should also be a place signifying the complex subject: *the influence of John Donne on 20th Century English poetry*.

A *third* requirement is that the order of both simple and complex subjects should be systematic and generally acceptable. By *systematic* I mean that all simple subjects having a common characteristic – whether of form or language or period, for example, in the class literature – should be grouped together; and that the placing of complex subjects should follow a coherent and constant plan. If, for example, the complex topic *20th Century novel* has been placed as a subdivision of *novel* in the form class of literature, then the topic *19th Century novel* should not appear as a subdivision of *19th Century* among the period divisions. Such systematization should be acceptable – that is, the order of simple subjects should follow an arrangement best suited to the needs of most users – whether it be for example 'conventional', geographical, chronological, or plain alphabetical. And for complex subjects – the placing should reflect consensus where it exists; and where it doesn't, some guide such as the concept of 'decreasing concreteness' should be employed.

Table II outlines a section of Dewey class 630 Agriculture to illustrate these points. It will be seen that three groups of simple subjects are systematically enumerated: one of processes, one of injuries, etc., and a third covering particular crops. It will also be noted that complex subjects made up of these elements are also catered for in a similarly systematic fashion. There is thus a clear place for both simple and complex subjects, and an order which is systematic and probably generally acceptable: as, for example, in the chronological order of processes, and the collocation of complex subjects under crop. This collocation surely meets a general need more effectively than if everything were brought together under process, scattering materials on crops: harvesting of wheat, oats, barley, etc., all collocated at harvesting. Thus this section satisfies literary warrant in its basic provisions and consensus in its order.

Now we can ask a further question: is it necessary to use synthetic devices to achieve the compounding of simple elements to cater for complex subjects found in literature? Theoretically the answer is No. Each of the complex subjects noted above could have been *enumerated* in the schedules. In practice this is impossible. Even schemes which are predominantly enumerative usually provide synthetic devices to cater for common form-division, space, and time elements – for clearly all of these would otherwise have to be enumerated at more or less every division in the schedules. Any attempt to enumerate complex subjects is in practice found to be selective: it could never hope to encompass the unpredictable multiple relationships found in literature. Additionally – though this need not *necessarily* follow – it is likely that the enumeration will be unsystematic: for example, the harvesting of potatoes may be found under potatoes, the harvesting of wheat under harvesting. This is because it becomes increasingly difficult as enumerative schemes grow for even those responsible for their development to descry the principles that underlie them – even if those principles were clearly understood in the first place. In the end few men are able to find their way through the labyrinth. Thus enumerative schemes are likely to have the following limitations in the schedules:

(i) omission of some simple and complex subjects, duplication of others;

(ii) conflicting principles underlying the placing of complex subjects.

The inevitable result of this is cross-classification – the situation where materials on the same subject are found in two or more places on the shelves or in the classified catalogue.

The Dewey classification has always incorporated numerous synthetic devices – they can be seen from the beginning in the common subdivisions, the geographical and historical schedules, within the class literature, and so on. The 17th edition has a table of thirty columns enumerating those parts of the schedules where synthesis is used. Recent editions show a marked tendency towards the systematic analysis of simple elements and a provision for synthesis, and we can say that the 'hospitality' to subjects has increased proportionately. Before this edition, for example, the complex subjects already illustrated in class 630 could not be specified.

Table III gives examples of entries from the Library of Congress catalogue 'Books: Subjects' to illustrate relative hospitality to subjects in various parts of Dewey and Congress schedules.

In the first group of examples, those from the field of English and American literature, Library of Congress exceeds Dewey in hospitality. By using the alphabetical device under periods it can cater for literary themes (society and the Arthurian legend) where Dewey has to remain content with placing these books under the period concerned. Note, however, in the case of Karolides, specification of theme is at the expense of period – in the Congress scheme this book will be separated from works on the American 20th Century novel. Here the classifier had to choose between period and theme: there is no allowance for combining the two as in the division for 17th and 18th Century English literature. Obviously, as subjects become narrower in enumerative schemes, the chances of listing every specific subject decrease. In this instance Dewey does rather better – it at least gives a standard priority order – language – form – period – topic, even though the precise topic (pioneer) cannot be specified.

The limits of enumeration are well illustrated in the second group of examples. In the case of cotton the Library of Congress enumerates a division for the process cotton spinning; for flax no such enumerated division is made and so books on flax spinning must jostle in alphabetic order with books on other aspects of flax. In Dewey, however, though spinning is not enumerated under any material, both cotton and flax can be divided by the general processes of textile manufacturers: the addition of the digits '22' in each case specifies 'spinning'. The maker of the scheme has not to consider whether to enumerate or not, whether to leave vacant numbers, and so on – once the provision for synthesis has been made; whether to specify 'spinning' or not is up to the classifier in his library.

Group 3 gives two similar illustrations. Here we have two instances of a common type of complex subject in medicine, both formed by fusion of two simple elements – the disease of an organ and the diagnosis of disease. In the first example the Library of Congress enumerates 'diagnosis' as a division of lung disease (though neither it nor Dewey can specify the particular kind of diagnosis); in the second case, however, having reached a more specific stage of disease – pneumoconiosis – Congress fails to enumerate X-ray diagnosis, or even the concept of diagnosis. With Dewey, however, we can add the special divisions at 616 to the numbers for pneumoconiosis and so arrive at a class commensurate with the subject of the book. Note that Dewey is superior in two respects here: it achieves *specificity* and also *consistency*: a book on X-ray diagnosis of pneumoconiosis will *always* be found with the disease. In the Congress scheme the priority is not clear and unless rules are carefully laid down another book on this topic might well be placed at X-ray diagnosis.

Another instance of both specific and consistent entry is found in the Peters example. At class 371 Dewey enumerates topics of an administrative or procedural nature in the field of education – but the ruling is given that wherever these topics apply to a particular *level* of education, then the level takes priority. Indeed provision is made for the synthesizing of complex subjects by adding to the number referring to level numbers from 371 signifying procedure. Thus 372 in the example stands for elementary education, whilst the 146 is taken from the schedule at 371 and stands for social guidance. The Library of Congress Classification for all its detail cannot cope and the classifier is left to make the uneasy decision as to whether to place the book at the number for elementary education or the one for counselling. In choosing the latter, as here, the classifier has probably flouted consensus – the book ought to be with elementary education. Perhaps the number for counselling appears, somehow, more precise.

The remaining examples give further illustrations of these points.

I should stress that I have chosen these examples as

illustrations. It would be a waste of time to try to persuade you that Dewey had the edge on Congress every time. There are many occasions when Congress happens to have enumerated the complex topic required, there are many occasions when Dewey fails to allow synthesis and fails also to give a clear indication as to which element in a compound is to take precedence.

Wherever the content of a field is relatively closed – as, for example, in certain areas of the arts (literary works of an author, for instance) enumeration may prove satisfactory. Nevertheless, in a world of ever-increasing complexity, I think that it can be argued that Dewey, insofar as it is a synthetic and systematic scheme, is on the side of the future. Indeed, if it is to remain a competitive scheme, it must move rapidly in this direction. As it loses weight so its capacity will increase, whilst enumerative schemes, like some prehistoric species, their bulk out-stripping thought, will move steadily towards extinction.

I have assumed throughout this talk the principle of specific classification. I have taken it for granted that we agree that classification scheme should provide as precise a place as possible for all the subjects found in books. However, I recognize that some will argue that classification can be regarded merely as a tool for broad shelf arrangement and that it is the role of the *catalogue* to assist in specific searching. This is a prevalent argument that needs to be examined.

Now whilst it could certainly be held that in the case of vast and rapidly growing copyright libraries where the stock is sealed off from the public, specific classification is not worth the effort, in the majority of libraries such as most of us are concerned with this is just not true. In the first place, a fair degree of specific classification is required for satisfactory browsing. As a user of libraries I can vouch for the fact that chaos has no advantages. This is particularly true in libraries using dictionary catalogues, for in such libraries the shelf order provides the only direct systematic approach to the collection.

The term 'browsing' may suggest an insignificant occupation. It is my belief that, on the contrary, systematic browsing plays a most important part in intellectual development, and that the provision for browsing is one of the most valuable of all library facilities. (It is one that, so far, seems unlikely to be appropriated by the computer.) However, if you don't accept the point, I would go on to argue that efficient reference work, at least in general public and university libraries, is dependent on systematic order in the sense outlined above. To give an instance: imagine that a reader has inquired after illustrations of Batik design. Clearly such an inquiry is easily answered if all books on that subject are collocated. If they are not, if Batik design isn't given a specific number so that the works are scattered alphabetically by author under a broader heading – say, textile design – then the only way to answer the inquiry is to list all the works and their shelf numbers from the catalogue before starting the search. Whether it is more economical to do this than to make a proper job of the classification in the first place clearly depends on the number of times the inquiry is made – and how can this be forecast?

But even this depends on the subject catalogue being specific. Now suppose that this were not the case – that books on Batik design were distributed alphabetically by author through the entries on textile design: without a cross reference from Batik the thing is hopeless. But even with a cross reference the librarian or reader now has to go through all the entries at TEXTILE DESIGN in the hope of discovering an unknown number of books on Batik – and then he has to note them before setting off to the broadly classified shelves.

Most librarians see reclassification as a choice between Dewey and Library of Congress. And whatever the classification scheme, a dictionary catalogue using Congress subject headings is increasingly popular. To illustrate these systems *Table IV* shows some twenty books classified by each scheme with the relevant subject headings, most of them (i.e. those not in square brackets) taken from the Library of Congress Catalog: Books: Subjects.

First the books are listed in the order of the schemes, then the subject headings are given and numbered. These numbers are also placed beside the books to indicate where the headings were used. The table would bear careful study but I will here make only a few brief points:

(i) Dewey's order is more generally coherent than that of Congress.

(ii) The order in Dewey is systematic. Congress relies heavily on the alphabet, and form divisions and author numbers. For example, types of libraries are grouped by relationship in Dewey; in Congress there is an alphabetical scatter – C for County, M for Municipal reference, R for Rural, S for School, V for Village, etc. The same is true for subject schemes of classification: L for Literature, M for Medicine, O for Oriental literature. Forms such as 'library catalogs and bulletins' and 'library reports' are frequently given precedence over subject.

(iii) Though Dewey does fail to provide specific class numbers – see for example 025.4 – both simple and quite complex topics are in many instances given a specific place – e.g. 027.82220942. On the other hand few of the Congress numbers are precise; even place divisions are often missing, and one wonders at the chaos that must be found at, for example, Z665 – Library Science.

(iv) Furthermore Congress fails to indicate priority orders. In Dewey we are told that where process and type of library conflict (as in Metcalf's *Planning academic and research library buildings*) the process is to be given priority. Histories, reports, etc., on libraries go with the type of library. By contrast in the Congress scheme Cornell University Handbook goes with *reports* (A/Z by name); New York State Library's Primer goes under general administration; the account of the reference network in Wisconsin is placed with US libraries, whilst Clapp's *Libraries of state-assisted institutions of higher education in Ohio* is to be found with university libraries. No doubt these placings have meaning in the Library of Congress but that is not the point at issue here.

(v) The subject headings are rarely precise. Without having to cite the plight of the public library (which has neither a place in the Congress classification scheme nor in the subject headings) we can see quite clearly that the broad nature of the headings combined with the broad shelf order is hardly conducive to information retrieval. Imagine, for example, someone wanting material on the history of the library profession in England. Books on this subject are to be found under the heading LIBRARY SCIENCE and they are distributed alphabetically by author at Z665 – Library Science – General works. In Dewey one can be sure of finding such works collocated at

020.942. One can only conclude that for librarianship at any rate Congress headings and Dewey classification will give better results than Congress headings and Congress classification.

Better results still would be achieved by using Dewey and either classified catalogue with a chain index or a dictionary catalogue with specific headings based on chain procedure – or augmented Congress headings.

So far we have been examining order: main class order and order within main classes. But it is not enough that order should exist: it must also be seen to exist. It must be seen by both classifiers and library users. In Dewey, order is clearly indicated by the following features:

(i) *Expressive notation,* that is, notation which for the most part expresses the successive stages of division. This is achieved by the addition of successive digits representing direct subdivision in the schedules and by synthetic devices – as illustrated in *Table V.*

Such notation is obviously an aid to browsing: the reader can follow the subject groups on the shelves much more easily than in schemes where notation is not expressive. Furthermore, clearer shelf-guiding is possible – to whatever level is required. Additionally, the cataloguer is assisted either in the production of a subject index for a classified catalogue or subject headings and references for a dictionary catalogue.

(ii) *Schedule layout:* The Dewey scheme has constantly improved its schedule layout in an effort to reveal not only the existing order but the thinking behind the order. This is achieved by typographic devices – type size, indentation, centred headings with black arrowheads, and so on. (Page 214 of the tables in the 17th edition illustrates these advantages.) In addition headings have been simplified to indicate the principle of division – as, for example, at 252.1 and 252.5 ('occasion' and 'classes of persons').

(iii) This example also shows further aids to the expression of order – namely the *notes* and *references.* These references remind the classifier of related fields (as under 250) – their use has been rationalized in recent editions of the scheme. The notes may outline the scope of a heading, by definition or by a listing of topics to be included (as at 252 and 252.35); or they may point out the use of further degrees of division by synthesis (as at

252.01/.09), giving examples; or they may indicate priority orders for complex subjects – e.g. at 252 'Class sermons on a specific subject with the subject'.

(iv) Such notes, along with the detailed *Introduction* which explains the main features of the scheme and its use, are invaluable in ensuring that the classifier understands the structure of the scheme and the scope of the various divisions.

(v) Finally there is the detailed relative index (the weaknesses peculiar to 17th edition index have been rectified). Dewey himself was rightly proud of this relative index – a forerunner of chain indexing.

These features go a long way towards ensuring a consistent and comprehensible order. I have emphasized what I consider to be the basic criteria in evaluating a classification scheme. It *is* important when buying a car to note the servicing facilities – but if the car hasn't an engine, what then? It seems to me that the Dewey engine is still ticking over, though there's an occasional knocking and it could no doubt do with a good tuning. And, the service facilities are not bad: Dewey numbers appear increasingly in Congress catalogues; the editorial staff seems to be relatively active; revisions appear with some regularity.

Librarians who have to choose between Congress and Dewey are in the dilemma of the proverbial lady facing death or a fate worse than death. If, for the sake of the analogy, we nominate Congress as death, then I think we may well find that the worse fate is not quite so unattractive a proposition after all.

TABLE I

Main Class Order in DC and LC

DC

Bibliography and Library
   science

Philosophy

Psychology

Religion

Social sciences, e.g.:
   Sociology
   Statistics
   Political science
   Economics
   Law
   Public administration
   Welfare and Associations
   Education
   Commerce
   Customs and Folklore

Language

Science, e.g.:
   Mathematics
   Physics
   Chemistry
   Biological sciences

Medicine

Technology, e.g.:
   Engineering
   Agriculture
   Business
   Chemical technology
   Manufactures
   Building

Fine arts – incl. Architecture
   & Music

Literature

Geography

Biography

History

LC

Philosophy

Psychology

Religion

History – auxiliary science incl.
   Biography followed by areas

Geography – incl. Travel and
   Physical geography, Anthropology, and Folklore

Social sciences, e.g.:
   Statistics
   Economics
   Transport and Communica-
      tion
   Commerce
   Finance
   Sociology – incl. Social
      history
   Associations, Societies
   Pathology – incl. Criminology
      Penology
   Socialism, Communism
   Political science – incl.
      Constitutional history,
      Administration, and Inter-
      national law
   Law
   Education

Music

Fine arts – incl. Architecture

Language and Literature

Science – e.g.:
   Mathematics
   Physics
   Chemistry
   Biological sciences

Medicine

Agriculture

Technology, e.g.:
   Engineering
   Building
   Chemical technology
   Manufactures

Military science, Naval science

Bibliography and Library science

TABLE II

Class 630 Agriculture:
An Illustration of Synthesis

The *processes* of crop production are enumerated, e.g.:
- 631.53 Propagation
- 631.55 Harvesting
- 631.56 Operations subsequent to harvesting: threshing, shelling, grading, etc.

Similarly *plant injuries and diseases, pests and their control* are enumerated at 632:
- 632.3 Bacterial diseases
- 632.52 Parasitic plants
- 632.7 Insect pests

At 633 specific *crops* are listed:
- 633.1 Cereal crops
- 633.11 Wheat
- 633.2 Forage crops
- 633.21 Bluegrasses

Complex subjects:
- 633.113 Propagation of wheat crops (the 3 from 631.53)
- 633.115 Harvesting of wheat crops (the 5 from 631.55)
- 633.1197 Insect pests in wheat crops (the 7 from 632.7 – added after the 9)

TABLE III

Examples Showing Hospitality to Subjects in DC and LC

The following examples of books and class numbers are taken from the Library of Congress Catalog – Books: Subjects.

Group 1

Brinkley, R. F. The Arthurian legend in 17th century English
           literature.
  DC: 820.9004:   Literature – English – 17th century
  LC: PR438.A7:   Literature – English – 17th century –
                            Arthurian

Tinker, C. B. The salon and English letters: the interrelations of
           literature and society in the age of Johnson.
  DC: 820.9006:   Literature – English – 18th century
  LC: PR448.S3:   Literature – English – 18th century –
                            Society

Karolides, N. J. The pioneer in the American novel, 1900–1950.
  DC: 813.52093: Literature – American – Novel – 20th century
                            – Special subjects
  LC: PS374.P5:   Literature – American – Forms – Prose –
                            Pioneers

Group 2

Johannsen, O. Handbuch der Baumwollspinnere.
  DC: 677.2122:   Manufactures – Textiles – Cotton –
                            Spinning
  LC: TS1577:   Manufactures – Textiles – Cotton – Spinning
Pringle, A. V. The theory of flax spinning.
  DC: 677.1122: Manufactures – Textiles – Flax – Spinning
  LC: TS1705:   Manufactures – Textiles – Flax – General
                            works

Group 3

Dahlgren, S. Transthoracic needle biopsy.
  DC: 616.24075: Medicine – Diseases – Lungs – Diagnosis
  LC: RC733:   Medicine – Diseases – Respiratory system –
                            Diagnosis

Liddell, F. D. K. Assessing the radiological progression of simple
pneumoconiosis with particular reference
to the periodic X-ray scheme . . .

DC: 616.244075572:   Medicine – Diseases – Lungs –
Pneumoconiosis – Diagnosis –
Radioscopic – X-ray

LC: RC773:   Medicine – Diseases – Lungs – Pneumoconiosis

Group 4

Peters, H. S. Random House program for elementary guidance
(i.e., Personnel service in elementary schools).

DC: 372.146:   Education – Elementary – Guidance and
counselling – Social guidance.

LC: LB1027.5:   Education – Teaching principles and practice
– Student guidance and counselling

Group 5

Fisher, R. M. The boom in office buildings: an economic study of
the past two decades.

DC: 338.47690523:   Economics – Production – Specific goods
and services – Buildings – Offices

LC: NA9000:   Architecture – Aesthetics and city planning

Location of Offices Bureau, London. Office costs and location.

DC: 338.476510942:   Economics – Production – Specific
goods and services – Offices –
England

LC: HF5547:   Business organization – Office organization
and management

Platt, R. Education for business management.

DC: 658.0071142:   Business – Management – Study and
teaching – Schools and courses colleges
and universities – Gt. Brit.

LC: HF20:   Economic history – Production – Study and
teaching

Deverell, C. S. Office personnel: Organization management.

DC: 658.3   Business – Management – Personnel – By level –
Office staff

LC: HF5547:   Business organization – Office organization
and management

Heckmann, J. Human relations in management.

DC: 658.4008:   Business – Management – Personnel – By
level – Executive – Collections

LC: HF5549:   Business organization – Personnel

TABLE IV

The Organization of Books on Librarianship by DC and LC, with LC Subject Headings

Dewey Order	S.H. by No.	Library of Congress Order	S.H. by No.
Library Science		*Libraries*	
Study and Teaching		Z *Library Science – General works*	
020.7		Z 665	
020.7 Bonn. Library education and training in developing countries	22	Z 665.A7 Ashworth. Handbook of special libraries and information work.	16,24
History		Z 665.P25 Palmer. From little acorns: the library profession in Great Britain.	24
020.9		*Library education – General and U.S.*	
020.942 Palmer. From little acorns: the library profession in Great Britain.	24	Z 668	
021 *The library*		Z 668.B68 Bonn. Library education and training	22
021.009 *Historical and geographical treatment.*		Z 668.P45 Perkins. A prospective teacher's knowledge of library fundamentals: a study of the responses made by 4,170 college seniors to tasks designed to measure familiarity with libraries.	23
021.009 Ollé. Library history.	5		
[021.009034] Vleeschauer. Library history of XIX Century (1750–1914).	6		
021.00954 Ohdedar. Growth of libraries in modern India, 1498–1836.	10	*Collections*	
022 *Physical plant of libraries*		Z 674	
022.3 *Planning*		Z 674.A75 Archer. Rare book collections: treatment and practical suggestions.	9
022.31 *By type of library*		Z 675 *Classes of libraries A–Z*	
022.317 *College and university*		Z 675.S3S34 School Library Association. The library and the primary school (England).	25
022[.317] Metcalf. Planning academic and research library buildings.	18,20		

Table IV (Continued)

Dewey Order	S.H.	Library of Congress Order	S.H.
Library economy		Z 675.U5C56 Clapp. The libraries of the state-assisted institutions of higher education in Ohio.	13,18
025.17 Treatment of special materials			
025.171 Mss., archival, rarities		Z 678 *Library administration and organization*	
025.171 Archer. Rare book collections: treatment and practical suggestions.	9	Z 678.N48 New York State Library. A primer of the public library system in N.Y. State.	4,12
025.4 Classification			
025.43 General schedules		Z 679 *Architecture*	
025.43 Batty. Introduction to Colon Classification.	1,2	Z 679.M38 Metcalf. Planning academic and research library buildings.	18,20
025.43 Dewey. Decimal Classification, 17th edition.	1,3	Z 696 *The collections, The books –*	
		Classification and notation	
025.430942 Davison. Classification practice in Britain...with special reference to Dewey.	1,3	Z 696.D296 Davison. Classification practice in Britain...with special reference to Dewey	1,3
025.5 Service to patrons		Z 696.D519 Dewey. Decimal classification. 17th edition.	1,3
025.52 Reference services			
025.52 Galvin. Problems in reference service: case studies.	8	Z 696.R26B8 Batty. Introduction to Colon Classification.	1,2
025.5209775 Garrison. A statewide reference network for Wisconsin libraries.	7,14,21	Z 711 *Reference work*	
		Z 711.G3 Galvin. Problems in reference service: case studies.	8
026 Special libraries			
026 Ashworth. Handbook of special librarianship and information work.	16	Z 718 *Libraries and schools*	

Table IV (Continued)

Dewey Order	S.H.	Library of Congress Order	S.H.
026.000942	17	Z 718.1 *Children's libraries. Children's depts. in public libraries, etc.*	
027 *General libraries*		Z 718.1.B8 Broderick. An introduction to children's work in public libraries.	15
027.4 *Public libraries*		Z 721 *Libraries – History – General works*	
027.474 Shera. Foundations of the public library ... movement in New England, 1629–1855.	11	Z 721.048 Ollé. Library history.	5
[027.4747] New York State Library. Development of New York's public library system.	4,12	Z 721.V54 Vleeschauer. Library history of XIX century (1750–1914).	6
[027.4747] New York. State Library. A primer of the public library system in New York State.	4,12	Z 731–876 *Library reports. History. Statistics*	
027.6 *Libraries for special groups, etc.*		Z 731.S55 Shera. Foundations of the public library ... movement in New England, 1629–1855.	11
027.62 *By age group*		Z 732 *United States A–Z by state*	
027.625 *Children*		Z 732.N7 New York. State Library. Development of New York's public library system.	4,12
027.625 Broderick. An introduction to children's work in public libraries.	15	Z 732.W8G3 Garrison. A statewide reference network for Wisconsin libraries.	7,14,21
027.7 *College and university libraries*		Z 733 *Individual libraries A–Z (By place or name)*	
027.709771 Clapp. The libraries of the state-assisted institutions of higher education in Ohio.	13,18	Z 733.C82A57 Cornell University. Handbook of the libraries.	19
027.7747 Cornell University. Handbook of the libraries.	19	Z 791 *Great Britain and Ireland*	

Table IV (Continued)

Dewey Order	S.H.	Library of Congress Order	S.H.
027.8 *School libraries*		Z 791.B9 Burkett. Special libraries and information services in the U.K.	17
027.8222 *Elementary schools*		Z 845 *Asia (A–Z)*	
027.82220942 School Library Association. The library and the primary school (England).	25	Z 845.I4038 Ohdedar. Growth of libraries in modern India, 1498–1836.	10
028 *Reading and reading aids*			
028.7 *Use of books and libraries as sources of information*			
028.7 Perkins. A prospective teacher's knowledge of library fundamentals: a study of the responsibilities made by 4,170 college seniors to tests designed to measure familiarity with libraries.	23		

Table IV (Concluded)

LC Subject Headings

1. Classification – Books.
2. Classification, Colon.
3. Classification, Dewey Decimal.
4. Libraries – Centralization.
5. Libraries – History.
6. Libraries – History – 19th Century.
7. Libraries – Reference Departments.
8. Libraries – Reference Departments – Case Studies.
9. Libraries – Special Collections – Rare Books.
10. Libraries – India – History.
11. Libraries – New England – History.
12. Libraries – New York (State).
13. Libraries – Ohio.
14. Libraries – Wisconsin.
15. Libraries, Children's.
    (Libraries, Children's *see also* School Libraries)

16. Libraries, Special.
17. Libraries, Special – Great Britain.
18. Libraries, University and College.
19. Libraries, University and College – Handbooks, etc.
20. Library Architecture.
21. Library Co-operation.
    (Library Education *see also* Library Schools)
22. Library Education – Asia.
23. Library Schools.
24. Library Science.
    (Library Science *see also* Classification – Books; and headings beginning with word "library")
    (Public libraries *see* Libraries)*
25. School Libraries.
    (School Libraries *see also* Libraries, Children's)

* Mr Angell informed the conference at which this paper was given that this unfortunate situation has now been changed to a *see also* from Libraries to Public libraries.

TABLE V

Expressive notation in DC

(1) 574   Biology
     574.1   Physiology
     574.19   Physics and chemistry of vital processes
     574.192   Biochemistry
     574.1925   Enzymes
     574.19255   Lipolytic enzymes

(2) 700   Art
     730   Sculpture and plastic arts
     731–735   Sculpture
     731.4   Technique
     731.45   Casting
     731.456   In bronze

(3) 350   Public administration
     351   Central government
     351.1–351.4   Civil Service
     351.1   Personnel management
     351.16   Conditions of employment ⎫
     351.162   Promotion of welfare, etc. ⎬ by synthesis
     351.1623   Welfare services ⎭

(4) 800   Literature
     810   American literature
     813   Fiction
     813.52   20th Century ⎫
     813.520925   Stream of consciousness ⎬ by synthesis ⎭

Index entries for (2) using chain procedure

Bronze casting: Sculpture	731.456
Casting techniques: Sculpture	731.45
Sculpture: Art	731–735
Art	700
Fine arts	700

Subject headings and references for (2) using chain procedure

Bronze casting – Sculpture
Casting techniques – Sculpture *see also* Bronze casting – Sculpture
Sculpture *see also* Casting techniques
Art *see also* Sculpture
Fine arts *see also* Art

Index

This index does not contain entries for items in the reading lists at the ends of chapters.

ct Comparative treatment
qv Further references will be found at the heading indicated

DATE DUE